VISUAL QUICKSTART GUIDE

MICROSOFT OFFICE 2004

FOR MAC OS X

Steve Schwartz

 **Peachpit Press**

Visual QuickStart Guide
Microsoft Office 2004 for Mac OS X
Steve Schwartz

Peachpit Press

1249 Eighth Street
Berkeley, CA 94710
(510) 524-2178
(800) 283-9444
(510) 524-2221 (fax)

Find us on the World Wide Web at: www.peachpit.com
To report errors, please send a note to errata@peachpit.com
Peachpit Press is a division of Pearson Education

Editor: Suzie Lowey
Production Editor: Lupe Edgar
Copyeditor: Elizabeth Welch
Compositor: Steve Schwartz
Indexer: FireCrystal Communications
Cover Design: Peachpit Press
Cover Production: George Mattingly / GMD

ISBN: 0-321-24747-7

9 8 7 6 5

Printed and bound in the United States of America

Dedication:

To the hard-working members of the
Macintosh Business Unit, Microsoft
Corporation for consistently producing
excellent products.

Special Thanks to:

- Suzie Lowey and Lupe Edgar (Peachpit Press) for professionally managing this project, while maintaining a sense of humor.

- Emily Glossbrenner (FireCrystal Communications) for producing another spectacular index on very short notice.

- Elizabeth Welch for her consummate copyediting skills.

- Jessica Sommer (Microsoft Corporation) for ensuring that I received software in a timely fashion and for providing answers to critical Office-related questions.

TABLE OF CONTENTS

TABLE OF CONTENTS

TABLE OF CONTENTS

TABLE OF CONTENTS

TABLE OF CONTENTS

INTRODUCTION

Welcome to *Microsoft Office 2004 for Mac OS X: Visual QuickStart Guide*. Feel free to turn immediately to the parts of the book that will be most helpful to you. If you're the thorough type, though, you might want to take a moment to read the next few pages. They list the basic skills you'll need—skills you almost certainly have if you've used the Mac for any length of time. We'll also take a look at what's new in this edition of Microsoft Office for Macintosh.

What You Already Know

This book assumes you have a basic understanding of the following Macintosh skills:

◆ How to turn the Mac on and off.

◆ How to use the mouse (move, point, click, double-click, and drag).

◆ How to use the elements of the OS X Desktop (menus, windows, icons, Dock, and Trash).

◆ How to use the common elements of applications (menus, toolbars, document windows, and buttons).

◆ How to manipulate windows (open, close, move, resize, minimize to the Dock, and switch among open windows).

◆ How to manipulate files (find, open, save, close, copy, and move).

◆ How to use the elements of dialog boxes (text fields, pull-down menus, check boxes, radio buttons, and tabs).

◆ How to use toolbars (viewing and hiding, using the icons and drop-down menus).

✔ Tip

■ If you'd like to explore any of these skills further or learn more about what your Mac can do, check out *The Little Mac Book* and *The Little iMac Book* (Robin Williams, Peachpit Press). And if you're new to Mac OS X (the operating system for which Office 2004 was designed), you might want to try *The Little Mac OS X Book* (also by Williams) and Maria Langer's *Visual QuickStart Guides* for Mac OS X.

How to Use This Book

This is a book for beginning and intermediate users of Microsoft Office for Macintosh. If you're using Office for the first time, switching from a Windows version to the Macintosh version, or already know the basics but want to get more out of your investment in Office, this book is for you. If you learn better from step-by-step instructions and lots of graphic examples than from reference manuals that just describe what the menu commands do, this book is also for you. Most of all, if you know what you want to do and want to get started in the shortest amount of time possible, this book is *definitely* for you.

I and the former authors of this title have worked hard to create a book that will let you turn to the directions for any procedure, learn what it does, and do it yourself. A screen shot illustrates every significant step. The goal is to give you all the information you need and none that you don't, making you productive as quickly as possible. Along the way, you'll find tips that offer helpful information about many of the procedures.

Each section has been designed to function independently; you almost never need to know one part of the subject to understand another. However, because many features are common to all Office programs, you'll find yourself recognizing elements and procedures you learned in one program and applying them to the others.

HOW TO USE THIS BOOK

About Word

Word 2004, the word-processing component of the Microsoft Office suite, is used to create letters, memos, invoices, proposals, reports, forms, brochures, catalogs, labels, envelopes, Web pages, and just about any other type of printed or electronically distributed document that you can imagine.

You can type text into Word and insert almost any kind of graphic, formatting the text and graphics into sophisticated documents with tables, running headers and footers, footnotes, cross-references, page numbers, tables of contents, and indexes. If your needs aren't that expansive, you can also create simple letters and memos with Word's easy-to-use features.

Word's approach, like that of the other applications in Office, is visual. As you work in a document, you see all the text, graphics, and formatting exactly as it will appear when you print.

Word works in concert with the other Office applications. It can display numbers and charts from Excel worksheets, as well as slides from PowerPoint. And you can flag Word documents for follow-up in your Entourage to-do list.

About Excel

Excel 2004, the Office spreadsheet application, is used to track, calculate, and analyze data. If you want to view numeric information graphically, you can use Excel to create professional charts in dozens of formats.

After typing numbers into a row-and-column cell grid in an Excel worksheet, you can enter formulas into adjacent cells that total, subtract, multiply, or divide the numbers. You can also enter *functions,* special Excel formulas that perform complex calculations—from sums and averages to sophisticated financial computations, such as net present value. Excel can even calculate complex statistics.

You can also use Excel to create, maintain, and import lists and databases. You can accumulate text and numeric records, as well as sort, search, filter, and extract data from a database. Excel works especially well with FileMaker Pro databases.

About PowerPoint

PowerPoint 2004 is the presentation component of Office. You use it to create slides, handouts, overheads, and any other materials you might use during a stand-up dog-and-pony show. You can even use PowerPoint to present *slide shows*—electronic presentations that you run on your computer screen or on a projection device in front of an audience.

PowerPoint comes with dozens of professionally designed templates that take care of the presentation's look, allowing you to focus on its message. It includes sample presentation outlines to help you get a start on the content.

PowerPoint's powerful arsenal includes bulleted and numbered text slides, graphs, tables, organization charts, clip art, animations and movies, and drawing tools.

If you need to convey your PowerPoint presentation to an even wider audience, you can convert it to a QuickTime movie or to a Web-based slide show that can be viewed with any Web browser.

About Entourage

Entourage 2004 helps you manage your life and your communications. Use it to send and receive email, read and post to discussion groups on the Internet, and maintain your calendar, address book, to-do list, and notes.

You can flag Office documents for follow-up in your to-do list, remind yourself of appointments and events, look up contact information in public directories, and link related Entourage items to one another.

✔ Tip

- For in-depth information on Entourage 2004, see my upcoming *Microsoft Entourage 2004 for Mac OS X: Visual QuickStart Guide.*

ABOUT POWERPOINT AND ENTOURAGE

What's New in Office 2004?

Microsoft Office 2004 for Macintosh has many new features. Here are some of the most significant ones.

What's new in all Office programs?

◆ The new Project Center enables you to organize and view Office materials related to a particular project. All projects are created in Entourage, but can be accessed from any Office application.

◆ The Office Toolbox provides access to key tools, such as the Scrapbook (an enhanced version of the Office Clipboard), Project Palette, Compatibility Report, and Word reference tools.

◆ New sections have been added to the Formatting Palette. For example, you can use the Add Objects section to insert clip art, tables, pictures, and other objects into the current document.

◆ Any graphic in a received Office document can be saved as a separate file.

◆ The Print dialog box now includes Quick Preview, a miniature preview of the printed document.

◆ The AutoRecover feature helps avoid data loss in the event of a crash.

◆ Filenames can be up to 255 characters long and can include Unicode (foreign language) characters, as can the files themselves.

◆ Using the AutoUpdate feature, Office can use the Internet to automatically check for updates to any of the applications and then download and install them.

What's new in Word 2004?

◆ A Notebook Layout view has been added, enabling you to take and organize notes, record audio notes, and more.

◆ The Project Gallery has been expanded by adding tabs that list all documents on which you've recently worked, active projects, and learning materials.

◆ Change tracking (for recording edits made to a document) has been revised and is much clearer than in previous versions of Word.

◆ When Word makes an AutoCorrect correction to your text or you use Paste to add material to a document, smart buttons appear that allow you to modify the new material's formatting.

◆ The Document Map has been replaced by the Navigation Pane, making it simple to quickly go to any page of interest. The pane can display a list of major document headings or thumbnails for all pages.

What's new in Excel 2004?

◆ The new Page Layout view allows you to view your worksheet onscreen exactly as it will look when printed.

◆ Smart buttons appear beneath cells to help you specify paste, insert, AutoFill, and error checking options.

◆ Excel 2004 can open XML files created in Excel 2000 or later. Worksheets can also be saved in XML Spreadsheet schema.

What's new in Entourage 2004?

◆ Support has been added for displaying message threads and for grouping messages according to various criteria, such as message date or subject.

◆ The Preview pane can now be placed to the right of the message headers.

◆ Email messages can optionally be created from any Word document and automatically formatted as HTML.

◆ Entourage is integrated in several ways with MSN Messenger. New contact information can be added to the address book of either or both programs. Every Entourage contact card contains a drop-down menu that you can click to log onto MSN Messenger and send instant messages to the contact.

◆ You can summon MapPoint to view a location map or driving directions to any contact in your address book.

◆ Support for Exchange servers, digital ID signatures, and message encryption has been added.

What's new in PowerPoint 2004?

◆ Presenter tools have been added, including an onscreen clock for timing presentations and a thumbnail view of your entire presentation.

◆ Using the Change Slides section of the Formatting Palette, you can quickly see how a new template design will look when applied to slides in the current presentation.

◆ Animations and transitions are compatible with those of PowerPoint for Windows and vice versa.

What's new in MSN Messenger?

◆ The new spam filter helps eliminate unwanted messages from strangers.

◆ MSN Messenger is integrated with Word's Track Changes feature, enabling you to send instant messages regarding edits made to a document by others.

◆ Integration with the Project Center is also provided, allowing you to message project team members concerning a particular document edit or comment.

◆ New *emoticons* (smileys) have been added.

◆ You can share files across firewalls.

WHAT'S NEW IN OFFICE 2004?

Part I:
Introduction

ESSENTIAL OFFICE TECHNIQUES

1

Many basic operations in Office 2004, such as starting a new document, opening an existing document, saving your work, using common interface elements, working with various types of content, and getting help, apply to more than one program. Rather than repeat this information throughout the book, we'll cover it here.

Launching Office Applications

You can launch Office applications in the same manner as other OS X applications— plus some Office-specific ways.

To launch an Office application:

◆ *Do one of the following:*

▲ Click the program icon in the Dock (**Figure 1.1**).

▲ Open the Microsoft Office 2004 folder (**Figure 1.2**) and double-click the program icon.

▲ Double-click an alias for the program.

▲ If the program has been saved as a *favorite*, choose its name from the Finder's Go > Favorites submenu.

▲ From the New tab of the Project Gallery in any open Office application, create a new document in another Office application.

The application launches. If it hasn't been disabled, the Project Gallery appears (see the next section).

Office program icons

Figure 1.1 If the Office programs are in the Dock, click the appropriate icon to launch the program.

Figure 1.2 You can also launch an Office application by double-clicking its file icon.

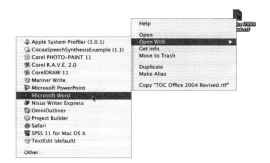

Figure 1.3 To open a compatible document in a specific Office application, choose the program from the Open With pop-up menu.

To launch an Office application while opening one or more documents:

◆ *Do one of the following:*

▲ Double-click a document file icon or a document alias that is associated with an Office application. (For example, double-clicking a Word document will launch Word—if it isn't already running—and open the document.)

▲ Select an Office document from the Finder's Go > Favorites submenu.

▲ Drag the icon of a compatible document onto an Office application icon. (For example, you can drag a compatible worksheet onto the Excel icon.)

▲ Select one or more document icons of the same type, (Control)-click one of them, and choose the appropriate Office application from the Open With submenu (**Figure 1.3**).

▲ Within Entourage or another email application, open an attached Office document.

The application launches and the selected document(s) open.

✔ Tip

■ There is no one right or preferred way to launch an Office application or open its documents. Use any method that's convenient at the moment. (Of course, the more methods you learn, the more likely you'll always find one that's convenient.)

LAUNCHING OFFICE APPLICATIONS

Using the Project Gallery

A feature introduced in Office 2001 called the *Project Gallery* gives you access to standard blank documents, as well as to templates and wizards that provide a substantial amount of document formatting and content. In Office 2004, the Project Gallery has been expanded to make it easy for you to open documents on which you've recently worked, current projects, and sample Office documents.

To use the Project Gallery:

1. *Do one of the following:*

▲ Launch an Office application. (If the Project Gallery hasn't been disabled, it opens on program launch.)

▲ Choose File > Project Gallery (or press [Shift][⌘][P]).

The Project Gallery opens.

2. *Do one of the following:*

▲ *To create a new document* for this or another Office application (regardless of whether it is currently running), click the New tab (**Figure 1.4**). Select Blank Documents from the Groups list, select a document type from the ones displayed on the right, and click Open.

▲ *To create a document from a template or wizard,* click the New tab (see Figure 1.4), select My Templates or another template or wizard category from the Groups list, select a template or wizard from the ones displayed on the right, and click Open.

▲ *To open a document on which you recently worked,* click the Recent tab (**Figure 1.5**). Select a time period from the Date pane, select a document from the ones listed, and click Open.

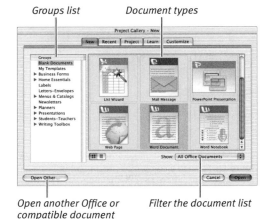

Groups list   Document types

Open another Office or compatible document   Filter the document list

Figure 1.4 To create a new document, select Blank Document and the icon for the type of document you want to create.

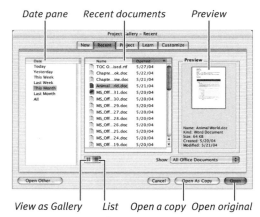

Date pane   Recent documents   Preview

View as Gallery   List   Open a copy   Open original

Figure 1.5 You can open any document on which you've previously worked by selecting it from the list on the Recent tab.

Figure 1.6 Set Project Gallery preferences on the Customize tab of the Project Gallery window.

▲ *To open a project file* created in the Project Center, click the Project tab, select a document, and click Open.

▲ *To learn more about Office 2004,* click the Learn tab, select a document, and click Open.

▲ *To open an existing document* (other than the ones displayed), click the Open Other button, select a document from the Open dialog box that appears, and click Open. (The Open Other button is available on all tabs.)

✔ Tips

■ You can view documents as a gallery (thumbnails) or a text list by clicking the appropriate icon at the bottom of the Project Gallery (see Figure 1.5).

■ You can limit the kinds of documents shown in the Project Gallery by picking a file type from the Show drop-down menu. For example, you can elect to view only Excel documents.

■ On the Recent tab, you can optionally open a *copy* of a recent document rather than the original—effectively treating the file as a template or stationery document. Select a file and click the Open As Copy button (see Figure 1.5).

■ To set preferences for the Project Gallery, click the Customize tab (**Figure 1.6**). For example, if you'd rather not see the Project Gallery every time you launch an Office program, remove the checkmark from Show Project Gallery at startup.

Creating a New Document

Unless you work exclusively with documents created by others, you'll also want to create new documents of your own. In all Office programs, you can create a new blank document in the following ways:

- ◆ **Word.** Choose File > New Blank Document.

- ◆ **PowerPoint.** Choose File > New Presentation.

- ◆ **Excel.** Choose File > New Workbook.

- ◆ **All.** Press ⌘Ⓝ.

✔ Tips

- ■ As explained in the previous section, you can also create a new document in the Project Gallery window. Click the New tab, select Blank Documents from the Groups list, select the type of Office document you want to create, and click Open (see Figure 1.4).

- ■ If you don't make a choice in the Project Gallery window and click Cancel to dismiss it, a new blank document is created for you automatically.

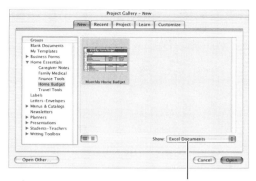

Show drop-down menu

Figure 1.7 Select a category in the left pane to view the available templates and wizards on the right. To restrict the list to application-specific templates and wizards, choose the application from the Show menu.

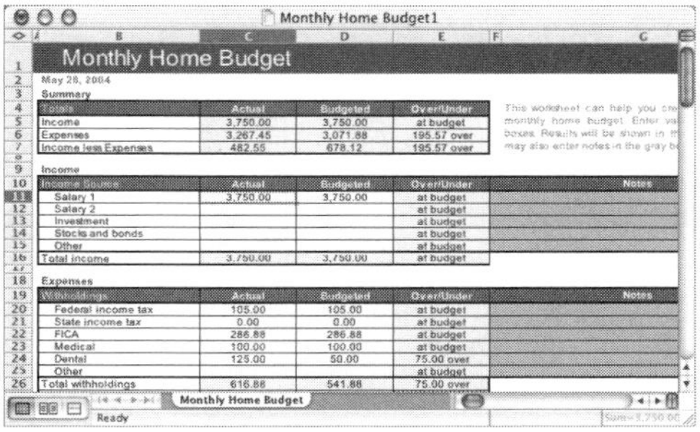

Figure 1.8 Although templates are more common for Word than for the other Office applications, this Excel worksheet is based on a template.

Templates and Wizards

Office 2004 provides a diverse collection of templates and wizards that you can use to create impressive documents without having to become a design professional.

Templates are formatted documents to which you add your own content. *Wizards* are short multiple-step or tabbed procedures that ask you questions about the document you want to produce and then create the document based on your answers. If you like, you can edit the resulting document when the wizard is finished.

Creating a document from a template

A *template* is a partially formed document that contains text, styles, and formatting. You can start a document with a template, and then modify the content and formatting.

To create a document from a template:

1. If the Project Gallery isn't already open, choose File > Project Gallery (Shift ⌘ P). The Project Gallery opens.

2. Click the New tab (**Figure 1.7**). In the Groups list, select the type of document you want to create. (To expand a category, click the triangle beside it.)

   Choices appear in the pane on the right.

3. Select a template from the ones displayed and click Open.

   A copy of the template opens (**Figure 1.8**).

4. Fill in the content, edit and format the document as necessary, and then save the document.

TEMPLATES AND WIZARDS

✔ Tips

- When creating a new document from a template, you're always working with a *copy*—not the original template. To remind you, Word names the copy *Document* rather than using the template's name. As long as you save the copy with a new name or in a different location, changes you make to the copy won't affect the template.

- You can also base a new document on any recently used Office document— effectively treating your own documents as templates. In the Project Gallery, click the Recent tab, select a document, and click the Open As Copy button.

TEMPLATES AND WIZARDS

Name the template

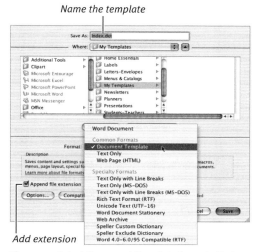

Add extension

Figure 1.9 Select Document Template (or a similarly named option) when saving a file as a template.

Saving a document as a template

You don't have to rely exclusively on the provided Office templates. You may occasionally find it useful to save your *own* documents as templates, enabling you to reuse them with minor changes as often as you like.

To save a document as a template:

1. Create an Office document with the desired formatting. Delete text and other material that you don't want saved as part of the template, while retaining any text you'll want to use in new documents.

    In a Word fax-form template, for example, you might leave your contact information intact and add a placeholder (such as "Message text here") for the message text.

2. Choose File > Save As.

3. In the dialog box that appears, choose Document Template from the Format drop-down menu (**Figure 1.9**).

4. Enter a name for the template in the Save As text box.

5. From the Where drop-down list, choose a location in which to save the template.

    Normally, you should accept the default folder (My Templates) for personal templates, but you're free to save them to other locations if you like.

6. Click the Save button.

    The document is saved as a template.

✔ Tips

- AutoText entries, macros, and custom toolbars (if any) are also saved as part of a template.

- For compatibility with Office for Windows, Mac template files may use these file extensions: Word (.dot), Excel (.xlt), and PowerPoint design (.pot).

TEMPLATES AND WIZARDS

Modifying an existing template

You can modify the templates provided with Office, as well as any files of your own that you've saved as templates. In this way, you can create templates that better serve your needs.

To modify a template:

1. In the Office application in which the template was created, choose File > Open (⌘O).

   The Open dialog box appears.

2. Choose *application name* Templates from the Show drop-down menu.

3. Navigate to the Templates folder within the Microsoft Office 2004 folder. Open additional folders as necessary until you find the template that you want to change (**Figure 1.10**).

4. Select the template and click Open.

5. Make any necessary edits and formatting changes to the template.

6. *Do one of the following:*
   - ▲ To replace the original template with the modified one, choose File > Save (⌘S).
   - ▲ To save the modified template without overwriting the original template, choose File > Save As, edit the template name (if desired), and save it in the My Templates folder or another folder of your choosing (**Figure 1.11**).

✔ Tip

- ■ Unless you're certain you'll never need the original template again, it's more prudent to modify a *copy* of the template, saving it with a new filename. To open a copy of a template for modification, choose Copy from the Open drop-down menu in the Open dialog box (see Figure 1.10).

Show templates only

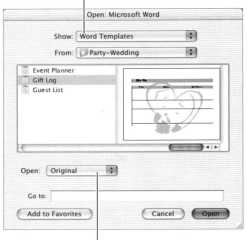

Open options

Figure 1.10 Select the template you want to modify.

Edit the filename

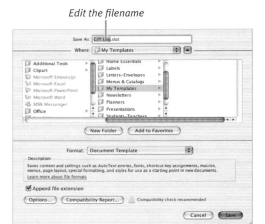

Figure 1.11 To avoid overwriting the original template, save the modified version using a different filename or in a different folder.

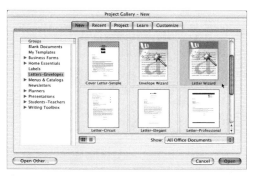

Figure 1.12 The Letter Wizard is selected in the Project Gallery.

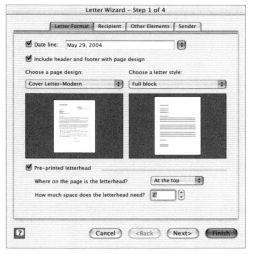

Figure 1.13 Enter the information requested by the wizard and set options as you wish.

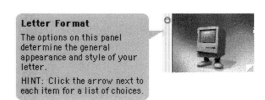

Figure 1.14 If you're confused, the Office Assistant may have some useful advice. (To enable it, choose Help > Use the Office Assistant).

Working with wizards

Wizards step you through the process of creating a specific type of document. They generally provide sample text that you can use, too. In Word, for example, you can use wizards to create letters, brochures, menus, catalogs, and labels.

To use a wizard:

1. If the Project Gallery window isn't open, choose File > Project Gallery (Shift ⌘ P).

2. On the New tab, select a category from the Groups list.

3. In the pane on the right, select the wizard for the type of document you want to create (**Figure 1.12**) and then click Open.

   The wizard appears (**Figure 1.13**).

4. Follow the steps presented by the wizard. Each step prompts you for more detail to help generate a customized document.

5. To complete the wizard, click Finish, Save & Exit, or OK. (Button labels vary.)

   The document now includes the information you entered and the options selected.

6. Make any necessary changes to the document and save the file.

✔ Tips

- Many wizards—but not all—include *Wizard* as part of the name.

- You can move from one section of a multi-page wizard to another by clicking Next, Back, or a specific tab.

- The Office Assistant provides helpful hints for some wizards (**Figure 1.14**).

TEMPLATES AND WIZARDS

Opening Existing Documents

Unless you use or refer to every document you create only once (a *very* unlikely occurrence), you'll need to open documents you've previously saved on disk.

To reopen a saved file:

1. Choose File > Open, click the Open icon on the Standard toolbar, or press ⌘O.

2. In the Open dialog box (**Figure 1.15**), navigate to the location where the file is stored.

3. From the Open drop-down menu (**Figure 1.16**), choose one of the following:

   ▲ **Original.** Open the original for editing.

   ▲ **Copy.** Open a copy for editing, protecting the original from changes.

   ▲ **Read-Only.** Open the document for viewing. If you edit the document, you can save the changes only if you use a different filename and/or location.

4. To open the document, double-click the document's filename or select the filename and click Open.

✔ Tips

■ If the file you want to open is one you've recently used, it may appear in the list of recent documents at the bottom of the File menu. If so, you can choose its name from the list to open it.

■ You can also open documents by choosing them from the Recent Items submenu of the Apple menu or from the Recent tab of the Project Gallery.

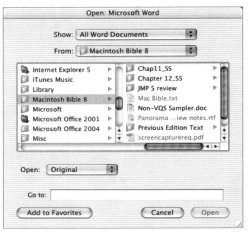

Figure 1.15 To open an existing document, choose it in the Open dialog box.

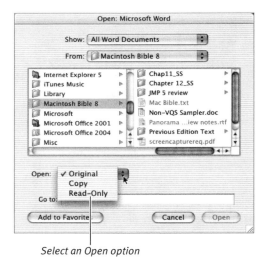

Select an Open option

Figure 1.16 Although you'll usually want to work with the original document, you can elect to open a copy or open the document in read-only mode.

OPENING EXISTING DOCUMENTS

Figure 1.17 To save the current document, you can click the Save icon on the Standard toolbar.

Expand or collapse the Where area

Figure 1.18 To save a new document or to save an old one using a new name or location, enter the necessary information in the Save As dialog box.

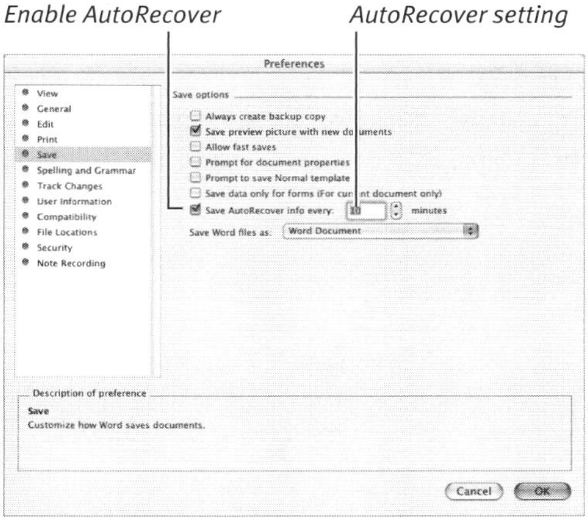

Saving Your Work

It's a good idea to save your work frequently. Doing so guards against data loss in the event that you must quit an Office program prematurely or restart your Mac.

To save your work:

1. Choose File > Save, press ⌘S, or click the Save icon on the Standard toolbar (**Figure 1.17**).

   If the document was previously saved, the new version of the file automatically overwrites the old one.

2. If this is the first time you've saved the document (or if you've chosen File > Save As), a Save As dialog box appears (**Figure 1.18**). Continue with the remaining steps.

3. Enter a filename in the Save As text box.

4. Choose a file format from the Format drop-down menu.

5. Click the Where drop-down menu to select a location in which to store the document. If you need to navigate to a drive or folder that isn't listed, click the triangle icon to expand the Where area.

6. Click Save or press [Return].

✔ Tips

- Each Office application proposes a default folder whenever you save your work. You can specify a different default folder in each program's Preferences.

- Word, Excel, and PowerPoint can be instructed to automatically save documents at user-defined intervals. This is known as *AutoRecover*. To enable AutoRecover and specify a time interval, choose *program name* > Preferences and select the Save category (**Figure 1.19**).

Enable AutoRecover   *AutoRecover setting*

Figure 1.19 By enabling AutoRecover, you can ensure that you never lose more than a few minutes' work.

Working with Text

Text is an important part of most Office documents. Whenever an application is ready for you to type text, a blinking insertion point appears in the document. Whatever you type appears at the insertion point.

Setting the text insertion point

To revise or add to existing text, you must move the insertion point to the spot where you want to make the change.

To set the insertion point:

◆ *Do one of the following:*

▲ Move the I-beam cursor to the spot where you want to position the insertion point. Click to set the insertion point (**Figure 1.20**).

▲ Press the arrow keys, Pg Up, Pg Dn, or any of the other keyboard shortcuts listed in **Table 1.1**.

✔ Tip

■ In Excel, the insertion point can be in the text box on the Formula Bar or in the cell (**Figure 1.21**), depending on where you're performing the text entry or editing.

Office lets you easily share information between its applications. The three main methods are to copy, embed, or link information from one application to another.

Insertion point   I-beam cursor

Figure 1.20 Whatever you type will appear at the insertion point.

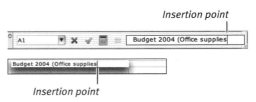

Insertion point

Insertion point

Figure 1.21 In Excel, the insertion point can be in the Formula Bar (top) or in the cell you're editing (bottom).

Table 1.1

Navigation Keyboard Shortcuts	
KEYSTROKE	MOVEMENT
⬆ or ⬇	Up or down one line
Option ⬅ or Option ➡	One word to the left or right
⌘⬅ or ⌘➡	Beginning or end of current line
⌘⬆ or ⌘⬇	Beginning of previous or next paragraph

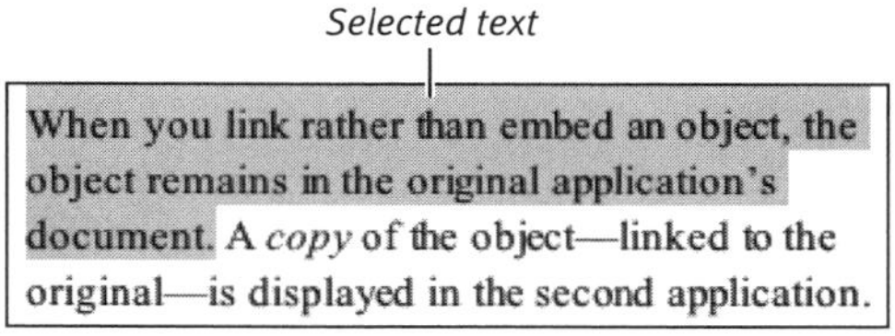

Selected text

> When you link rather than embed an object, the object remains in the original application's document. A *copy* of the object—linked to the original—is displayed in the second application.

Figure 1.22 Click and drag to create a text selection. The selected text is highlighted.

Selecting text

Before you can edit, replace, delete, or format text, you must first *select* it. Any operation you then perform will affect the selected text.

To select text using the mouse:

◆ *Do any of the following:*

▲ Click at one end of a section of text to set the insertion point and drag to the other end to select the text (**Figure 1.22**). A selection can be as little as one character or can contain many consecutive paragraphs.

▲ To select text on consecutive lines, click to set the insertion point at the beginning of the selection and either drag through the lines you want to select or Shift-click at the end of the selection.

▲ You can make multiple, noncontiguous text selections. You might, for example, want to select several headings to simultaneously apply the same formatting to them. Hold down ⌘ to make multiple selections.

▲ Double-click anywhere within a word to select it. Triple-click anywhere within a paragraph to select it.

✔ Tips

■ A preference setting ensures that the entire first and last word of a selection are highlighted. If you want to be able to select *parts* of words, choose *program name* > Preferences, select the Edit heading, and remove the checkmark from When selecting, automatically select entire word.

■ To select an entire line of text in a Word document, click in the left margin of the line. To select multiple lines, click in the margin to the left of a line and then drag down through the lines.

WORKING WITH TEXT

To select text using the keyboard:

1. Use the arrow keys or mouse to set the insertion point at one end of the text that you want to select.

2. Hold down [Shift] and press arrow keys (or the keys shown in Table 1.1) to extend the selection.

✔ Tips

■ Use [Shift][Option][←] or [Shift][Option][→] to select a word at a time.

■ Use [Shift][↓] or [Shift][↑] to select multiple lines of text.

■ To select from the insertion point to the beginning or end of the current line, press [Shift][⌘][←] or [Shift][⌘][→], respectively.

Replacing text

To replace text in a document or dialog box, select the text and type over it. Doing so simultaneously deletes the text and replaces it with the new text. (It isn't necessary to first delete the old text.)

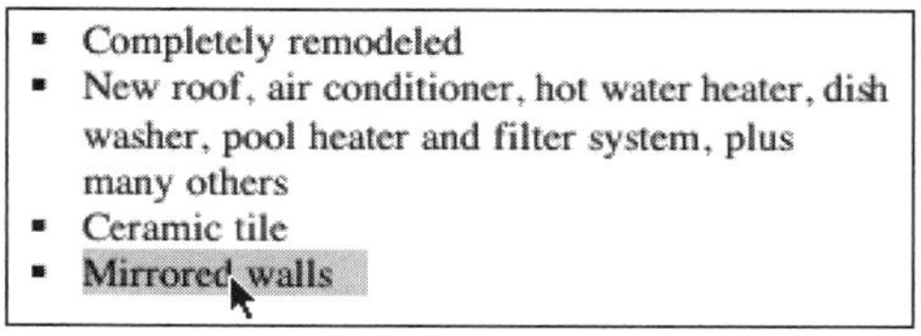

- Completely remodeled
- New roof, air conditioner, hot water heater, dish washer, pool heater and filter system, plus many others
- Ceramic tile
- Mirrored walls

Figure 1.23 When the cursor is moved over a text selection, it becomes an arrow pointer.

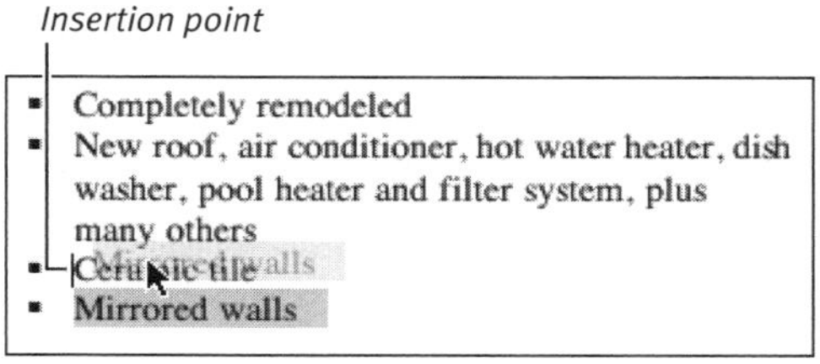

Insertion point

- Completely remodeled
- New roof, air conditioner, hot water heater, dish washer, pool heater and filter system, plus many others
- Ceramic tile
- Mirrored walls

Figure 1.24 Drag the arrow pointer to the destination. An insertion point shows where the dragged text will appear.

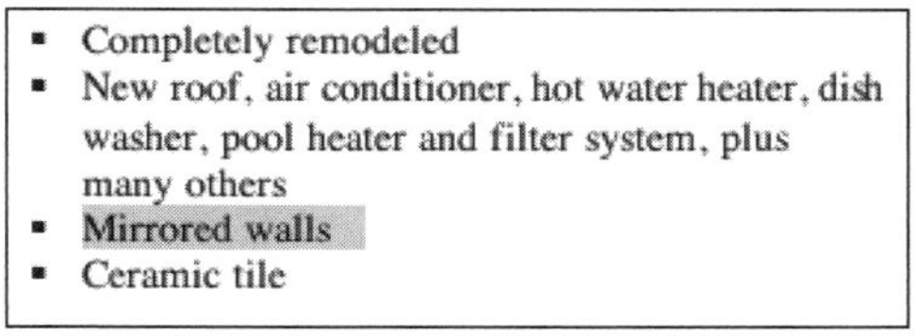

- Completely remodeled
- New roof, air conditioner, hot water heater, dish washer, pool heater and filter system, plus many others
- Mirrored walls
- Ceramic tile

Figure 1.25 Release the mouse button to drop the text. The "Mirrored walls" bullet has been moved up one paragraph.

Moving text

To move text in a document, you can either use the Edit > Cut and Edit > Paste commands or drag and drop. *Drag and drop* is like a simplified cut and paste, accomplished by selecting text and then dragging it to a new location in the document. You can even drag text from one document to another or from one application window to another.

To drag and drop text:

1. Select the text to be moved.

2. Place the cursor over the selected text.

   The cursor changes to an arrow pointer (**Figure 1.23**).

3. Press and hold the mouse button, and drag the pointer to the destination.

   An insertion point indicates the spot where the dragged text will reappear (**Figure 1.24**).

4. Release the mouse button to drop the text at the new location (**Figure 1.25**).

✔ Tips

- To *copy* text rather than move it (leaving the original text intact), press Option as you drag.

- A drag and drop between documents is treated as a copy rather than a cut. That is, following the operation, the original material remains in the source document.

- You can also use drag and drag to copy or move other kinds of objects, such as graphics and charts.

- Because OS X doesn't support *clippings* (an OS 9 feature), you cannot use drag and drop to drag a text selection from Office 2004 onto the desktop.

WORKING WITH TEXT

Working with Pictures and Other Objects

Drawings, charts, WordArt, clip art, scanned images, and other items you can select in an Office document are *objects*. After selecting an object (by clicking or dragging through it), you can reposition it on the page by dragging. You can also drag objects into other documents—including documents in other applications. To copy rather than move an object, hold down (Option) as you drag.

To format an object, you must select it and then choose a formatting command, as described in the following steps.

To format an object:

1. Select the object that you want to format.

2. *Do one of the following:*

   ▲ Choose a command or click an icon on the Formatting Palette (**Figure 1.26**), the Drawing toolbar (**Figure 1.27**), or the object-specific toolbar (**Figure 1.28**) that appears when you select the object.

   ▲ Double-click the object to open a relevant formatting dialog box.

   ▲ Choose an appropriate command (such as Picture) from the Format menu.

✔ Tips

■ If neither the Formatting Palette nor the necessary toolbar is visible, you can display them by choosing the appropriate command from the View menu.

■ For more information about using the Formatting Palette, see the next section.

■ For assistance with text formatting, see Chapter 5.

Figure 1.26 When you select an object, the Formatting Palette displays commands that are relevant to formatting the object.

Figure 1.27 You can modify many objects by choosing commands and options from the Drawing toolbar.

Selected object
WordArt toolbar

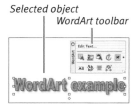

Figure 1.28 When you select an object (such as this WordArt text in a Word document), an object-specific toolbar generally appears.

WORKING WITH PICTURES AND OTHER OBJECTS

Close button   *Title bar*

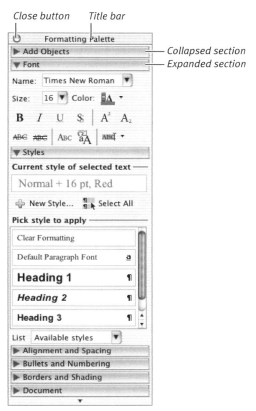

— *Collapsed section*
— *Expanded section*

Figure 1.29 Click a triangle icon to collapse or expand a section of the Formatting Palette.

Figure 1.30 One way to show or hide the Formatting Palette is to click its toolbar icon.

- To change the behavior of the Formatting Palette (making it automatically fade or minimize after a set period of inactivity, for instance), choose Tools > Customize > Customize Formatting Palette.

The Formatting Palette

A relatively recent addition to Office, the Formatting Palette (**Figure 1.29**) is a floating palette that you can use to quickly format selected text, graphics, and even the document. Because you can position it anywhere onscreen, it's often more convenient to use than the menus and toolbars. The Formatting Palette is available in Word, PowerPoint, and Excel.

The sections in the Formatting Palette change to reflect what you're currently doing. For example, the Font section only appears when you're working with text.

To use the Formatting Palette:

- If the Formatting Palette isn't visible, choose View > Formatting Palette or click the Formatting Palette icon on the Standard toolbar (**Figure 1.30**).

  When enabled, the Formatting Palette command is preceded by a checkmark. To disable the Formatting Palette, choose the same command again or click its *close button* (the red button in its title bar).

- To move the Formatting Palette, click its title bar and drag it to a new location.

- You can expose or collapse sections of the Formatting Palette by clicking the triangles.

- To apply a Formatting Palette command, click an icon, make a choice from a drop-down menu or list, or enter a number or other appropriate data in a text box.

✔ Tips

- When typing an entry in a text box, it is sometimes necessary to complete it by pressing [Return].

- Most—but not all—of the Formatting Palette commands require that you first select text or an object.

Using the Format Painter

The Format Painter (**Figure 1.31**) is a recent addition to Office's formatting tool arsenal. Using it, you can copy the formatting of selected text and objects and apply it to other text and objects.

Figure 1.31 Click the Format Painter icon on the Standard toolbar.

To use the Format Painter:

◆ *Do any of the following:*

- ▲ To copy character formatting from one text string to another, select the source string, click the Format Painter toolbar icon, and then drag-select the target text string.

- ▲ To copy a paragraph format, select the entire source paragraph (including the paragraph mark at its end), click the Format Painter toolbar icon, and then click anywhere in the target paragraph (or drag through multiple paragraphs).

- ▲ To copy object formatting, select the source object, click the Format Painter toolbar icon, and then click the target object.

Format Painter

Figure 1.32 Double-click the Format Painter icon to lock it.

✔ Tips

- ■ To copy formatting to *multiple* objects, text strings, or paragraphs, double-click the Format Painter toolbar icon (**Figure 1.32**). One by one, apply the formatting to as many target objects, text strings, or paragraphs as you wish. When you've finished, click the Format Painter toolbar icon again.

- ■ In Excel, you can use the Format Painter to quickly format a range of cells. Some of the copied formatting includes any applied number format (such as Currency with two decimal places), cell shading, and borders.

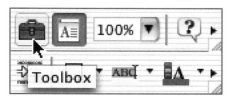

Figure 1.33 Click the Toolbox icon on the Standard toolbar.

Close button   Selected component

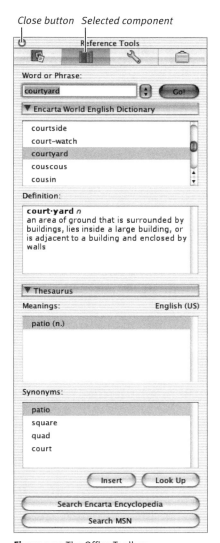

Figure 1.34 The Office Toolbox.

The Office Toolbox

Office 2004 provides access to several useful utilities in a new window called the Office Toolbox. In this section, you'll learn about the Scrapbook and Compatibility Report. For information on the Reference Tools (dictionary, encyclopedia, and thesaurus), see Chapter 3. Using the Project Palette is discussed in Chapter 27.

To open or close the Office Toolbox:

1. To open the Office Toolbox, click the Toolbox icon on the Standard toolbar (**Figure 1.33**) or choose Tools, followed by Scrapbook, Reference Tools, Compatibility Report, or Project Palette.

    The Office Toolbox opens (**Figure 1.34**), displaying the section you last used or the section you specifically chose. To switch to another tool, click its icon at the top of the window.

2. To close the Office Toolbox, click the Toolbox icon again or click the window's close button.

THE OFFICE TOOLBOX

The Scrapbook

In recent versions, Office provided its own Clipboard that you could use to temporarily store multiple items copied or cut from Word, Excel, and PowerPoint documents. The items were available for pasting into *any* Office document—not merely documents from the same application.

In Office 2004, the Office Clipboard is gone—replaced by a more robust utility known as the Scrapbook. The Scrapbook can store material that is currently selected within an Office document, copied or cut material that is in the OS X Clipboard, or complete files.

To add an item to the Scrapbook:

1. Open the Office Toolbox and, if necessary, click the Scrapbook icon.

   The Scrapbook appears (**Figure 1.35**).

2. *Do one of the following:*

   ▲ Select an item in an open Office document, such as text, a graphic image or other object, or a cell range. Drag the item into the Scrapbook or click the Scrapbook's Add button.

   ▲ To add the contents of the OS X Clipboard as a Scrapbook item, click the down arrow beside the Add button and choose Add from Clipboard (**Figure 1.36**).

   ▲ To add a file as a Scrapbook item, click the down arrow beside the Add button and choose Add File (see Figure 1.36). In the Choose a File dialog box that appears, select the file that you want to add and click Choose.

   The material is added as a new Scrapbook item (referred to as a *clip*).

Scrapbook icon   Filter menu   View menu

Figure 1.35 Use the Scrapbook to store text and graphic clips.

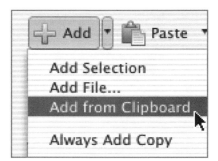

Figure 1.36 Click the Add drop-down menu to add information from the Clipboard or a file.

THE OFFICE TOOLBOX

Figure 1.37 Additional options are available in the Paste drop-down menu.

To insert a clip into a document:

1. *Optional:* Click in an active document to place the insertion point where you want to paste the Scrapbook clip.

2. In the Scrapbook, select a clip to be pasted. The selected item is shaded in blue.

3. *Do one of the following:*

   ▲ Click the Paste button at the bottom of the Scrapbook window. The clip is added to the document at the current cursor location.

   ▲ Drag the clip to the desired location in the document and release the mouse button.

   ▲ Click the down arrow beside the Paste button (**Figure 1.37**) and choose Paste as Plain Text. The selected text clip is pasted, but its formatting is ignored.

   ▲ Click the down arrow beside the Paste button (see Figure 1.37) and choose Paste as Picture. The clip is pasted into the document as a graphic object.

✔ Tip

■ To simultaneously paste multiple—but not *all*—Scrapbook items into a document, ⌘-click to select the items and then click Paste. You can also use this technique to delete multiple items.

THE OFFICE TOOLBOX

To organize your Scrapbook clips:

1. Select a clip in the Scrapbook.

2. *Do any of the following:*

   ▲ To filter the list to show only certain clips, choose a command from the drop-down menu at the top of the window (**Figure 1.38**). To restore the complete list, choose All.

   ▲ To change the clip display mode, choose List, Detail, or Large Preview from the View drop-down menu (see Figure 1.35).

   ▲ To add a descriptive name to a clip, double-click the clip. Replace the selected clip name with one of your choosing.

   ▲ To associate a clip with a category, project, or keywords, expand the Organize section of the Scrapbook. Choose a category and/or project from the drop-down lists. To add keywords, type them in the Keywords text box. Separate multiple keywords with commas.

   ▲ To delete a clip, select it and click the Delete button at the bottom of the window.

   ▲ To delete all or just the visible clips from the Scrapbook, click the down arrow beside the Delete button, choose the appropriate command, and confirm the deletion in the dialog box that appears.

Figure 1.38 Choose a filter option from the first drop-down menu. Then enter any other requested information (presented as a drop-down menu or text box).

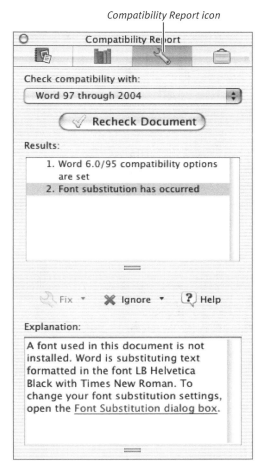

Compatibility Report icon

Figure 1.39 Use the Compatibility Report section of the Office Toolbox to determine if the current document has potential compatibility problems.

The Compatibility Report

Corporate users have long been concerned about the cross-platform compatibility of their documents, as well as whether users of older versions of Office will be able to read ones created in the newest version. In Office 2004, this should be less of a concern because users can check any document for potential compatibility issues and optionally correct them.

To create a compatibility report:

1. In Office 2004, open the document you want to check.

2. Open the Office Toolbox and, if necessary, click the Compatibility Report icon at the top of the Office Toolbox window.

3. If you know what version of Office that the document's intended recipient uses, select it from the drop-down list.

4. Click the Check Document button.

   Compatibility issues, if any, appear in the Results text box (**Figure 1.39**). The button label changes to "Recheck Document."

5. One by one, select each numbered item that appears in the Results text box.

   An explanation of the compatibility issue appears in the Explanation text box.

6. For each compatibility issue, you can click Fix or Ignore.

   However, as shown in Figure 1.39, not all issues can be corrected in this manner. Some must be fixed manually by following the Explanation text.

✔ Tip

■ Excel's Preferences has a Compatibility section where you can specify whether worksheets should automatically be checked for compatibility problems.

THE OFFICE TOOLBOX

Undoing Actions

If you make a mistake while working on a document, you can frequently correct it by *undoing* the action. You can either choose the Edit > Undo command or click the Undo toolbar icon (if available). Office 2004 programs support unlimited Undos.

To undo one or more actions:

1. To undo your most recent action, you can do any of the following:
   ▲ Choose Edit > Undo *action name*.
   ▲ Press ⌘Z.
   ▲ Click the Undo icon on the Standard toolbar (**Figure 1.40**).

2. To undo *multiple* recent actions, you can do any of the following:
   ▲ Repeatedly choose Edit > Undo *action name*, press ⌘Z, or click the Undo toolbar icon.
   ▲ Click the down arrow beside the Undo toolbar icon and select the actions that you want to correct (**Figure 1.41**).

   In order from most to least recent, each action is undone.

3. To reverse the effect of one or more Undo commands, do any of the following:
   ▲ Choose Edit > Redo.
   ▲ Press ⌘Y.
   ▲ Click the Redo toolbar icon (see Figure 1.40).
   ▲ Click the down arrow beside the Redo toolbar icon and choose the number of actions you want to redo (see Figure 1.41).

✔ Tip

■ Redo and Repeat share the same keyboard shortcut. You can repeat your most recent command by choosing Edit > Repeat or by pressing ⌘Y.

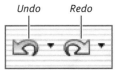
Undo   Redo

Figure 1.40 Undo and Redo icons are on the Standard toolbar.

Undo menu

Figure 1.41 Open the Undo menu and choose the actions to undo.

UNDOING ACTIONS

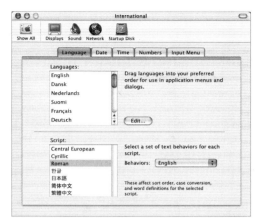

Figure 1.42 Use the International System Preferences to instruct OS X and the Office applications to support languages other than English on your computer.

Figure 1.43 Check the languages that you want OS X and Office to support.

Figure 1.44 Select a language dictionary for Word to use for spelling checks.

Working in Other Languages

Office 2004 has improved its Unicode language support, enabling it to display a wider variety of foreign (non-Roman) characters than in any previous version. You can view and edit documents in many languages, mix languages in a document, and set preferences to match the conventions and requirements of particular languages. You can also use foreign characters in filenames.

To use a foreign language:

1. Choose System Preferences from the Apple menu and click the International icon.

2. On the Language tab of the International dialog box (**Figure 1.42**), click the Edit button to add languages to the Languages list (**Figure 1.43**). After adding a language, you can change the list's order by dragging items up or down in the Languages list.

3. Click the other tabs to set your preferred date, time, and number styles, as well as the keyboard layout.

4. Close the dialog box.

5. In Word, choose Word > Preferences.

6. In the Preferences dialog box, click the Spelling and Grammar heading and then click the Dictionaries button.

   The Custom Dictionaries dialog box appears.

7. Select a language from the Languages drop-down list (**Figure 1.44**) and click OK.

8. Click OK to dismiss the Preferences dialog box.

Flagging Files for Followup

You can flag any Office document for followup at a later time. For instance, if you want to be reminded to review a budget worksheet two hours before the scheduled meeting, you can flag it for followup. At the appointed date and time, a reminder will pop onscreen. The Office Notifications program (see Chapter 23) is responsible for displaying all Office-related reminders.

To flag a document for followup:

1. Make the document active in the Office program in which it was created and then do one of the following:
   ▲ Click the Flag for Follow Up icon on the Standard toolbar (**Figure 1.45**).
   ▲ Choose Tools > Flag for Follow Up.
   The Flag for Follow Up dialog box appears (**Figure 1.46**).

2. Specify the date and time at which you want to be reminded, and then click OK.
   The flagged document is recorded as a new Entourage task.

3. At the designated time, a reminder dialog box will appear (**Figure 1.47**). Click the document's name to launch the appropriate Office application and open the document.

Figure 1.45 You can click the Flag for Follow Up icon on the Standard toolbar.

Figure 1.46 Specify a followup date/time and click OK.

Document link

Figure 1.47 To open the document, click its link in the Office Notifications dialog box.

Preference categories   *Preference settings*

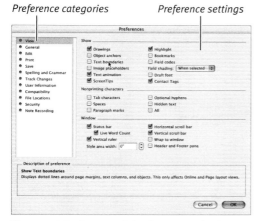

Figure 1.48 Preferences dialog boxes contain three panes: categories (left), options for the selected category (right), and a description of the option over which the cursor is presently hovering (bottom).

Customizing and Setting Preferences

Although the Office applications are pre-configured in a way that will suit the average user's needs, you're free to customize them, if you wish. There are two ways to do this:

◆ Modify the settings in the application's Preferences dialog box (available in all Office applications).

◆ Customize the application's toolbars, menus, Formatting Palette, and keyboard shortcuts (available in Word, PowerPoint, and Excel).

To change Preferences for a program:

1. With the program running, choose *program name* > Preferences (for example, Word > Preferences).

   The Preferences dialog box appears (**Figure 1.48**).

2. Select a Preferences category in the left pane.

   All related preferences appear to the right. When the cursor is rested over a preference, an explanation of the preference appears in the bottom pane.

3. Change preferences as you wish.

4. Repeat Steps 2 and 3 for other Preferences categories, if desired.

5. Click OK to put the new Preferences settings into effect.

✔ Tip

■ In general, the recommended approach to altering most preferences is to use each program for a while—until you are familiar with the way that you and the program work. *Then* make your changes.

CUSTOMIZING AND SETTING PREFERENCES

To customize an Office application:

1. With the application running, choose Tools > Customize, followed by the component that you want to change.

A dialog box for the component appears.

2. **Default toolbars.** To specify toolbars that should automatically be displayed, click the Toolbar tab of the Customize Toolbars/Menus dialog box (**Figure 1.49**).

From the Save in drop-down menu, choose the current document (to associate the toolbars with only that document) or a style sheet name, such as Normal (to associate the toolbars with all documents that are based on that style sheet). Then click check boxes to indicate the toolbars that should be displayed.

3. **Customized toolbars and menus.** You can customize toolbars and menus by adding icons, controls, and commands to them. (To modify a toolbar, the toolbar must be onscreen. You can display it by clicking its check box on the Toolbars tab of the dialog box.) Click the Commands tab of the Customize Toolbars/Menus dialog box (**Figure 1.50**).

Word only: From the Save in drop-down menu, choose the current document (to associate the toolbars with only that document) or a style sheet name, such as Normal (to associate the toolbars with all Word documents based on that style sheet).

All programs: Do any of the following:

▲ To add an icon to a toolbar, select it in the Commands pane and drag it to the desired location on the toolbar. (*Note:* To create a custom toolbar from scratch, click the New button.)

▲ To add a command to a menu, drag the command from the Commands pane onto the menu title in the

Figure 1.49 Add and remove checkmarks to specify which toolbars will automatically appear with the current document or style sheet.

Figure 1.50 To add a command to a menu, drag it from the dialog box into the destination menu.

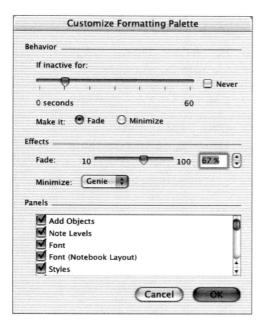

Figure 1.51 If you wish, you can customize the Formatting Palette for any application.

Figure 1.52 Use the Customize Keyboard dialog box to create new keyboard shortcuts for Word or Excel.

miniature menu bar (found just above the toolbars). The menu will drop down. Drag the command to its destination position within the menu and then release the mouse button.

4. **Customized Formatting Palette.** In the Customize Formatting Palette dialog box (**Figure 1.51**), you can remove panels (by clearing their check boxes) and change the fading/minimizing behavior.

5. **Customized Keyboard (Word and Excel only).** In the Customize Keyboard dialog box (**Figure 1.52**), you can add or change keyboard shortcuts for Word and Excel commands. In the Categories list, select a menu category; in the Commands list, select the command whose shortcuts you want to change. The current shortcuts assigned to that command (if any) are displayed.

For Word only. From the Save changes in drop-down menu, choose the current document (to associate the shortcuts with only that document) or a style sheet name, such as Normal (to associate the shortcuts with all Word documents based on that style sheet).

Do any of the following:

▲ To add a new keyboard shortcut, click in the Press new shortcut key text box, press the key combination, and then click Add or Assign. (Be certain that no other command is already associated with the key combination before you click Add or Assign!)

▲ To remove a keyboard shortcut, select it in the Current keys list and click Remove.

▲ To restore the default keyboard shortcuts, select the style sheet or document name from the Save changes in drop-down menu and then click Reset All.

Getting Help

Office 2004 provides many sources of help (**Figure 1.53**).

◆ You can get pop-up ScreenTips (also called ToolTips) for toolbar icons and parts of the document window.

◆ You can activate the Assistant and have it answer your typed queries.

◆ You can view the included sample files and other learning materials.

◆ You can use the detailed online help included with each application.

◆ You can visit Microsoft's Web site for other information.

To display a ScreenTip or ToolTip:

1. You can enable or disable ScreenTips separately for each Office program.

   Do the following:

   ▲ **Word.** Choose Word > Preferences. On the View tab, enter or remove the checkmark from ScreenTips.

   ▲ **Excel or PowerPoint.** Choose Tools > Customize > Customize Toolbars/ Menus. In the Customize dialog box (**Figure 1.54**), enter or remove the checkmark from Show ScreenTips on toolbars. (You may also wish to check or uncheck Show shortcut keys in ScreenTips.)

   ▲ **Entourage.** Choose Entourage > Preferences, select the General heading, and enter or remove the checkmark from Show ToolTips.

2. With ScreenTips or ToolTips enabled, move the pointer over any icon, button, or other Office element, and then wait a second or two.

   A yellow ScreenTip appears (**Figure 1.55**).

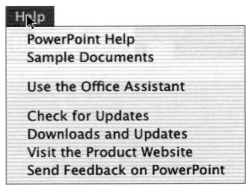

Figure 1.53 Most help sources are available directly from each Office application's Help menu.

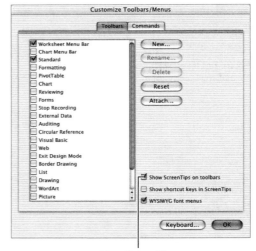

Show ScreenTips

Figure 1.54 ScreenTips in Excel and PowerPoint are governed by this check box in the Customize dialog box.

Figure 1.55 When you rest the cursor over most Office components, a ScreenTip appears.

What would you like to do?

- Create form letters by using the Data Merge Manager
- About data merge
- About data merge data sources
- About fields
- Field codes: MergeRec field

create a form letter

Options   Cancel   **Search**

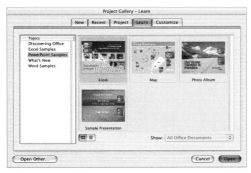

Figure 1.56 In the Assistant's search dialog box, type a question or search string and click Search.

To use the Assistant:

1. If the Assistant isn't presently visible, choose Help > Use the Office Assistant.

2. Click the Assistant to request help.

3. Type a question or search string, and then press [Return] or click Search.

The Assistant will interpret your query and present a list of options (**Figure 1.56**).

4. Click a suggested topic to open Microsoft Office Help to that subject.

✔ Tip

- You can customize the Assistant by clicking the Options button (see Figure 1.56). The Office Assistant dialog box opens. On the Gallery tab, you can select a different Assistant (if others are installed).

To view sample files and other Office learning materials:

1. *Do one of the following:*

▲ Choose Help > Sample Documents.

▲ Open the Project Gallery (File > Project Gallery) and click the Learn tab (**Figure 1.57**).

2. Select a topic from the Topics pane.

3. In the right side of the dialog box, select the item that you want to view.

4. Click the Open button.

The document opens in the associated Office application, in your default Web browser, or your default PDF viewer.

✔ Tip

- To read the Office 2004 manual, select the Discovering Office topic. Select What's New for a rundown of the new features introduced in Office 2004.

Figure 1.57 Click the Learn tab of the Project Gallery to open sample files and similar materials.

GETTING HELP

To use application help documents:

1. Choose Help > *program name* Help.
   The Microsoft Office Help window opens (**Figure 1.58**).

2. *Do one of the following:*
   - ▲ In the toolbar at the top of the Help window, click Contents to display a list of major topics in the left pane.
   - ▲ Click Index to get an alphabetical list of key entries in Office Help.
   - ▲ Click Search to search for keywords. If the Assistant is active, it will handle the search request; if not, the search query will appear in the left pane of the Microsoft Office Help window (see Figure 1.58).

3. Click an item in the left pane to display its help text or to expand it to display a list of subtopics, any of which you can click to view the associated help text.

4. To navigate backward and forward through multiple help screens, click the arrow icons in the Microsoft Office Help toolbar. In the body of the window, underlined blue text is a clickable link to another Help section. Special terms are also shown in blue, but have no underlining). Click a term to view its definition.

✔ Tips

- ■ To view an Office application's Web site using your default Web browser, choose Help > Visit the Product Website.

- ■ To check for available updates to the current Office application, choose Help > Check for Updates. To learn more about available updates and other downloads, choose Help > Downloads and Updates.

Figure 1.58 Your primary source of detailed help (other than this book) is Microsoft Office Help.

OFFICE 2004 AND THE INTERNET

2

Microsoft Office has features that let you tap into the power of the Internet. This chapter shows you how to incorporate Internet links (known as *hyperlinks*) within your documents, so you can direct readers to the Web to see a graphic, hear an audio file, or read additional information on a topic. For example, a Word letter about your summer vacation could contain a link to a Web site where you posted pictures.

You'll also learn how to perform the following Internet-related activities:

◆ Without leaving Word, Excel, or Power-Point, send the current document in email.

◆ Fetch Web pages from within Word.

◆ Save any Office document or your Entourage calendar in HTML format so you can publish it on the Web. Because the resulting files can be viewed in any browser, you can also give or email them to anyone who doesn't use Office.

◆ Check for software updates to Office.

◆ Visit the Office Web site, use its resources, and download useful files.

Adding Hyperlinks

Including clickable links (called *hyperlinks*) in your Office documents is a handy way to enhance content. When clicked, a hyperlink will launch a browser to display a particular Web page, open a document located on your hard disk, or address a new message in your email program.

To create a Web page hyperlink in a Word, Excel, or PowerPoint document:

1. *Do one of the following:*
   ▲ Position the insertion point where you want to insert a text link.
   ▲ Select existing text or an object that you want to designate as the link.

2. Choose Insert > Hyperlink (⌘K). The Insert Hyperlink dialog box appears (**Figure 2.1**).

3. If it isn't selected, click the Web Page tab.

4. *Do one of the following:*
   ▲ Type or paste the Web address in the Link to text box.
   ▲ If you've previously linked to the desired address, select it from the drop-down list.
   ▲ If the address is a bookmarked site in your browser or you recently viewed the page, you can select it by clicking the Favorites or History button, respectively.

5. *Optional:* The text in the Display text box is what will appear on the document page. By default, the Link to text is displayed. To specify different text, edit as desired.

6. *Optional:* When the cursor is rested over a hyperlink, a pop-up ScreenTip appears (**Figure 2.2**). By default, the Link to text is displayed. Click ScreenTip to customize the text that appears.

Select a recently used address

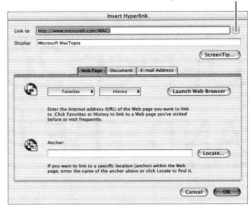

Figure 2.1 You can create a link in the current document that—when clicked—will open a Web page, a document on disk, or a new email message.

http://www.siliconwasteland.com

Figure 2.2 A ScreenTip automatically appears when you rest the cursor over a hyperlink.

Figure 2.3 To link to a specific location on a Web page, select it from the named bookmarks in the list.

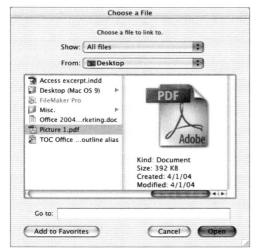

Figure 2.4 Select the document file to which you want to link.

7. *Optional:* To link to a specific spot on the Web page (called a *bookmark* or *anchor*), click the Locate button. Note that the Web page designer must have already created the anchor. You cannot arbitrarily select a link spot.

   In the dialog box that appears (**Figure 2.3**), select a bookmark and click OK.

8. Click OK to create the hyperlink.

To create a document hyperlink in a Word, Excel, or PowerPoint document:

1. *Do one of the following:*
   - ▲ Position the insertion point where you want to insert a text link.
   - ▲ Select existing text or an object that you want to designate as the link.

2. Choose Insert > Hyperlink (⌘K).

   The Insert Hyperlink dialog box appears (see Figure 2.1).

3. On the Document tab, click Select.

   The Choose a File dialog box appears (**Figure 2.4**).

4. Select a file and click Open.

   To restrict listed files to one type, select a file type from the Show drop-down list.

5. *Optional:* The text in the Display text box is what will appear on the document page. By default, the Link to text is displayed. To specify different text, edit as desired.

6. *Optional:* When the cursor is rested over a hyperlink, a pop-up ScreenTip appears (see Figure 2.2). By default, the Link to text (i.e., the file path) is displayed. Click ScreenTip to customize the pop-up text.

7. *Optional:* To link to a bookmarked spot in the document, click the Locate button. In the dialog box that appears, select a bookmark and click OK.

8. Click OK to create the hyperlink.

To create an email hyperlink in a Word, Excel, or PowerPoint document:

1. *Do one of the following:*

   ▲ Position the insertion point where you want to insert a text link.

   ▲ Select the text or object that you want to designate as the link.

2. Choose Insert > Hyperlink ($\mathcal{H}$ K).

   The Insert Hyperlink dialog box appears (see Figure 2.1).

3. Click the E-mail Address tab.

4. *Do one of the following:*

   ▲ Type or paste the recipient's email address in the To text box.

   ▲ Select an address from the Recent Addresses drop-down list.

   ▲ To look up an address in your default email program, click Launch E-mail Application.

5. *Optional:* Enter a subject for the message in the Subject text box.

6. *Optional:* The text in the Display text box is what will appear in the email message. By default, the Link to text is displayed. To specify different text, edit as desired.

7. *Optional:* When the cursor is rested over a hyperlink, a pop-up ScreenTip appears (see Figure 2.2). By default, the Link to text (i.e., the email address) is displayed. Click ScreenTip to customize the pop-up text.

8. When the settings are satisfactory (**Figure 2.5**), click OK.

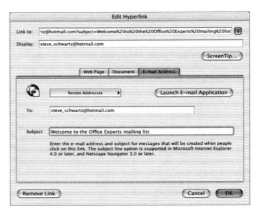

Figure 2.5 Specify the intended recipient's email address and the text for the Subject line.

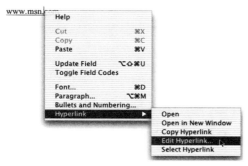

Figure 2.6 To modify the selected link, choose Hyperlink > Edit Hyperlink.

To create a hyperlink in an Entourage document:

◆ Type or paste the complete link address into the message. The following examples illustrate the proper syntax.

▲ `http://www.msn.com` (Web address)

▲ `ftp://ftp.microsoft.com` (FTP site)

▲ `mailto:roadrunner@cox.net` (email address)

Whether or not the link will be clickable depends on the capabilities of the recipient's email program.

To edit a hyperlink:

1. *Do one of the following:*

▲ Ctrl-click the hyperlink text or object to reveal the pop-up menu. In Word or PowerPoint (**Figure 2.6**), choose Hyperlink > Edit Hyperlink. In Excel, choose Hyperlink.

▲ Select all or part of the hyperlink. Choose Insert > Hyperlink (⌘K).

The Edit Hyperlink dialog box appears, identical to the Insert Hyperlink dialog box (see Figure 2.1).

2. Make the necessary changes and click OK.

To remove a hyperlink:

1. *Do one of the following:*

▲ Ctrl-click the hyperlink text or object to reveal the pop-up menu. In Word or PowerPoint (**Figure 2.6**), choose Hyperlink > Edit Hyperlink. In Excel, choose Hyperlink.

▲ Select all or part of the hyperlink. Choose Insert > Hyperlink (⌘K).

The Edit Hyperlink dialog box appears, identical to the Insert Hyperlink dialog box (see Figure 2.1).

2. Click Remove Link and then click OK.

ADDING HYPERLINKS

✔ Tips

- When clicked, a Web or email hyperlink automatically launches the person's default Web browser or email program.

- A document hyperlink can be made to *any* document on your hard disk—not just to Office documents. When clicked, the appropriate application will launch and then open the designated document.

- You can create a clickable table of contents in any lengthy Word document. First, assign a bookmark to every major heading. Then create a document hyperlink from each table of contents entry to the appropriate bookmark.

- You can also create a hyperlink by typing it directly into a document or by copying it from another source (such as the Address box of your Web browser, a link on a Web page, or embedded in an email message) and then pasting it into the document.

- For typed hyperlinks to be recognized in Word, AutoCorrect must be set to transform eligible text into links. Choose Tools > AutoCorrect, click the AutoFormat As You Type tab, and ensure that Internet paths with hyperlinks (**Figure 2.7**) is checked.

- For a Web page hyperlink to work when clicked, you must be on a computer that has an Internet connection.

- Deleting hyperlinked text or a hyperlinked object simultaneously deletes the link.

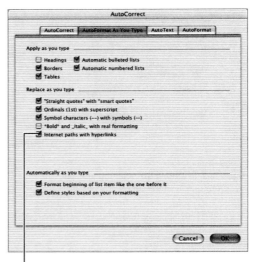

Convert addresses to hyperlinks

Figure 2.7 Word ignores typed hyperlinks unless this option is enabled.

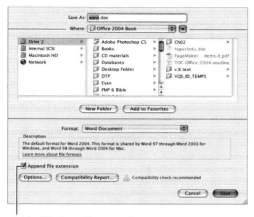

Add a Windows file extension

Figure 2.8 When sending attachments to Windows users, click the Append file extension check box to add the appropriate extension.

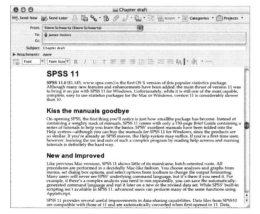

Figure 2.9 If you know that the recipient doesn't have Office or a compatible program, you can send the document as formatted HTML.

Emailing an Office Document

With an email program such as Microsoft Entourage (see Part V), you can send your documents to others. Using the Send To command in Word, PowerPoint, or Excel, you can send the currently open document as an *attachment* (a file delivered with an email message) or as a formatted HTML message.

To send an Office document as an email attachment:

1. *Optional:* Choose File > Save As to save the document. If you intend to send it to someone who is using Windows, click the Append file extension check box (**Figure 2.8**).

2. *Do one of the following:*

▲ Choose File > Send To > Mail Recipient (as Attachment).

▲ Choose File > Send To > Mail Recipient (as HTML).

Your default email program launches and creates a new message with the document already attached or converted to HTML (**Figure 2.9**).

3. Select recipients, write the message text, and send the message.

✔ Tips

■ The OS X email programs supported by these commands are Entourage, Apple's Mail, Mailsmith, and Eudora. If another email program is set as your default, the Send To commands will not be available.

■ If multiple people use your computer, you may need to switch *identities*. Quit all Office programs, launch Entourage, choose Entourage > Switch Identity, and click Switch in the dialog box that appears. In the next dialog box, select your identity and click OK.

EMAILING AN OFFICE DOCUMENT

Other Internet Capabilities

Office 2004 has additional Internet capabilities that you may want to explore. Here are some of the most interesting ones:

◆ Use Word's File > Open Web Page command (**Figure 2.10**) to fetch Web pages from the Internet.

◆ You can create Web pages from Word, PowerPoint, or Excel documents using the File > Save as Web Page command, enabling you to publish the pages on the Internet or a company intranet. If you have friends or coworkers who don't use Office, they can view the resulting documents in any browser. For an example of saving an Office document as a Web page, see Chapter 19.

◆ You can use the File > Save as Web Page command in Entourage to save your calendar as a series of Web pages (**Figure 2.11**). If you publish the pages to a Web site, you (and others, if you wish) can refer to the calendar from any Internet access point—while on vacation or a business trip, for example.

◆ Use the File > Web Page Preview command to quickly determine how the current Word, PowerPoint, or Excel document will look if saved as a Web page.

◆ The Help menu has commands that open your Web browser to display information from the Internet.

　▲ Choose Help > Check for Updates to launch Microsoft AutoUpdate (**Figure 2.12**).

　▲ Choose Tools > Tools on the Web to visit the Mactopia Web site. You can get assistance with Office programs and use the site resources, such as encyclopedias and trip planners.

Select a recently used address

Figure 2.10 Type, paste, or select the address of the Web page that you want to open.

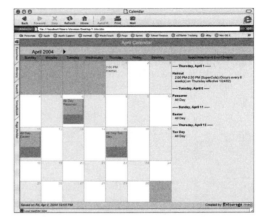

Figure 2.11 You can select a date range from your Entourage calendar and save it as a set of Web pages.

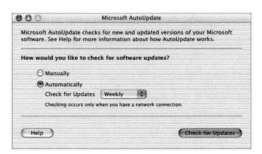

Figure 2.12 You can configure AutoUpdate to check for Office updates on a regular schedule or just run it manually whenever you wish.

Launch browser

Figure 2.13 You can view and download clip art from Microsoft's Web site.

▲ Choose Help > Visit the Product Web Site or Help > Downloads and Updates to go to the Office section of the Mactopia Web site or to the downloads area, respectively.

◆ You can download additional clip art images by choosing Insert > Picture > Clip Art and then clicking Online in the Clip Gallery window (**Figure 2.13**).

◆ If you need to perform Internet activities from within Word, Excel, or PowerPoint, display the Web toolbar (**Figure 2.14**) by choosing View > Toolbars > Web.

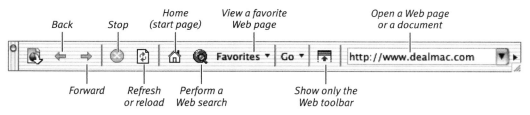

Back   Stop   Home (start page)   View a favorite Web page   Open a Web page or a document

Forward   Refresh or reload   Perform a Web search   Show only the Web toolbar

Figure 2.14 Using the Web toolbar, you can perform common Web activities in Office applications.

Part II:
Microsoft Word

WORKING WITH WORD

Normally, the first chapter in a Part covers a program's basic features, such as how to create, open, and save documents, edit text, and the like. However, because many of these features and techniques are common to *all* Office applications, they've already been discussed at length in Chapter 1.

Expanding on the material in Chapter 1, this chapter covers additional elementary features that are specific to Word. While you can get along fine without mastering the material in this chapter, having a familiarity with it will make your Word experience more productive.

Other chapters in Part II explain document and text formatting, how to include images in your Word documents, designing tables, and employing more advanced features to create professional-looking documents for use in home, school, and business.

The Word Window

If this is the first time you've used Word, you should start by familiarizing yourself with the Word window and its components (**Figure 3.1**). They'll be referred to throughout the chapters in Part II of this book.

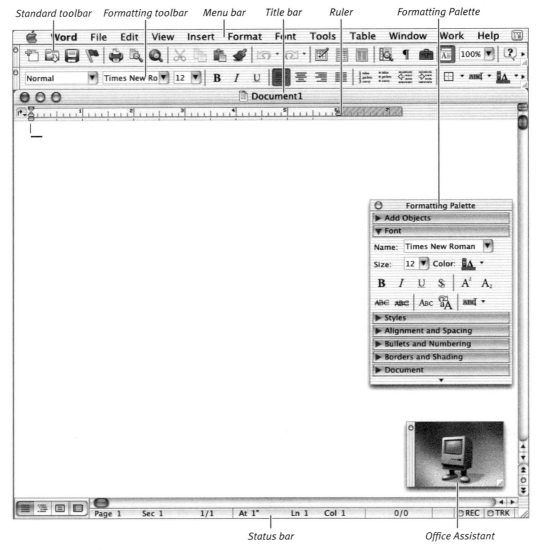

Figure 3.1 The Word window.

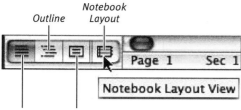

Figure 3.2 You can change to most views by clicking am icon at the bottom of the document window.

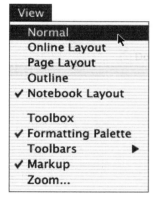

Figure 3.3 You can also change views by choosing a command from the View menu.

Changing views

Changing the layout often requires that you view a document in different ways. You can select from Normal, Online Layout, Page Layout, Outline, Notebook Layout, and Master Document views. **Table 3.1** explains each view's purpose.

To change views:

◆ *Do one of the following:*

  ▲ Click the Normal, Outline, Page Layout, or Notebook Layout icon in the bottom-left corner of the document window (**Figure 3.2**).

  ▲ Choose a view from the View menu (**Figure 3.3**).

✔ Tips

■ Master Document view is only accessible from the View menu.

■ Although Page Layout view constantly displays useful layout information (such as margins, page breaks, and so on), writing in Word is usually fastest when done in Normal view.

■ To use "click and type" (discussed later in this chapter), you must switch to Page Layout, Online Layout, or Notebook Layout view.

THE WORD WINDOW

Table 3.1

Word Document Views	
VIEW	PURPOSE
Normal	Shows text formatting in a simplified page layout that lends itself well to most standard writing tasks.
Outline	Shows the document's structure and allows you to rearrange text by dragging headings.
Page Layout	Shows the document as it will look when printed, including the page borders, margins, headers and footers, columns, and frames that contain images.
Online Layout	Shows the document as it would appear in a Web browser.
Notebook Layout	Used to quickly record notes and ideas (both in text and audio form).
Master Document	Enables you to form a compound document composed of individual documents.

Using the navigation pane

Introduced in Office 2004, you can use the navigation pane to quickly move to any page or heading in the current document. As such, it is especially useful in long documents, such as manuals and reports.

To use the navigation pane:

1. To show or hide the navigation pane (on the left side of the document window), choose View > Navigation Pane or click the Navigation Pane icon on the Standard toolbar.

2. The navigation pane has two display modes, determined by your choice from the drop-down menu above the pane (**Figure 3.4**).
   - ▲ **Thumbnail.** Displays miniature representations of document pages.
   - ▲ **Document Map.** Displays headings in the current document.

   You can switch between display modes by choosing the other command.

3. To jump to a new location in the current document, do one of the following:
   - ▲ When Thumbnail is chosen, click a page thumbnail.
   - ▲ When Document Map is chosen, click a heading.

✔ Tips

- You can change the width of the navigation pane by dragging the divider to the left or right.

- In Document Map view, you can control the specific heading levels displayed by (Control)-clicking in the navigation pane (**Figure 3.5**). Choose a Show Heading command to display all headings that are that level or higher. You can also expand and collapse heading levels as needed.

Menu   Divider

Figure 3.4 Use the navigation pane to navigate large documents.

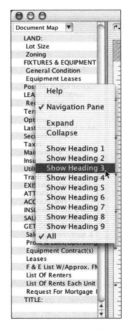

Figure 3.5 Choose a Show Heading command to specify the heading levels to be displayed.

Entering Text

If you're new to computing, you'll find that entering text in a word processing document is only a little different than using a typewriter—different but *much* simpler.

As in most computer programs, the blinking vertical line (called the *insertion point*) indicates where the next character you type will appear. Type as you would with a typewriter. The main differences include the following:

- You press [Return] only to begin a new paragraph—*not* to begin a new line in the same paragraph.

- You'll note that the lines of a paragraph are automatically adjusted to include as many words as possible. This occurs via a feature known as *word wrap.* If you add or delete text in a paragraph, the entire paragraph rewraps to accommodate the changes.

- Typing a word processing document does not have to be a linear process—as it must with a typewriter. For example, although you *can* backspace over errors (by pressing [Delete]), you can also just select incorrect text and type over it. (The first character you type automatically deletes the selected text.)

- You can click anywhere within existing text to change the insertion point. Then you can insert more text at that spot, correct an error, or perform other edits.

✔ Tip

- For additional information concerning text entry, see Chapter 1.

ENTERING TEXT

Click and type

Click and type is a Word feature that can be thought of as a form of automatic paragraph formatting. You can click in any blank area of your document to enter text at that spot. In a new document, for example, you could click near the right margin or halfway down the page. Click and type is not available in Normal or Outline view.

To enable and use click and type:

1. Choose Word > Preferences.

   The Preferences dialog box appears.

2. Select the Edit heading in the left side of the dialog box to display the Edit preferences (**Figure 3.6**).

3. Click the Enable click and type check box, and then click OK.

4. Switch to a view in which click and type is supported: Page Layout, Online Layout, or Notebook Layout.

5. Move the cursor to a blank spot on the page where you'd like to type.

   As you move, the cursor changes shape to reflect the type of paragraph formatting that will be applied to the text (**Figure 3.7**). The shapes include align left, align right, center, left indent, left text wrap, and right text wrap.

6. Double-click to set the new insertion point and begin typing.

   Word inserts the necessary blank paragraphs and tabs to fill the document to the beginning of the new text.

Enable or disable click and type

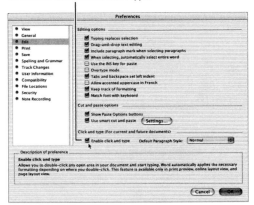

Figure 3.6 Enable click and type in the Edit section of the Preferences dialog box.

 Figure 3.7 The click and type cursor changes to show the paragraph formatting that will be applied.

ENTERING TEXT

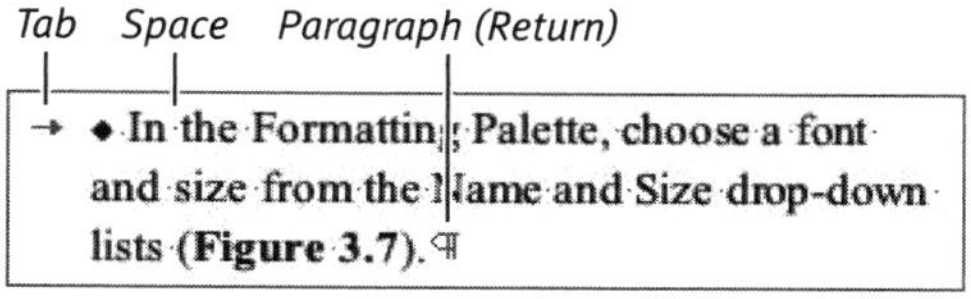

Tab   Space   Paragraph (Return)

→   ♦ In the Formatting Palette, choose a font
and size from the Name and Size drop-down
lists (**Figure 3.7**). ¶

Figure 3.8 When displayed, non-printing characters
are a faint gray.

Figure 3.9 The Show/Hide
¶ icon is the paragraph
symbol.

Table 3.2

Non-printing Characters	
SYMBOL	CHARACTER
· (dot)	Space
→▪	Tab
◂┘	Line break (new line, same paragraph)
¶	End of paragraph

Showing/Hiding Non-printing Characters

Non-printing characters indicate where you
ended a paragraph, pressed (Spacebar), or
pressed (Tab) (**Figure 3.8**). You can show or
hide non-printing characters as you work on
a Word document. Being able to see non-
printing characters is especially helpful when
you're trying to locate multiple tab characters
where only one should be or when you're
looking for errant punctuation, such as blank
paragraphs or extra spaces. See **Table 3.2** for
a complete list of non-printing characters.

To show/hide non-printing characters:

♦ Click the Show/Hide ¶ icon on the
Standard toolbar (**Figure 3.9**).

✔ Tips

■ The Show/Hide ¶ icon is a toggle. Click
it once to show non-printing characters
and a second time to hide them.

■ Showing non-printing characters is
particularly useful in the proofing/editing
stage—after you've finished the writing.
(Having non-printing characters visible
while *creating* a document, on the other
hand, can be distracting.)

SHOWING/HIDING NON-PRINTING CHARACTERS

Editing: Beyond the Basics

As mentioned previously, the basic editing techniques were discussed in Chapter 1. In this section, you'll learn to search for and replace text, use Office's AutoText feature to automatically enter text for you, and use smart buttons to speed common editing and formatting tasks.

Finding and replacing text

You can instruct Word to search for and optionally replace words or phrases. For example, if you can't remember the page on which you referred to Apple's annual report, you could perform a Find on the phrase "annual report." Or suppose your company has recently changed its name from Bob's Plumbing to Widgets Inc. Using the Replace command, you can replace every instance of the old name with the new one. Refer to **Table 3.3** (on the next page) for a list of special Find options.

To find text:

1. Choose Edit > Find or press ⌘ F.

   The Find and Replace dialog box appears (**Figure 3.10**). The Find tab is selected.

2. Type a search string in the Find what box.

3. *Do one of the following:*

   ▲ To find the next instance of the search string, click Find Next.

   Word searches for the string, starting from the current insertion point. If it finds the string, it is automatically highlighted in the document (**Figure 3.11**).

   ▲ To find and highlight *all* instances of the search string, click the check box to Highlight all items found in, choose an option from the drop-down menu (such as Main Document or Current Selection), and click Find All.

Enter search string

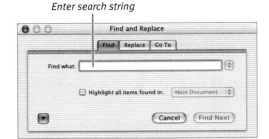

Figure 3.10 Type the text you want to find in the Find what text box.

Highlighted match   *Search string*

Figure 3.11 When a Find or Find and Replace search locates a match, Word scrolls as necessary to highlight the found text.

Show/hide additional options

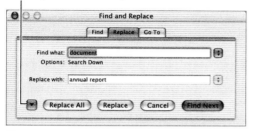

Figure 3.12 Type the search string in the Find what box and the replacement text in the Replace with box.

4. *Do one of the following:*

▲ To search for the next occurrence of the text string (when searching for individual occurrences), click Find Next. Repeat as necessary to find additional matches.

▲ If you're done searching, click the Cancel button or the close box.

To replace text:

1. *Do one of the following:*

▲ Choose Edit > Replace ([Shift][⌘][H]). The Find and Replace dialog box appears. The Replace tab is selected (**Figure 3.12**).

▲ Choose Edit > Find ([⌘][F]). The Find and Replace dialog box appears. Click the Replace tab.

2. Type a search string in the Find what text box.

3. In the Replace with text box, type the replacement string and click Find Next.

Word searches for the text. If it finds an instance of the string, that instance is highlighted in the document.

4. Click Replace to replace the text or Find Next to search for the next occurrence of the search string.

Repeat this step until you're done or until Word notifies you that it has finished searching the document.

EDITING: BEYOND THE BASICS

Table 3.3

Special Find Options	
OPTION	DESCRIPTION
Match case	Finds words that contain the same combination of upper- and lowercase characters
Find whole words only	Finds only complete words (for example, "art" finds only "art," not "artist")
Use wildcards	Allows you to enter a code to specify a special character combination to find (for example, "?" will match any single character)
Sounds like	Finds text that sounds like the search string
Find all word forms	Finds all variations of the chosen word (for example, "apple" and "apples")

✔ Tips

- When performing a Replace, you can click Replace All to simultaneously replace all occurrences of the search string.

- When performing a new Find, you can repeat a search by clicking the arrow to the right of the Find what text box. Search terms you've previously used appear in this drop-down list.

- Click the triangle in the bottom-left corner of the dialog box to display additional search options (**Figure 3.13**). For instance, Finds are normally case insensitive. If you want to find terms that match a specific capitalization, click the Match case check box. To hide the additional search options, click the triangle again.

- You can also base a search on a particular font, effect, or style by choosing options from the Format drop-down menu. For example, you could replace all instances of Arial Italic text with Helvetica Italic (**Figure 3.14**).

- To specify a search direction (down, up, or all) or to search all open documents (rather than just the active one), choose an option from the drop-down menu at the top of the expanded search options.

- To include a special character such as a tab or paragraph mark in a search, open the Special menu and choose a character (**Figure 3.15**). The symbol for the chosen character is automatically added to the search string. (In this example, ^t is inserted to represent a tab character.)

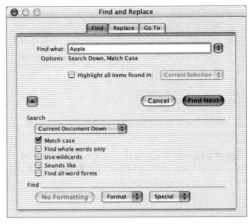

Figure 3.13 Click the triangle to expand the Find and Replace dialog box to show advanced search options.

Figure 3.14 By including only format options in the Find what and Replace with boxes, you can replace one font with another throughout a document.

Figure 3.15 To include a special character in a Find or Replace string, choose it from this menu.

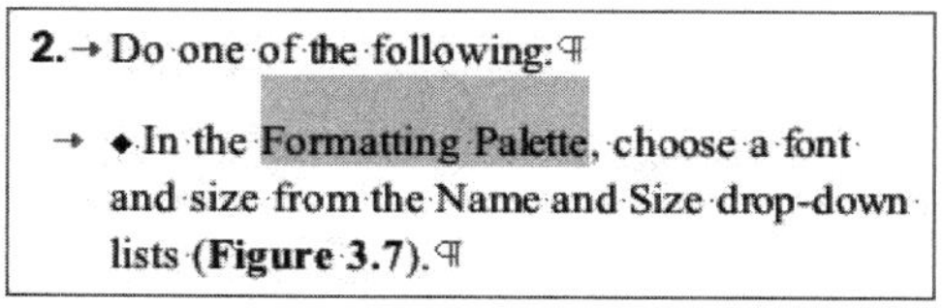

2. → Do one of the following: ⁊

→ ◆ In the Formatting Palette, choose a font and size from the Name and Size drop-down lists (**Figure 3.7**). ⁊

Figure 3.16 Select the text that will become the new AutoText entry.

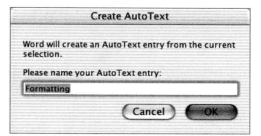

Figure 3.17 The Create AutoText dialog appears and suggests a name for the new entry. Edit it as desired.

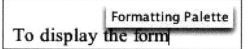

Figure 3.18 Whenever you type four characters that Word recognizes as a possible AutoText entry, you are offered the opportunity to insert it in the document.

Automatically entering text

The AutoText feature is designed to save you from repetitively typing text. AutoText enables you to quickly insert any amount of text into a document—from one word to multiple paragraphs.

To create an AutoText entry:

1. In the active document, select the text from which you want to create an AutoText entry (**Figure 3.16**).

The selected text must consist of at least five characters.

2. Choose Insert > AutoText > New.

The Create AutoText dialog box appears and suggests a name (**Figure 3.17**).

3. *Optional:* Replace the suggested name with one of your own.

If you want to be able to insert the entry using AutoComplete, make sure that the name contains at least four characters.

4. Click OK to add the text to the list of available AutoText entries.

To insert an AutoText entry:

1. As you type, Word watches for the name of an AutoText entry. When it detects one, a yellow box containing the AutoText entry's name appears (**Figure 3.18**).

2. *Do one of the following:*

▲ To accept the AutoText replacement, press [Enter] or [Return].

▲ To ignore the proposed AutoText replacement, continue typing.

EDITING: BEYOND THE BASICS

✔ Tips

- You can use AutoText to enter lengthy medical, legal, or technical terms. AutoText is also great for writing letters that have the same opening and closing lines.

- You can also include graphics, such as a logo, in an AutoText entry.

- To save a formatted paragraph as an AutoText entry, be sure to include the paragraph mark at the end of the paragraph in your selection. Otherwise, the entry will be inserted as plain text. (To view paragraph marks, click the Show/ Hide ¶ icon in the Standard toolbar.)

- To delete an AutoText entry, choose Insert > AutoText > AutoText. On the AutoText tab of the AutoCorrect dialog box (**Figure 3.19**), select the entry and click Delete.

- You can also make an AutoText insertion by choosing Insert > AutoText > AutoText, selecting the entry from the list in the AutoCorrect dialog box (see Figure 3.19), and clicking Insert.

- Another way to make an AutoText entry is by choosing it from one of the Insert > AutoText submenus (**Figure 3.20**). Word provides dozens of common AutoText entries to get you started. You'll find your personal entries in the template in which they were stored; typically, this is the Normal template.

- By default, the names of your Entourage contacts are also available as AutoText entries. To exclude them, choose Insert > AutoText > AutoText, and check the Exclude contacts check box in the AutoCorrect dialog box (see Figure 3.19).

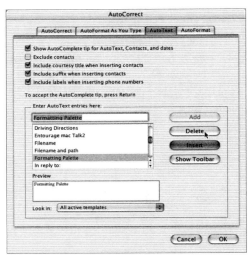

Figure 3.19 You can delete AutoText entries, as well as specify the classes of entries to use, in the AutoCorrect dialog box.

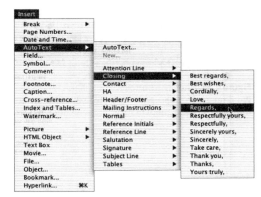

Figure 3.20 You can also insert an AutoText entry by choosing it from an Insert > AutoText submenu.

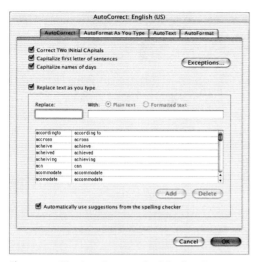

Figure 3.21 The AutoCorrect tab of the AutoCorrect dialog box contains the list of items that will automatically be corrected in your documents.

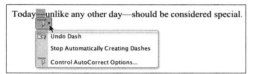

Figure 3.22 When the button appears, click it to open the drop-down menu.

Working with smart buttons

To make certain edits more flexible, Word and Excel provide smart buttons. A *smart button* is a pop-up icon that—when clicked—displays a menu of options. There are two types of smart buttons: AutoCorrect Options and Paste Options.

The Replace list of words, phrases, and symbols in the AutoCorrect dialog box (**Figure 3.21**) determines which text will automatically be substituted for other text as you type. For instance, if you type (c), a copyright symbol (©) is substituted. Common typos, such as ones caused by transposing letters, are also corrected. After an autocorrection has occurred, you can click the AutoCorrect Options button to modify the correction.

Paste Option buttons are immediately available after pasting or using drag and drop. You can specify that the pasted or dropped text keep its original formatting or that it adopt the formatting of surrounding text.

To use an AutoCorrect Options button:

1. After an autocorrection, move the cursor over the corrected text.

   A blue underline appears under the text.

2. Move the cursor over the blue underline to reveal the AutoCorrect button. Click the button to open the drop-down menu (**Figure 3.22**).

3. *Do one of the following:*

   ▲ Choose Undo or Change back to restore the original, uncorrected text.

   ▲ Choose Stop automatically correcting *condition* to prevent future instances from being corrected and to delete the item from the Replace list.

   ▲ Choose Control AutoCorrect Options to modify your AutoCorrect settings (see Figure 3.22).

To use a Paste Options button:

1. Immediately following most paste or drag-and-drop operations, a Paste Options button appears (**Figure 3.23**).

2. Click the button to reveal the drop-down menu.

3. *Do one of the following:*

   ▲ Choose Keep Source Formatting to keep the original formatting for the pasted or dropped text.

   ▲ Choose Match Destination Formatting to change the text formatting of the pasted or dragged text to match that of the surrounding text and paragraph.

   ▲ Choose Keep Text Only to strip all previously applied formatting from the pasted or dropped text. (For instance, text that was colored red and italicized would be reduced to plain, black text.)

✔ Tips

■ There is no time limit for clicking an AutoCorrect Options button. As long as you haven't closed and reopened the document, an AutoCorrect Options button will be available for every autocorrection made during the current session.

■ On the other hand, a Paste Options button must be used immediately. You must take advantage of it while it's visible.

■ For some users, Paste Options buttons are a distraction or nuisance. To prevent them from constantly popping up, choose Word > Preferences. In the Edit section of the Preferences dialog box (**Figure 3.24**), remove the checkmark from Show Paste Options buttons.

■ After undoing an autocorrection, you can later "redo" the correction by clicking the button and choosing Redo AutoCorrect.

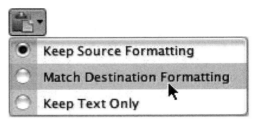

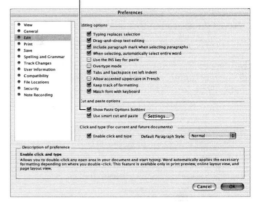

Figure 3.23 A Paste Options button allows you to control the formatting of pasted text.

Paste Options buttons setting

Figure 3.24 You can enable or disable Paste Options buttons in the Preferences dialog box.

EDITING: BEYOND THE BASICS

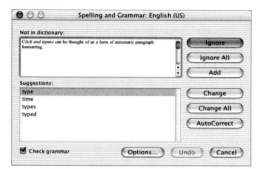

Figure 3.25 Word suggests corrections for most spelling and grammatical issues that it identifies.

Proofing Your Work

It's a good idea to check your work before letting anyone else see it. Word 2004 provides tools you can use to check your spelling and grammar, find synonyms when you're stuck for a word, and look up word definitions.

To check spelling and grammar:

1. Choose Tools > Spelling and Grammar or press (Option)(⌘)(L).

   The Spelling and Grammar dialog box appears (**Figure 3.25**). The spelling checker searches for possible misspellings, and the grammar checker identifies questionable grammar.

2. As it examines the document, Word stops at each questionable word or phrase. For each instance, do one of the following:

   ▲ To accept one of the entries in the Suggestions list, highlight the suggestion and click Change.

   ▲ You can manually edit the text in the upper text box. Click Change to accept the edits or Undo Edit to revert to the original text.

   ▲ To leave the word or phrase as is and continue the spelling check, click Ignore. To ignore all instances of the word or phrase in the current document, click Ignore All.

   ▲ To add the current spelling of a flagged word to your user dictionary and simultaneously accept the new spelling as correct, click Add. (Adding a word will prevent Word from flagging it as a misspelling in other documents.)

   continues on next page

3. When a suspected grammatical error is identified, the dialog box and its options change (**Figure 3.26**). For each such error, do one of the following:

▲ To ignore the error for this or all instances in the document, click Ignore or Ignore All, respectively.

▲ To accept a selected correction in the Suggestions box, click Change.

▲ You can manually edit the text. After doing so, click Change to accept the edits or Undo Edit to revert to the original text.

▲ To examine the next sentence (without making a judgment on the current problem), click Next Sentence.

An alert box appears when the spelling and grammar checks are complete.

4. Click OK to dismiss the alert box.

✔ Tips

■ You can restrict a spelling and grammar check to selected text by selecting the text prior to choosing the Spelling and Grammar command.

■ To disable grammar checking, remove the checkmark from the Check grammar check box in the Spelling and Grammar dialog box (see Figure 3.26). Word will then only check for spelling errors.

■ Unless you've changed the Spelling and Grammar's Preferences (**Figure 3.27**), Word automatically checks your spelling as you type. Suspect words are marked with squiggly red underlining.

■ As you type, Word automatically corrects common misspellings. You can add your own words to the AutoCorrect list by choosing Tools > AutoCorrect. Enter the misspelling in the Replace box and the correctly spelled word in the With box.

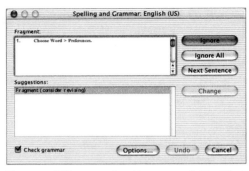

Figure 3.26 When questionable grammar is identified, you can ignore this instance or all instances. Or you can skip this instance and jump to the next sentence.

Mark suspected errors in text

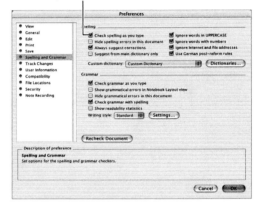

Figure 3.27 To instruct Office to automatically mark misspelled words as you type, ensure that this Spelling Preferences item is checked.

Selected word

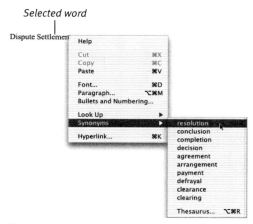

Figure 3.28 To quickly replace a word with a synonym, (Control)-click the word and choose a synonym from the ones presented.

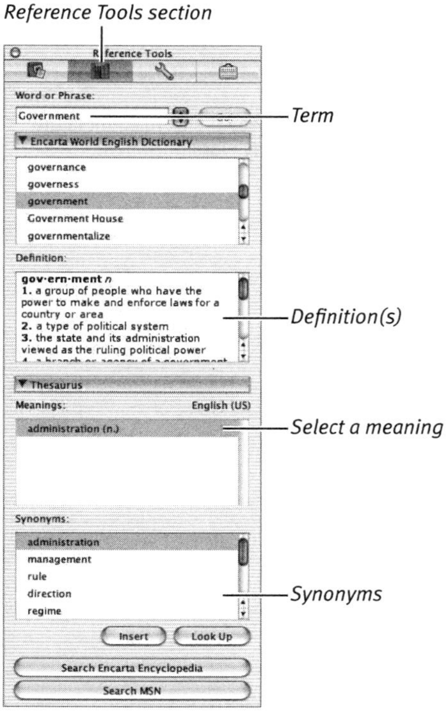

Reference Tools section

— *Term*

— *Definition(s)*

— *Select a meaning*

— *Synonyms*

Figure 3.29 The Reference Tools section of the Office Toolbox contains both the thesaurus and dictionary.

To find synonyms:

◆ *Do one of the following:*

▲ To perform a quick lookup, (Control)-click the word or phrase you wish to replace and select a replacement from the Synonyms submenu (**Figure 3.28**).

▲ Select the word or phrase you wish to replace and choose Tools > Thesaurus ((Option)(⌘)(R)). The Office Toolbox opens (**Figure 3.29**), displaying information for the highlighted word or phrase. Select the closest meaning from the Meanings list, select a synonym from the Synonyms list, and click Insert.

✔ Tips

■ To view a definition or meanings for the selected synonym, click Look Up.

■ You can also use the Office Toolbox to *manually* check for synonyms. In the Word or Phrase text box, type or paste the word/phrase you wish to examine and click Go. To insert a selected synonym at the current insertion point, click Insert.

To look up a word's definition:

1. *Do one of the following:*

▲ Select the word in your document and choose Tools > Dictionary.

▲ (Control)-click the word and choose Look Up > Definition from the pop-up menu that appears.

The Office Toolbox opens (see Figure 3.29).

2. If necessary, expand the Encarta World Dictionary section of the Office Toolbox. The definition for the selected word appears in the Definition text box.

PROOFING YOUR WORK

✔ Tips

- You can also type or paste words into the Word or Phrase box to view a definition.

- You can use the Web to expand the information available to you concerning the text in the Word or Phrase text box. Click the Search Encarta Encyclopedia button to read related encyclopedia articles or click Search MSN to perform a general Web search for the term.

Calculating a word count

Sometimes you may need to know the exact word count or similar statistics for a document. For example, word count is important when you're writing to a particular length, as is often the case with magazine articles and homework assignments. Word can calculate this information for you.

To calculate the word count:

1. *Do one of the following:*
   - ▲ To calculate statistics for a particular portion of the document, begin by selecting that part of the document.
   - ▲ To calculate statistics for an entire document, ensure that nothing is currently selected.

2. Choose Tools > Word Count.

   The Word Count dialog box appears (**Figure 3.30**). It contains information about your document, including the page count and the number of words, lines, and paragraphs in your document

✔ Tip

- In the bottom-right corner of every document window are two numbers (**Figure 3.31**). The first is the word in which the insertion point is located, counting from the beginning of the document. The second is the total words in the document.

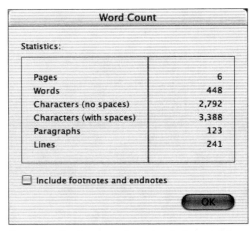

Figure 3.30 To view a word count and other useful statistics about your document, choose Tools > Word Count.

Total words

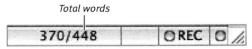

Figure 3.31 You can also see the word count in the bottom-right corner of any Word document.

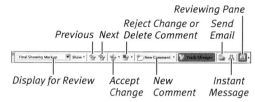

Reviewing Pane

Reject Change or   Send
Previous   Next   Delete Comment   Email

Display for Review   Accept   New   Instant
Change   Comment   Message

Figure 3.32 When track changes is enabled (the darkened icon), the Reviewing toolbar is extremely useful.

Reviewing Pane   *Edit/comment balloons*

Figure 3.33 You'll do most of your work with Final Showing Markup chosen. You can accept or reject changes, as well as make other necessary edits.

Tracking Changes

Not every Word document is the product of a single person. Occasionally (or perhaps frequently) you may collaborate with others. For instance, you might be creating a group report for school, working on a departmental budget with members of your staff, or writing a magazine or journal article that needs to incorporate an editor's comments. Word has features that enable the author to review the comments and changes of others, as well as to accept or reject each one.

To track changes to a document:

1. Choose View > Toolbars > Reviewing.

   The Reviewing toolbar appears (**Figure 3.32**).

2. Click the Track Changes toolbar icon on the Reviewing toolbar.

   When Track Changes is enabled, the toolbar icon is darkened. Any changes you make to the document will automatically be recorded and tracked.

3. Choose one of these display options from the Display for Review drop-down menu:

   ▲ **Original.** Display the original, unedited document (as it would look if all changes were rejected).

   ▲ **Original Showing Markup.** Display insertions and formatting changes in balloons. Deleted text remains visible.

   ▲ **Final.** Display the document as if all changes have been accepted.

   ▲ **Final Showing Markup.** Display deletions in balloons. Insertions and formatting changes remain visible in the document text (**Figure 3.33**).

   continues on next page

TRACKING CHANGES

4. To insert a comment, select the text on which you want to comment (or position the insertion point). Choose Insert > Comment or click the New Comment toolbar icon.

A new comment line is added to the Reviewing Pane at the bottom of the document window. Enter your comment.

5. To delete a comment or reject an edit, do one of the following:

▲ Select the edit or comment in the Reviewing Pane. Click the Reject Change/Delete Comment toolbar icon.

▲ Click the Reject button (the *X*) in the associated balloon (**Figure 3.34**).

▲ Control-click the comment/edit in the body of the document and choose Reject Change or Delete Comment from the pop-up menu that appears.

6. To accept an edit, do one of the following:

▲ Select the edit in the Reviewing Pane. Click the Accept Change toolbar icon.

▲ Click the Accept button (the checkmark) in the associated balloon.

▲ Control-click the edit in the body of the document and choose Accept Change from the pop-up menu that appears.

✔ Tips

■ You can jump directly from one edit or comment to the next by clicking the Next and Previous toolbar icons.

■ To show or hide the Reviewing Pane, click the Reviewing Pane toolbar icon.

■ You can send email or an instant message to the author of a selected comment or edit by clicking a toolbar icon.

■ To alter the Track Changes preferences, (**Figure 3.35**), click the Show toolbar icon and choose Preferences.

Reject
Accept

Figure 3.34 You can accept or reject an edit, as well as delete a comment, by clicking an icon in the related balloon.

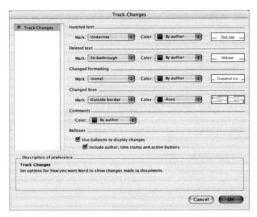

Figure 3.35 Although the default settings will usually suffice, you're free to modify the Track Changes preferences.

TRACKING CHANGES

Section menu   *Select a printer*

Figure 3.36 Set options for the current print job in the Print dialog box.

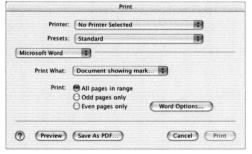

Figure 3.37 Set Word-specific options, such as printing a document showing changes, in the Microsoft Word section of the Print dialog box.

Printing Word Documents

Like other applications in the Office 2004 suite, Word offers a plethora of print options. The following step list covers the ones that you are most likely to use.

To print a Word document:

1. Open the Word document that you want to print.

2. *Optional:* To print only part of the current document, select that text.

3. Choose File > Print (⌘P).

   The Print dialog box appears (**Figure 3.36**), open to the Copies & Pages section.

4. Select a connected printer from the Printer drop-down list.

5. Specify the number of copies and range of pages to print.

   The Selection option for Pages is only available if you preselected part of the document in Step 2.

6. *Optional:* To alter Page Setup options (paper size, orientation, and paper feed method), click the Page Setup button.

7. *Optional:* To set Word-specific options, choose Microsoft Word from the drop-down menu. In the Microsoft Word section of the dialog box (**Figure 3.37**), choose an option from the Print What drop-down menu. If you're doing two-sided printing, you can also elect to print just the odd or even pages. Choose Copies & Pages from the drop-down menu to return to the main Print dialog box screen.

8. Turn the printer on, and then click the Print button.

   The print job is routed to the selected printer.

✔ Tips

- You can preview a document printout onscreen by choosing File > Print Preview. It's often a good idea to request a print preview prior to printing. You can use it to ensure that page breaks, margins, and the like are as you expect.

- To print the complete document using the current print settings, click the Print icon on the Standard toolbar. Printing commences immediately—without displaying the Print dialog box.

- If you save a document after printing it, the print settings are saved, too. This makes it easy for you to repeat a complex print job.

- To share a Word document with a friend or colleague who doesn't have Word, click the Save As PDF button rather than Print. A cross-platform PDF file will be generated that can be opened in Preview or Adobe Reader. The recipient will be able to read the document onscreen and print it, if desired.

PRINTING WORD DOCUMENTS

DOCUMENT
FORMATTING

Unlike character and paragraph formatting (discussed in Chapter 5), *document formatting* applies to an entire document (or, in some cases, to a section of a document). You can use document formatting commands to alter the page orientation, set margins, or specify a custom paper size on which to print a memo or an envelope, for example.

You can add columns to create a newsletter, divide a document into sections (as you might do for a manual or report), and force pages and columns to break exactly where you want. As you choose new settings, Word automatically adjusts the text to fit the specified orientation, margins, paper size, columns, and so on.

Paper Size and Orientation

Word's default printout setting is 8 ½" x 11" *portrait* (vertical orientation). The choices you make for paper size and orientation are applied to the current document only. New documents revert to the default settings.

To change paper size or orientation:

1. Choose File > Page Setup.

   The Page Setup dialog box appears (**Figure 4.1**).

2. Choose Page Attributes from the Settings drop-down menu. Select a destination printer from the Format for list of installed printers.

3. To set the page orientation, click the portrait icon for a standard vertical printout or a landscape icon for a horizontal printout.

4. *Do one of the following:*

   ▲ Select a standard size from the Paper Size drop-down list.

   ▲ To specify a nonstandard paper size, choose Custom Paper Size from the Settings drop-down menu, click the Use custom page size check box, and enter the dimensions in the Width and Height text boxes (**Figure 4.2**). Specify a paper feed method by clicking the appropriate icon and radio button, and then click OK.

5. *Optional:* To proportionately scale the printout to better fit the current paper size, enter a number in the Scale text box. The default entry is 100 (for 100%).

6. Click OK to close the dialog box.

   The document is modified to match the new Page Setup settings.

Select a printer   Paper type and size

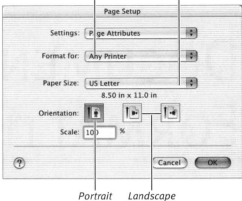

Portrait   Landscape

Figure 4.1 Specify a paper size and orientation in the Page Setup dialog box.

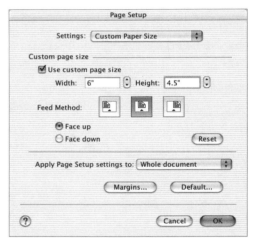

Figure 4.2 You can create a custom paper size if you need to print on nonstandard paper.

✔ Tip

■ To see how the new settings will affect the printed version of the document, switch to Page Layout view (View > Page Layout) or choose File > Print Preview.

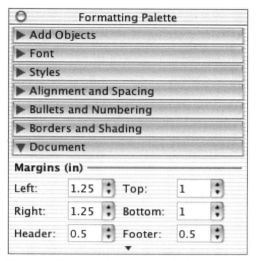

Figure 4.3 You can set basic margins in the Document section of the Formatting Palette.

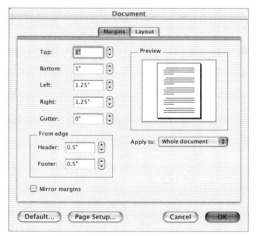

Figure 4.4 The Document dialog box provides more extensive margin options.

Margins

Margins are the blank borders around the document page. Although Word has default margin settings, you can vary the margins to fit the dictates of the current document— when printing on an unusual-sized paper or if you need to squeeze a few extra lines of text onto each page, for instance.

To change the margins:

◆ *Do one of the following:*

▲ Expand the Document section of the Formatting Palette. In the Margins area (**Figure 4.3**), enter new Left, Right, Top, and/or Bottom margins.

▲ Choose Format > Document. On the Margins tab of the Document dialog box (**Figure 4.4**), enter margin settings and click OK.

The new margin settings are applied to the document.

✔ Tips

■ The Document dialog box (see Figure 4.4) has other margin options that you may find useful:

▲ Specify a gutter margin if you're preparing the document for binding. (The *gutter* is extra space added to the edges or tops of pages that will be bound. This prevents the binding from obscuring the printing.)

▲ Click the Mirror margins check box when creating a book, magazine, or other two-sided publication. This makes the outer margin on left pages match those of right pages, while also creating matching inner margins.

■ Margin settings are generally applied to an entire document. However, you can set different *indents* for selected paragraphs in the Paragraph dialog box.

Headers and Footers

Headers and footers display the same reference information at the top or bottom of every document page. You can include any information you want, such as your name, document title, current date, or page numbers, for example.

To insert headers and footers:

1. Choose View > Header and Footer.

   Word switches to Page Layout view (**Figure 4.5**), and the Header and Footer toolbar appears (**Figure 4.6**).

   Views are discussed in Chapter 3.

2. You can edit the header or the footer. To switch between them, click the Switch Between Header and Footer toolbar icon or click in the element you want to edit.

3. A header or footer can contain any combination of text, graphics, and special features, such as page numbers or today's date. Type the necessary text and insert special items by clicking toolbar icons.

4. Use tabs to separate and position header and footer elements.

5. Click the Close button on the Header and Footer toolbar when you're done editing.

Header and Footer toolbar

Figure 4.5 Create the header or footer by typing and clicking icons on the Header and Footer toolbar.

✔ Tips

- Headers and footers are only visible in Page Layout view (View > Page Layout). In Page Layout view, you can edit an existing header or footer by simply double-clicking in the appropriate area of the page. Double-click in the body text when you're through editing.

- As with other text, you can apply character formatting to header and footer elements, such as changing fonts or adding boldface.

- You can make additional room for a header or footer by adjusting margins. See "Margins," earlier in this chapter.

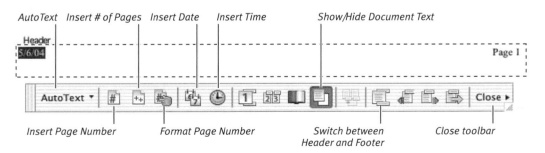

Figure 4.6 The Header and Footer toolbar.

HEADERS AND FOOTERS

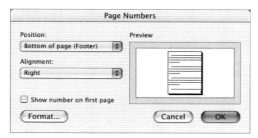

Figure 4.7 Indicate where you want the page numbers to appear, their alignment, and whether the first page will be numbered.

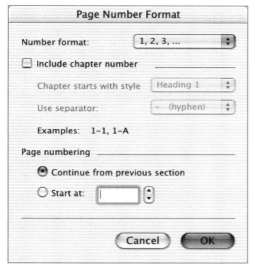

Figure 4.8 The Page Number Format dialog box provides additional options, such as whether to use chapter-relative page numbering.

Page Numbers

Page numbers in the header or footer improve a document's organization and make it easy for readers to keep their place.

To number a document's pages:

1. Choose Insert > Page Numbers.

   The Page Numbers dialog box appears (**Figure 4.7**).

2. Specify the page number's position and alignment.

   ▲ You can place numbers in the header or footer (Position) and align them to the right, left, or center (Alignment).

   ▲ The Inside and Outside alignment choices apply if you have mirrored pages, as when creating a book.

3. If you want the first page's number to be displayed, click the Show number on first page check box. Otherwise, the first visible number will be on the second page.

4. To set or change the page number format, click the Format button. The Page Number Format dialog box appears (**Figure 4.8**). *Do any of the following:*

   ▲ Choose a numbering style from the Number format drop-down menu.

   ▲ To use chapter-relative numbering (as in 13-1, 13-2, and so on), click the Include chapter number check box, and then choose a style and separator from the two drop-down menus.

   ▲ You can also choose to continue page numbering from a previous section or designate a starting page number.

   Click OK to close the Page Number Format dialog box.

5. Click OK to close the Page Number dialog box.

✔ Tip

■ You can edit the header or footer to precede the page number with the word Page (see Figure 4.6).

Inserting Page Breaks

Word inserts an *automatic page break* whenever text fills the page. In Normal view, an automatic page break is shown as a horizontal dotted line. If you want a page to break *before* you've filled the page (to avoid splitting a table across two pages, for example), you can insert a *manual page break*.

To insert a page break:

1. Position the insertion mark at the beginning of the line where you want the new page to start.

2. Choose Insert > Break > Page Break.

✔ Tips

- To delete a manual page break in Normal view, select the break (**Figure 4.9**) and press (Delete). To delete a manual page break in Page Layout view, position the insertion mark just before the first character of the new page and press (Delete).

- You cannot delete or move an automatic page break. You can, however, insert a manual page break above it.

- Use Widow/Orphan control to ensure that Word doesn't leave a single line of text at the page top or bottom when it breaks a page. Select the errant paragraph, choose Format > Paragraph, click the Line and Page Breaks tab in the Paragraph dialog box (**Figure 4.10**), check Widow/Orphan control, and click OK. Word will repaginate as necessary to eliminate the widow or orphan text.

- To prevent a heading and the following paragraph from being split across two pages, select the heading, choose Format > Paragraph, click the Lines and Page Breaks tab, and check the option to Keep with next (see Figure 4.10).

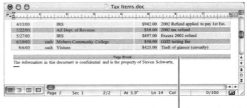

Selected manual page break

Figure 4.9 To remove a manual page break in Normal view, begin by selecting the page break.

Widow/Orphan control   *Keep paragraphs together*

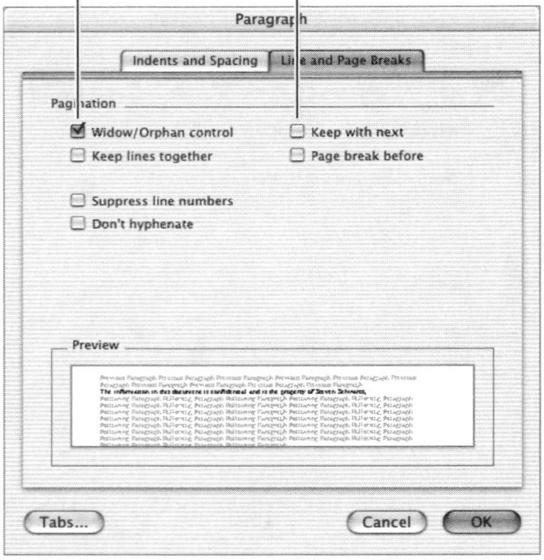

Figure 4.10 In the Paragraph dialog box, you can tell Word to handle widows and orphans and prevent two paragraphs from being split between pages.

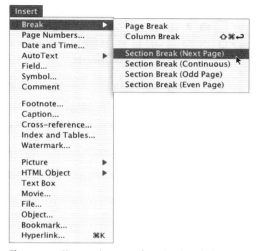

Figure 4.11 Choose the type of section break that you want to insert.

Creating Multiple Sections

A document can contain multiple sections, each with different document formatting attributes, such as different margins, page numbering schemes, and headers and footers. For example, an annual report might contain different sections for the title page, introduction, body, and financial information.

A new document contains only one section until you insert a section break. See **Table 4.1** for section break options.

To create multiple sections:

1. Place the insertion mark where you want the new section to begin.

2. Choose Insert > Break and select one of the section break types from the submenu (**Figure 4.11**).

   In Normal view, Word inserts a double line marked with the text "Section Break," followed by the specific type of break (**Figure 4.12**).

continues on next page

Section break indicator

| 6/10/03 | cash | Mohave Community College | $50.00 | GED testing fee |
| 8/6/03 | cash | Visions | $425.00 | Theft of glasses (casualty) |

Section Break (Next Page)
The information in this document is confidential and is the property of Steven Schwartz,

Figure 4.12 The new section break appears.

Table 4.1

Section Breaks

BREAK TYPE	DESCRIPTION
Next Page	Starts a new section at the top of the next page.
Continuous	Starts a new section without moving the text after the section break to a new page. If the previous section has multiple columns, Word evens out the column bottoms.
Odd Page	If the section break falls on an even page, Word starts the new section on the next page. Otherwise, it leaves the next even page blank and starts the new section on the next odd page.
Even Page	If the section break falls on an odd page, Word starts the new section on the next page. Otherwise, it leaves the next odd page blank and starts the new section on the next even page.

CREATING MULTIPLE SECTIONS

✔ Tips

■ Like page breaks, the "Section Break" indicator text and double lines are only visible in Normal and Outline views.

■ To remove a section break, switch to Normal view, highlight the section break, and press [Delete].

■ To apply document formatting options to a section, select some text in the section and choose Format > Document. The Document dialog box appears. Click the appropriate tab (**Figure 4.13**), alter the layout and margin settings, choose Selected sections from the Apply To drop-down menu, and click OK.

■ You can also open the Document dialog box by double-clicking the section break marker that ends the section you want to format.

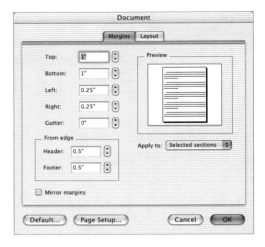

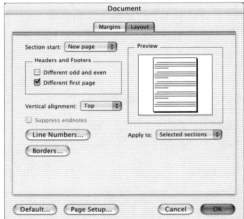

Figure 4.13 To set new formatting for a selected section, make the necessary changes on the Margins (top) and Layout (bottom) tabs of the Document dialog box.

Enter the number of
columns wanted...

...or click one of
these presets

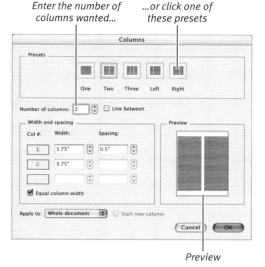

Preview

Figure 4.14 In addition to specifying the number of columns, you can set column and gutter widths in the Columns dialog box.

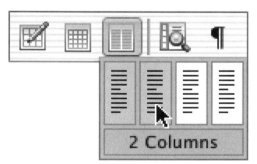

Figure 4.15 Click the Columns toolbar icon and drag to set the number of columns.

Figure 4.16 By clicking and dragging the column-related ruler icons, you can change column settings.

Multiple Columns

A new Word document normally starts as a single large column. However, if you want to lay out a newsletter or break up your text with pictures, for example, you can create additional columns.

To set up multiple columns:

1. Choose Format > Columns.

    The Columns dialog box appears (**Figure 4.14**).

2. In the Columns dialog box, click one of the Presets or enter a number in the Number of columns text box.

3. *Optional:* To add a vertical line between each pair of columns, click the Line between check box.

4. In the Width and spacing section of the dialog box, for each column specify the width and space between. (To make all columns the same width, click the Equal column width check box.)

5. Choose an option from the Apply to drop-down menu.

6. Click OK.

✔ Tips

- You can also set the number of columns by clicking the Columns icon on the Standard toolbar and then dragging until you reach the requisite number of columns (**Figure 4.15**).

- After creating multiple columns, you can change the number of columns or other column-related settings by returning to the Columns dialog box.

- You can manually change column widths or spacing by clicking and dragging icons in the horizontal ruler (**Figure 4.16**).

MULTIPLE COLUMNS

5

TEXT FORMATTING

In Chapter 4, you learned to apply document-level formatting, such as setting the page size, orientation, and margins. In this chapter, you will discover the many ways that you can format the text in your documents. There are two types of formatting that can be applied to selected text: character and paragraph.

◆ *Character formatting* refers to the font, size, styles, and color applied to—and that only affects—selected text within a paragraph.

◆ *Paragraph formatting* concerns itself with formatting that affects entire paragraphs. In addition to setting a default font for the paragraph, formatting can include line spacing, space before and after the paragraph, alignment, and so on.

To make it simpler to format a document's text consistently, you can define and apply character and paragraph styles, as explained at the end of this chapter.

Character Formatting

You can change the look of selected text by applying different font, size, style, and color formatting. You can format text in several ways, as described below. Use any method that's convenient for you.

To apply character formatting:

1. Select the text that you want to format.

   Using normal selection techniques, you can select individual characters, words, paragraphs, or the entire document.

2. *Do any of the following:*

   ▲ In the Font section of the Formatting Palette (**Figure 5.1**), select any combination of font, size, color, highlighting, and style effects.

   ▲ Select font, size, color, highlighting, and style options from the icons and drop-down menus on the Formatting toolbar (**Figure 5.2**).

   ▲ Choose Format > Font or press ⌘D. On the Font tab of the Font dialog box (**Figure 5.3**), select font, size, color, and effects, and then click OK.

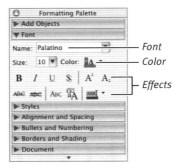

Figure 5.1 You can apply most types of character formatting by selecting options from the Formatting Palette.

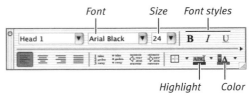

Figure 5.2 Basic character formatting options can be selected from the Formatting toolbar.

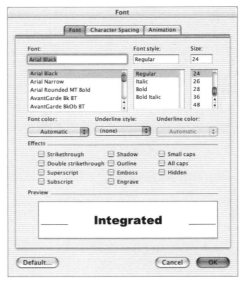

Figure 5.3 For more complex formatting needs, you can select options from the Font dialog box.

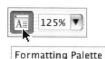

Figure 5.4 You can show or hide the Formatting Palette by clicking this toolbar icon.

Figure 5.5 You can change the case of selected text by selecting an option in this dialog box.

Table 5.1

Font Effect Keyboard Shortcuts

SHORTCUT	DESCRIPTION
⌘ B	Boldface
⌘ I	Italic
⌘ U	Underline
⌘ Shift K	Small caps
⌘ Shift A	All capital letters
Shift F 3	Cycle through case selections

✔ Tips

■ To show or hide the Formatting Palette, choose View > Formatting Palette or click the Formatting Palette icon on the Standard toolbar (**Figure 5.4**). To show or hide the Formatting toolbar, choose View > Toolbars > Formatting.

■ To restore selected text to the standard font and size for the paragraph, select the text and choose Clear Formatting from the Style drop-down list on the Formatting Palette or the Formatting toolbar.

■ To increase the size of selected text to the next listed size for the font in use, press ⌘ Shift >. To decrease the size, press ⌘ Shift <.

■ You can use keyboard shortcuts (**Table 5.1**) to apply the most common font effects to selected text.

■ The font style icons (such as Bold), as well as their keyboard shortcuts, work as toggles. Issue them once to apply the formatting; issue them a second time to remove the formatting.

■ You can change the letter case of selected text by choosing Format > Change Case. Select an option from the Change Case dialog box (**Figure 5.5**) and click OK.

■ Applying a bold or italic effect to selected text is *not* the same as using the actual bold or italic version of a font, if one is available. By choosing the bold version of a font (AGaramond Bold or B Helvetica Bold, for example), you will normally get more aesthetically pleasing and typographically correct text.

CHARACTER FORMATTING

Paragraph Formatting

Some formatting is paragraph-specific. That is, rather than affecting individual words or sentences, it affects the entire paragraph. Common paragraph formatting that you can apply includes setting the alignment, indents, line spacing, and tab stops. You can also create bulleted or numbered lists, as well as add borders or shading.

Setting paragraph alignment

Each paragraph in a document can be aligned left, center, right, or justified (**Figure 5.6**), as explained below.

◆ *Left* is the most common alignment setting and is the default. Text in a left-aligned paragraph is flush with the left margin and ragged on the right margin.

◆ *Center-aligned* paragraphs are horizontally centered between the left and right margins and are ragged on both sides. Center alignment is frequently used for titles and section heads.

◆ *Right-aligned* paragraphs are flush with the right margin and ragged on the left.

◆ *Justified* paragraphs are aligned flush with both the left and right margins; you'll often see this in a newspaper. The spacing between words is automatically adjusted as needed to maintain the flush margins.

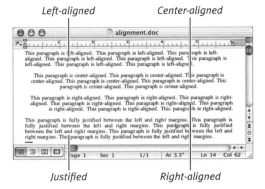

Left-aligned *Center-aligned*

Justified *Right-aligned*

Figure 5.6 These are the paragraph alignments that are available in Word.

New vs. Existing Text

You can apply formats to text and paragraphs before or after you've typed them.

◆ When you apply a character or paragraph format to existing text, only that text is affected.

◆ When you apply a character format before you type, all text that follows will have the same format until you choose another character format.

◆ When you apply a paragraph format before you type, its format dictates the format of following paragraphs.

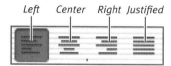

Figure 5.7 One of the quickest ways to set alignment is to click an icon on the Formatting toolbar.

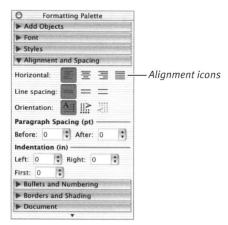

Alignment icons

Figure 5.8 You can also click an alignment icon on the Formatting Palette.

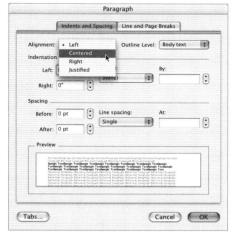

Figure 5.9 Although it's more convenient when you have multiple options to set, you can also set alignment in the Paragraph dialog box.

To set alignment for a paragraph:

1. Select one or more paragraphs whose alignment you want to change.

2. *Do one of the following:*

   ▲ Click an alignment icon on the Formatting toolbar (**Figure 5.7**).

   ▲ Expand the Alignment and Spacing section of the Formatting Palette and click an alignment icon (**Figure 5.8**).

   ▲ Choose Format > Paragraph. The Paragraph dialog box appears. On the Indents and Spacing tab, choose an alignment from the Alignment drop-down menu (**Figure 5.9**) and click OK.

   The selected paragraph(s) are aligned as directed.

✔ Tip

■ When you're typing and press Return to end a paragraph, the next paragraph automatically takes on the alignment of the paragraph you just completed.

PARAGRAPH FORMATTING

Indenting paragraphs

An *indent* is space between a paragraph and the left or right margin. Indents can be used to set off quotations from surrounding text (left and right indents), format body paragraphs in a business letter or school report (first line indents), and to create bulleted or numbered lists (hanging indents).

Before setting an indent, you must first select the paragraph(s). Selecting a paragraph for formatting is different from selecting a word. You don't have to select the *entire* paragraph; it's sufficient to just click somewhere within it. To select multiple contiguous paragraphs, drag through them. To select multiple non-contiguous paragraphs, you can ⌘-double click a word in each one.

You can modify paragraph indents using the Formatting Palette, the Paragraph dialog box, or the ruler. You can create the following types of indents in Word:

◆ *Left* indents the paragraph from the left margin.

◆ *Right* indents the paragraph from the right margin.

◆ *First line* indents only the first line of the paragraph.

◆ *Hanging* indents the entire paragraph except for the first line.

To indent paragraphs using the Formatting Palette:

1. Select the paragraph(s).

2. In the Formatting Palette, expand the Alignment and Spacing section.

3. In the Indentation subsection, set the Left, Right, and/or First indent (**Figure 5.10**).

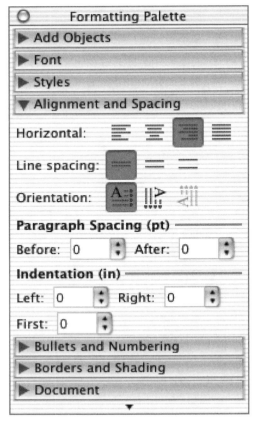

Figure 5.10 You can specify a left, right, or first line indent in the Indentation area of the Formatting Palette (found in the Alignment and Spacing section).

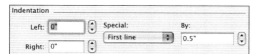

Figure 5.11 For greater precision in setting indents, use these options on the Indents and Spacing tab of the Paragraph dialog box.

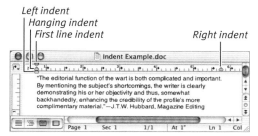

Figure 5.12 Align the main three indent markers to create a block (useful for quotations).

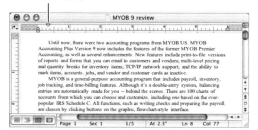

Figure 5.13 You can move the First Line Indent marker slightly to the right to create a paragraph style that is commonly used in business and education.

To indent paragraphs using the Paragraph dialog box:

1. Select the paragraph(s).

2. Choose Format > Paragraph or press Option ⌘ M.
The Paragraph dialog box appears.

3. Switch to the Indents and Spacing tab.

4. *Do any of the following:*

▲ In the Indentation section of the tab (**Figure 5.11**), change the values for Left and/or Right. The numbers correspond to the ruler that appears above the document window.

▲ To set a first line or hanging indent, choose First line or Hanging from the Special drop-down menu and then enter a value in the By text box.

5. Click OK to apply the new settings to the selected paragraph(s).

To indent paragraphs using the ruler:

◆ To create a uniform or flush indent, move the First Line Indent marker so it is directly above the Hanging and Left Indent markers (**Figure 5.12**). Then click and drag the square base of the Left Indent marker. The three markers will move together.

◆ To set a first line indent, move the First Line Indent marker (**Figure 5.13**). Note that it moves independently of the other indent markers.

◆ To set a hanging indent, move the First Line Indent marker to the left of the Left Indent marker and move the Hanging Indent marker to the position where the indent will begin.

◆ To set the indent for the right side of the paragraph, move the Right Indent marker.

PARAGRAPH FORMATTING

✔ Tips

- Click the Decrease Indent or Increase Indent icons on the Formatting toolbar (**Figure 5.14**) or the same icons in the Bullets and Numbering section of the Formatting Palette to decrease or increase the left indent.

- When entering text for the first line of a paragraph that's formatted with a hanging indent, enter the bullet character or number, press Tab, and then type the paragraph text. If the paragraph has multiple lines, all lines after the first will automatically align to the Hanging Indent marker.

- Word also has options for *directly* creating numbered and bulleted lists, as explained later in this chapter.

Figure 5.14 Click these toolbar icons to decrease or increase a paragraph's left indent by 0.5".

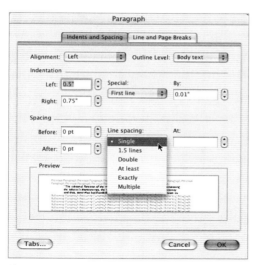

Figure 5.15 For more precise line spacing needs, you can choose a setting from the Line spacing drop-down menu in the Paragraph dialog box.

Setting line spacing

Being able to modify line spacing is especially useful if you're creating a document that has a space restriction or when it must follow line-spacing requirements set by an editor or teacher. The most common line spacings are single, 1.5, and double. You can also specify an exact value.

To set line spacing for a paragraph:

1. Select the paragraph or paragraphs for which you want to set line spacing.

2. *Do one of the following:*
   ▲ In the Formatting Palette, expand the Alignment and Spacing section, and then click one of the Line spacing icons (see Figure 5.10).
   ▲ Choose Format > Paragraph. The Paragraph dialog box appears. On the Indents and Spacing tab, choose a line spacing option from the Line spacing drop-down menu (**Figure 5.15**) and click OK.

✔ Tips

■ Line spacing is a paragraph—not a document—formatting option. When you set line spacing, it is applied only to the currently selected paragraphs. To apply the same line spacing to an entire document, choose Edit > Select All (or press ⌘Ⓐ) prior to setting the line spacing.

■ The Paragraph dialog box has additional line spacing options. *At least* is designed to accommodate graphics and large font sizes. It sets line spacing to the minimum amount necessary to prevent clipping the tops of text. *Exactly* generates a fixed line spacing of a set amount. *Multiple* enables you to increase or decrease line spacing by a percentage. A setting of 1.2 would increase line spacing by 20 percent, for example.

Setting tab stops

Tab stops are often used to align text and numbers in nice, neat columns. For example, you can create tables in which the entries are aligned on their left edges, right edges, or decimal points (**Figure 5.16**).

To set tabs:

1. Select the paragraph(s) for which you want to set tab stops.

2. Click the tab alignment icon to the left of the ruler to choose the type of tab you'd like to set (**Figure 5.17**).

3. Click the ruler at the location where you'd like to place the tab stop.

   If the placement is off, you can drag the marker to another spot on the ruler.

4. To add more tab stops for the selected paragraph(s), repeat Steps 2 and 3.

5. If the selected paragraphs don't already contain tabs, insert them as necessary by pressing Tab. Affected text will conform to the new tab settings.

✔ Tips

- If you want more precise tab settings, choose Format > Tabs and set tabs in the Tabs dialog box (**Figure 5.18**). You can also select a *leader character* (such as a string of periods) that will separate the two text strings. Leaders are frequently used in menus to separate items from prices, for example.

- You can remove a tab stop by dragging it off the ruler. To remove all manually placed tab stops for selected paragraphs, click Clear All in the Tabs dialog box.

- The Bar option shown in Figures 5.16 and 5.17 isn't for aligning text. It inserts a vertical bar at the chosen ruler location.

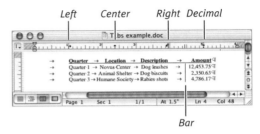

Figure 5.16 By judiciously choosing and setting tab stops, you can create perfectly aligned tables.

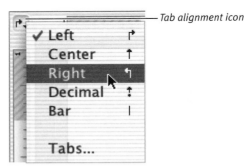

Figure 5.17 Choose a tab style from this pop-up menu in the upper-left corner of the document window.

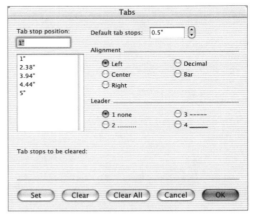

Figure 5.18 To set tab stops precisely or to specify a leader character, use the Tabs dialog box.

PARAGRAPH FORMATTING

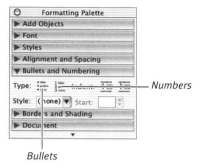

Numbers

Bullets

Figure 5.19 Click an icon to enable or disable bullets or numbers for the selected paragraph(s).

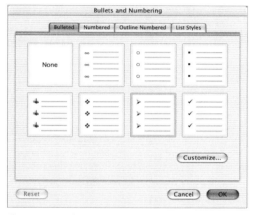

Figure 5.20 Select one of these bullet styles. To use a different character or otherwise alter the bullet settings, click the Customize button.

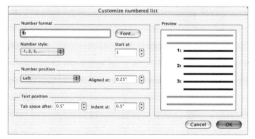

Figure 5.21 In this dialog box, you can change the font, style, alignment, and spacing of numbered lists.

Bulleted and numbered lists

Bullets help break text into readable chunks, making it simpler for a reader to find or digest important points. Word also lets you generate numbered lists, such as points in a contract. The procedures for adding bullets and numbers are very similar. You can apply bullets and numbering to paragraphs before or after you've typed the text.

To create bulleted or numbered lists:

◆ *Do one of the following:*

▲ To use the default bullet or numbering style for selected paragraphs, click an icon in the Bullets and Numbering section of the Formatting Palette (**Figure 5.19**) or the same icon on the Formatting toolbar.

▲ Choose Format > Bullets and Numbering. On the Bulleted (**Figure 5.20**) or the Numbered tab of the Bullets and Numbering dialog box, select a bullet or numbering style and click OK.

The paragraph series becomes a bulleted or numbered list.

✔ Tips

■ You can remove bullets or numbers by selecting the paragraphs and clicking the Bullets or Numbering icon again.

■ To choose a special bullet character (such as a picture from your hard disk), set the bullet's distance from the text, or specify a new font and format for numbers, click the Customize button in the Bullets and Numbering dialog box. Set options in the dialog box that appears (**Figure 5.21**) and then click OK.

■ To quickly change the bullets or numbers in a list, double-click any bullet character or number in your text. The Bullets and Numbering dialog box will open.

PARAGRAPH FORMATTING

Applying borders and shading

Borders and shading can add style to a document or serve to highlight an important paragraph. You can set a border around selected pages, paragraphs, or text. You can do the same with shading.

To apply a border or shading:

1. Select the text to which you'd like to add a border or shading.

2. Choose Format > Borders and Shading. The Borders and Shading dialog box appears (**Figure 5.22**).

3. *Do one of the following:*
   - ▲ To add a border around selected text or selected paragraphs, click the Borders tab.
   - ▲ To add a border around one or more pages, click the Page Border tab.

4. Select a border type: None, Box, Shadow, 3-D, or Custom.

5. *Optional:* If you don't like the default settings, you can specify a different line style, color, and/or width for the border.

6. *Optional:* To adjust the offset that separates the border from the text on each side, click the Options button (**Figure 5.23**).

7. On the Shading tab (**Figure 5.24**), select a shading color in the Fill section and a shading pattern in the Patterns section.

8. From the Apply to drop-down menu, choose the part of the document to which you want to apply the border and/or the shading, and then click OK.

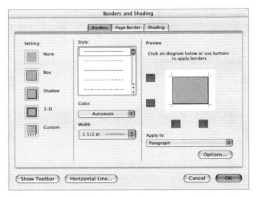

Figure 5.22 Add a border or shading to selected text in the Borders and Shading dialog box.

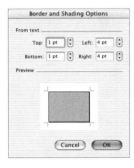

Figure 5.23 You can change the offset between each border edge and the text.

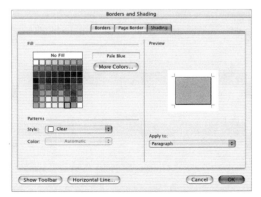

Figure 5.24 Select the shading color and a pattern on the Shading tab.

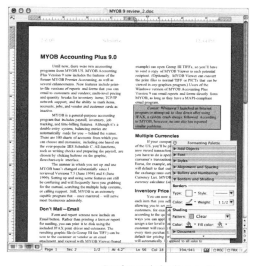

Border and shading options

Figure 5.25 You can also set border and shading options in the Formatting Palette.

✔ Tips

■ You can also select borders and shading settings from the Formatting Palette (**Figure 5.25**).

■ To add borders only to specific sides, switch to the Borders or Page Border tab of the Borders and Shading dialog box, and then click those sides in the Preview area. You can make each side a different line style, color, and width.

■ You can remove any line by clicking it in the Preview area of the Borders tab. To remove *all* borders, set Setting to None. You can also clear all borders by setting Type to No Border. (Click the Type icon in the Formatting Palette to see this choice.)

Using Word Styles

A *style* contains text-formatting settings. Using styles, you can quickly apply a set combination of formatting to characters or paragraphs. A paragraph style named Head A, for example, can contain all the formatting for one type of heading, such as its font, space after, and alignment. To format text as a heading, you select the heading and then choose the Heading A style from the Style list.

Character styles contain font formatting and are applied to selected characters. *Paragraph styles* are applied to entire paragraphs and contain both font and paragraph formatting. When no specific style is applied, paragraphs use the Normal style and text is formatted with the Default Paragraph Font style.

To apply a style:

1. Display the Formatting toolbar or the Formatting Palette by choosing View > Toolbars > Formatting or View > Formatting Palette.

2. Select the characters or paragraphs that you want to format.

3. On the Formatting toolbar (**Figure 5.26**) or the Formatting Palette (**Figure 5.27**), select a character or paragraph style from the Style drop-down list.

✔ Tips

■ One important reason for using styles is that doing so ensures consistency in the way a document is formatted.

■ In the Style lists, paragraph styles are denoted by the ¶ character.

■ To quickly remove paragraph or character formatting from selected text, select the Clear Formatting style.

■ You can make noncontiguous text selections by ⌘-clicking.

Figure 5.26 You can select a style from the Style list on the Formatting toolbar...

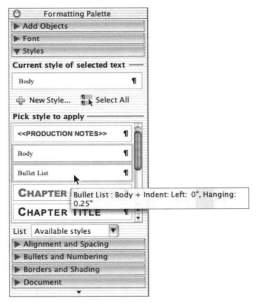

Figure 5.27 ...or from the Style list on the Formatting Palette.

Figure 5.28 Click the current style and choose New Style from the drop-down menu.

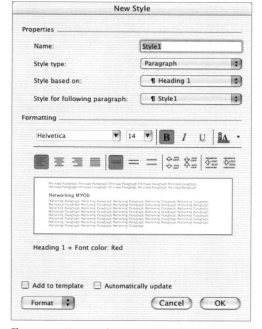

Figure 5.29 Name and create new styles in the New Style dialog box.

Creating a paragraph style

Generally, you should create paragraph styles if you know you'll need to use the same types of paragraphs throughout a document. As explained in the steps that follow, styles are easiest to create "by example."

To create a paragraph style using the Formatting toolbar:

1. Apply font and paragraph formatting to a paragraph and then select the paragraph.

2. Click the current style name in the Style list on the Formatting toolbar.

3. Type the new style name in place of the old one and press Return.

   This sets the selected text to the newly named style and adds the new style to the Style list for the current document.

To create a paragraph style using the Style dialog box:

1. Apply font and paragraph formatting to a paragraph, and then select or position the insertion mark within the paragraph.

2. *Do one of the following:*

   ▲ Choose Format > Style. In the Style dialog box, click the New button.

   ▲ In the Styles section of the Formatting Palette, click the New Style button or click the down arrow beside the Current style of selected text (**Figure 5.28**) and choose New Style.

   The New Style dialog box appears (**Figure 5.29**).

3. Enter a name for the new style in the Name text box.

4. Ensure that Paragraph is the Style type and that the *original* style for the selected paragraph is shown as the Style based on.

continues on next page

5. The Style for following paragraph is the style that Word will automatically apply whenever you use the new style and then press ⸢Return⸥ to create a new paragraph. Select a style from the drop-down list.

6. *Optional:* If there is additional character or paragraph formatting that you wish to include as part of the style definition, specify it in the Formatting section of the dialog box.

7. Click OK to complete the style definition and add it to the Style drop-down lists.

When you save the document, the new style is saved as part of the document.

✔ Tip

- The new style is *not* automatically applied to the original paragraph. Normally, you'll want to apply it to the paragraph when you return from the New Style dialog box.

To modify a paragraph style:

1. Select the paragraph and apply desired font and/or paragraph formatting changes.

2. Select the previously applied style from the Style drop-down list.

The Modify Style dialog box appears (**Figure 5.30**).

3. Click the Update the style to reflect recent changes? radio button and then click OK.

Every paragraph that is currently format-ted with this style will be reformatted to match the revised style definition. Other styles based on the modified style will also change as appropriate.

✔ Tip

- You can also modify a style by opening its drop-down menu in the Formatting Palette and choosing Modify Style (see Figure 5.28).

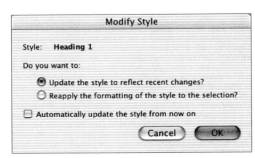

Figure 5.30 In the Modify Style dialog box, you can update the style based on the currently selected text or reapply the original style to the selected text (to remove new formatting).

Formatting options   Name the style

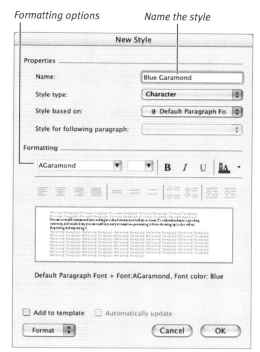

Figure 5.31 Name the new character style and make any necessary changes to the formatting.

Creating a character style

Use character styles to apply consistent formatting to selected text. You can apply character styles within a paragraph that already has a paragraph style. The style will only affect the selected word(s) and will only add formatting, such as font and size.

To create a character style:

1. Select the formatted text from which you want to create a new character style.

2. *Do one of the following:*
   ▲ Choose Format > Style. In the Style dialog box, click the New button.
   ▲ In the Styles section of the Formatting Palette, click the New Style button or click the down arrow beside the Current style of selected text (see Figure 5.28) and choose New Style.
   The New Style dialog box appears (**Figure 5.31**).

3. In the Name text box, enter a name for the new style (or accept the proposed name).

4. Choose Character from the Style type drop-down menu.

5. As necessary, select additional character formatting options from the first row of the Formatting section.

6. Click OK to dismiss the New Style dialog box.
   The new character style is added to the Style drop-down lists.

✔ Tip

■ You aren't required to specify *all* formatting options for a character style. For example, if you only select blue as the color while leaving the font information blank, the applied style will simply color selected text without changing its font.

USING WORD STYLES

97

Deleting styles

Although there's little harm in retaining styles that aren't being used in the current document, you're free to delete any style that you've defined. Deleting unnecessary styles can help minimize the clutter in a lengthy Style list. (Note, however, that the default Word styles *cannot* be deleted.)

To delete a style:

1. *Do one of the following:*

   ▲ Choose Format > Style. Select the style name in the Style dialog box (**Figure 5.32**) and click Delete.

   ▲ In the Pick style to apply section of the Formatting Palette, click the down arrow beside the style you want to delete. Choose Delete from the menu that appears.

   A confirmation dialog box appears (**Figure 5.33**).

2. Click Yes to delete the style.

3. If the deletion was initiated in the Style dialog box (Step 1), click Cancel or Apply to dismiss the dialog box.

Defined styles for the document   Delete the style

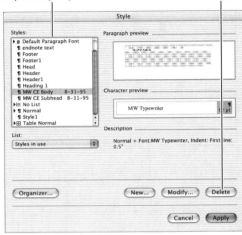

Figure 5.32 Select a style from the Styles list and click the Delete button.

Figure 5.33 Click Yes to confirm the style deletion.

Styles in current document

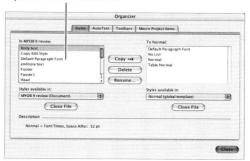

Figure 5.34 Use the Organizer dialog box to copy styles from one document or template into another.

Select styles to be copied

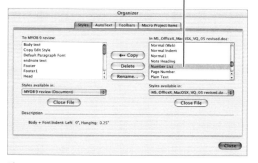

Figure 5.35 From the list on the right, select the styles that you want to copy into the original document.

Importing styles

Styles that you've defined are only available in the document(s) in which they've been saved. If you'd like to reuse some of these styles, you can import them into other documents.

To import styles:

1. Open the document or template into which you want to import styles.

2. Choose Format > Style.

   The Style dialog box appears (see Figure 5.32).

3. Click the Organizer button.

   The Organizer dialog box appears (**Figure 5.34**), showing the document's defined styles in the left pane. (Click the Styles tab if it isn't currently displayed.)

4. Click the Close File button beneath the right pane.

5. Click the Open File button beneath the right pane.

   The Choose a File dialog box appears.

6. Navigate to the folder that contains the file from which you want to import styles, select the file, and click Open. The styles from this document appear in the right pane of the Organizer dialog box.

   By default, the Show list is set to only show Word Templates. If importing from a standard Word file rather than a template, choose All Word documents from the Show drop-down menu.

7. In the right pane (**Figure 5.35**), select the styles you want to import and click the Copy button.

   You can ⌘-click to select multiple styles.

8. Click Close to dismiss the dialog box.

   The imported styles are now a part of and available for use in the document.

USING WORD STYLES

ADDING GRAPHICS

You can add graphics to a Word document in several ways:

◆ You can choose an image from the included clip art collection.

◆ You can insert images from your hard disk, such as scans, digital photos, or pictures that you've downloaded from the Web or received in email.

◆ You can scan an image directly into a document or transfer photos from your digital camera.

◆ You can use Word's drawing tools to create your own graphics or add predefined shapes called *AutoShapes*.

◆ You can add artistic text called *WordArt* to your documents.

✔ Tip

■ When scanning images to include in your documents, be aware that most published graphics are copyrighted and cannot be legally used without the permission of the copyright holder. Exceptions are books of royalty-free clip art, as well as royalty-free clip art and photographs that are distributed on disc or electronically.

Inserting Clip Art and Other Images

Clip art, photos, and scans can add color and visual interest to a document. Clip art is great if you're creating a brochure, advertising an event, or hosting a party. And, of course, nothing beats the realism of including your own photographs and scans in a document—whether they're inserted from disk or added directly from a connected TWAIN-compliant digital camera or scanner.

To insert clip art into a document:

1. Choose Insert > Picture > Clip Art or, if the Drawing toolbar is visible, click the Insert Clip Art toolbar icon.

   The Clip Gallery window appears (**Figure 6.1**).

2. Select a clip art category from the list on the left, and then click to select a picture from the ones displayed.

3. *Optional:* To preview the selected image at full size in a separate window, click the Preview check box.

4. Click Insert to insert the picture into your document.

   The picture appears in the document at the current insertion mark.

5. *Optional:* To change the picture's size or format settings, select the picture.

   The Picture toolbar appears (**Figure 6.2**) or—if the Formatting Palette is open—the Picture toolbar's tools are added to the Formatting Palette.

6. *Optional:* Make any necessary edits, as explained in "Image Editing," later in this chapter.

Category list

Preview in a separate window

Figure 6.1 Pick from the many high-quality images in the Clip Gallery window.

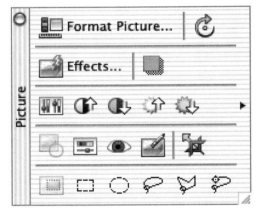

Figure 6.2 Use the Picture toolbar to edit, format, apply special effects, or specify a text wrap method for the selected image.

Filter the file list

Figure 6.3 Select a picture from your hard disk. (Many pictures display a preview when selected.)

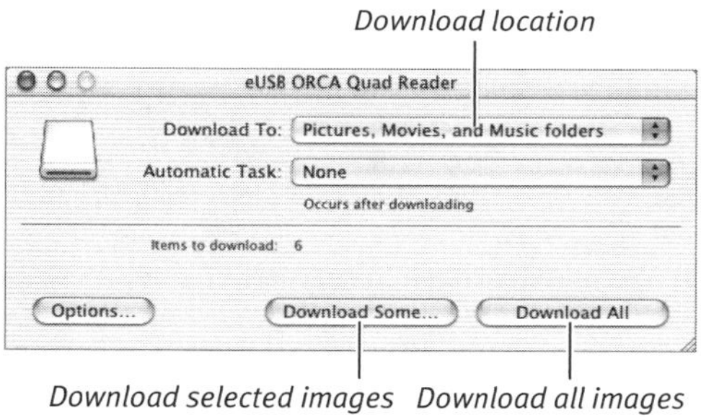

Download location

Download selected images   *Download all images*

Figure 6.4 You can also use OS X's Image Capture to transfer images to your hard disk.

To insert a picture from disk:

1. Choose Insert > Picture > From File or, if the Drawing toolbar is visible, click the Insert Picture toolbar icon.

The Choose a Picture dialog box appears.

2. Navigate to the drive and folder that contains the picture, select it (**Figure 6.3**), and click Insert.

The image is added to the document.

To insert a picture directly from a TWAIN scanner or digital camera:

1. Choose Insert > Picture > From Scanner or Camera.

2. In the Insert Picture from Scanner or Camera dialog box, select the name of your scanner or digital camera from the Device list.

3. Click the Acquire button.

The scanner or camera's image-transfer software launches.

4. Scan an image as you normally would or select an image that's stored in your camera.

✔ Tips

■ When inserting a picture from disk, you can filter the file list to show only pictures of a particular type (such as JPEG, TIFF, or EPS) by choosing that file format from the Show drop-down list.

■ If your camera, scanner, or memory card reader isn't recognized by the From Scanner or Camera command, you may be able to use Image Capture (found in the Applications folder) to move the images to your hard disk (**Figure 6.4**).

■ You can proportionately resize any image by clicking and dragging a corner handle. To resize non-proportionately, drag any middle handle.

INSERTING CLIP ART AND OTHER IMAGES

Setting Text Wrap

All images—whether clip art, photos, shapes, or AutoShapes—are objects. An object's *wrapping style* (also known as *text wrap*) determines how it's displayed and interacts with surrounding text.

Objects can be in-line or floating. An *in-line object* is part of a paragraph and is subject to the paragraph's formatting. As an example, you might include artwork for an icon you want readers to recognize and embed it in a sentence (**Figure 6.5**). *Floating objects,* on the other hand, can be freely moved about the page and are not tied to a paragraph.

To set wrapping style for an object:

1. Select the object, and open the Format Picture dialog box by doing one of the following:
   ▲ Double-click the object.
   ▲ Click the Format Picture icon on the Picture toolbar.
   ▲ Click the Draw icon on the Drawing toolbar and choose Format Picture from the pop-up menu that appears.
   ▲ Choose Format > Picture.

2. In the Format Picture dialog box, click the Layout tab (**Figure 6.6**).

3. *Do one of the following:*
   ▲ To designate the selected object as in-line, click the In line with text icon.
   ▲ To designate the selected object as floating, click one of the other text wrap icons or click Advanced to choose from other wrapping styles.

4. Click OK.

✔ Tip

■ If a newly inserted object is only partially displayed, it has the wrong wrapping style, such as "In line with text."

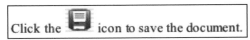

Figure 6.5 In-line graphics are treated as part of the paragraph in which they're embedded.

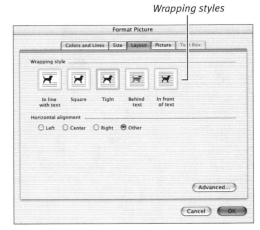

Figure 6.6 Click an icon to specify a wrapping style for the currently selected object.

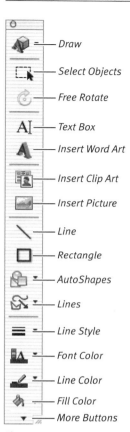

Figure 6.7 The Drawing toolbar.

Figure 6.8 Select a line style and thickness.

Drawing Lines and Shapes

You can use lines to separate text, create callouts for charts and images, or begin building shapes. You can add a variety of predefined shapes to a document, too.

To draw lines or shapes, you use the Drawing toolbar (**Figure 6.7**). If the toolbar isn't visible, you can display it by choosing View > Toolbars > Drawing. Keep this toolbar handy; we'll be using it throughout the chapter.

To draw lines:

1. Click the Line icon on the Drawing toolbar.

2. Click in your document where you want to start the line, hold down the mouse button, and drag to complete the line.

3. With the line still selected, click and hold the Line Style icon on the Drawing toolbar (**Figure 6.8**), and then choose from the thickness and style options.

✔ Tips

■ To change a line's length or direction, select the line, click a handle at either end, and drag. To move a line to a new position, click and drag the line's middle.

■ To draw a line from its center (rather than from an end point), press (Option) as you drag.

■ To create a special line (such as an arrow or curve), select a line type from the Lines toolbar icon and then draw the line.

■ To format a line (changing its color or adding endcaps, for example), select new settings from the Drawing toolbar. If you want to make multiple changes, click the Line Style icon in the Drawing toolbar and choose More Lines. In the Format AutoShape dialog box that appears, set the desired formatting options.

To draw a shape:

1. To draw a predefined shape (called an AutoShape), click the AutoShapes icon on the Drawing toolbar and choose a shape from a submenu (**Figure 6.9**).

2. Click and drag to draw the selected shape.

✔ Tips

- You can click the Rectangle icon or choose Oval from the More Buttons icon on the Drawing toolbar to create rectangles, squares, ovals, and circles.

- To draw a proportional AutoShape or shape (creating a square or circle instead of a rectangle or oval, for example), press Shift as you drag.

- To draw an AutoShape or shape from its center, press Option as you drag.

- By picking options from the Formatting Palette, you can change the line style and thickness, color, and angle of a selected shape.

- Many AutoShapes contain one or more yellow diamonds that you can drag to change an aspect of the shape (**Figure 6.10**).

- To delete a line, arrow, or shape, select it and press Delete.

- Another way to create an AutoShape is to choose Insert > Picture > AutoShapes. An AutoShapes toolbar appears from which you can select a shape to draw.

- To replace a selected AutoShape with another, click the Draw icon in the Drawing toolbar, and choose a replacement shape from the Change AutoShape submenus.

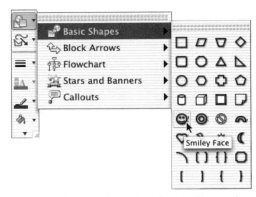

Figure 6.9 Choose a shape from the AutoShape submenus.

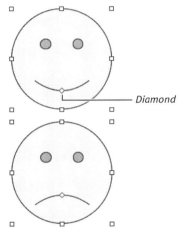

Figure 6.10 Many AutoShapes contain a yellow diamond that you can drag to modify the shape.

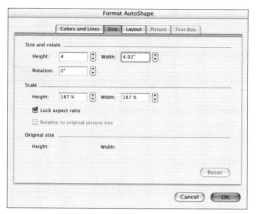

Figure 6.11 Use options on the Size tab of the Format AutoShape dialog box to precisely resize a shape.

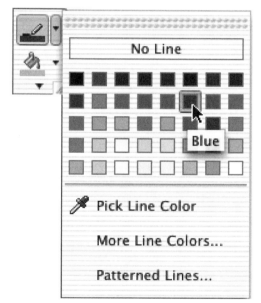

Figure 6.12 Select a color from the Line Color palette. To use a color from another object, click Pick Line Color. To remove the line, click No Line.

Shape Editing

You can change the size of shapes or Auto-Shapes, as well as embellish them with color, shadows, and three-dimensional effects.

To resize a shape:

- ◆ *Do any of the following:*
  - ▲ To resize an object non-proportionately, click and drag any handle.
  - ▲ To resize an object proportionately, press (Shift) as you drag a corner handle.
  - ▲ To resize an object from its center, press (Option) as you drag any handle. Press (Shift)(Option) as you drag to proportionately resize from the center.
  - ▲ Open the Format AutoShape dialog box. (Double-click the shape, choose Format > AutoShape, or click the Draw icon on the Drawing toolbar and choose Format AutoShape.) Click the Size tab (**Figure 6.11**). Enter a new height and width or scaling percentages. To resize proportionately, click the Lock aspect ratio check box.

To color a line or shape:

1. Click a line or shape to select it.

2. *Do any of the following:*
   - ▲ Click the down arrow beside the Line Color icon on the Drawing toolbar to display the Line Color palette (**Figure 6.12**). Select a color. The color is applied to the line or to the shape's outline.
   - ▲ Click the down arrow beside the Fill Color icon on the Drawing toolbar to display the Fill Color palette. Select a color. The color will fill any empty area of the selected shape.

To apply a shadow or 3-D effect to a shape:

1. Click a shape to select it.

2. Click the More Buttons down arrow at the end of the Drawing toolbar. Choose an option from the Simple Shadows or 3-D menu to specify the location and direction of the shadow or effect.

✔ Tips

- The Line Color and Fill Color toolbar icons display the most recent color you've used. To apply that color to another line or shape, simply click the Line Color or Fill Color icon.

- Some shapes can accept both a line and fill color; others can accept only one or the other.

- A shadow can be applied to any type of image (shape, clip art, or photo). The 3-D effect can only be applied to shapes.

- Shadows and 3-D effects (**Figure 6.13**) are mutually exclusive; you can apply one or the other, but not both.

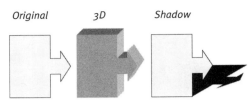

Original   *3D*   *Shadow*

Figure 6.13 You can apply a 3-D or shadow effect to any shape or AutoShape.

SHAPE EDITING

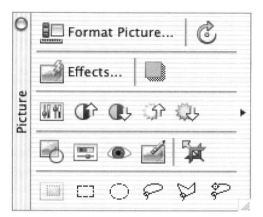

Figure 6.14 Image-editing commands can be selected from the Picture toolbar.

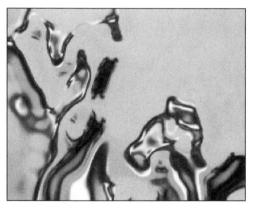

Figure 6.15 Some effects, such as Chrome, can render a photo's subject matter unrecognizable.

Image Editing

Word has a variety of image-editing tools that you can use to correct and edit digital photos, scans, and other *bit-mapped* (dot-based) pictures. Depending on your needs, you may find that a more advanced image-editing application is unnecessary.

To edit a picture:

1. *Optional:* A picture can be edited in place in the Word document or in a separate window. To open the picture in its own window, select the picture and choose Edit > Edit Picture (or Edit > Picture Object > Open).

2. Edit commands can be chosen from the Picture toolbar (**Figure 6.14**) or the Formatting Palette. If necessary, open one of these by choosing View > Toolbars > Picture or View > Formatting Palette.

3. Choose commands from the Picture toolbar or Formatting Palette:

   ▲ Click Format Picture to set text wrap or precisely adjust the image size, cropping, contrast, or brightness.

   ▲ Click the Free Rotate icon and drag any of the green corner handles to rotate the picture to a new angle.

   ▲ Click the Effects icon to apply a special effects filter to the entire image or to a selected area (**Figure 6.15**).

   ▲ Click the Simple Shadow icon to add a shadow behind the image.

   ▲ Click the Image Control icon to convert the picture to grayscale or black and white. To dim the picture's colors so it recedes into the background, choose Watermark.

   continues on next page

Image Editing

▲ Click a Contrast or Brightness icon to increase or reduce the appropriate property. Additional clicks intensify the effect.

▲ To make all areas with a specific color in the picture transparent (allowing that color to blend with the background), click Set Transparent Color and select the color with the eyedropper cursor that appears.

▲ To adjust colors or their saturation, click the Color Adjustment icon. In the dialog box that appears (**Figure 6.16**), select the color that you want to adjust (red, green, or blue) or select Saturation. Then drag the slider to a new setting or click one of the preview images. Click Apply to apply the new color settings to your image.

▲ To eliminate red eye from a photo, click the Fix Red Eye icon and then click in the red portion of the eye. Repeat until all red is eliminated.

▲ To eliminate a scratch from a photo or scan, click the Remove Scratch icon and then click the start and end points of any straight segment of the scratch. Repeat as necessary for additional segments.

▲ To crop a picture (removing unnecessary material from around the subject, for example), click the Crop icon. Then click a handle and drag.

▲ Use the selection tools to select a portion of an image for editing. After a selection has been made, you can copy, cut, or apply a filter to it. You can also create a cutout from the selection (**Figure 6.17**) by clicking the Cutout icon.

✔ Tip

■ It's easier to correct red eye and scratches if you zoom in on the area.

Item to adjust   *Adjustment slider*

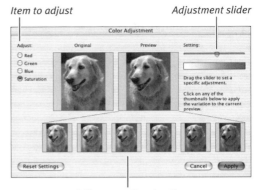

Adjustment thumbnails

Figure 6.16 In the Color Adjustment dialog box, click the radio button for the color or attribute you want to adjust, and then click the thumbnail that most closely matches the desired adjustment.

Figure 6.17 A cutout is a crop based on a selection—in this case, a circular one.

IMAGE EDITING

Insertion mark

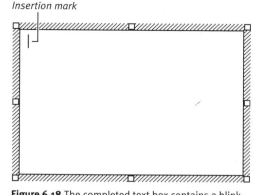

Figure 6.18 The completed text box contains a blinking insertion mark, indicating that it's ready to receive your typed or pasted text.

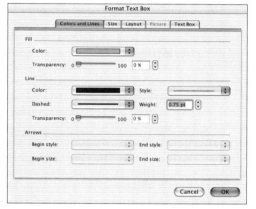

Figure 6.19 In the Format Text Box dialog box, you can adjust a text box's size, color, margins, and so on.

Creating Text Boxes

In Word, you can create text boxes that—unlike normal text—are objects. A *text box* is a rectangular or square container for text (perfect for emphasizing a quote, for example). You can edit the size, shape, color, and other aspects of a text box, just as you can with a graphic.

To create a text box:

1. Click the Text Box icon on the Drawing toolbar.

2. To draw a text box, click and drag from one corner to the opposite corner. When you release the mouse button, the text box is completed (**Figure 6.18**).

3. Type or paste your text.

4. For precise control over the text box's formatting (such as fill and line color, wrap, and margins), double-click one of its sides or choose Format > Text Box.

5. Set options in the Format Text Box dialog box (**Figure 6.19**), and click OK.

✔ Tips

- To create a square text box, press (Shift) as you draw.

- You can change the size and shape of a text box by dragging any handle.

- You can change the location of a text box by moving the pointer over one of its sides and dragging.

- To delete a text box, click one of the sides so that the insertion point inside disappears, and then press (Delete).

- You can change the font, size, color, and alignment of text in a text box. Select the text and choose formatting commands from Word's menus, the Formatting toolbar, or the Formatting Palette.

Creating Artistic Text

WordArt is graphically formatted text that Word can display in a number of preset, artistic styles. After creating WordArt, you can modify or fine-tune it using the WordArt toolbar.

To insert WordArt:

1. Choose Insert > Picture > WordArt or click the Insert WordArt icon on the Drawing toolbar.

2. Select a style from the WordArt Gallery (**Figure 6.20**) and click OK.

    The Edit WordArt Text dialog box appears (**Figure 6.21**).

3. Replace the placeholder text with your own text. Set the font, size, and style and click OK.

    Your WordArt-formatted text and the WordArt toolbar appear (**Figure 6.22** and **Figure 6.23**).

To modify WordArt:

1. Select the WordArt.

2. *Do any of the following:*

    ▲ To resize WordArt, drag any of its handles. To move WordArt, move the pointer over the text itself. When the pointer changes to a hand, click and drag the WordArt to a new spot.

    ▲ To manually change the text angle, click and drag the yellow diamond.

    ▲ To alter the WordArt text, double-click the WordArt or click the Edit Text icon.

    ▲ To change the WordArt style, click the WordArt Gallery icon and select a replacement style.

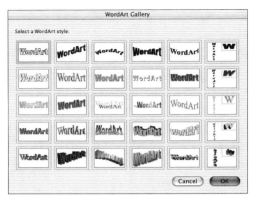

Figure 6.20 Choose a WordArt style from the WordArt Gallery window.

Figure 6.21 Replace the sample text with your own text. You can also set the font, size, and style.

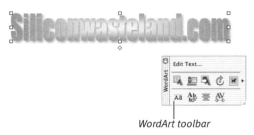

WordArt toolbar

Figure 6.22 Your text is formatted to match the selected WordArt style.

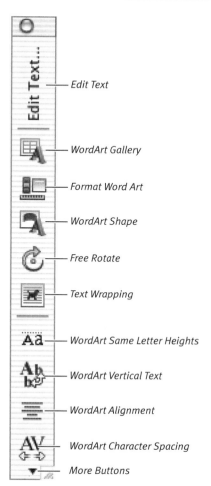

Edit Text

WordArt Gallery

Format Word Art

WordArt Shape

Free Rotate

Text Wrapping

WordArt Same Letter Heights

WordArt Vertical Text

WordArt Alignment

WordArt Character Spacing

More Buttons

Figure 6.23 The WordArt toolbar.

Figure 6.24 You can change the characters in normal WordArt (top) so that they all are the same height (bottom). Note that punctuation marks are also considered characters.

▲ To precisely control the WordArt's appearance, click the Format WordArt icon. Make any desired changes in the Format WordArt dialog box that appears.

▲ To change the shape of the curve(s) to which the WordArt is bound, click the WordArt Shape icon and select a shape from the palette that appears.

▲ To change the angle of the WordArt, click the Free Rotate icon. Then drag any of the green corner handles that appear around the WordArt.

▲ To set the manner in which surrounding text wraps around the WordArt, click the Text Wrapping icon. (For more information, see "Setting Text Wrap," earlier in this chapter.)

▲ To make all characters the same height (**Figure 6.24**), click the WordArt Same Letter Heights icon. If you don't like the effect, click the icon again to reverse it.

▲ To switch between horizontal and vertical text, click the WordArt Vertical Text icon.

▲ To specify a different paragraph alignment or spacing between characters, click the WordArt Alignment or the WordArt Character Spacing icon.

CREATING ARTISTIC TEXT

CREATING TABLES

It's easy to create tables in Word documents. With the click of a button, you can create and begin entering information into a table. Tables can be included in sales reports, research projects, or data analyses. Or a table may consist of only a list of names and phone numbers. We'll discuss creating simple tables first, and then move on to building more complex tables.

The procedures in this chapter assume that you're working with an existing Word file. If you don't have a document open, do one of the following:

◆ To add a table to an existing document, choose File > Open, press ⌘O, or click the Open toolbar icon.

◆ To create a table in a new document, choose File > New Blank Document, press ⌘N, or click the New Blank Document toolbar icon.

Creating a Simple Table

The process of creating a table includes specifying the number of rows and columns, entering text or data, and formatting the table and cells.

To create a simple table:

1. Position the insertion point in your Word document where you want the table to appear.

2. Click the Insert Table icon on the Standard toolbar.

3. In the pop-up palette, drag to specify the desired number of columns and rows (**Figure 7.1**).

   An unformatted table appears (**Figure 7.2**). If you don't want to format the table immediately (or at all), you can begin entering your text and data. Otherwise, continue with Step 4.

4. To apply a predefined format to the table, choose Table > Table AutoFormat.

   The Table AutoFormat dialog box appears (**Figure 7.3**).

5. Select a table style from the Formats list.

   You can choose from simple structures, tables with or without headers, three-dimensional tables, and colored tables. A sample of the selected style appears in the Preview window.

6. Set the formatting options in the bottom section of the dialog box as desired.

7. Click OK.

   The formatting is applied to the table (**Figure 7.4**).

Insert Table icon

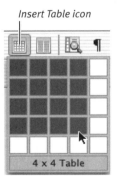

Figure 7.1 Drag in the pop-up palette to specify the table size.

Figure 7.2 An unformatted table appears in the Word document.

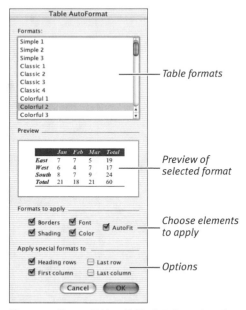

Figure 7.3 Choose Table > Table AutoFormat, and then choose a format from the Formats list.

Figure 7.4 Your formatting choices are applied to the table.

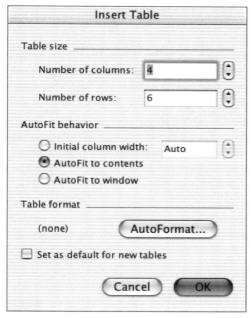

Figure 7.5 In the Insert Table dialog box, specify the number of columns and rows for the table.

✔ Tips

■ You can simultaneously insert and format a table by choosing Table > Insert > Table. In the Insert Table dialog box (**Figure 7.5**), specify the numbers of columns and rows, and set the initial column widths. To select a table format, click AutoFormat.

■ You can apply table formatting at any point—regardless of whether you've begun entering data.

CREATING A SIMPLE TABLE

117

Entering Data

After you've placed the table in a document, you can enter your information.

To enter data in a table:

1. To insert data into a cell, click in the cell and then type.

   As you type, the text wraps within the cell as necessary. The entire row will become taller if it needs to accommodate multiple lines of text (**Figure 7.6**).

2. After completing the entry in the first cell, press Tab to move to the cell to its right, and type text in that cell.

   When you reach the rightmost cell of a row, pressing Tab moves the insertion mark to the first cell of the next row.

✔ Tips

■ Press Shift Tab to move back one cell.

■ If there is already text in a cell when you Tab into it, the text is automatically selected. If you wish, you can delete the entire cell entry by pressing Delete or typing over it.

■ You can move directly to any cell by clicking in it.

■ When you finish entering data in the last cell of the table, you can press Tab to create a new row, if you wish.

■ Use normal editing procedures to alter and format the information in the cells.

Cell with excess text

Figure 7.6 If you enter text that's wider than the cell width, the row height expands as needed to fully display the text.

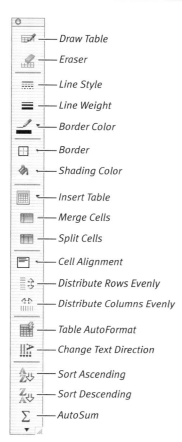

- Draw Table
- Eraser
- Line Style
- Line Weight
- Border Color
- Border
- Shading Color
- Insert Table
- Merge Cells
- Split Cells
- Cell Alignment
- Distribute Rows Evenly
- Distribute Columns Evenly
- Table AutoFormat
- Change Text Direction
- Sort Ascending
- Sort Descending
- AutoSum

Figure 7.7 Tables and Borders toolbar.

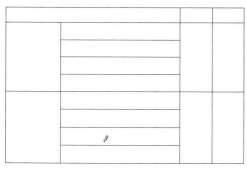

Figure 7.8 Click the Draw Table icon on the Tables and Borders toolbar, and then click and drag to create the table outline.

Building a Table from Scratch

If you have a complex table in mind, you can use Word's tools to draw your own.

To build a table from scratch:

1. Choose Table > Draw Table.

   The Tables and Borders toolbar appears (**Figure 7.7**).

2. Click the Draw Table icon on the toolbar, and then drag the table's outline in the document.

   Click where you want one corner, drag diagonally to the opposite corner, and then release the mouse button.

3. Use the Draw Table tool to draw the interior cell boundaries (**Figure 7.8**).

4. When you're done working on the table and ready to begin entering text, click the Draw Table tool icon again.

✔ Tips

- If the Tables and Borders toolbar does *not* appear automatically, you can open it by clicking the Tables and Borders icon on the Standard toolbar or by choosing View > Toolbars > Tables and Borders.

- If you change your mind about a line and want to erase it, click the Eraser icon on the Tables and Borders toolbar, and then click the line you want to erase. (When drawing with the Draw Table tool, you can temporarily switch to the Eraser tool by pressing (Shift).)

- To remove a line you've just drawn, choose Edit > Undo, press ⌘Z, or click the Undo icon on the Standard toolbar.

Editing the Table Structure

Once you have created the skeleton of the table, you can fine-tune it. The Tables and Borders toolbar simplifies the process.

To edit the table structure:

◆ *Do any of the following:*

▲ To move a line, click and drag it to a new location (**Figure 7.9**).

▲ To change the style, width, or color of a line, choose new options from the Line Style, Line Weight, and Border Color menus on the Tables and Borders toolbar (**Figure 7.10**). Click any line in the table to apply the new settings to that line. New lines that you draw will also use those settings.

▲ To distribute cell heights or widths evenly, click outside the table to clear the tool selection. Then click and drag through the cells you want to adjust, and click the Distribute Rows Evenly or Distribute Columns Evenly icon on the Tables and Borders toolbar (**Figure 7.11**).

▲ To set row heights or column widths precisely, select the cells you want to modify and then choose Table > Table Properties. On the Row, Column, or Cell tab of the Table Properties dialog box (**Figure 7.12**), enter the preferred dimensions and click OK.

▲ You can change the table width by entering a value in the Preferred width text box on the Table tab of the Table Properties dialog box. You can also change the size of a table manually by dragging the table's bottom-right corner.

▲ To move a table, click the symbol in its upper-left corner and drag the table to a new location.

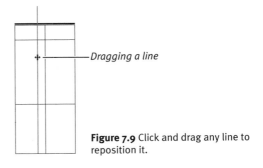

Figure 7.9 Click and drag any line to reposition it.

Line Style   Line Weight   Border Color

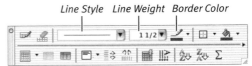

Figure 7.10 To draw or alter the lines in a table, select options from the Tables and Borders toolbar.

Distribute Rows Evenly   Distribute Columns Evenly

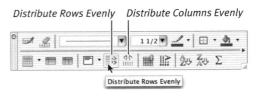

Distribute Rows Evenly

Figure 7.11 You can even up selected rows or columns.

Figure 7.12 The Table Properties dialog box.

EDITING THE TABLE STRUCTURE

Figure 7.13 To set alignment for data in selected cells, choose an option from the Cell Alignment palette.

Figure 7.14 To change the orientation of a cell's text, select the cell and click the Change Text Direction icon.

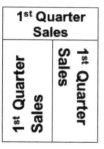

Figure 7.15 You can orient cell text in these directions.

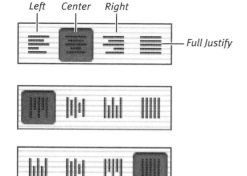

Figure 7.16 To set the alignment of text in selected cells, click these icons on the Formatting toolbar.

Aligning Table Data

Using the Tables and Borders toolbar, you can also change the alignment or orientation of data.

To change the alignment or orientation of cell data:

◆ *Do any of the following:*

▲ Select the cells whose alignment you want to change. Click the Cell Alignment icon on the Tables and Borders toolbar and select the desired alignment from the pop-up palette (**Figure 7.13**).

▲ To change the orientation of data within cells, select the cells you want to orient. Click the Change Text Direction icon on the Tables and Borders toolbar (**Figure 7.14**) repeatedly until you get the desired orientation. There are three possible orientations (**Figure 7.15**).

✔ Tip

■ You can also set the alignment of selected cells by clicking one of the four alignment icons on the Formatting Palette or the Formatting toolbar. The alignment icons presented (**Figure 7.16**) depend on the text direction in the selected cell(s).

Working with Numeric Data

Word tables have the calculation capabilities of Excel worksheets. For example, you can use the AutoSum tool to total columns or rows of numeric values. And using the Table > Formula command, you can insert a formula into any cell.

Figure 7.17 To create a row or column total, click in the cell to the right of the row or beneath the column, and then click the AutoSum icon.

To total a row or column:

◆ *Do any of the following:*

▲ To total values in a column, click in the cell below the numbers you're adding, and then click the AutoSum icon on the Tables and Borders toolbar (**Figure 7.17**).

▲ To total values in a row, click in the cell to the right of the numbers you're adding, and click the AutoSum icon.

✔ Tips

■ If you need a blank row for your totals, click in the last row and choose Table > Insert > Rows Below. To add an extra column, click in the rightmost column and choose Table > Insert > Columns to the Right.

■ You can perform other calculations with table values. Click in an empty cell where you want to display the result, choose Table > Formula, enter a formula in the Formula dialog box (**Figure 7.18**), and click OK. The calculation result appears in the cell.

■ You can choose functions from the Paste function drop-down list (see Figure 7.18).

■ Cells can be referenced as if they were in a worksheet. For example, the top five cells in the first column would be referenced as (A1:A5).

■ To view the formula in a cell, select the cell and choose Table > Formula.

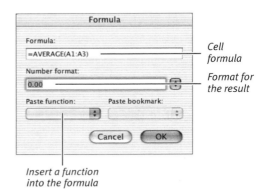

Figure 7.18 Choose Table > Formula and enter a formula in the Formula dialog box.

■ Table formulas do not automatically recalculate. To force a recalculation, reapply the AutoSum or formula to the result cell or (Control)-click the cell and choose Update field from the pop-up menu.

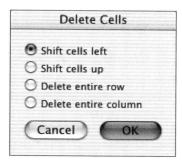

Figure 7.19 In the Delete Cells dialog box, indicate how to adjust the remaining cells after the deletion.

Deleting Cells

You can easily remove cells from a table. You can delete an entire table, full rows or columns, or only selected cells.

To delete table cells:

◆ *Do any of the following:*

▲ To delete an entire table, click any cell and choose Table > Delete > Table.

▲ To delete entire rows or columns, select one or more cells from the row(s) or column(s), and then choose Table > Delete > Rows or Table > Delete > Columns.

▲ To delete specific cells in a table, select the cells and choose Table > Delete > Cells. The Delete Cells dialog box appears (**Figure 7.19**). You can delete entire rows or columns. Or you can delete only the selected cells, moving the rest up or to the left (to close up the deletion).

✔ Tips

■ You can also make the Delete Cells dialog box appear by selecting the desired cell(s), Control-clicking in the selection, and choosing Delete Cells from the pop-up menu that appears.

■ Deleting a cell, row, or column is not the same as simply clearing the cells' contents. The Delete commands actually *remove* selected cells, rows, or columns from the table. To *clear* one or more cells of the data they contain, select the cells and choose Edit > Clear > Contents.

■ If you accidentally delete a table or any part of it, you can restore the deleted portions by immediately choosing the Edit > Undo command, pressing ⌘Z, or clicking the Undo toolbar icon.

DELETING CELLS

Merging and Splitting Cells

Using the Merge Cells command, you can combine two or more adjacent cells into a single cell (to create extended column or row headings, for example). Similarly, you can use the Split Cells command to split a single cell into multiple cells. Split Cells is also useful for restoring previously merged cells to their original multi-cell structure.

To merge cells:

1. Select adjacent cells to be merged (**Figure 7.20**).

2. Choose Table > Merge Cells or click the Merge Cells icon on the Tables and Borders toolbar (see Figure 7.7).

   The cells merge (**Figure 7.21**).

To split a cell:

1. Select the cell that you want to split into multiple cells.

2. Choose Table > Split Cells or click the Split Cells icon on the Tables and Borders toolbar (see Figure 7.7).

   The Split Cells dialog box appears (**Figure 7.22**).

3. Specify the number of columns and rows into which to split the cell, and then click OK.

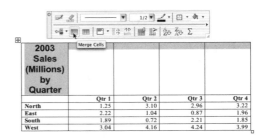

Figure 7.20 Select the cells you want to merge (in this case, the top row) and then click the Merge Cells icon.

Merged cells

2003 Sales (Millions) by Quarter			
	Qtr 1	Qtr 2	Qtr 3	Qtr 4
North	1.25	3.10	2.96	3.22
East	2.22	1.04	0.87	1.96
South	1.89	0.72	2.21	1.85
West	3.04	4.16	4.24	3.99

Figure 7.21 The cells merge, creating a single cell for the table's title.

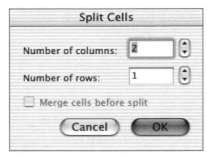

Figure 7.22 When splitting a cell, you must specify the number of resulting rows and columns.

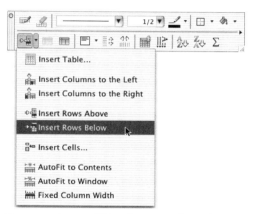

Figure 7.23 Insert additional rows or columns by clicking the down arrow beside the Insert Table icon.

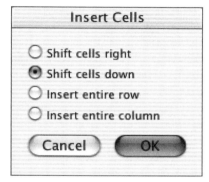

Figure 7.24 When you insert new cells in a table, you must indicate how it will affect the other cells.

✔ **Tips**

■ To insert multiple columns or rows, select the desired number of new columns or rows and then issue the Insert command.

■ The Standard toolbar contains an Insert Table/Columns/Cells icon that changes depending on what is currently selected in the table.

Adding Rows and Columns

Another way you can change a table layout is by inserting additional rows, columns, or cells.

To insert a new row:

1. Click a cell in the row that will serve as the reference for the new row.

2. You can either choose Table > Insert Rows Above or Table > Insert Rows Below, or click the down arrow beside the Insert Table icon on the Tables and Borders toolbar and choose the same command (**Figure 7.23**).

   The new row appears.

To insert a new column:

1. Click a cell in the column that will serve as the reference for the new column.

2. Select Table > Insert Columns to the Left or Table > Insert Columns to the Right, or choose the command from the Tables and Borders toolbar (see Figure 7.23).

   The new column appears.

To insert new cells:

1. Select the cell or cells that will serve as the reference for the new cell(s).

2. Choose Table > Insert > Cells, or choose the same command from the Tables and Borders toolbar (see Figure 7.23).

   The Insert Cells dialog box appears (**Figure 7.24**).

3. Select an option and click OK.

   The new cells are inserted into the table, and the table is adjusted as necessary.

ADDING ROWS AND COLUMNS

Nesting Tables

Nested tables are tables within tables. They can be handy if you have a special subcategory of information that the table needs to reflect. Inserting a nested table is similar to creating a new table.

To insert a nested table:

1. Click in your current table to select a place to insert the nested table (**Figure 7.25**).

2. Click the Insert Table icon on the Standard toolbar (see Figure 7.1) and drag to specify the number of rows and columns for the nested table.

   A nested table appears within your original table (**Figure 7.26**).

✔ Tip

■ You can also insert a nested table by choosing the Table > Insert > Table command or by clicking the Insert Table icon on the Tables and Borders toolbar. For instructions, refer to the first tip following "Creating a Simple Table," earlier in this chapter.

Selected cell

	Species	Jan.-June	July-Dec.
Cats	Abyssinian	37	45
	Burmese	12	17
Dogs	Retriever	52	55
	Corgi	23	18
	Total	124	135

Figure 7.25 Select the location where the nested table will be inserted.

Nested table

	Species	Jan.-June	July-Dec.
Cats	Abyssinian	37	45
	Burmese	12	17
Dogs	Retriever	52	55
	Golden / Blonde		
	Corgi	23	18
	Total	124	135

Figure 7.26 The nested table is created within the original table.

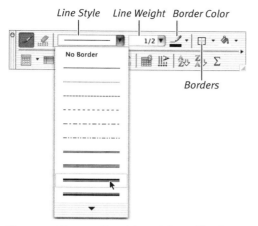

Line Style *Line Weight* *Border Color*

Borders

Figure 7.27 Choose a line style, weight, and border color from the Tables and Borders toolbar.

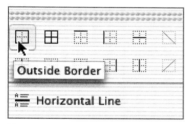

Figure 7.28 From the Borders pop-up palette, choose a border option to apply to the selected cells.

2003 Sales (Millions) by Quarter			
	Qtr 1	Qtr 2	Qtr 3	Qtr 4
North	1.25	3.10	2.96	3.22
East	2.22	1.04	0.87	1.96
South	1.89	0.72	2.21	1.85
West	3.04	4.16	4.24	3.99

Figure 7.29 A table with varied line styles and shade fills often looks more professional.

Borders and Cell Shading

Borders are the lines surrounding cells. *Shading* is fill within cells. The Table > Table AutoFormat command offers a collection of templates for borders and shading that you can apply to a table (discussed in "Creating a Simple Table," earlier in this chapter). If you prefer, you can follow the procedure below to set cell borders and shading manually.

To set borders and shading manually:

1. Select the cells whose borders or shading you want to set or change.

2. From the Tables and Borders toolbar, choose a line style, weight, and border color (**Figure 7.27**).

3. Click the Border icon on the Tables and Borders toolbar, and then pick the type of border, such as top, bottom, left, right, or outside, you wish to apply to the selected cells (**Figure 7.28**).

4. To apply shading to the selected cells, click the Shading Color icon on the Tables and Borders toolbar and choose a color from the drop-down palette.

   The completed table can contain any combination of borders and shading (**Figure 7.29**).

✔ Tip

- Word provides another way to draw lines that you may find simpler. From the Tables and Borders toolbar, choose a line style, weight, and border color. Then click the Draw Table icon. Each table line that you click or drag/draw with the pencil cursor will take on the specified settings.

BORDERS AND CELL SHADING

127

Converting Text to a Table

You can convert existing text in a Word document into a table.

Figure 7.30 Select the text you want to convert into a table, and then choose Table > Convert > Convert Text to Table. (In this instance, the text is tab delimited.)

To convert text to a table:

1. Select the lines of existing text you want to convert into a table (**Figure 7.30**).

2. Choose Table > Convert > Convert Text to Table.

   The Convert Text to Table dialog box appears (**Figure 7.31**).

3. Specify the number of columns and rows that the resulting table will contain.

4. *Optional:* Click AutoFormat to select a format for the table.

5. Click OK to generate the table.

   The selected text is converted into a table (**Figure 7.32**). To adjust the formatting and style, see "Editing the Table Structure" and "Borders and Cell Shading," earlier in this chapter.

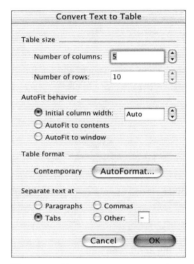

Figure 7.31 If necessary, you can set conversion options in the Convert Text to Table dialog box.

✔ Tips

- To allow Word to convert selected text *automatically* into an appropriate table, click the Insert Table toolbar icon.

- To convert multiple paragraphs into a table, select those paragraphs and choose Table > Convert > Convert Text to Table. Select Paragraphs as the text separator in the Convert Text to Table dialog box.

- If you're converting tab-delimited text into a table, make sure the text doesn't have multiple tab characters between items that should be in adjacent columns—even if removing the extra tabs makes the spacing look wrong.

- You can convert a selected table back into text by choosing Table > Convert > Convert Table to Text.

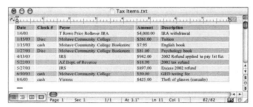

Figure 7.32 The selected text is converted into a Word table.

OTHER WORD FEATURES

Many people—perhaps most—only use Word for traditional word-processing tasks, such as writing letters, memos, and the occasional report. However, Word also has a host of ancillary features and capabilities that you may occasionally find useful. In this chapter, you'll learn to do the following:

◆ Use the Contact toolbar to add contact information from your Office Address Book to Word documents

◆ Create labels and envelopes

◆ Design catalogues, menus, and newsletters

◆ Use the Data Merge Manager to create merge documents, such as personalized form letters

◆ Use Outline View to create outlines

◆ Use the new Notebook Layout View to help organize your thoughts

Using the Contact Toolbar

Using the Contact toolbar, you can quickly add name, address, and other contact information from your Office Address Book to letters, labels, and envelopes. (The Office Address Book is normally maintained in Entourage but is also accessible from Word.)

To use the Contact toolbar:

1. Choose View > Toolbars > Contact.

   The Contact toolbar appears above the document window (**Figure 8.1**).

2. To insert a contact into your document, position the insertion point where you'd like to insert the contact information.

3. Choose the contact name from the Contacts drop-down menu.

   The contact's name appears in the document at the insertion point.

4. If you've recorded a street address, phone number, or email address for the contact, you can also insert that information into the document by clicking the Include Address, Include Phone, or Include E-mail toolbar icon.

Select a contact *Create a new contact* *Insert address* *Insert phone number* *Insert email address*

Figure 8.1 You can use the Contact toolbar to insert contact names and other information from the Office Address Book into your documents.

AutoText suggestion

Figure 8.2 If you begin typing the name of a person who is in your Address Book, Word will offer to insert his or her name.

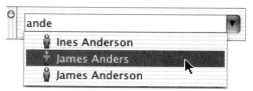

Figure 8.3 To quickly find a desired contact record, type part of the individual's name in the Contacts box.

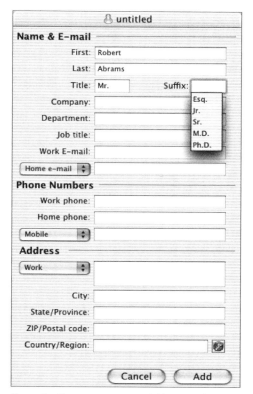

Figure 8.4 You can create new Address Book contact records from within Word.

✔ Tips

■ You can also enter a contact's name using Word's AutoText feature (see Chapter 3). Start typing the person's name in your document. If the name is in your Address Book, Word will suggest it (**Figure 8.2**). Press (Enter) or (Return) to accept the name, or continue typing if it's not the right one.

■ If you have many entries in your Address Book, the Contacts drop-down list may not display them all. To see other entries, type part of the person's name in the Contacts text box. The contact list will show all possible matches for what you've typed, enabling you to choose the desired contact (**Figure 8.3**).

■ To create a new contact record, click the Add icon on the Contact toolbar. Enter the information in the dialog box that appears (**Figure 8.4**) and then click Add. (For more information on creating Address Book contacts, refer to Chapter 21.)

Creating Labels

Word provides label templates that you can use to create many kinds of labels, such as mailing labels, videotape labels, and name badges. Using the Labels wizard, you can generate a single label or an entire sheet of the same label that will print on popular label manufacturers' stock.

To create labels:

1. *Do one of the following:*

   ▲ If the Project Gallery isn't open, choose File > Project Gallery ([Shift][⌘][P]). On the New tab, select Labels from the Groups list (**Figure 8.5**), select the Mailing Label Wizard, and click OK.

   ▲ Create a new document by choosing File > New Blank Document ([⌘][N]), and then choose Tools > Labels.

   The Labels wizard appears (**Figure 8.6**).

2. Click the Options button to open the Label Options window (**Figure 8.7**). Specify the type of printer you'll use, the label manufacturer, and the label's part number. Click OK.

3. Enter the address or other appropriate text in the Address text box of the Labels wizard.

   To insert your own mailing address (from your identity in the Entourage Address Book), click the Use my address check box.

4. Click a radio button to indicate the desired printing option: Full page of the same label or Single label. (In the latter case, you must also specify the label row and column on which you want to print.)

5. *Optional:* You can alter the font, size, and style of selected text by clicking Font. To set special print options, click Customize.

6. Click OK.

   The labels appear in a new document.

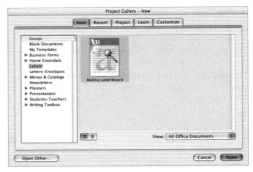

Figure 8.5 You can select the Mailing Label Wizard (Labels wizard) from the Project Gallery dialog box.

Enter label text   Set label type Set font

Figure 8.6 Design your label in the Labels wizard.

Part numbers   Manufacturers

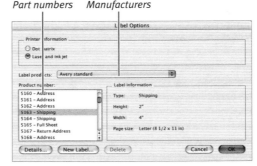

Figure 8.7 Select the label manufacturer, part number, and the printer you'll use.

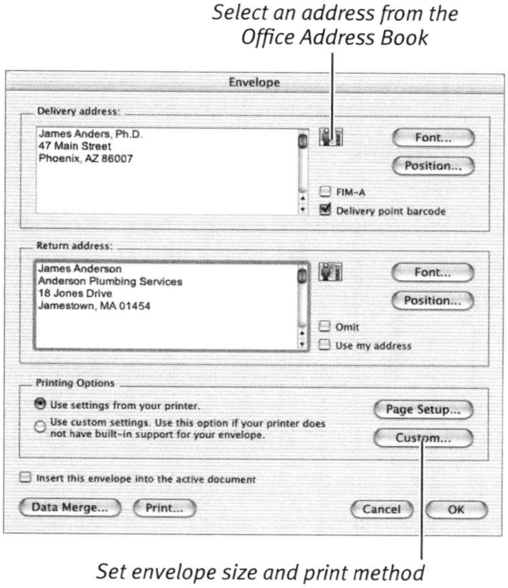

*Select an address from the
Office Address Book*

Set envelope size and print method

Figure 8.8 Specify the delivery address, the return address (if any), and formatting options.

Printing Envelopes

The Envelope wizard can extract the mailing address from a letter and format it so you can print an envelope. Alternatively, you can use the Envelope wizard to create and print *any* envelope; it doesn't matter whether the address is extracted from an open document, chosen from the Office Address Book, or entered by hand.

To create an envelope:

1. *Do one of the following:*
   ▲ Choose Tools > Envelopes.
   ▲ In the Project Gallery, select the Letters-Envelopes category and then select the Envelope wizard.

   The Envelope wizard appears (**Figure 8.8**). If the active Word document contains a single address, the wizard automatically uses it as the delivery address.

2. If the active Word document *doesn't* contain a delivery address, you can type one in the Delivery address text box. You can also pick one from the Office Address Book by clicking the icon beside the text box.

3. By default, your address from the Office Address Book is used as the return address.
   ▲ To use a different return address, remove the checkmark from the Use my address check box. Then type a new return address or click the Address Book icon to select a return address from the Office Address Book.
   ▲ To omit the return address (if you're using preprinted envelopes, for example), click the Omit check box.

4. *Optional:* Click the Font and Position buttons to make any necessary changes to the format and position of the delivery and return address.

continues on next page

PRINTING ENVELOPES

5. In the Printing Options section of the wizard, click a radio button to specify whether the envelope will be printed using standard settings for your printer or, in the case of an unsupported envelope size, whether custom settings are necessary.

6. Click the Page Setup button to specify the printer to use, envelope size, and printer feed method (**Figure 8.9**). Click OK.

7. *Do one of the following:*

   ▲ If you're satisfied with the formatting and are ready to print the envelope, click Print.

   ▲ If you want to make further changes to the envelope (reducing the line spacing in the addresses or adding a logo, for example), click OK. The envelope is displayed as a new, editable Word document (**Figure 8.10**).

✔ Tips

■ If the active Word document contains more than one address, highlight the delivery address in the document before choosing the Envelopes command or the Envelope wizard.

■ The Delivery point barcode option in the Envelope dialog box prints a machine-readable version of the zip code on the envelope. This assists the USPS in processing the letter.

■ If you are creating reply envelopes, you can have Word print an FIM code by clicking the FIM-A check box in the Envelope dialog box. FIMs are necessary *only* for business reply mail. Check with the USPS for more information.

■ You can apply fonts selectively. To use a different font or style for just the recipient's name, for example, select the name before clicking the Font button.

Printer feed methods   Choose an envelope type

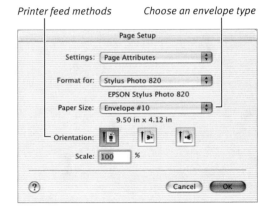

Figure 8.9 Use the Page Setup dialog box to set print options.

Figure 8.10 Rather than route the envelope directly to your printer, you can generate it as an editable Word document.

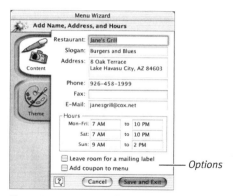

Figure 8.11 Enter text information and options on the Content tab.

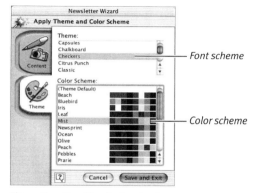

Figure 8.12 Specify a font and color scheme on the Theme tab.

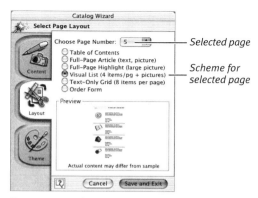

Figure 8.13 On the Layout tab, select a layout scheme for each page.

Catalogs, Menus, and Newsletters

Catalogs, menus, and newsletters are fun to make because you can really use your creativity. Word simplifies the process by providing wizards for creating these kinds of documents. (See Chapter 1 for more information about wizards and templates. Refer to Chapter 6 for help with adding and working with graphics.)

To create a catalog, menu, or newsletter:

1. Open the Project Gallery by choosing File > Project Gallery ((Shift)(⌘)(P)).

2. In the Category list, select Newsletters or select Catalogs or Menus from the Menus & Catalogs topic.

3. Select a template for the catalog, menu, or newsletter, and then click OK.

   The Catalog, Menu, or Newsletter Wizard appears, as appropriate.

4. Enter your information in the wizard:
   - ▲ In the Menu Wizard, enter the name and address of the restaurant and its hours of operation (**Figure 8.11**). Pick a color scheme on the Theme tab.
   - ▲ In the Newsletter Wizard, enter the title, address, and layout information. Select a font theme and color scheme on the Theme tab (**Figure 8.12**).
   - ▲ In the Catalog Wizard, enter the title and number of pages, specify the contents of each page on the Layout tab (**Figure 8.13**), and select a font theme and color scheme on the Theme tab.

5. Click Save and Exit.

   Your data and settings are transferred to the Word document. Replace the text and graphic placeholders with your material.

The Data Merge Manager

Word provides help for creating mail merge letters, labels, and envelopes. It can assist you in creating the *main document* (containing placeholders for the information that changes with each copy), creating or opening the *data source* (for example, a collection of names and addresses), and printing the merged documents. In this example, we'll show you how to create form letters using records in the Office Address Book as the data source for the merge.

To create merged documents:

1. Create or open the document you'll use as the main document (**Figure 8.14**).

   You can use a form letter, a label layout, or an envelope layout, for example.

2. Choose Tools > Data Merge Manager.

   The Data Merge Manager palette opens (**Figure 8.15**).

3. In the Main Document section of the Data Merge Manager palette, click Create. Then choose a merge type (such as Form Letters) from the drop-down menu that appears.

Recipient's address here   *Salutation here*

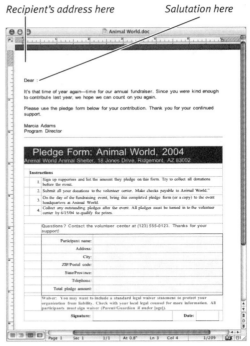

Figure 8.14 This form letter will serve as the main document. Space has been left for the recipient's address and the salutation.

Document type to be created

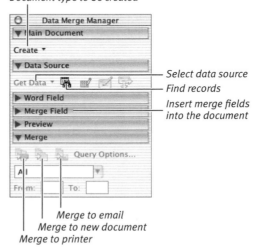

Select data source
Find records
Insert merge fields into the document

Merge to email
Merge to new document
Merge to printer

Figure 8.15 Use the Data Merge Manager to create merge letters, labels, and envelopes.

THE DATA MERGE MANAGER

▼ Merge Field

Drag and drop into document:

First_Name	Last_Name	Suffix
Title	Full_Name	E_Mail
Address	Street	City
State_or_Province	Country	Zip_Code
Phone	Fax	Mobile_Phone
Job_Title	Company	Department

Figure 8.16 After you select the data source, a list of the merge fields it contains appears. Drag the necessary fields into position in the main document.

«First_Name» «Last_Name»
«Street»
«City», «State_or_Province» «Zip_Code»

Dear «First_Name»:

James Anders
47 Main Street
Phoenix, AZ 86007

Dear James:

Figure 8.17 In the document, field names (top) are surrounded by brackets (« and »). To view the document with the merge data in place (bottom), click the View Merged Data icon in the Preview section.

Merge menu

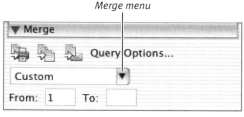

▼ Merge

🖳 🖳 🖳 Query Options...

Custom ▼

From: 1   To:

Figure 8.18 In the Merge section, indicate the records you want to merge.

4. Expand the Data Source section, click Get Data, and then choose one of the following from the drop-down menu:

- ▲ **New Data Source** steps you through the process of creating a data source from scratch.

- ▲ **Open Data Source** lets you use data from an existing Word or Excel document.

- ▲ **Office Address Book** uses contact information from your Address Book.

- ▲ **FileMaker Pro** lets you import data from selected fields in an existing FileMaker Pro 5, 5.5, or 6.0 database.

After you've created or opened the data source, the Merge Field section of the Data Merge Manager expands to list the fields in the data source—in this case, the Office Address Book (**Figure 8.16**).

5. Drag the merge fields from the Data Merge Manager into the proper positions in the main document (**Figure 8.17**).

The merge fields are placeholders for data from the data source. You can place merge fields on separate lines, together on the same line, or embedded within the text of the main document.

6. If necessary, format the merge fields and add any required spacing or punctuation.

For example, for the last line of an address, you'd separate City, State, and Zip merge fields with a comma and spaces, like this:

«City», «State» «Zip»

7. Specify which records to merge by choosing an option from the Merge menu of the Data Merge Manager (**Figure 8.18**).

Choose *All* to merge all records in the data source, *Current Record* to merge only the record number selected in the Preview section, or *Custom* to specify a particular range of records.

continues on next page

THE DATA MERGE MANAGER

8. When the merge document is complete, do one of the following:

▲ Click the Merge to Printer button (see Figure 8.15) to print immediately.

▲ Click the Merge to New Document button to create a Word document that you can edit and print later.

▲ Click the Merge to E-Mail button to send the merge document(s) to Entourage's Outbox for transmission as email (**Figures 8.19** and **8.20**).

✔ Tips

■ At times, you may want to create a merge for just one record. To locate the desired record, click the Find Record icon in the Data Source section of the Data Merge Manager. For more complex record-selection needs, click the Query Options button in the Merge section.

■ Before completing the merge, it's a good idea to preview the data to make sure that the right fields were selected and the formatting looks okay. Expand the Preview section of the Data Merge Manager, click the View Merged Data icon, and click the arrow icons to review some of the merge records displayed as part of the main document.

■ If you aren't certain whether you've chosen the correct records, merge to document. After doing so, scan the resulting document, delete unnecessary records, edit any incomplete ones, and *then* print.

— *Email address field*
— *Message subject*
— *Message format*

Figure 8.19 Set options in the Mail Recipient dialog box prior to merging to email.

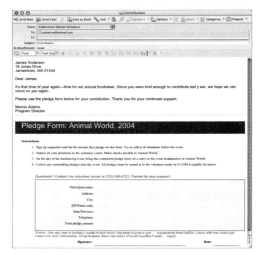

Figure 8.20 When you merge to email, each message generated by the merge is placed in Entourage's Outbox, ready for sending. If necessary, you can edit the messages in Entourage.

Figure 8.21 You can switch to Outline View by clicking an icon at the bottom of the document.

Working with Outlines

Most of us remember creating outlines in high school or college. Sometimes it was because we were forced to do so as part of an assignment; other times it was because we found them a useful—or essential—means of organizing our thoughts for a paper, presentation, or project. If you still find outlines useful or want to explore the ease with which computer-based outlines can be created and organized, try out Word's Outline View.

To create an outline:

1. In a new document, switch to Outline View by clicking the Outline View icon in the bottom-left corner of the document window (**Figure 8.21**) or by choosing View > Outline.

   The Outlining toolbar (**Figure 8.22**) automatically appears.

2. Type your first item and press ⌐Return⌐.

   Word marks it as a Level 1 item, formatted as Heading 1. Each subsequent item (created by pressing ⌐Return⌐ to generate a new paragraph) will be at the same level as the previous item.

   continues on next page

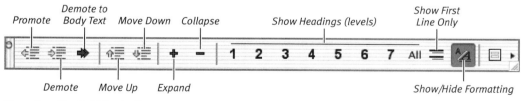

Figure 8.22 The Outlining toolbar.

3. To change a selected item's level, you can do any of the following:

▲ Click the Promote toolbar icon or press ⌃Control⌃Shift⌃← to raise an item's level by one.

▲ Click the Demote toolbar icon or press ⌃Control⌃Shift⌃→ to lower an item's level by one.

▲ Move the cursor over a point's outline symbol (+ or -). When the cursor changes to a plus (**Figure 8.23**), you can drag the item to the left or right to promote or demote it to the desired level.

▲ Click the Demote to Body Text toolbar icon to change an item into body text. (This is useful for writing notes and comments related to the item above.)

4. To move an item and all its subordinate items to a new location in the outline, select the item and use drag and drop to move the item(s) to the destination.

5. To change your view of the outline, you can do any of the following:

▲ To expand/show all levels, click the All toolbar icon or press ⌃Control⌃Shift⌃A.

▲ Click a level number on the toolbar to show only levels that are at that same level or higher.

▲ To expand or collapse a selected item by one level, click the Expand or Collapse toolbar item. Each additional click shows or hides one more level.

▲ To hide/show an item's subordinate items, double-click its plus (+) symbol.

✔ Tips

■ To delete a selected item, press ⌈Delete⌋.

■ Outline View is designed to make it easy to move material around. You can use it to reorganize normal documents, too.

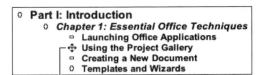

Item to be moved

Figure 8.23 You can promote, demote, or move an item by clicking its outline symbol and then dragging the item to a new position or location.

Other Outliners

While Outline View can certainly serve your basic outlining needs, there are other very capable outliners available for Mac OS X. They have features such as multiple columns (for recording notes, dates, and other items related to each outline point), calculation capabilities, and advanced point-numbering abilities.

If you'd like to learn more about two of my favorite OS X outliners, check out:

◆ *OmniOutliner* (www.omnigroup.com)

◆ *NoteBook* (www.circusponies.com)

WORKING WITH OUTLINES

Figure 8.24 You can either convert the current document to a notebook or create a new, blank notebook.

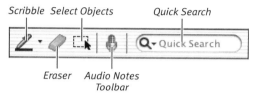

Figure 8.25 The Standard toolbar is replaced by one with these additional note-related icons and controls.

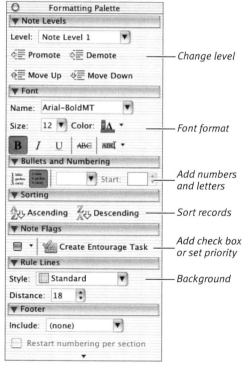

Figure 8.26 Note sections are added to the Formatting Palette.

Using Notebooks

New in Office 2004, the Notebook Layout View is used—like Outline View—to organize your thoughts concerning projects, reports, and many other activities. To facilitate the note-taking process, you can insert pictures, freehand drawings, and audio notes. To help arrange your notes, each notebook has side tabs that you can label as you wish.

Working with notebooks is very similar to working with outlines. In fact, it may help you to think of a notebook as simply a variation of an outline.

To create a notebook:

1. With a new or existing Word document active, click the Notebook Layout View icon in the bottom-left corner of the document window or choose View > Notebook Layout.

   If you don't already have a document open in Notebook Layout View, a dialog box appears (**Figure 8.24**).

2. *Do one of the following:*
   - ▲ Click Convert to change the current document into a notebook.
   - ▲ Click Create New to open a new document as a notebook.

   The document is converted to a notebook or a new one is created. The Standard toolbar is replaced by the Notebook Layout View Standard toolbar (**Figure 8.25**). Note sections are added to the Formatting Palette (**Figure 8.26**).

3. To enter a note, type as you would in a normal document. To begin a new note, press Return.

   Notes can contain multiple lines of text and will automatically wrap as needed.

   continues on next page

4. Like outline items, notes can be indented to denote subordinate items. To indent (demote) a selected note, press ⟨Tab⟩ as many times as necessary or click the Demote icon on the Formatting Palette. To promote a note to a higher level, press ⟨Shift⟩⟨Tab⟩ or click the Promote icon.

5. To rearrange notes, do the following:

▲ To move a note and all its subordinate notes to another location, click the symbol to the left of the note to select it and then use drag and drop to move the notes(s) to the desired location (**Figure 8.27**).

▲ Select (or click in) a note and click the Move Up or Move Down icon on the Formatting Palette.

▲ Change the current indent level of a selected note by pressing ⟨Tab⟩ or ⟨Shift⟩⟨Tab⟩.

6. To add an image or QuickTime movie to a notebook page, choose Insert > Movie or choose an option from the Insert > Picture submenu.

Images and movies can either be in-line or floating objects (determined by the object's wrapping style). Choose Format > Picture. Select a wrapping style on the Layout tab of the Format Picture dialog box (**Figure 8.28**) and then click OK.

7. Use the Scribble tool to add freehand drawings to a notebook page.

▲ To draw in the current color and line width, click the Scribble toolbar icon.

▲ To set a new pen color and/or line width, click the down arrow beside the Scribble icon and choose new settings (**Figure 8.29**).

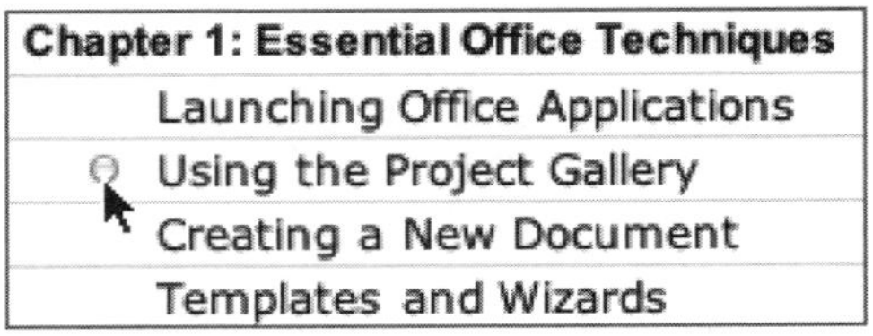

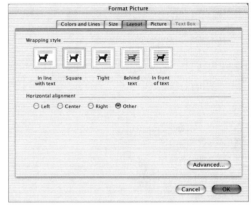

Figure 8.27 When you move the cursor over the left side of a note, a selection symbol appears. You can click the symbol and drag the note to a new location or change its indentation.

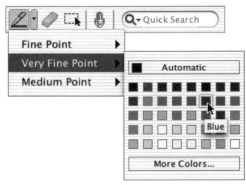

Figure 8.28 Select a text wrap style by clicking an icon. To view other wrap options, click the Advanced button.

Figure 8.29 Use the Scribble tool to make freehand drawings on a notebook page.

Chapter 1
Chapter 2
Chapter 3
+

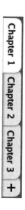

Figure 8.31 Click the plus (+) tab to add a page to the notebook.

8. To add an audio note, click the Audio Notes Toolbar icon. The Audio Notes toolbar appears (**Figure 8.30,** bottom of this page).

   Do the following:

   ▲ Select the note that will be linked to the recording.

   ▲ When you're ready to begin, click the Start Recording button and speak into your connected microphone. Click Stop to end the recording. A speaker icon appears beside the note.

   ▲ To listen to an audio note, click the speaker icon. Stop or pause playback by clicking a toolbar icon.

9. To search for text, type a search string in the Quick Search box (see Figure 8.25) and press Return. All matching instances are highlighted. (Matches on other tabs are indicating by highlighted tabs.)

✔ Tips

- As is the case with outlines, you can freely work with a notebook in other views.
- Note text can be formatted by applying fonts, styles, and selective numbering. Select a note or text string and choose formatting commands from the Format menu, Font menu, or Formatting Palette.
- To add a page to a notebook, click the plus (+) tab (**Figure 8.31**). To change a tab's label, select the tab text and edit it.
- To delete an object, click it with the Eraser tool or select it and press Delete.

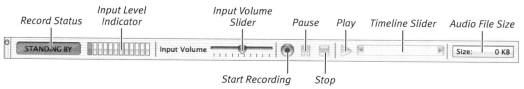

Record Status
Input Level Indicator
Input Volume Slider
Pause
Play
Timeline Slider
Audio File Size
STANDING BY
Input Volume
Size:
0 KB
Start Recording
Stop

Figure 8.30 Use the Audio Notes toolbar to create and play audio notes.

Part III: Microsoft Excel

SPREADSHEET ESSENTIALS

As you probably know, Excel is Office 2004's *spreadsheet* application. By working in a grid of columns and rows called a *worksheet*, you can create lists, perform complex calculations, and graph selected data.

In this chapter, we'll explore the basic topics that you'll need to understand in order to begin using Excel:

- ◆ Creating new workbooks
- ◆ Entering data into cells and navigating a worksheet
- ◆ Using AutoFill to intelligently fill ranges
- ◆ Editing cell contents and performing Find/Replace procedures
- ◆ Documenting worksheets with comments
- ◆ Naming cell ranges
- ◆ Importing text files
- ◆ Working with workbooks and sheets
- ◆ Printing workbooks, worksheets, and selected ranges

Creating a New Workbook

A new Excel document is called a *workbook*.
Every workbook consists of one or multiple
pages known as *worksheets* (or *sheets*).

To create a new workbook:

◆ *Do either of the following:*

▲ When you launch Excel, the Project
Gallery appears (**Figure 9.1**). To create
a new workbook, click the New tab. By
default, the Blank Documents group is
selected, as is the Excel Workbook
thumbnail. Click the Open button.

▲ If Excel is already running, choose
File > New Workbook, press ⌘N, or
click the New icon on the Standard
toolbar.

A new workbook appears (**Figure 9.2**).

✔ Tips

■ On Excel's launch, if you close the Project
Gallery without opening a new or existing
workbook, a new workbook is automatically created.

■ Whether the Project Gallery appears at
startup is determined by a setting in the
General section of Excel's Preferences
(**Figure 9.3**). The number of sheets in a
new workbook is also determined by a
setting in this dialog box.

To open Preferences, choose Excel >
Preferences. (The command is only available if a workbook is currently open.)

■ You can also open the Project Gallery
while Excel is running. Choose File >
Project Gallery (⇧⌘P).

■ It isn't necessary to close any open workbooks before creating a new one.

■ While you can keep adding worksheets to
a single workbook, it's more usual to create
a new workbook for each new project.

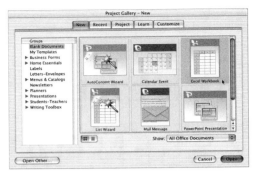

Figure 9.1 On program launch, you can create a new
workbook in the Project Gallery by pressing Return.

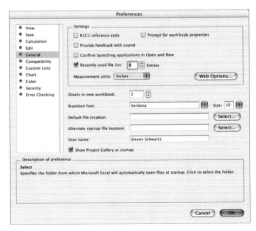

Figure 9.2 A new workbook appears.

Figure 9.3 In the General section of Preferences, check
Show Project Gallery at startup.

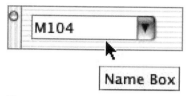

Figure 9.4 Type the cell address in the Name Box.

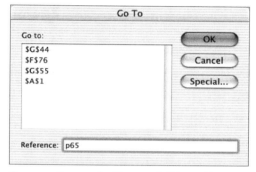

Figure 9.5 Type a cell address and click OK. (If the address was recently used, you can select it from the Go to list.)

Table 9.1

Keyboard Navigation Shortcuts	
SHORTCUT	**ACTION**
⬆, ⬇, ⬅, ➡	Move to the adjacent cell (up, down, left, or right)
Pg Up, Pg Dn	Move up or down one screen
Option Pg Dn, Option Pg Up	Move right or left one screen
Tab, Shift Tab	Move right or left one cell
Enter, Shift Enter	Move down or up one cell
Return, Shift Return	Move down or up one cell
Home	Move to first cell of the row
Control Home	Move to cell A1

Worksheet Navigation

Excel windows work as they do in most other Macintosh applications—with some additional tricks to get you where you want to go.

A sheet is divided into a grid of columns and rows (see Figure 9.2). The intersection of a given column and row is known as a *cell*. Every column is labeled with a letter (shown in its heading) and every row with a number. The combination of a column letter and row number uniquely identifies each cell, such as G7 or D103. This combination is known as a *cell address*.

To move to a cell:

◆ *Do one of the following:*

▲ Scroll as necessary to display the desired cell and then click the cell.

▲ Use the keyboard to navigate to the cell, as explained in **Table 9.1**.

▲ Type the cell address in the Name Box on the Formula Bar (**Figure 9.4**), and then press Return or Enter.

▲ Choose Edit > Go To (Control G). In the Go To dialog box (**Figure 9.5**), enter the cell address in the Reference text box and then click OK.

The cell you click or move to becomes the *active cell*. The address appears in the Name Box, and the corresponding column letter and row number are highlighted.

✔ Tips

■ You can use the scroll bars to scroll through a worksheet without changing the active cell.

■ You can press Control Delete to return directly to the active cell.

■ If it's not visible, you can display the Formula Bar by choosing View > Formula Bar.

Entering Data into Cells

Data entry is primarily a click-and-type procedure, as explained in the following steps.

To enter data into a cell:

1. Click a cell to make it active (**Figure 9.6**).

2. In the cell or the Formula Bar, type the text, number, date, or formula (**Figure 9.7**).

   As explained in Chapter 11, formulas must begin with an equal sign (=).

3. *Do one of the following:*

   ▲ Complete the entry by pressing a navigation key, such as (Return) or (Enter) to move down or (Tab) to move right.

   ▲ To complete the entry without changing the active cell, click the Enter icon on the Formula Bar.

   Excel evaluates the cell contents and then formats it appropriately.

✔ Tips

■ To complete a cell entry, you can also use the keyboard shortcuts shown in Table 9.1.

■ If you change your mind about a cell entry, press (Esc) or click the Cancel icon on the Formula Bar. If the cell was originally empty, it is cleared; if it contained data or a formula, the data or formula is restored.

■ If a new text entry you're typing matches one or more others in the same column, Excel provides a drop-down AutoComplete list of all matches. Click one to accept it, or keep typing to ignore the list.

■ Some numbers, such as Zip Codes, are best treated as text rather than numbers. Doing so enables you to preserve any leading zeros, such as 01701. (If recorded as a number, Excel drops the leading zero.) To prevent this, format the cells as Text prior to entering the data.

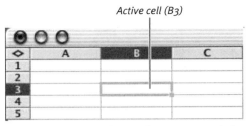

Active cell (B3)

Figure 9.6 The current (or active) cell is surrounded by a thick, gray border. Its column and row heading are highlighted.

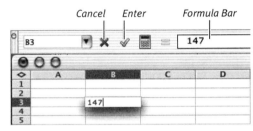

Cancel   Enter   Formula Bar

Figure 9.7 You can type directly into the active cell or into the text box on the Formula Bar.

Entering Data into a Range

If you know the cell range into which you'll be entering data, you can speed up the process by selecting the range.

After you complete the entry for each cell, press (Tab) to move to the next cell to the right or press (Return) or (Enter) to move to the next cell down. When a row or column of the range has been completed, the cursor automatically moves to the beginning of the next row or column.

| 30 | June 28, 2004 |
| 31 | |

Figure 9.8 Move the cursor over the lower-right edge of the cell. It becomes the fill cursor.

30	June 28, 2004
31	
32	
33	
34	
35	
36	
37	
38	
39	
40	
41	
42	July 8, 2004
43	

Figure 9.9 Drag to select the range you want to fill.

30	June 28, 2004
31	June 29, 2004
32	June 30, 2004
33	July 1, 2004
34	July 2, 2004
35	July 3, 2004
36	July 4, 2004
37	July 5, 2004
38	July 6, 2004
39	July 7, 2004
40	July 8, 2004

Figure 9.10 When you release the mouse button, the new data appears.

Using AutoFill

When you need to fill a range of cells with consecutive numbers, dates, days of the week, or items that follow a specific pattern (such as every four days), you can employ AutoFill to automatically enter the sequence.

To AutoFill a range of cells:

1. In the first cell, type the first number, word, or date of the series.

   Examples include 105, Sunday, March, 6/30/04, April 1, 2005, or Qtr 1.

2. If the series isn't apparent from the initial cell entry, enter the next item in the series in an adjacent cell (the column to the right or the row below).

3. Select the initial cell or cells. Then move the pointer over the lower-right corner of the lowest or rightmost cell. It becomes the *fill cursor* (**Figure 9.8**). Drag to extend the sequence, as desired (**Figure 9.9**).

   As you drag past each cell, the value that will be filled in the current cell is shown in a yellow ScreenTip.

4. Release the mouse button when the destination cells have been selected.

   The sequence appears in the selected cells (**Figure 9.10**).

✔ Tips

■ If AutoComplete doesn't work, it has probably been disabled (in the Edit section of the Preferences dialog box).

■ To fill a series of cells with the same text or numeric data, such as CA or 0.082, use an Edit > Fill command rather than AutoFill. You can also use the Fill commands to extend a series of calculated values.

Editing Cell Data

The easiest way to change a cell's contents is to select the cell and then type over the current data. But if the cell contains a formula or a lengthy text string, it's often faster to edit the current contents rather than retype.

To edit a cell's contents:

1. *Do one of the following:*

   ▲ Click the cell to select it. (Selecting a cell automatically selects its *entire* contents.) Type to replace/overwrite the contents.

   ▲ Double-click the cell to set the insertion point in the cell's text (**Figure 9.11**).

   ▲ Click the cell to select it. Set the insertion point in the text displayed in the Formula Bar (**Figure 9.12**).

2. Edit the contents in the cell or in the Formula Bar using the same techniques as you would if editing text in Word.

   For example, you can delete the previous character or a selection by pressing (Delete), insert additional characters, or move left or right within the contents by pressing the left- or right-arrow key.

3. To complete the edit, move to another cell; click the Enter icon on the Formula Bar; or press (Return), (Enter), (Tab), or another navigation key.

✔ Tips

- To cancel a revision and leave the original contents of the cell intact, press (Esc) or click the Cancel icon on the Formula Bar (see Figure 9.7).

- If you edit a formula or cell data that is referenced by a formula, any affected cells are recalculated when you complete the edit.

Figure 9.11 You can edit cell data directly in the cell...

Insertion point

Figure 9.12 ...or in the text box on the Formula Bar.

EDITING CELL DATA

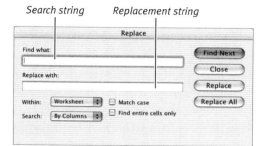

Figure 9.13 Enter Find what and Replace with strings in the text boxes.

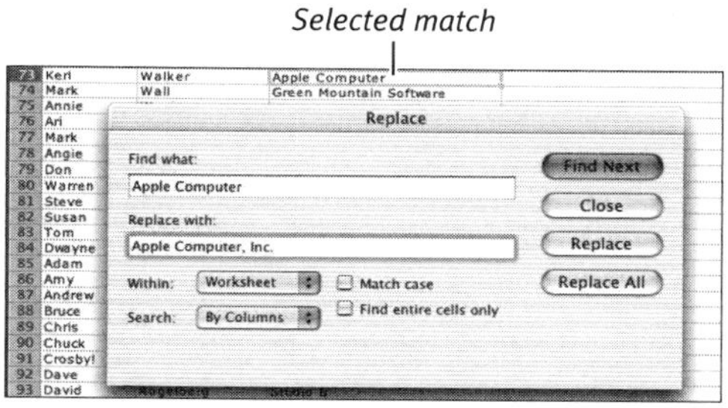

Figure 9.14 When a match is found, Excel scrolls to it and selects the cell.

Finding and Replacing Data

Another way to edit a worksheet is to use the Replace command to search for a string and replace it with another.

To perform a Find/Replace:

1. *Optional:* To restrict your search to a specific part of the worksheet, select that range.

2. Choose Edit > Replace.

   The Replace dialog box appears (**Figure 9.13**).

3. Enter a search string in the Find what text box and a replacement string in the Replace with text box.

4. From the Within drop-down menu, choose Worksheet to search only the active sheet or Workbook to search all sheets.

5. From the Search drop-down menu, choose By Rows or By Columns, depending on how the data is arranged.

   For example, to replace an old company name or address with a new one in a worksheet that restricts those items to one or two columns, a By Columns search is best. If the text could be found in any column, on the other hand, a By Rows search might be better.

6. *Optional:* Click one or both check boxes to restrict matches to those with identical letter case (Match case) or where the Find what string is the *only* data in the found cell (Find entire cells only).

7. To begin the search, click Find Next.

   If Excel finds a match, it highlights it in the worksheet (**Figure 9.14**).

continues on next page

FINDING AND REPLACING DATA

8. For each match, do one of the following:

▲ To replace this match with the Replace with string, click Replace.

▲ To skip this match and look for the next one, click Find Next.

▲ To skip this match and end the search immediately, click Close.

Repeat this step to find and handle any additional matches in the worksheet or workbook.

✔ Tips

■ To simultaneously search for and replace all instances of the match, you can click Replace All at any time. Note, however, that you will not be given an opportunity to view the changes individually, since they are made *en masse*.

■ You can undo a Replace All by immediately choosing Edit > Undo Replace (⌘ Z).

■ As a sanity check following a Replace All, you may want to perform a Find (Edit > Find), search for the replacement string, and see if they all look appropriate to you.

■ The Find what string can also include *wild card characters*, as follows:

▲ **Question mark (?).** A substitute for any single character. For example, s?ng would find sang, sing, song, and sung.

▲ **Asterisk (*).** A substitute for any number of characters (including none). For example, John* would find John, Johnny, and Johnson; that is, any text string that begins with John.

Figure 9.15 If specified in Preferences, the User name is automatically attached to each comment.

Comment indicator

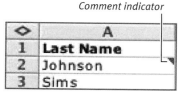

Figure 9.16 A commented cell is marked with a tiny triangle.

Figure 9.17 A comment appears when you move the cursor over the cell to which it is attached.

Edit   Next   Show All
Comment Comment Comments

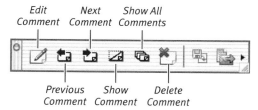

Previous   Show   Delete
Comment Comment Comment

Figure 9.18 The Reviewing toolbar contains commands for working with comments.

Adding Cell Comments

To help document the assumptions underlying a calculation or to explain the meaning of a complex formula, you can attach a *comment* to any cell. Comments are visible only when you want them to be.

To create and manage comments:

1. To attach a comment to a cell, select the cell and choose Insert > Comment.

   A text box appears. If set in the General section of the Preferences dialog box (**Figure 9.15**), the User name appears in the text box to identify the comment's author. If you wish, you can delete it.

2. Enter your comment in the box. When you're finished, click any other cell.

   The comment text box closes and a small triangle appears in the cell's upper-right corner to show that it has an associated comment (**Figure 9.16**).

3. To view comments, do one of the following:
   - ▲ To view a specific comment, rest the cursor over the cell (**Figure 9.17**).
   - ▲ To view all the comments in a worksheet, choose View > Comments. (To hide the comments, choose View > Comments again.)

✔ Tips

- When you choose View > Comments, the Reviewing toolbar appears (**Figure 9.18**). You can use the toolbar to cycle through the comments, create new comments, delete or edit comments, and so on.

- You can resize a comment box by dragging any of its surrounding handles when creating or editing the comment.

- Since a comment is an object, you can format it—changing its font or color, for example.

Naming Cell Ranges

To make it easy to find a particular cell range, create a chart from it, or reference it in a formula, you can assign a name to any cell or range. Such names are referred to as *range names*, *named ranges*, or *names*.

For example, you could assign the name April to a column of April sales figures, and refer to it in a formula by name: =SUM(April) rather than =SUM(D3:D14). You can assign a name to a single cell, a subset of a column or row, a group of cells that spans several rows or columns, or a group of nonadjacent cells.

To name a cell range:

1. Select the cells that you want to name.

2. In the Name Box on the Formula Bar (**Figure 9.19**), enter the name you wish to assign to the selected cells and press ⌷Enter⌷ or ⌷Return⌷.

✔ Tips

- The first character of a name must be a letter or an underscore (_). Names may contain multiple words, but they cannot contain spaces. Use an underscore instead, such as Tax_Pct.

- You cannot name a cell while you're changing its contents.

- You can also assign a name to a *constant* (as explained in the following tip), such as defining SalesTaxPct as =0.075.

- Another way to define names is to choose Insert > Name > Define. In the Define Name dialog box (**Figure 9.20**), enter a name, specify a range or constant in the Refers to text box, and click Add. (As shown, constants must begin with an equal sign.) Click OK when you're done.

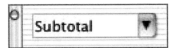

Figure 9.19 In the Name Box, enter a name for the selected cell or cell range.

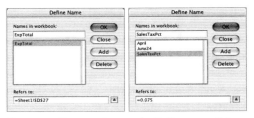

Figure 9.20 You can also use the Define name dialog box to create names that reference selected cells (left) or a constant (right).

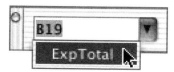

Figure 9.21 To go to a named range, you can select it from the Name Box drop-down list.

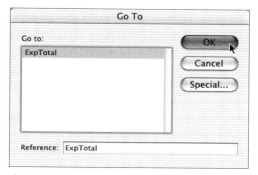

Figure 9.22 You can also go to a named range by selecting it in the Go To dialog box.

■ Another reason to create names is so that you can quickly jump to key areas of a worksheet. To go to a named range, you can do any of the following:

▲ Select the name from the Name Box's drop-down list (**Figure 9.21**).

▲ Type the name in the Name Box text box.

▲ Choose Edit > Go To. In the Go To dialog box (**Figure 9.22**), select the name and click OK.

■ From a given worksheet, you can refer to named ranges in other worksheets of the same workbook.

Importing Data from a Text File

Typing data isn't the only way to fill cells. You can import data from a variety of external sources. In Chapter 14, procedures for importing data from a FileMaker Pro database and from Web pages are presented. In this section, you'll learn how to import data from an ordinary text file. Since most major applications can save data or tables as *tab-delimited text files*, it's a very common format for data exchange.

To import data from a text file:

1. In the source program (such as a database, spreadsheet, or word-processing program), export or save the file in a delimited format, such as tab- or comma-delimited.

   In a delimited file, fields are separated from one another by a special character, such as a tab or comma. Each record is a single paragraph, ending with a Return character.

2. Drag the icon of the exported file onto the Excel program icon. (If Excel is on the Dock, you can drag it onto that icon, for example.)

   Excel attempts to open and interpret the file as a new worksheet (**Figure 9.23**).

3. Examine the resulting worksheet. If it is satisfactory, save it as a normal Excel file. (Choose File > Save As and select the Excel 97-2004 & 5.0/95 workbook format.)

Figure 9.23 Check the new worksheet to see if the data appears to have been reasonably interpreted.

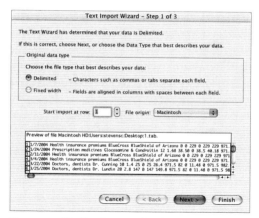

Figure 9.24 The Text Import Wizard presents a series of dialog boxes in which you specify the format of the text file being imported.

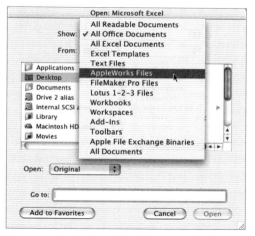

Figure 9.25 In the Open dialog box, open the Show menu to view a list of Excel-compatible file types.

✔ Tips

- If the result of the drag-and-drop procedure is *not* satisfactory, you can import the data using the Text Import Wizard. Choose Data > Get External Data > Import Text File and follow the Wizard's directions (**Figure 9.24**). The Text Import Wizard can import virtually any consistently delimited file, as well as one in which the data consists of fixed-width fields.

- If you attempt to use the File > Open command to import a text file, the Text Import Wizard is automatically invoked.

- When data is exported as text from most applications, any formulas contained in the source data are lost. Instead, the *results* are exported. Thus, following the import into Excel, you may need to reconstruct the formulas in the worksheet.

- Excel can also open some types of files in their original, native format, such as FileMaker Pro databases and AppleWorks worksheets. When possible, this is the preferred method of importing data into Excel.

  For a list of compatible file types, choose File > Open and click the Show menu in the Open dialog box (**Figure 9.25**).

IMPORTING DATA FROM A TEXT FILE

Working with Workbooks

As mentioned earlier in this chapter, an Excel file is called a *workbook*. By default, every workbook contains three *worksheets* (or *sheets*). As you'll learn in this section, you can switch from one sheet to anther, rename sheets, add more sheets to a workbook as they are needed and delete unnecessary ones, reference data in any sheet from any other sheet, and consolidate multiple sheets.

Switching sheets

Many of your workbooks will consist of only one sheet that you're using. But in those instances when you're using multiple sheets, it's simple to switch from one to another.

To change the active sheet:

◆ At the bottom of the workbook window (**Figure 9.26**), click the named tab of the sheet you want to display.

The selected sheet becomes active.

✔ Tips

■ If the tab of the desired sheet isn't visible, click the arrow icons to scroll through the tabs.

■ You can rearrange the order of sheets by dragging their tabs to the left or right.

Scroll icons   Active Sheet   Sheet tabs

Summary | January | February | March | April | Sheet6 | Shee

Ready

Figure 9.26 To make a different sheet active, click its tab at the bottom of the document window.

Selected sheet name

Figure 9.27 Double-click a sheet name to select it for renaming.

Naming sheets

You can replace the default sheet names (Sheet1, Sheet2, and so on) with more informative names, such as Advertising, October Budget, Personnel, or Summary.

To rename a sheet:

1. Double-click the tab of the sheet you want to rename.

   The current sheet name is selected (**Figure 9.27**).

2. Type a new sheet name or edit the current name. To complete the process, click anywhere else in the worksheet or press Return or Enter.

   Sheet names can be a maximum of 31 characters long and may include spaces.

✔ Tip

■ To select a sheet's name for editing or renaming, you can also choose Format > Sheet > Rename. Or you can Control-click the tab and choose Rename from the pop-up menu that appears. (However, since double-clicking a tab is more direct, it's unlikely that you'll ever use these alternate procedures.)

Adding and Deleting Sheets

There are two ways to add or delete sheets from a workbook: using menu commands and by Control-clicking a sheet tab.

◆ To add a new sheet, choose Insert > Worksheet, or Control-click a sheet tab and choose Insert from the pop-up menu that appears.

◆ To delete an unwanted sheet, make the sheet active and choose Edit > Delete Sheet, or Control-click the sheet's tab and choose Delete from the pop-up menu that appears.

Viewing multiple sheets

Sometimes you may want to view several sheets at the same time. You can accomplish this by opening each sheet in a separate window and then arrange the windows so you can see them all.

To view multiple sheets simultaneously:

1. Choose Window > New Window.

   A second copy of the workbook opens in a new window.

2. In the copy, click the tab of the sheet you want to view.

3. Choose Window > Arrange.

   The Arrange Windows dialog box appears (**Figure 9.28**).

4. Select a window arrangement and click OK.

   ▲ **Tiled.** Arrange windows so that all are visible and as large as possible (**Figure 9.29**).

   ▲ **Horizontal, Vertical.** Arrange windows in horizontal or vertical strips.

   ▲ **Cascade.** Display all windows at full size, cascading downward to the right. Each window overlaps the next, leaving an edge exposed so you can easily switch between them by clicking an edge.

5. To work in a given window, click in it to make it active.

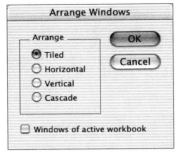

Figure 9.28 Select an arrangement option and click OK.

Figure 9.29 This is an example of three tiled windows.

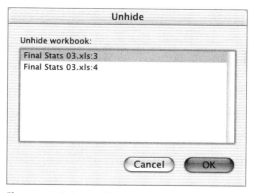

Figure 9.30 Select a window to unhide and click OK.

✔ Tips

■ The Window arrangement commands are also designed for arranging *different* open workbooks—not only multiple copies of a single workbook.

■ To make the active workbook fill the screen, click the zoom icon (the green plus) in its title bar. Click the zoom icon a second time to restore the window to its previous size and screen location.

■ To temporarily hide the active window, do one of the following:

▲ Click the minimize icon (the yellow minus) in the title bar, double-click the title bar, choose Window > Minimize Window, or press ⌘M. The window is moved to the Dock.

▲ Choose Window > Hide.

To restore a window from the Dock, click its icon in the Dock. To restore a window that was hidden with the Hide command, choose Window > Unhide. In the Unhide dialog box (**Figure 9.30**), select the window that you want to reveal and click OK.

■ If one or more windows are covered by windows from other programs or the Finder, you can reveal them by choosing Window > Bring All to Front.

■ The names of all open workbooks (including copies) are listed at the bottom of the Window menu. You can make any open workbook or copy active by choosing it from this menu.

WORKING WITH WORKBOOKS

Referring to data on other sheets

Formulas aren't restricted to cell references that are in the current worksheet. They can also reference data from other sheets.

To refer to another sheet:

1. Click the destination cell for the formula. Type an equal sign (=) to start the formula.

2. As necessary within the formula, do one of the following to refer to a cell or range in another sheet:
   ▲ Switch to the appropriate sheet and select the cell or range.
   ▲ Type the cell reference in the form:
   sheetname!range
   August!C17, for example.

3. If it isn't finished, continue building the formula. To add references to other sheets, repeat Step 2. To complete the formula, press [Return] or [Enter].

✔ Tips

■ If you have named ranges in other sheets, you can enter their names in formulas without worrying about which sheet the data is on. Excel will find the range on any sheet in the current workbook. (See "Naming Cell Ranges," earlier in this chapter.)

■ It's a good idea to display the Formula Bar while constructing or editing formulas that reference other sheets. Doing so ensures that you can always see the current state of the formula (**Figure 9.31**). To display the Formula Bar, choose View > Formula Bar.

References to other sheets

Figure 9.31 If displayed, the Formula Bar shows the current state of the formula.

Consolidating worksheets

When various sheets of a workbook contain data that you want to summarize, you can sum or perform other calculations across those sheets, placing the results in a consolidation sheet. Record-keeping workbooks are often organized in a way that makes them amenable to such calculations. For example, a bookkeeping workbook might have a separate worksheet for every month of the year, followed by a single sheet in which totals and averages across all sheets are displayed.

Excel supports a variety of consolidation methods, including the following:

▲ **By position.** Requires that the sheets be identically organized. Each referenced cell or range must be in the same location on every sheet.

▲ **3-D referencing.** There is no requirement that the sheets be identically organized.

▲ **By category.** The referenced data uses the same row and column labels, but can be located in different places on the various worksheets.

As examples of consolidation calculations, we'll look at manually creating a consolidation by position and using the Consolidate dialog box to guide a 3-D referencing consolidation.

To consolidate by position:

1. Create or select a sheet for the consolidation. On that sheet, click the destination cell for the formula. Type an equal sign (=) to begin the formula.

2. Enter a supported function, followed by an open parenthesis (**Figure 9.32**).

   Supported functions are SUM, AVERAGE, AVERAGEA, COUNT, COUNTA, MAX, MAXA, MIN, MINA, PRODUCT, STDEV, STDEVA, STDEVP, STDEVPA, VAR, VARA, VARP, VARPA.

3. Click the tab of the first sheet in the consecutive set of sheets. Select the cell or range to include in the formula.

4. Hold down (Shift) and click the tab of the last consecutive sheet that you want to include in the calculation.

   This assumes, of course, that each sheet in the set contains the same data in the selected cell or range.

5. Press (Return) or (Enter) to complete the formula.

   Click the formula cell in the consolidation sheet to view the formula (**Figure 9.33**).

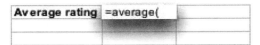

Figure 9.32 Start the formula as you normally do, but restrict yourself to the supported functions.

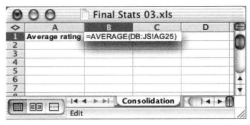

Figure 9.33 Return to the consolidation sheet and click the cell to examine the formula.

Function menu   *Select cell or range*

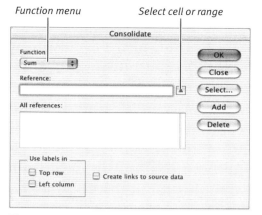

Figure 9.34 You can use the Consolidate dialog box to guide the creation of the necessary formulas.

Figure 9.35 This sheet uses six consolidation formulas to summarize expenses across a series of sheets.

✔ Tips

■ The Consolidate dialog box retains the most recently used references. To create additional formulas that reference *other* cells, you'll have to delete or edit the entries in the All references box.

■ To apply a different function to the *same* references (see Figure 9.35, for example), select a new destination cell, choose the new function, and click OK.

To create a consolidation formula using the Consolidate dialog box:

1. Click the upper-left cell of the range in the worksheet where you want to consolidate the data.

2. Choose Data > Consolidate.

   The Consolidate dialog box appears (**Figure 9.34**).

3. Choose a function from the drop-down Function menu.

4. For each sheet that you want to include in the consolidation, enter a reference to the pertinent cell(s) in the Reference text box.

   You can type the reference (or a range name), manually click the cell(s), or click the selection icon.

5. After entering each reference, click Add.

   The new reference is added to the list in the All references box.

6. *Optional:* If you're identifying ranges by column or row headings, click the appropriate radio button in the Use labels in section of the dialog box.

7. *Optional:* To maintain a link between the referenced cells and the consolidation formula, click the Create links to source data check box.

   Doing so will cause the consolidation formula to automatically update if any of the referenced cells change. Do *not* check this box if you want the current result to remain unchanged.

8. Click OK.

   The consolidated data appears in the destination cell of the consolidation sheet (**Figure 9.35**).

WORKING WITH WORKBOOKS

Printing Worksheets and Workbooks

Excel provides a multitude of tools and options to ensure that you can print exactly what you want. Printing is a two-step process: setting Page Setup options and page breaks, and printing the desired material.

To set page orientation and breaks:

1. To view or change the page orientation, choose File > Page Setup. On the Page tab of the Page Setup dialog box (**Figure 9.36**), click Portrait or Landscape and then click OK to close the dialog box.

   Changing the orientation will change the amount of material that will fit per page, as well as where page breaks fall.

2. *Optional:* To print only part of a worksheet, select it now. If you also want to save the selection as the sheet's new *print area* (so it will be remembered the next time you print), choose File > Print Area > Set Print Area.

3. Switch to Normal or Page Layout view to get a rough idea of where page breaks will occur in the printout. For a more accurate preview or to adjust the margins, choose File > Print Preview (**Figure 9.37**).

   In Normal view, page breaks are indicated by dashed lines. In Page Layout view, page breaks are shown as new pages.

4. *Optional:* To manually adjust page breaks (ensuring that key data isn't split between pages or to make data fit within the page width, for example), choose View > Page Break Preview or click the Page Break Preview icon. Drag the page break lines to new positions, if desired (**Figure 9.38**).

   Note that if you drag a break right or down (to fit additional rows or columns), Excel will scale the printout as needed.

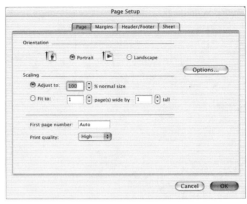

Figure 9.36 Select a page orientation by clicking the appropriate radio button.

Click to end the preview

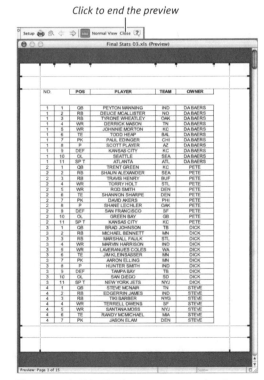

Figure 9.37 In Print Preview, you can examine the page breaks and adjust margins by dragging.

PRINTING WORKSHEETS AND WORKBOOKS

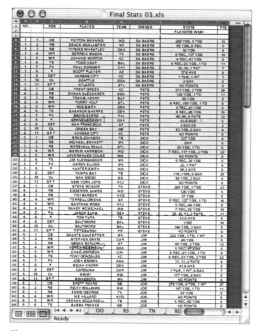

Figure 9.38 In Page Break Preview, you can change the page breaks by dragging them to new positions.

Quick Preview area

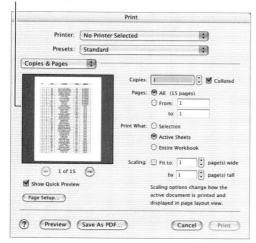

Figure 9.39 Set options in the Print dialog box.

To print a selected range, worksheet, or workbook:

1. *Optional:* To print only part of the active worksheet, select it now.

   If you want to print an entire worksheet, workbook, or a saved print area (see the previous set of steps), this isn't necessary.

2. Choose File > Print, click the Print toolbar icon, or press ⌘P.

   The Print dialog box appears (**Figure 9.39**), open to the Copies & Pages section.

3. Select a connected printer from the Printer drop-down list.

4. Specify the number of copies and range of pages to print.

5. Click a radio button (Selection, Active Sheets, or Entire Workbook) to specify the Print What setting.

6. *Optional:* The Quick Preview area shows the pages that will be printed, given the current Print and Page Setup settings. Click the arrow icons beneath the Quick Preview to view the pages to be printed, margins, and page breaks.

   If necessary, you can modify the Pages range (Step 4) or any other options in the dialog box.

7. Turn the printer on, and then click the Print button.

   The print job is routed to the selected printer.

FORMATTING WORKSHEETS

While raw data typed in a monospaced font into fixed-width columns is fine for many worksheets, it isn't satisfactory for *all* worksheets. Excel provides a variety of formatting tools and procedures that you can apply to dress up any worksheet. With minimal effort, you can turn the ordinary into presentation-quality material.

Setting Column and Row Sizes

You can change the width of selected columns, as well as the height of selected rows, as your data dictates. This is particularly useful when you need to accommodate large fonts (row height) or lengthy text strings that spill over into adjacent columns (column width).

To manually adjust a column's width:

1. Move the pointer over the right edge of the heading of the column whose width you wish to change.

   The pointer changes to a double arrow (**Figure 10.1**).

2. Click and drag to the right or left (**Figure 10.2**).

   As you drag, a ScreenTip appears, showing the current width of the column in characters (approximate) and the default unit of measure.

3. Release the mouse button to complete the procedure.

4. Repeat Steps 1–3 until the column is the desired width.

To manually adjust a row's height:

1. Move the pointer over the bottom edge of the row whose height you wish to change.

   The pointer changes to a double arrow.

2. Click and drag up or down.

   As you drag, a ScreenTip appears, showing the current height of the row in points and the default unit of measure. (There are 72 points per inch.)

3. Release the mouse button to complete the procedure.

4. Repeat Steps 1–3 until the row is the desired height.

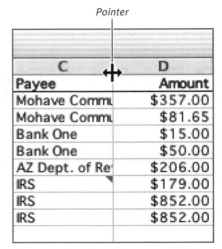

Figure 10.1 Move the pointer over the right edge of the column header. It changes to a double arrow.

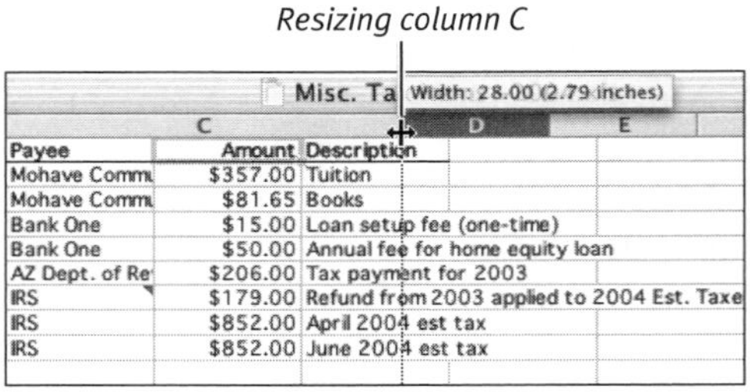

Figure 10.2 Drag right or left to change the column width.

SETTING COLUMN AND ROW SIZES

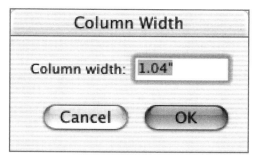

Figure 10.3 Use the Column Width (or Row Height) dialog box to enter a precise width or height.

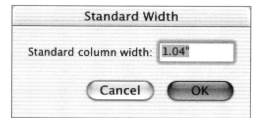

Figure 10.4 You can define a new default column width that will automatically be applied to blank and new columns.

✔ **Tips**

■ To adjust a column width or row height to automatically accommodate the contents (the widest or highest entry, respectively), double-click the column heading's right border or the row heading's bottom border.

■ To set *multiple* columns or rows to the same width or height, select the columns or rows by dragging across their headings. Then drag the edge of any selected column or row heading. All selected columns or rows will change uniformly.

■ You can also set width or height by choosing commands from the Format menu, as follows:

  ▲ To set a column width to the width required to fully display the longest test string, click the column heading and choose Format > Column > AutoFit Selection. To set the column width to that of a specific cell, select the cell and choose the same command.

  ▲ To set the width or height for selected columns or rows, choose Format > Column > Width or Format > Row > Height. In the dialog box that appears (**Figure 10.3**), enter the new size (in the default measurement unit), and click OK.

  ▲ To set a new default column width for the worksheet, choose Format > Column > Standard Width, enter the new width (**Figure 10.4**), and click OK.

SETTING COLUMN AND ROW SIZES

Reorganizing a Worksheet

You can insert and delete rows, columns, and cells, as well as copy or move data from one area of the worksheet to another.

Inserting and deleting columns and rows

With a single command, you can insert or delete one or multiple rows or columns.

To insert new rows or columns:

1. *Do one of the following:*
   - ▲ To insert a single row or column, select any cell in the row or column where you'd like the new row or column to appear (**Figure 10.5**).
   - ▲ To insert multiple rows or columns, select contiguous cells where you'd like the new rows or columns to appear.

2. Choose Insert > Rows or Insert > Columns. The new rows or columns appear. The worksheet adjusts to accommodate them.

To delete rows or columns:

1. *Do one of the following:*
   - ▲ To delete a single row or column, select any cell in the row or column that you want to delete.
   - ▲ To delete multiple rows or columns, select contiguous cells in the rows or columns that you want to delete.

2. Choose Edit > Delete.
   The Delete dialog box appears (**Figure 10.6**).

3. Select Entire row or Entire column.

4. Click OK.
   The worksheet adjusts to accommodate the deleted row(s) or column(s).

Selected cell

◇	A		B
1	Date		Check #
2	1/20/04		Disc
3	1/20/04		Disc
4	2/12/04		Cash
5	2/12/04		3033
6	4/11/04		3051
7	4/11/04		✛
8	4/11/04		3052
9	6/14/04		
10			

Figure 10.5 Click the cell where you want to insert the column or row.

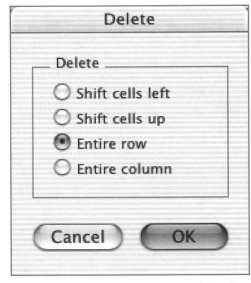

Figure 10.6 Indicate whether you'd like to delete the entire row or column.

Figure 10.7 Another way to insert or delete rows or columns is to select headings, [Control]-click one, and choose Insert or Delete from the pop-up menu.

✔ Tips

- Rather than selecting one or more cells prior to inserting rows or column, you may find it less confusing to select row or column *headings*.

- You can also [Control]-click a column or row heading and choose Insert or Delete from the pop-up menu (**Figure 10.7**). You can use this technique for multiple insertions and deletions, too. Simply select more than one row or column before you [Control]-click one of them.

- Although it's sufficient to select only cells prior to deleting rows or columns, it's more expedient to select *entire* rows or columns by clicking their heading. When you choose Edit > Delete, the selected rows or columns are instantly deleted—without displaying the Delete dialog box.

Inserting and deleting cells

When you insert or delete one or more cells, Excel needs to know how to adjust the data in adjacent cells. You indicate your choice in either the Insert or Delete dialog box.

To insert blank cells:

1. Select a cell or a contiguous group of cells where you want to insert empty cells.

2. *Do one of the following:*
   ▲ Choose Insert > Cells.
   ▲ Control-click one of the selected cells and choose Insert from the pop-up menu that appears.

   The Insert dialog box appears (**Figure 10.8**).

3. Select either Shift cells right or Shift cells down (referring to how the worksheet will be adjusted following the insertion).

4. Click OK.

To delete selected cells:

1. Select a cell or a contiguous group of cells that you want to delete.

2. *Do one of the following:*
   ▲ Choose Edit > Delete.
   ▲ Control-click one of the selected cells and choose Delete from the pop-up menu that appears.

   The Delete dialog box appears (see Figure 10.6).

3. Select Shift cells left or Shift cells up.

4. Click OK.

   The worksheet adjusts to fill in the hole left by the deleted cell(s).

✔ Tip

■ To clear a cell's contents rather than deleting the cell, press Delete or choose a command from the Edit > Clear submenu.

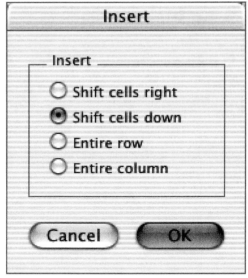

Figure 10.8 Select a Shift option to apply to affected areas of the worksheet following the insertion.

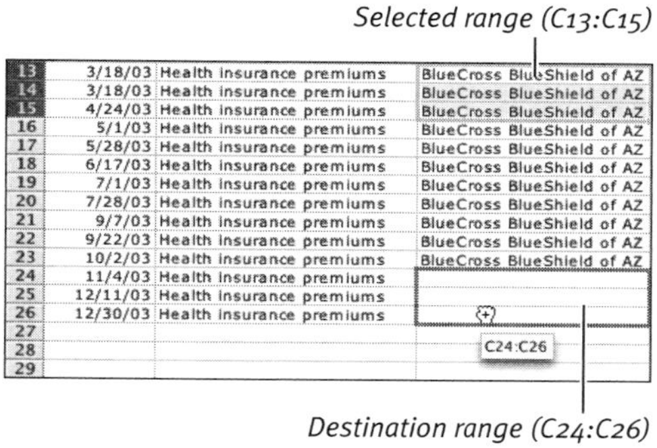

Selected range (C13:C15)

Destination range (C24:C26)

Figure 10.9 A plus symbol appears in the hand to indicate that Excel is copying rather than moving the range.

Copying and moving data

Excel's support of *drag and drop* makes it especially easy to move or copy data.

A drag-and-drop copy is a nondestructive procedure; the original cells remain unaltered. A drag-and-drop move, on the other hand, *is* a destructive procedure. It is the same as performing a Cut and then a Paste; that is, the contents of the original cells are deleted.

To move or copy a cell range:

1. Select a cell range to move or copy.

2. Move the pointer over the edge of the range; it becomes a hand.

3. *Do one of the following:*

   ▲ To copy the cells, press Option while dragging to the destination. A small plus sign (+) appears inside the hand pointer to indicate that you are copying rather than moving the data (**Figure 10.9**).

   ▲ To move the cells, drag them to the destination.

   A yellow ScreenTip appears to indicate the destination.

4. Release the mouse button to copy or move the cell range to the new location.

REORGANIZING A WORKSHEET

Working with Large Sheets

There are two helpful procedures you can use when working with large worksheets. First, you can freeze column and/or row headings to prevent their information from moving offscreen when you scroll. Second, you can split a worksheet into multiple panes. Doing so enables you to display and independently scroll through two or four regions of the worksheet. You can split a sheet horizontally, vertically, or in both directions.

To freeze column and/or row headings:

1. *Do one of the following* (**Figure 10.10**):

   ▲ To freeze only rows, click the row heading that is immediately below the rows you want to freeze.

   ▲ To freeze only columns, click the column heading that is immediately to the right of the columns you want to freeze.

   ▲ To freeze both rows and columns, select the cell immediately below and to the right of the rows and columns you want to freeze.

2. Choose Window > Freeze Panes.

   Gray lines appear in the worksheet to mark the frozen areas (**Figure 10.11**).

✔ Tips

■ You cannot freeze panes when in Page Layout View. If they're currently frozen, they will be removed if you switch to Page Layout View.

■ When working with frozen panes, pressing Control Home selects the cell in the upper-left corner of the unfrozen data range rather than cell A1.

■ To unfreeze the panes, choose Window > Unfreeze Panes.

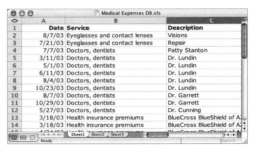

Figure 10.10 To freeze the top row of column headings, select row 2. To freeze the Date column (A), select column B. To freeze both, select cell B2.

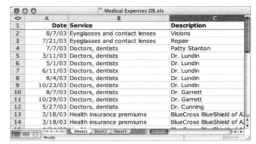

Figure 10.11 In this worksheet, both row 1 and column A are frozen. No matter what direction you scroll, row 1 and column A will remain onscreen.

Figure 10.12 A worksheet can be split into two or four panes.

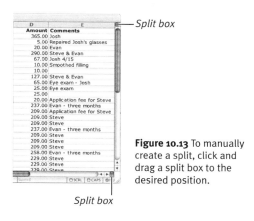

Split box

Figure 10.13 To manually create a split, click and drag a split box to the desired position.

Split box

Split bar

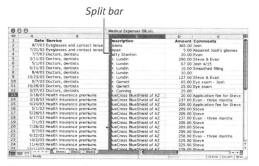

Figure 10.14 To adjust a split, drag the split bar or box to a new position.

To automatically split a sheet into four panes:

1. Click the cell that you want to become the upper-left corner of the bottom-right pane.

2. Choose Window > Split.

   The worksheet is split into four panes (**Figure 10.12**).

3. *Optional:* To adjust any split, click and drag its split bar or split box to a new position.

To manually split a sheet into multiple panes:

1. Each sheet has two split boxes—found at the top of the vertical scroll bar and the right end of the horizontal scroll bar (**Figure 10.13**).

2. *Do one or both of the following:*

   ▲ Drag the split box that's above the vertical scroll bar downward to split the sheet into two horizontal panes.

   ▲ Drag the split box to the right of the horizontal scroll bar to the left to split the sheet into two vertical panes.

   A ghost of the split bar appears as you drag.

3. Release the mouse button when the split bar is positioned correctly (**Figure 10.14**).

4. *Optional:* To adjust a split, click and drag its split bar or split box to a new position.

✔ Tip

■ To remove all splits, choose Window > Remove Split. To remove an individual split, drag its split bar or box off the right or top edge of the worksheet.

WORKING WITH LARGE SHEETS

Worksheet Formatting

The remainder of this chapter discusses ways that you can make your worksheets more attractive and readable by applying global or selective formatting.

Automatic range formatting

The easiest way to make a sheet presentable is to apply an AutoFormat. An AutoFormat creates a complete look for a range of cells by setting the font, text alignment, number formatting, borders, patterns, colors, and so on. Excel offers a variety of AutoFormat styles, each with a different look.

To AutoFormat a range of cells:

1. Select the cell range that you want to format.

2. Choose Format > AutoFormat.

   The AutoFormat dialog box appears (**Figure 10.15**).

3. Select an AutoFormat style from the scrolling list.

   A sample of the selected format appears in the center of the dialog box.

4. *Optional:* To select the specific formatting attributes that will be applied, click the Options button.

5. Click OK.

   The AutoFormat style is applied to the selected range (**Figure 10.16**).

✔ Tips

■ To remove an AutoFormat style immediately after applying it, choose Edit > Undo or click the Undo toolbar icon.

■ To remove an AutoFormat style later, select the range, follow Steps 2 and 3, and choose None from the list of AutoFormat styles.

AutoFormat styles   *Sample*

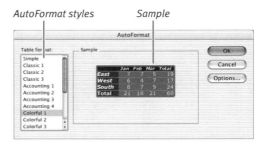

Figure 10.15 Select an AutoFormat style from the scrolling list.

Figure 10.16 This is a worksheet after an AutoFormat style was applied to it.

Figure 10.17 Specify a criterion to be satisfied. Click Format to specify the formatting that will be applied.

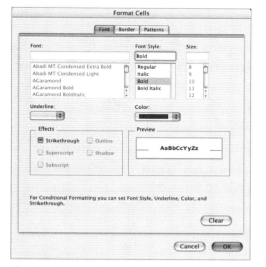

Figure 10.18 Select formatting options from the tabs of the Format Cells dialog box.

Cells with conditional formatting (column D)

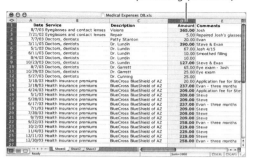

Figure 10.19 When you close the Conditional Formatting dialog box, the cells are evaluated. Those that satisfy the criterion are reformatted.

Conditional formatting

Using *conditional formatting*, you can apply different formats to selected cells, depending on their value or whether they meet some other criteria. For example, you could specify that sales figures above a certain dollar amount should be colored blue to make them easy to spot.

To apply conditional formatting to cells:

1. Select the cells you wish to format.

2. Choose Format > Conditional Formatting. The Conditional Formatting dialog box appears (**Figure 10.17**).

3. *Do one of the following:*

   ▲ From the first drop-down menu, choose Cell value is to create a criterion based on the values in the selected cells.

   ▲ From the first drop-down menu, choose Formula is to base the criterion on a true/false formula which references *other* cells.

4. Complete the criterion by specifying a cell value or formula, and click the Format button.

   The Format Cells dialog box appears (**Figure 10.18**).

5. Click the tabs at the top of the dialog box and select the combination of font, border, and pattern formats that you want to apply to cells that meet the criterion. Click OK when you are done.

6. Click OK to close the Conditional Formatting dialog box.

   The cells are evaluated and formatted accordingly (**Figure 10.19**).

✔ Tips

- You can set additional criteria (up to a total of four) by clicking the Add button. If more than one criterion is satisfied by a given cell, the formatting specified by the first criterion satisfied will be applied.

- You can copy conditional formats—like any other format—to other cells using the Format Painter tool (**Figure 10.20**).

Formatting text

Excel offers a wide range of formatting options that you can apply to text. You can specify a font, color, effects (such as boldface or italic), and an alignment for selected cells.

To format text:

1. Select the cell or cells you want to format.

2. *Do any of the following:*

   ▲ Choose Format > Cells, press ⌘①, or Control-click one of the selected cells and choose Format Cells from the pop-up menu.

   In the Format Cells dialog box (**Figure 10.21**), set formatting options on the Alignment and Font tabs, and click OK.

   ▲ Select formatting options by clicking icons on the Formatting toolbar (**Figure 10.22**).

✔ Tip

- If the Formatting toolbar isn't visible, you can display it by choosing View > Toolbars > Formatting.

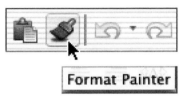

Figure 10.20 Select a conditionally formatted cell, click the Format Painter toolbar icon, and click/paint the cells to which the format should be applied.

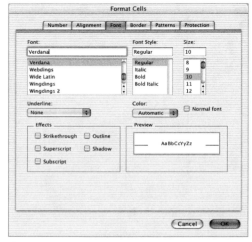

Figure 10.21 Select font and alignment settings from the appropriate tabs.

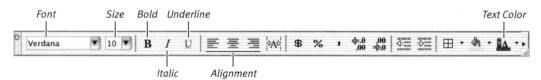

Figure 10.22 Text formatting options can be selected from the Formatting toolbar.

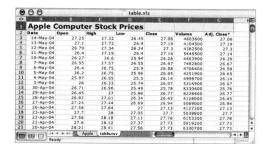

Figure 10.23 Select the group of cells within which the text will be centered—in this case, cells A1:G1.

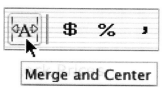

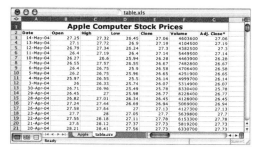

Figure 10.24 After selecting the cells, click the Merge and Center toolbar icon.

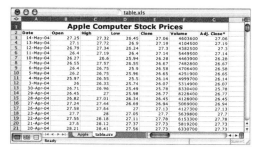

Figure 10.25 The Merge and Center results in a single cell containing a centered text string.

To center text across a group of cells:

1. Type a title or other text into the leftmost cell of the cell group.

2. Select the cell group; that is, the cells within which you want to center the text string (**Figure 10.23**).

3. Click the Merge and Center icon on the Formatting toolbar (**Figure 10.24**).

   The selected cells are merged into a single cell and the text is centered within it (**Figure 10.25**).

Formatting numbers, dates, and times

Worksheets often contain columns of numbers, dates, and times. While the default formatting that Excel applies will occasionally suffice, you can also apply *specific* number, date, or time formatting to such cells.

To format numbers, dates, or times:

1. Select cells that contain a number, date, or time.

2. *Do one of the following:*

   ▲ Click a number-formatting icon on the Formatting toolbar (**Figure 10.26**).

   ▲ Choose Format > Cells (⌘1). On the Number tab of the Format Cells dialog box (**Figure 10.27**), select a Category and then select formatting options.

✔ Tips

■ Number formatting is in *addition* to any text formatting applied to the cells, such as font, color, and effects.

■ Unless you select a special number format, Excel formats numbers with the General format.

■ If you enter a number preceded by a dollar sign (**$**), Excel automatically applies Currency formatting. If you enter a number followed by a percent sign (**%**), Excel applies Percentage formatting.

■ You can save number formatting as a *style*. See "Using Styles," at the end of this chapter.

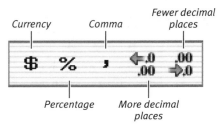

Figure 10.26 Number-formatting commands can be selected from the Formatting toolbar.

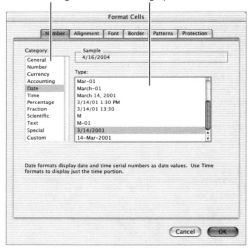

Figure 10.27 In the Format Cells dialog box, you can set very precise formats for cells that contain numbers, dates, or times.

Borders icon

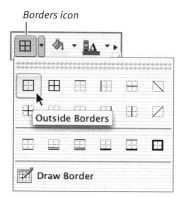

Figure 10.28 You can quickly select a border style from the Borders icon on the Formatting toolbar.

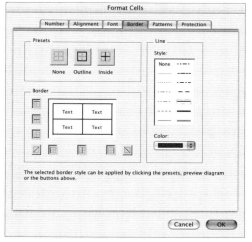

Figure 10.29 Select one or more borders by clicking icons, specify a line style, and choose a border color.

Cell borders and shading

A *border* is a line (or lines) at the edge of a cell. You can use borders to divide the information on the sheet into logical regions or highlight data of special interest. *Shading* is a pattern or color used to fill selected cells.

To apply a border to a cell or range:

1. Select the cell or range to which you'd like to apply a border.

2. *Do one of the following:*

▲ To apply the most recently used border to the selected cell(s), click the Borders icon on the Formatting toolbar.

▲ Click the down arrow beside the Borders icon on the Formatting toolbar and select a border (**Figure 10.28**).

▲ Choose Format > Cells (⌘①). On the Border tab of the Format Cells dialog box, select a border, a line style, and a color (**Figure 10.29**). Click OK to apply the border to the selected cells.

✔ Tip

■ To remove borders from a selected range, click the down arrow beside the Borders icon on the Formatting toolbar and select the No Border icon.

WORKSHEET FORMATTING

185

To apply shading to a cell or range:

1. Select the range to which you'd like to add shading.

2. Choose Format > Cells (⌘①), or Control-click one of the selected cells and choose Format Cells from the pop-up menu.
   The Format Cells dialog box appears.

3. Click the Patterns tab (**Figure 10.30**).

4. *Do one or both of the following:*
   ▲ To apply a solid color to the selected cells, click a color or gray swatch.
   ▲ To apply a pattern to the selected cells, open the Patterns palette and select a pattern.

   The color and/or pattern are applied to the selected cell range.

✔ Tips

■ You can quickly select a solid color shading from the Fill Color drop-down menu on the Formatting toolbar (**Figure 10.31**).

■ AutoFormat styles often include shading as part of their definition.

■ If the shading makes it difficult to read the cell contents, you may be able to correct this by changing the text color to one that contrasts with the shading. Against a dark shading, a light color (or white) often works well (**Figure 10.32**).

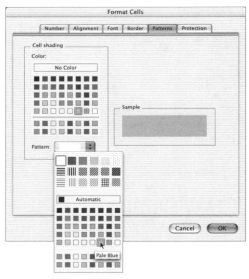

Figure 10.30 Select a color and/or pattern to apply as shading to the selected cells.

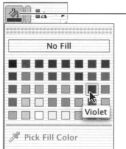

— *Fill Color icon*

Figure 10.31 You can click this toolbar icon to pick a fill color to apply to the currently selected cells.

White text and dark shading

Figure 10.32 Light-colored text is easy to read against solid, dark shading.

WORKSHEET FORMATTING

Style name menu

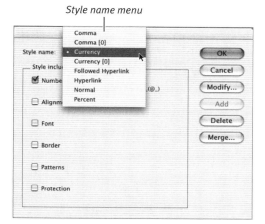

Figure 10.33 Choose an existing style from the Style name menu.

New style name

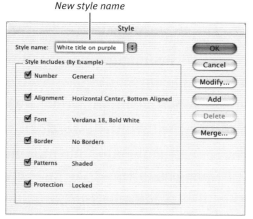

Figure 10.34 When you enter a new style name, Excel automatically displays the formatting attributes that will be considered part of the style (based on the selected cell's formatting).

Using styles

A *style* is a preset formatting combination. You can apply an existing style to selected cells or create your own styles.

To apply an existing style to selected cells:

1. Choose Format > Style.

   The Style dialog box appears.

2. Choose a style from the pull-down Style name menu (**Figure 10.33**).

3. Click OK to apply the style to the selected cells.

✔ Tips

- When a [0] follows a style name in the Style name menu, Excel formats the data with zero decimal places.

- By default, Excel assigns cells the Normal style unless you specify a different style. To change the default cell formatting, modify the Normal style.

To create a new style:

1. Format a cell as desired and then select it.

   See "Formatting text" and "Formatting numbers, dates, and times," earlier in this chapter.

2. Choose Format > Style.

3. Type a new style name in the Style name box (**Figure 10.34**).

   Excel displays the attributes with which the current cell is formatted.

4. To remove attributes from the new style definition, click to remove their checkmarks.

5. Click OK to save the new style definition.

✔ Tips

- You can import the styles from another open workbook into the current one by clicking the Merge button in the Style dialog box. Select the other workbook in the Merge Styles dialog box (**Figure 10.35**) and click OK.

- To modify an existing style, select the style from the Style name menu and then click the Modify button. In the Format Cells dialog box, specify new formatting and click OK.

- You can delete styles that you no longer need by selecting them in the Style dialog box and clicking Delete.

  Note, however, that you cannot delete the Normal style. And if you delete the Comma, Currency, or Percent style, they will no longer be available on the Formatting toolbar. (In general, it's best to restrict style deletions to styles you've created.)

- If you delete a style that's currently in use in the worksheet, style-related formatting will be removed from the affected cells.

Figure 10.35 Select the open workbook whose styles you want to merge into the current worksheet.

WORKSHEET FORMATTING

FORMULAS AND FUNCTIONS

Calculations are the way Excel "does the math." Even if you're only using Excel to keep lists, you may have numbers on which you'd like to perform some calculations (for example, totaling the number of items sold or computing bowling averages). Excel excels at calculations of this sort and provides tools to save you time and effort.

For instance, suppose you want to calculate the total of a column of numbers. You would create a *formula* in the cell beneath the column. The formula might look like this: `=SUM(B2:B12)`

All formulas begin with an equal sign (=), which enables Excel to distinguish them from text or a number. When you've finished entering the formula and move to another cell, Excel evaluates the formula based on any *functions* used (such as SUM) and the data to which it refers (cells B2 through B12). What's now shown in the cell is no longer the formula but its *result;* in this case, the total of the numbers in the specified cells.

Formula Basics

To add two numbers, you could select a cell and type =23+43. To add the contents of two cells, you use their addresses in the formula, as in =B3+B4. (The addresses are referred to as *cell references;* that is, you're referring to the cells by their addresses.) The cell into which you type the formula displays the result of the calculation as soon as you move to a different cell.

If data in any referenced cell changes, the result instantly changes. This quick recalculation lets you perform what-if analyses. Just change any of the numbers in the referenced cells to see how the changes affect the results.

Formulas can consist of any combination of data, cell references, functions, and operators (such as +, -, and /). The following steps illustrate how to create a simple formula.

To create a simple formula:

1. *Optional:* You can create or edit formulas in the cell or in the Formula Bar, whichever you find more convenient. To use the Formula Bar, choose View > Formula Bar.

2. Select the cell in which you want to create the formula and type an equal sign (=), either in the cell or in the Formula Bar (**Figure 11.1**).

3. *Do one of the following:*
   - ▲ Type the first number or cell reference to include in the formula.
   - ▲ Click the first cell you want to reference in the formula. (When creating or editing a formula, clicking a cell results in the cell's address being inserted into the formula.)

4. Type an operator, such as + or /.
   See **Table 11.1** for a list of common arithmetic operators.

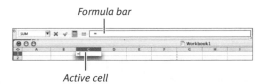

Formula bar

Active cell

Figure 11.1 You can create or edit a formula in the cell or in the Formula Bar.

Table 11.1

Arithmetic Operators	
OPERATOR	ACTION
+	Addition
–	Subtraction
*	Multiplication
/	Division
%	Percentage
^	Exponentiation

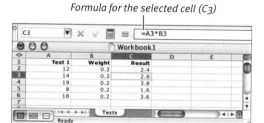

Formula for the selected cell (C3)

Figure 11.2 A cell normally displays the result rather than the formula. To view the formula, double-click the cell or select the cell and check the Formula Bar.

5. *Do one of the following:*

▲ Type the final number or cell reference you want to include in the formula.

▲ Click the final cell that you want to reference in the formula.

6. Press ⌗Return⌗ or ⌗Enter⌗ to complete the formula and show the result (**Figure 11.2**).

✔ Tips

■ You can combine numbers and cell references in a formula, such as =C2*2.5 (the contents of cell C2 multiplied by 2.5).

■ After the initial element in a formula has been typed or inserted, clicking a cell automatically adds the contents of the cell to the current formula. For example, if a formula currently contains =17 and you click cell A4, the formula becomes =17+A4.

■ If adjacent cells require a similar formula, you can copy the formula from cell to cell. See "Copying a Formula to Adjacent Cells," later in this chapter.

FORMULA BASICS

About Precedence

Here's a fact of spreadsheet life. Few formulas consist only of two cell references or numbers separated by an operator. They're often considerably more complex. And while it might make your life simpler if formulas were evaluated from left to right, that isn't necessarily the case. Instead, spreadsheets follow established rules of *precedence* when evaluating formulas. These strict rules determine the order in which a formula's components are combined.

For example, suppose you see the following formula:

= 3 + 7 * 2

If evaluated from left to right, the result would be 20. The *actual* result, however, is 17. This is the case because operators with a higher precedence (such as multiplication) are always evaluated before operators with a lower precedence (such as addition). Thus, our example is calculated by multiplying 7 times 2 and then adding 3, resulting in 17. **Tables 11.2** shows the precedence for the various operators.

To avoid forcing you to rearrange numbers, cell references, and operators, Excel lets you alter the evaluation order for a formula by enclosing items in parentheses. Such items are automatically treated as being of higher precedence. If you use multiple sets of nested parentheses, they are evaluated from innermost to the outermost set.

By adding parentheses to our simple formula, as in = (3 + 7) * 2, we can now force it to be evaluated from left to right. Although addition is of lower precedence than multiplication, the parentheses will make it be evaluated by first adding 3 and 7 and then multiplying that result by 2, yielding 20. See **Table 11.3** for more examples.

Table 11.2

Precedence of Operators (from highest to lowest)	
OPERATOR	MEANING
–	Negation (-5)
%	Percentage
^	Exponentiation
* and /	Multiplication, division
+ and –	Addition, subtraction
&	Concatenation (for combining text strings)
=, <, >, <=, >=, <>	Comparison (equal, less than, greater than, less than or equal, greater than or equal, not equal)

Table 11.3

Precedence Examples		
EXAMPLE	EVALUATION	RESULT
2 * 3 + 4	(6) + 4	10
2 + 3 * 4	2 + (12)	14
2 * (3 + 4)	2 * (7)	14
(7 – 2) * (3 * 4)	(5) * (12)	60
30 – (2 * 3) * 4	30 – (6 * 4)	6

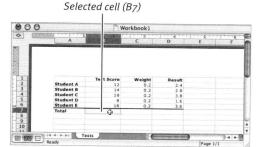

Figure 11.3 Click to select the cell in which the formula will be created.

Figure 11.4 Drag to select the cells you want to total with the Sum function; in this case, B2 through B6.

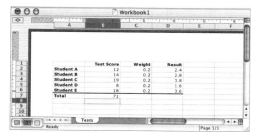

Figure 11.5 After completing the formula, the total of cells B2 through B6 (71) is displayed in cell B7.

Using Functions

Functions are shortcuts for common or complex calculations that would be difficult to create with a basic formula. Excel's more than 200 built-in functions enable you to perform financial, statistical, logical, and text-based calculations.

Functions accept values (called *arguments*), perform an operation on them, and then return one or more values. After reviewing the following examples, see **Table 11.4** at the end of this chapter for a list of common functions.

Totaling a column

Perhaps the simplest function-based calculation one can perform—and certainly the most common—is that of totaling a column of numbers using the Sum function. (Sum can also be used to total rows or any combination of adjacent and nonadjacent cells.)

To total a column using Sum:

1. Click the cell in which you want the sum to appear (**Figure 11.3**).

   Although this will generally be the cell immediately beneath the column of numbers, there's no requirement that it be so.

2. Enter an equal sign (=) to start the formula, type the word sum, and type an open (left) parenthesis.

3. Drag down the column of numbers that you want to total—from the first to the last number (**Figure 11.4**).

4. Type the closing (right) parenthesis, and press Return or Enter to complete the formula (**Figure 11.5**).

   You don't actually have to type the closing parenthesis before pressing Return or Enter. Excel will do it for you.

Using AutoSum

To make it easier to perform virtually any computation on a column or row, Excel provides the AutoSum feature. When used directly beneath a column or to the right of a row, AutoSum determines the proper cell range by examining the data.

To perform a column or row calculation using AutoSum:

1. Click the empty cell directly beneath a column or to the right of a row.

2. *Do one of the following:*

   ▲ To calculate the total of the column or row using the Sum function, click the AutoSum toolbar icon.

   ▲ Click the down arrow beside the AutoSum toolbar icon. Choose a function (such as Sum or Average) from the drop-down menu (**Figure 11.6**).

   The complete formula is shown (**Figure 11.7**).

3. *Do one of the following:*

   ▲ Press (Return) or (Enter) to accept the selected range and display the result.

   ▲ Edit the formula (changing the range, for example). Then press (Return) or (Enter) to display the result.

✔ Tips

■ AutoSum defaults to operating on columns. If it finds suitable data above the destination cell, it performs a column calculation. If not, it attempts to operate on a row.

■ To quickly perform a calculation for a set of adjacent columns, select the empty cell beneath each of the columns before choosing an AutoSum function. Excel will insert a formula in each selected cell.

AutoSum icon

Figure 11.6 Select a function from the AutoSum drop-down menu. (To use a more advanced function, choose More Functions.)

Figure 11.7 The formula (including the AutoSum-selected range) is displayed.

Figure 11.8 There's no need to memorize function names and their arguments. Click the Paste Function toolbar icon.

Click to select data from the worksheet

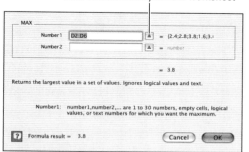

Figure 11.9 The Paste Function tool explains the selected function and has text boxes in which you can type or paste the argument data. You can click a triangle button to select data from the worksheet.

Including nonadjacent cells

While column- and row-base calculations are commonplace, there's no requirement that a formula operate on adjacent cells. Referenced cells can be scattered all over a worksheet or workbook. The following example shows one way to enter nonadjacent cell references into a formula, such as =MAX(A3,A5,D17).

To use nonadjacent cells in a formula:

1. Click the cell in which you want to place the formula and type an equal sign (=).

2. Enter a function (such as Max), followed by an open left parenthesis.

3. Click the cell that contains the first argument to the function.

   You can also type the cell reference, such as G17.

4. Enter a comma.

5. Click the next cell whose value you want to include or type its cell reference.

6. Repeat Steps 4 and 5 until you've included the necessary cells.

7. Press (Return) or (Enter) to complete the formula.

✔ Tips

- A formula can contain a combination of discrete cells *and* ranges, such as =SUM(B2,B4,B9:B11). This formula will add the contents of cells B2, B4, and B9 through B11.

- When you need help entering a formula, you can click the Paste Function icon on the Standard toolbar (**Figure 11.8**). The Paste Function tool (**Figure 11.9**) lists the arguments required by the function and lets you select the necessary cells and ranges by pointing and clicking in the worksheet.

The Calculator

Excel provides a useful tool called the Calculator that you can use to create and edit formulas. Like most such tools, using it is entirely optional. However, you may find it more convenient than typing formulas directly into cells.

To build a formula with the Calculator:

1. Click the cell where you want to insert the formula.

   You can also select a cell that already contains a formula, if you wish to edit it.

2. Choose Tools > Calculator or click the Calculator icon on the Formula Bar.

   The Calculator appears (**Figure 11.10**). An equal sign (=) is automatically inserted to begin the formula.

3. Click buttons to build the formula. As you click and add elements to the formula, they appear in the Calculator's formula pane.

   You can also type directly into the formula pane, adding necessary elements and performing edits.

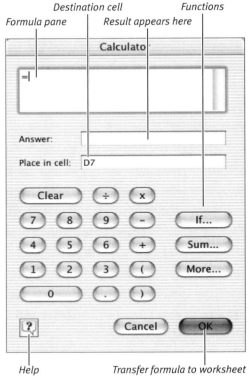

Figure 11.10 You can create and edit formulas using the Calculator.

Specify the conditional test

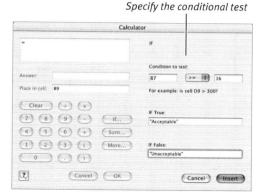

Figure 11.11 Specify the If test by typing or selecting cells and choosing a condition from the drop-down menu. You must also specify what will happen in the event of a true or false test result.

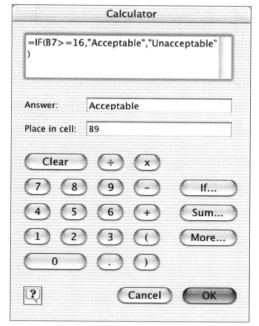

Figure 11.12 Creating a formula based on an If function is simple when using the Calculator.

4. While creating or editing a formula, you can do any of the following:

   ▲ Click buttons to build the formula.

   ▲ To insert a cell reference, click the cell or range in the worksheet.

   ▲ Click Sum to add a Sum function to the formula. A pane opens to the right, containing a text box in which to list the cells or range to be summed. Click, ⌘-click, and/or drag through the cells to be totalled. Click Insert to transfer the Sum function into the formula pane.

   ▲ Click If to add a conditional test to the formula. Specify the conditional test, a true result, and a false result (**Figure 11.11**). Click Insert to transfer the If function into the formula pane (**Figure 11.12**).

   ▲ To use a different function, click More. The Paste Function window appears, displaying the list of Excel functions. Choose a function and click OK. A new window appears (see Figure 11.9), prompting for arguments. Enter or select the arguments from the worksheet and then click OK. The function is transferred to the formula pane of the Calculator.

   When the Calculator is able to convert the formula into a number, the result appears in the Answer box.

5. When the formula is finished, click OK to transfer it into the designated cell (that is, the Place in cell).

✔ Tip

■ When entering a text result for an If function (see Figure 11.11), it isn't necessary to surround the text with quotation marks. Excel will automatically add them.

Copying a Formula to Adjacent Cells

You'll sometimes want to perform the same calculation for additional columns or rows. For example, in a worksheet that shows sales by region, you may wish to display a total for every column of sales figures. Rather than rebuild the formula from scratch, you can copy it to adjacent cells. Excel changes the formula automatically to refer to each column or row's data.

To copy a formula to adjacent cells:

1. Click the cell containing the formula.

2. Drag the fill handle at the lower-right corner of the cell across the adjacent cells to which you want to copy the formula (**Figure 11.13**).

   The formula's results appear in the cells and the Auto Fill Options button appears (**Figure 11.14**).

3. *Optional:* To change the format in the destination cells, click the Auto Fill Options button and choose a formatting option from the drop-down menu.

✔ Tips

- Check copied formulas for accuracy if you refer in the formula to any cells in columns or rows other than the ones containing the formula. Excel sometimes guesses incorrectly about your intentions.

- The operation described above can also be accomplished by using a Fill command. Select the first cell and drag to select the destination cells. Then choose Edit > Fill > Right or Edit > Fill > Down, as appropriate.

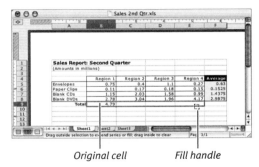

Original cell   *Fill handle*

Figure 11.13 From the original cell (B9), click and drag the fill handle across the destination cells (C9–E9). (To perform this copy operation on rows, such as the averages in column F, you would drag down.)

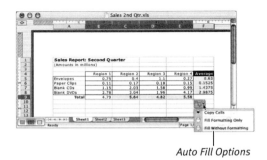

Auto Fill Options

Figure 11.14 The results appear in the destination cells (C9–E9). Click the Auto Fill Options button to review formatting options.

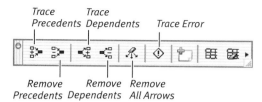

Trace Precedents *Trace Dependents* *Trace Error*

Remove Precedents *Remove Dependents* *Remove All Arrows*

Figure 11.15 The Auditing toolbar.

Figure 11.16 The arrow shows that the formula in cell F7 depends on the four cells in the range B7:E7.

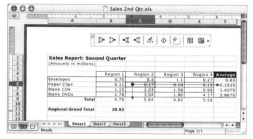

Figure 11.17 The arrows show that cell C6 is used in two formulas, found in cells C9 and F6.

Auditing a Worksheet

To avoid erroneous results from incorrect formulas, Excel supplies a comprehensive set of auditing commands. By selecting a cell and then choosing the appropriate command, you can locate the following in a worksheet:

- ◆ **Precedents.** Locate all cells that provide data to the currently selected formula.

- ◆ **Dependents.** Locate all formulas that draw data from the currently selected cell.

- ◆ **Errors.** To identify the source of an error (such as #N/A), you can locate all cells that provide data to the selected formula.

To audit a worksheet:

1. *Optional:* Choose View > Toolbars > Auditing to display the Auditing toolbar (**Figure 11.15**).

2. *Do any of the following:*

   ▲ To locate precedents, select the cell that contains the formula. Choose Tools > Auditing > Trace Precedents or click the Trace Precedents toolbar icon. Arrows appear in the worksheet, showing formula dependencies (**Figure 11.16**).

   Choose the Trace Precedents command again to see if an additional level of precedents exists.

   ▲ To locate dependents (formulas that draw data from a given cell), select the data cell. Choose Tools > Auditing > Trace Dependents or click the Trace Dependents toolbar icon. Arrows appear in the sheet, showing the formulas that include the selected cell (**Figure 11.17**).

continues on next page

AUDITING A WORKSHEET

▲ To trace an error, click the cell that contains the error. An Error button appears. To identify the error type, rest the cursor on the Error button. To identify the cell(s) involved in the error, select the error cell and choose Tools > Auditing > Trace Error, click the Trace Error toolbar icon, or click the Error button and choose Trace *error condition*.

✔ Tips

■ To clear the arrows, choose Tools > Auditing > Remove All Arrows or click the Remove All Arrows toolbar icon.

■ There are other auditing options that you may wish to explore, such as correcting circular references and locating *invalid data* (cells that violate validation rules).

AUDITING A WORKSHEET

Table 11.4

Function Examples	
SYNTAX	DESCRIPTION
AVERAGE(number1, number2, ...)*	Calculates the average (arithmetic mean) of the arguments
DATE(year, month, day)	Provides the serial number of a particular date
DAYS360(start_date, end_date, method)	Calculates the number of days between two dates based on a 360-day year (used in some accounting functions)
DDB(cost, salvage, life, period, factor)	Provides the depreciation of an asset for a specified period using the double-declining balance method or another specified method
FV(rate, nper, pmt, pv, type)	Calculates the future value of an investment
IRR(values, guess)	Provides the internal rate of return for a series of cash flows
MAX(number1, number2, ...)	Calculates the maximum value in a list of arguments
MEDIAN(number1, number2, ...)	Calculates the median (the middle value) of the given numbers
MIN(number1, number2, ...)	Calculates the smallest number in the list of arguments
NOW()	Provides the serial number of the current date and time
NPV(rate, value1, value2, ...)	Calculates the net present value of an investment based on a series of periodic cash flows and a discount rate
PMT(rate, nper, pv, fv, type)	Calculates the periodic payment for an annuity or loan
PV(rate, nper, pmt, fv, type)	Calculates the present value of an investment
ROUND(number, num_digits)	Rounds a number to a specified number of digits
SUM(number1, number2, ...)	Calculates the sum of all numbers in the list of arguments
STDEV(number1, number2, ...)	Estimates standard deviation based on a sample
TODAY()	Provides the serial number of today's date
VAR(number1, number2, ...)	Estimates variance based on a sample
VALUE(text)	Converts text to a number

*The expression (number1, number2, ...) can also be specified as a range, such as C25:C47.

WORKING WITH LISTS

Figure 12.1 When you transform a data range into a list (or create a list from scratch), Excel displays it with a special frame and attaches a drop-down menu to each column/field heading.

It's long been known that many users create worksheets that are simply lists of information, such as address data and club membership rosters. Such lists typically include few calculations, if any. A spreadsheet program is very adept at managing lists—considerably more so than a word processing program (the formerly preferred program for list management).

In recognition of the fact that people use spreadsheets to create and manage lists, Microsoft introduced the List Manager as a feature of Excel 2001. This chapter explains how to use the List Manager to create and maintain lists (**Figure 12.1**).

You should note that Excel lists are essentially databases. If you intend to create lists in Excel, you'll also want to learn about Excel's database features, discussed in Chapter 14.

✔ Tip

■ Excel Help offers several excellent general tips for creating lists:

▲ Include only one list per worksheet—unless the lists are far apart. If a list will contain many rows, consider dedicating the worksheet to it.

▲ Keep critical non-list data above or below the list. Data to the left or right may be hidden when you filter the list.

Creating a List

You can create a list by converting an existing data range or by using the List Manager to guide the list's creation.

To create a list:

1. *Do one of the following:*

   ▲ To create a list in a new worksheet, open the Project Gallery (File > Project Gallery), select the Blank Documents group, click the List Wizard icon, and click Open.

   ▲ To create a new list in an existing worksheet, click the cell where you want the list to begin and choose Insert > List.

   ▲ To convert an existing data range into a list, click any cell within the range and choose Insert > List.

   ▲ Start entering your list into a worksheet. A dialog box (**Figure 12.2**) will appear after you enter a few rows of data, offering to invoke the List Manager. Click Yes to convert the data to a list, skipping the steps below.

   In all but the last option, the List Wizard appears (**Figure 12.3**).

2. In Step 1 of the List Wizard, select one of these options for the data source:

   ▲ **None.** A list will be created from scratch.

   ▲ **Excel worksheet.** Use existing data from the specified range, converting it into a list. If the data already has column labels, be sure to check My list has headers.

   ▲ **External data source.** Select this option and click the Get Data button to import the list data from an external file. (This option requires installed ODBC drivers.)

Figure 12.2 When it appears that you're creating a list, Excel offers to help set it up.

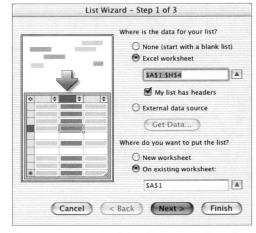

Figure 12.3 In Step 1, tell the List Manager where the data (if any) resides and where to create the list.

CREATING A LIST

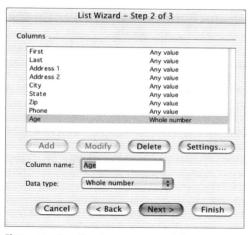

Figure 12.4 Specify column names and data types.

Figure 12.5 Name the list, indicate whether to add a totals row, and specify an AutoFormat style.

Figure 12.6 The List toolbar.

3. Indicate where the list should be placed:
   - ▲ **New worksheet.** Create the list in a new, blank worksheet.
   - ▲ **On existing worksheet.** The upper-left corner of the list will begin at the specified cell.

   Click Next. Step 2 appears (**Figure 12.4**).

4. *Do one of the following:*
   - ▲ If the list is based on existing data, select each column, select a data type from the drop-down Data type list, optionally edit the column name, and click Modify to record the changes.
   - ▲ If the list is being created from scratch, enter each column name, select a data type from the drop-down Data type list, and click Add. (The order in which columns are added will match their order in the list.)

5. *Optional:* To set formatting, conditional formatting, or validation options for the current field, click Settings. Repeat for other fields as necessary.

   Click Next to continue.

6. In Step 3 (**Figure 12.5**), name the list and indicate whether you want a totals row. You can also choose an AutoFormat style.

7. Click Finish.

   The list appears on the worksheet, starting at the designated cell (see Figure 12.1).

✔ Tips

- When your list appears, the List toolbar also appears (**Figure 12.6**). You can use it to modify any list element.

- When converting existing data to a list, you can still add, delete, and modify columns in Steps 4 and 5.

- To convert a list back to normal data, click the List icon on the List toolbar and choose Remove List Manager.

Entering and Editing Data

Cells in a list are the same as other worksheet cells. You can use normal editing techniques to enter, delete, and modify list cell contents. In addition, you may find the following editing information useful.

To edit list data:

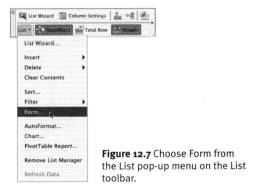

◆ To add new data to a list, you can use either of the following techniques:

▲ Type data into each cell as you would in any worksheet. Press ⟨Tab⟩ or ⟨Shift⟩⟨Tab⟩ to move to the next or previous cell. When you complete a row, a new row appears at the bottom of the list.

▲ Choose Data > Form, or click the List icon on the List toolbar and choose Form (**Figure 12.7**). Use the Form dialog box to enter new records (**Figure 12.8**).

◆ To delete a selected *record* (list row), you can do either of the following:

▲ Choose Edit > Delete Row, or click the List icon in the List toolbar and choose List > Delete > Row.

▲ To clear the contents of the row without deleting it, choose Edit > Clear > Contents, or click the List icon and choose List > Clear Contents.

Figure 12.7 Choose Form from the List pop-up menu on the List toolbar.

Figure 12.8 You can optionally use a form to enter new records, edit existing records, or delete records.

✔ Tips

■ As you begin typing a cell entry, a list of previous entries for the column that begin with the same characters appears. You can select one of these items as a data-entry shortcut.

■ Refer to Chapter 14 for information on using forms for data entry and editing.

Adding List Columns

If necessary, you can add new columns to an existing list. Click a cell where you want to insert the column. Then click the Insert Column icon on the List toolbar or choose Insert > Columns. To complete the process, edit the column name.

To add a blank column to the end of a list, widen the list frame so it shows a blank, gray area on the right side and then click the (New Column) text.

Table formats   Preview of selected format

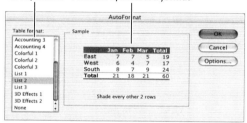

Figure 12.9 Select a format to apply to the list.

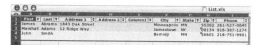

Figure 12.10 This is a list to which an AutoFormat table style has been applied.

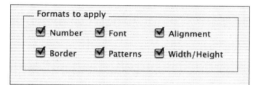

Figure 12.11 Click Options to reveal this section at the bottom of the AutoFormat dialog box, enabling you to selectively apply formatting options to the list.

Formatting a List

After you've entered the list data (or at least have a good start on it), you may want to format the list. In addition to the standard cell-formatting options (such as bold, italic, font, size, borders, and shading), there are formats that you can apply to the entire list.

To format an entire list:

1. Click any cell in the list.

2. Choose Format > AutoFormat or click the List icon on the List toolbar and choose AutoFormat.

   The AutoFormat dialog box appears (**Figure 12.9**).

3. Click any of the Table format styles in the left pane to see a preview of the format. Select a format and click OK.

   The format is applied to the list (**Figure 12.10**).

✔ Tips

- If you click the Options button in the AutoFormat dialog box, you can selectively enable or disable AutoFormat elements, such as borders and cell patterns (**Figure 12.11**).

- After formatting a list with AutoFormat, you can still apply normal cell and text formatting.

- To get the full effect of your list's new appearance, click the Visuals icon on the List toolbar to hide the frame graphics. Click the icon a second time to restore the list frame.

- To learn how to format individual cells, cell ranges, and particular columns or rows, see Chapter 10.

FORMATTING A LIST

205

Filtering a List

As your list grows, you may occasionally want to view only rows that meet certain criteria. You can filter a list in this manner to generate a data subset for printing, charting, or record deletion, for example.

To apply an AutoFilter to a list:

1. Set the list for AutoFilter by choosing Data > Filter > AutoFilter or by clicking the Autofilters icon on the List toolbar.

   When enabled, every column title is followed by a pair of arrows and the Autofilters toolbar icon is darkened.

2. Click the AutoFilter arrows beside the column on which you want to filter and choose a filtering option from the drop-down menu (**Figure 12.12**).

   Only records that match the criterion are shown; the others are temporarily hidden.

3. *Optional:* To further filter the list, you can set additional criteria for other columns.

4. To restore all or some of the currently hidden records, do one of the following:

   ▲ To show all list records, choose Data > Filter > Show All, or click the List toolbar icon and choose Filter > Show All.

   ▲ If you've applied multiple filters, click the AutoFilter arrows for the filter you wish to remove and choose Show All.

✔ Tips

■ If you want to edit records with missing data for a given column, choose Show Blanks.

■ For additional filtering techniques and tips, see Chapter 14.

AutoFilter arrows

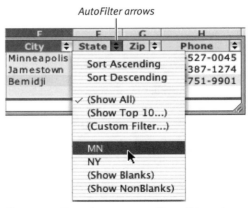

Figure 12.12 To apply or remove a filter, click a column's AutoFilter arrows and choose an option from the drop-down menu that appears.

FILTERING A LIST

Sort Ascending

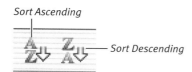
Sort Descending

Figure 12.13 The Standard toolbar has icons that you can click to perform an ascending or descending sort.

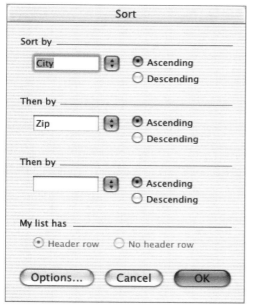

Figure 12.14 Specify the fields by which you want to sort. Each sort can be ascending or descending.

Sorting a List

You can sort a list by the values in one or more columns. Excel allows you to sort on the basis of the contents of a single column or multiple columns. When sorting on multiple columns, each additional column serves as a tie-breaker. For instance, you could sort on State and on Zip Code. This would group each state's records together, while breaking them into subgroups for each zip code.

To perform a simple sort:

◆ *Do one of the following:*

▲ Click any cell within the column on which you want to sort. Click the Sort Ascending or Sort Descending icon on the Standard toolbar (**Figure 12.13**).

▲ With AutoFilter enabled, click the AutoFilter arrows beside the column on which you want to sort. Choose Sort Ascending or Sort Descending from the drop-down menu (see Figure 12.12).

The list rows are rearranged.

To perform a complex sort:

1. Click any cell in the list.

2. Choose Data > Sort, or click the List toolbar icon and choose Sort.

   The Sort dialog box appears (**Figure 12.14**).

3. Select the primary sort field from the Sort by drop-down list, and click the Ascending or Descending radio button.

4. Select additional sort columns from the Then by drop-down lists, and set each to either Ascending or Descending.

5. Click OK to perform the specified sorts.

   continues on next page

✔ Tips

- When sorting by day or month, you can sort in calendar order instead of alphabetically. Click Options in the Sort dialog box. In the Sort Options dialog box that appears (**Figure 12.15**), choose a day or month format from the First key sort order list. (Note that such a custom sort can only be applied to the *primary* sort field.)

- The Sort Options dialog box is also where you can specify column sorts (rather than the usual row sorts). In the Orientation section of the dialog box (see Figure 12.15), select Sort left to right and then click OK. In the Sort dialog box, the Sort by and Then by drop-down lists will now contain row identifiers.

- To sort by field names in a column sort, choose Row 1. This can be very helpful when working with a list that has many fields/columns.

- Some sort operations cannot be undone. If a sort results in an unwanted sort order and no Undo command is available, close the worksheet without saving it.

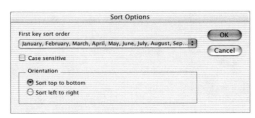

Figure 12.15 Use the Sort Options dialog box to specify a custom sort or to execute a column-based sort.

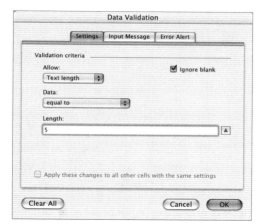

Figure 12.16 Specify a validation criterion on the Settings tab of the dialog box.

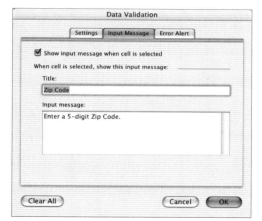

Figure 12.17 Enter an optional pop-up message to direct users who tab or click into a cell in this column.

Figure 12.18 When a Stop error message appears, the user can click Retry to correct the error or Cancel to delete the errant cell entry.

Data Validation

Excel allows you to set a validation criterion for any field/column to ensure that only valid data is entered. For example, a Zip Code field could be restricted to entries of exactly five digits. Validation tests are automatically applied as you add items to the list. You can set validation options when creating a list or afterwards (described in the following steps).

To set validation options:

1. Click a cell in the column for which you'd like to set validation criteria.

2. Choose Data > Validation.
   The Data Validation dialog box appears (**Figure 12.16**).

3. On the Settings tab, set a validation criterion by making choices from the drop-down lists and typing in the text box(es).

4. *Optional:* To prevent blank entries in the column, remove the checkmark from Ignore blank.

5. *Optional:* If you want a pop-up message to appear whenever you enter a cell in the column, click the Input Message tab. Enter a title and message text (**Figure 12.17**).

6. *Optional:* To enter an error message that will appear whenever validation fails, click the Error Alert tab. Enter a title and message text, and choose a message style from the Style drop-down menu:

   ▲ **Stop.** Prevent further work until the error is corrected.

   ▲ **Warning.** Offer a choice of correcting or accepting the entered data.

   ▲ **Information.** Display only explanatory text.

   Click OK when you're done. If an incorrect value is later entered into a cell in this column, the error message (if there is one) is displayed (**Figure 12.18**).

✔ Tips

- You can also set validation criteria by invoking the List Wizard.

- If you can't remember which columns have validation criteria, choose Edit > Go To. In the Go To dialog box, click Special. In the Go To Special dialog box (**Figure 12.19**), select Data Validation/All and click OK. Excel highlights the letters of all columns for which a data validation criterion has been set.

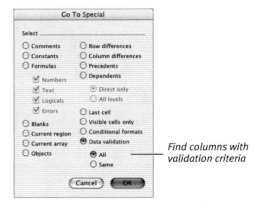

Find columns with validation criteria

Figure 12.19 Click Data Validation and All to identify columns for which you've set validation criteria.

13

CHARTS AND GRAPHS

Numeric information is often easiest to understand when presented graphically. In Excel, you can create a default chart with a single keystroke or create a more complex chart by using the helpful Chart Wizard. You can choose from nearly two dozen chart styles, including bar, column, line, area, pie, scatter, bubble, and radar charts—and many of them can be 3-D.

After Excel has generated a chart, you can tailor it to suit your needs. You can add, edit, or delete titles, labels, legends, and gridlines. You can also add, change, or remove color, patterns, or shading, as well as change the scale, labeling, and look of the axes. If you later edit a chart's source data, the chart will automatically reflect the new values.

✔ Tip

- Don't be afraid to experiment with options you don't completely understand. You can undo almost any modification by choosing Edit > Undo or by clicking the Undo icon on the Standard toolbar.

Creating Charts

Are you curious about how you can create a chart with one keystroke? It's preceded by a mouse operation, but it still takes only one keystroke to create a column chart with the default settings. For more complex charts and greater control of the options, you can use the Chart Wizard.

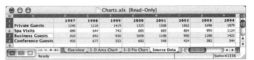

Figure 13.1 Select the data to be charted. In this example (Charts from the Learn tab of the Project Gallery), hotel stays by guests are selected.

To create a default chart:

1. Select the data from which you want to create a chart (**Figure 13.1**).

2. Press F11 to create the chart.

   Unless you've changed the default chart type, a column chart appears in a new sheet (**Figure 13.2**).

To create a chart with the Chart Wizard:

1. *Optional:* Select the data from which you want to create a chart.

   You can preselect the data or specify it later as part of the Chart Wizard process.

2. Click the Chart Wizard icon on the Standard toolbar or choose Insert > Chart. The Chart Wizard appears (**Figure 13.3**).

3. Select a chart type from the Standard Types or Custom Types tab. Click Next.

   You can preview any selected chart on the Standard Types tab by clicking the Press and Hold to View Sample button.

4. On the Data Range tab of the Chart Source Data screen (**Figure 13.4**), confirm the data range, indicate whether the series is in rows or columns, and click Next.

   ▲ If you preselected the labels and data in Step 1, ensure that the correct Series in radio button is selected.

   ▲ If you didn't preselect the labels and data or you need to modify your selection, type the range in the Data range text box or select it in the worksheet.

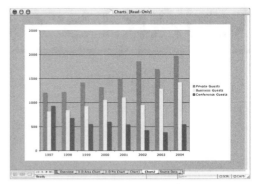

Figure 13.2 An attractive column chart is generated, complete with colored bars, axis labels, and a legend.

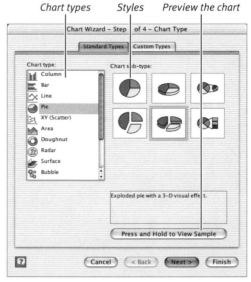

Figure 13.3 Select a chart type from the list on the left and then select a style from the ones displayed.

CREATING CHARTS

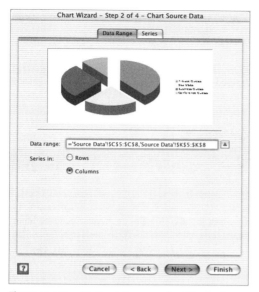

Figure 13.4 Specify the data source for this chart.

Figure 13.5 You can create the chart on a new sheet or embed it as an object on a current worksheet.

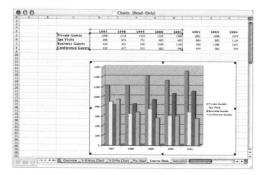

Figure 13.6 Example of an embedded/floating chart.

5. Click the tabs of the Chart Options screen and specify settings for elements such as the chart and axis labels, legend placement, optional data labels, and so on. Click Next to continue.

   The tab labels and options depend on the type of chart you're creating.

6. On the Chart Location screen (**Figure 13.5**), click a radio button to embed the chart in an existing worksheet or create it in a separate sheet. Click Finish.

   The completed chart appears—either as a separate sheet or as a floating object (**Figure 13.6**) embedded on the same sheet as the source data or another sheet in the current workbook.

✔ Tips

- You can change the default chart type from a column chart to any other type that you use frequently. Select an existing chart in any worksheet and then choose Chart > Chart Type. In the Chart Type dialog box, select a chart type and style, and then click the Set as Default Chart button.

- To chart nonadjacent data (as is shown in Figure 13.1, for example), press ⌘ while drag-selecting cells.

CREATING CHARTS

Modifying Charts

While a newly created chart may be perfect for your needs, you can also modify or embellish it as desired. Using a variety of techniques, you can change virtually any chart element, the data series, or even the chart type/style.

To modify a chart element:

1. To open a formatting dialog box for a given chart object, do any of the following:

   ▲ Double-click the chart object.

   ▲ Select the chart object and click the Chart toolbar's Format *selected object* icon (**Figure 13.7**).

   To display the Chart toolbar, choose View > Toolbars > Chart.

   ▲ Open the Chart Objects menu on the Chart toolbar and choose the object that you want to modify. Click the Format *selected object* toolbar icon (see Figure 13.7).

   ▲ Select a chart object and choose the first command from the Format menu (**Figure 13.8**).

2. In the dialog box that appears (**Figure 13.9**), make the necessary changes and click OK.

✔ Tips

- You can resize or move some chart elements, such as the legend and title. To resize a selected element, drag one of its handles. To move an element, click and drag it to a new location. (You can also move or resize an *entire* embedded chart.)

- To add a title, expand the Chart Options section of the Formatting Palette, select Chart Title from the drop-down menu in the Titles sub-section, and then type the title in the text box. You can edit a title in the same text box or on the chart.

Chart Objects   Format selected object

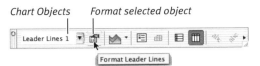

Figure 13.7 The Chart toolbar.

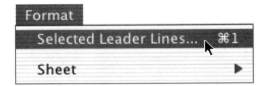

Figure 13.8 The wording of the first Format command changes to reflect the currently selected object(s).

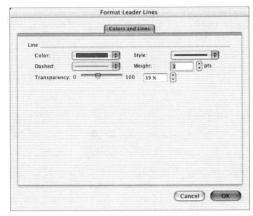

Figure 13.9 A Format dialog box specific to the selected object(s) appears.

MODIFYING CHARTS

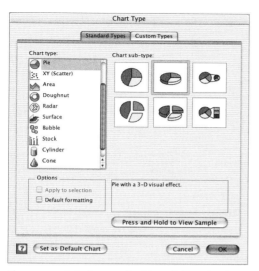

Figure 13.10 Select a new chart type (left) and style (right), and then click OK.

Figure 13.11 You can also select a new chart type from the Chart Type drop-down menu.

To change the chart type:

1. Make the chart active by selecting the chart or any of its elements.

2. *Do one of the following:*
   ▲ Choose Chart > Chart Type. In the Chart Type dialog box that appears (**Figure 13.10**), select a new chart type and style.
   ▲ Open the Chart Type menu on the Chart toolbar, and select a new chart type and style (**Figure 13.11**).

   The chart is transformed as specified.

✔ Tips

■ The Chart > Chart Type command offers more type and style options than the Chart Type drop-down menu on the Chart toolbar.

■ When the Chart Type drop-down menu is open, you can open the Chart Type dialog box by choosing More Types.

MODIFYING CHARTS

To change the data series for an embedded chart:

◆ To change any of the values in the current data series so they are reflected in the chart, edit the source data.

◆ To remove a data series from a chart, select the series in the chart and press [Delete].

◆ To change the data for a chart that's on the same sheet as the source data, start by selecting the chart. (Click in the blank area surrounding the chart or choose Chart Area from the Chart Objects menu of the Chart toolbar.) The current source data is indicated by colored rectangles (**Figure 13.12**).

Do any of the following:

▲ To select a different contiguous series of the same size, move the cursor over any edge of the blue source data rectangle. When the cursor changes to a hand, drag the rectangle to select another data range.

▲ To increase or decrease the data range, move the cursor over a corner of the blue rectangle and then drag.

▲ You can also add contiguous or noncontiguous data to the chart by selecting it in the worksheet, moving the cursor over the selection until it changes to a hand, and then dragging the selection onto the chart.

▲ You can also edit the data range by choosing Chart > Source Data or by clicking the Edit icon in the Chart Data section of the Formatting Palette. On the Data Range tab of the Source Data dialog box (**Figure 13.13**), enter a new range or select the range directly in the worksheet.

Labels   Data   Labels

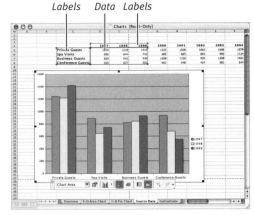

Figure 13.12 When you select a chart that is on the same sheet as its source data, the current labels and data are surrounded by colored rectangles.

Type or select a range

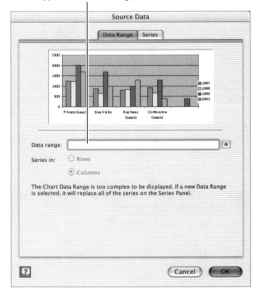

Figure 13.13 Enter a new source data range.

MODIFYING CHARTS

Select labels on the worksheet

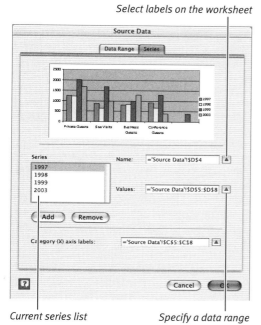

Current series list　　*Specify a data range*

Figure 13.14 You can selectively remove or add data series on the Series tab of the Source Data dialog box.

Figure 13.15 You can edit the data range for a selected series in the Formula Bar.

▲ You can also make changes on the Series tab of the Source Data dialog box (**Figure 13.14**). To remove a series, select it in the Series list box and click Remove. To add a series, click Add. Then click the triangle icon beside the Values text box and drag to select the new data values in the worksheet. Click the triangle icon again to record the values. Finally, to name the new series, type a name in the Name text box or—by clicking the triangle to the right of the text box—select the name in the worksheet.

To change the data series for a sheet chart:

◆ To change any of the values in the current data series so they are reflected in the chart, edit the source data.

◆ To remove a data series from a chart, select the series in the chart and press [Delete].

◆ To edit a single data series, select the series in the chart. References to the cells that contain data for the series appear in the Formula Bar (**Figure 13.15**). Edit the references to change the data source.

◆ To edit the source data for a series, edit the data for the entire chart, or add or remove a series, select any part of the chart and do one of the following:

▲ Choose Chart > Source Data.

▲ Click the Edit icon in the Chart Data section of the Formatting Palette.

▲ Select the entire chart, [Control]-click it, and choose Source Data from the pop-up menu that appears.

Make any desired changes in the Source Data dialog box (see Figures 13.13 and 13.14), as explained in the prior step list.

MODIFYING CHARTS

To format all or a selected data series:

◆ To change the color of *all* data series, select the chart or any object on it. In the Chart Colors, Fills, and Lines section of the Formatting Palette (**Figure 13.16**), select a new color scheme and/or a series color option.

◆ To format a single data series, select the series on the chart or by name from the Chart Objects menu on the Chart toolbar.

Do one of the following:

▲ On the Formatting Palette, select new settings from the Fill options and Line options sections.

▲ Select new settings in the Format Data Series dialog box (**Figure 13.17**) and click OK.

To display the dialog box, double-click an element in the data series, select a series element and choose Format > Selected Data Series, select a series element and click the Format Data Series icon on the Chart toolbar, or [Control]-click an element in the data series and choose Format Data Series from the pop-up menu.

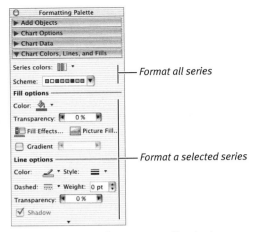

Format all series

Format a selected series

Figure 13.16 You can format one or all series by selecting options on the Formatting Palette.

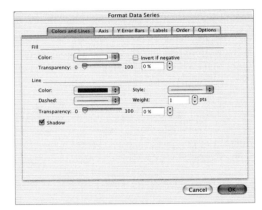

Figure 13.17 To format a single series, you can also set options in the Format Data Series dialog box.

MODIFYING CHARTS

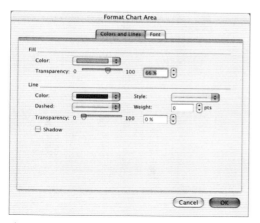

Figure 13.18 You can alter the formatting of the chart area in this dialog box.

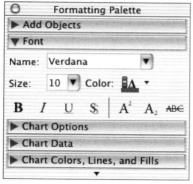

Figure 13.19 You can choose a new font for the axis labels, legend, and chart title.

Figure 13.20 You can choose chart elements by name from the Chart Objects toolbar menu.

To format the chart area:

◆ You can format the chart area using the Format Chart Area dialog box (**Figure 13.18**) or the Formatting Palette.

　▲ Open the Format Chart Area dialog box by double-clicking the chart area, selecting the chart area and choosing Format > Selected Chart Area, or selecting the chart area and clicking the Format Chart Area icon on the Chart toolbar.

　　On the Colors and Lines tab, set the fill color and transparency for the area that surrounds the chart. Options chosen from the Line section apply to the border around the chart. Click the Font tab to select a font for the axis labels, legend, and chart title.

　▲ More advanced options are provided on the Formatting Palette. Select the chart area, open the Chart Colors, Lines, and Fills section of the Formatting Palette, and choose new settings from the Fill options and Line options areas (see Figure 13.16). You can change the font used for the axis labels, legend, and chart title by selecting settings from the Font section of the Formatting Palette (**Figure 13.19**).

✔ Tips

■ As you'll quickly discover, you can use the same techniques to format *any* chart element. Select the element by clicking it or choosing it from the Chart Objects menu on the Chart toolbar (**Figure 13.20**). Then click the Format *object name* toolbar icon or select options from the Formatting Palette.

■ First, format the most general elements (such as the chart area) and then the individual elements within that area (such as the axis labels).

To add or remove other chart elements:

◆ *Do any of the following:*

▲ You can delete virtually any chart element (even a data series) by selecting it on the chart and pressing Delete.

▲ To delete elements such as the title or legend, click the element's border and press Delete.

▲ To add or remove the legend, click the Legend icon on the Chart toolbar.

▲ To display the source data as part of a chart (**Figure 13.21**), click the Data Table icon on the Chart toolbar.

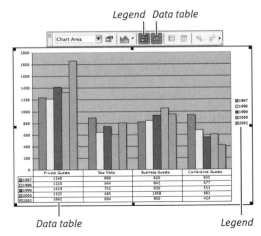

Legend Data table

Data table   *Legend*

Figure 13.21 You can display or remove the legend or source data by clicking a Chart toolbar icon.

MODIFYING CHARTS

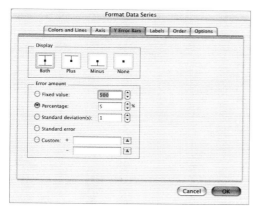

Figure 13.22 You must decide whether the error bars will be based on a fixed amount, a percentage, or variance from or standard error of the mean.

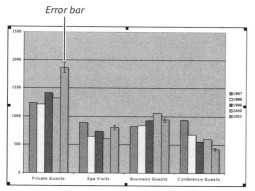

Figure 13.23 These error bars show ±5% for each element in the 2002 data series.

Adding error bars and trendlines

Error bars are lines drawn through data points to indicate the possible range of uncertain values (the "plus or minus" uncertainty). A *trendline* is a smooth line or curve drawn through the points of a data series to indicate a trend.

To add error bars to a data series:

1. Select the data series to which you want to add error bars.

2. *Do one of the following:*
   - ▲ Click the Format Data Series icon on the Chart toolbar.
   - ▲ Choose Format > Selected Data Series (⌘ 1).
   - ▲ Instead of selecting the data series, quickly double-click any element of it.

   The Format Data Series dialog box appears.

3. Click the Y Error Bars (**Figure 13.22**) or X Error Bars tab, set options, and click OK.

   The error bars appear (**Figure 13.23**).

✔ Tip

■ Chart types that accept only Y error bars include 2D area, bar, column, and line. Chart types that accept either X or Y error bars include x-y (scatter) and bubble charts.

MODIFYING CHARTS

To display a trendline for a data series:

1. Select a data series for which you want to display a trendline.

2. Choose Chart > Add Trendline.

   The Add Trendline dialog box appears (**Figure 13.24**).

3. Select a trendline type, specify the data series to which it will be applied, and click OK.

   The trendline appears (**Figure 13.25**).

✔ Tips

- To remove a trendline, select it and press Delete.

- You can plot *multiple* trendlines for a single data series, if you wish.

- To set different options for a trendline, double-click it. On the tabs of the Format Trendline dialog box, you can change the trendline's width, style, and color; switch to a different kind of trendline; or set advanced options.

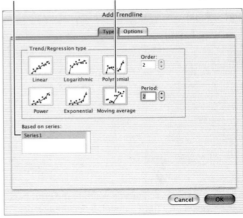

Based on this series   Selected trendline type

Figure 13.24 Select a trendline type and indicate the data series to which it will be applied.

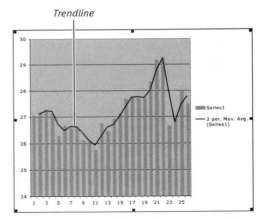

Trendline

Figure 13.25 You can add a moving average trendline to chart the movement of stock.

DATABASE TECHNIQUES

Figure 14.1 Records appear in rows; fields appear in columns.

As you know, Office 2004 doesn't include a dedicated database application. However, unless you work with extremely large data sets or need a complex or relational database, Excel can probably provide all the database power that you require.

In Excel, you enter data in rows. Each row is a *record* (one complete set of information). Each column is a *field* that contains one type of information for the record (**Figure 14.1**), such as a last name, Social Security number, or annual salary, for example. Rather than enter information directly into the worksheet cells, you can use an Excel "fill-in-the-blanks" form to make it easier to enter, edit, delete, and search for data. You can also import databases created in other programs, such as FileMaker Pro or Microsoft SQL Server.

After you enter the data, you can sort it, view only the information that matches certain criteria, and calculate group totals or other summary statistics.

Creating a Database

There are two ways to create a database in a worksheet. First, as explained in Chapter 12, you can use the List Manager. Second, you can create a database manually by entering the data in contiguous rows and columns, as explained below.

Note that *any* area of a worksheet can be considered a database as long as every data column has a label (which is treated as the field name) and the rows and columns are contiguous. A single blank row or column— even in the middle of an extensive data set—marks the edge of the database. Records beneath a blank or fields to the right of a blank column are not considered part of the database.

To manually create a database:

1. In either a new or an existing worksheet, enter the field names at the top of a group of adjacent columns.

2. Enter the data into the rows below the field names (see Figure 14.1).

✔ Tips

■ Press [Tab] when you complete a cell to move to the next cell to the right. Press [Enter] or [Return] when you complete a cell to move to the cell directly below.

■ When you later want to create more records, add them directly below the last data row (**Figure 14.2**).

■ There's nothing in the "rules" that requires you to dedicate an entire worksheet to a database. You can create a database as a separate area within any general-purpose worksheet or include multiple databases in a single worksheet, for example.

Next record goes here

Figure 14.2 You add a new record in the blank row immediately beneath the last record.

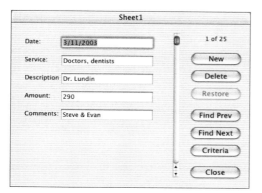

Figure 14.3 You can use a data form to create new records, edit the data in existing records, and delete unwanted records.

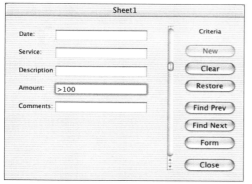

Figure 14.4 Enter search criteria in one or more fields. In this example, records in which the Amount field is greater than $100 will be identified as matches.

✔ Tips

- A form always opens to the first record in the database, regardless of the record that is selected when you choose Data > Form.

- A form can display up to 32 fields.

Using a Form for Data Entry

As explained in the previous section, you can manually create new records by adding rows at the bottom of the database. You can also use forms to speed data entry and make the process more like working in a traditional database application.

To use a form for data entry:

1. Click any cell in the database.

2. Choose Data > Form.

   A data entry form appears (**Figure 14.3**).

3. With the form displayed, you can do any of the following:

   ▲ To flip through the records in their current sort order, click Find Next, Find Prev, or the up- and down arrows at the bottom of the scroll bar. To go directly to a record of interest, drag the scroll box/slider.

   ▲ To create a new record, click the New button or drag the scroll box down to the blank record at the end of the database (labeled "New Record"). Enter the new data by typing and tabbing from field to field. When you're done, press ⌐Return⌐ to add the record.

   ▲ To edit a record, display it, make the desired changes, and press ⌐Return⌐.

   ▲ Click Delete to delete the current record.

   ▲ To view only specific records, click Criteria. In the form that appears, enter search criteria (**Figure 14.4**). Click Find Next and Find Prev to view the matching records. To resume working with the entire database, click Criteria, Clear, and Form.

4. To dismiss the form and record changes made to the current record (if any), click Close.

Database Operations

In any database, you can sort the records, *filter* (display only records that match certain criteria), and calculate subtotals.

To sort a database:

1. Click any cell in the database and then choose Data > Sort.

2. In the Sort dialog box (**Figure 14.5**), select a field name from the Sort by drop-down list.

3. To sort from smallest to largest or earliest to latest, click the Ascending radio button. To sort from largest to smallest or latest to earliest, click Descending.

4. To perform additional sorts on the data, select fields from the Then by drop-down lists. Specify an Ascending or Descending sort for each field.

5. Select the Header row radio button to prevent Excel from treating the field labels as a data row that should also be included in the sort.

6. Click OK to sort the database.

✔ Tips

- When sorting on multiple fields, specify fields in order of their importance. The second and third fields are tie breakers. For example, if you sort on Last Name, you could use First Name as the second sort field. If you sorted only on Last Name, all Johnsons would be grouped together, but their first names wouldn't be in a useful order.

- To sort by days of the week or month names, click the Options button (**Figure 14.6**). To create your own custom sort order lists, go to the Custom Lists section of the Preferences dialog box.

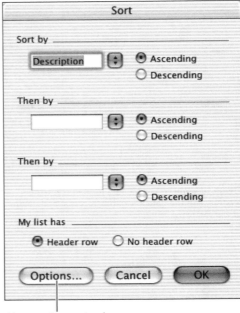

Use a custom sort order

Figure 14.5 Specify sort criteria in the Sort dialog box.

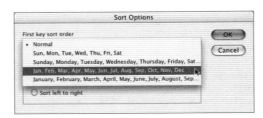

Figure 14.6 Select a custom sort order from the ones displayed in this drop-down list.

Figure 14.7 Select a filter criterion from a field's drop-down list.

Figure 14.8 The database is filtered to show only the records that match the selected criterion.

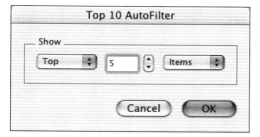

Figure 14.9 You can display the top (highest/most recent) or bottom (lowest/oldest) numeric or date values in a field by setting options in this dialog box.

To filter a database:

1. Click any cell in the database and then choose Data > Filter > AutoFilter.

2. Click an AutoFilter arrow to the right of any field and choose a filter criterion (**Figure 14.7**).

   The database is filtered to display only those records that match the criterion (**Figure 14.8**).

3. *Optional:* Select additional criteria by clicking the AutoFilter arrows beside other fields.

   Effects of filtering criteria are cumulative.

4. *Do one of the following:*

   ▲ To remove the effects of all currently applied filters but continue filtering, choose Data > Filter > Show All.

   ▲ To end filtering, choose Data > Filter > AutoFilter.

✔ Tips

- In a filtered database, row numbers of extracted records appear in blue, as do the AutoFilter arrows of criterion fields.

- To reverse the effect of an applied filter, choose Show All from its AutoFilter list.

- In addition to filtering, you can sort by a field by choosing Sort Ascending or Sort Descending from the field's AutoFilter list.

- To display a specific number or percentage of the highest or lowest values in a field, choose Show Top 10 from the AutoFilter drop-down list. Set options in the Top 10 AutoFilter dialog box (**Figure 14.9**) and click OK.

- To create a complex filter for a single field, choose Custom Filter from the AutoFilter drop-down list. To specify more complex criteria, choose Data > Filter > Advanced Filter.

To display subtotals or other grouping statistics:

1. Sort the database by the appropriate field(s) to create the groups of data on which to calculate subtotals (or another statistic).

2. Select any cell in the database and then choose Data > Subtotals.

   The Subtotal dialog box appears (**Figure 14.10**).

3. Select a break field from the At each change in drop-down list.

   A subtotal or other statistic will appear each time this field's value changes.

4. Select the mathematical or statistical function to calculate from the Use function drop-down list.

5. From the list box, click the check box for each field to which the function will be applied.

6. Make any desired changes in the remaining options and click OK.

   The function is applied to each subgroup in the database (**Figure 14.11**).

✔ Tips

- You can click the controls to the left of the database to show only the grand total, only subtotals, or mixtures of subtotals and data (**Figure 14.12**).

- To eliminate the subtotals, choose Data > Subtotals, click Remove All (see Figure 14.10), and then click OK.

Figure 14.10 Set subtotal options.

Figure 14.11 The function is calculated and displayed (in bold) for each data group.

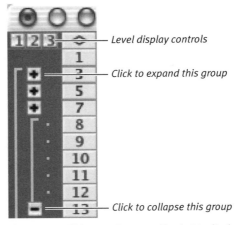

Level display controls

Click to expand this group

Click to collapse this group

Figure 14.12 Click controls to specify what to display.

Working with External Databases

As you learned in Chapter 9, you can open or import text files into Excel. Excel also provides tools to import data directly from FileMaker Pro 5 through 6, as well as retrieve data from the Web.

Importing from FileMaker Pro

Keep the following in mind when importing FileMaker Pro data into Excel 2004:

◆ Only files from FileMaker Pro 5.0, 5.5, and 6.0 are supported. In addition to the database file, you must have a working copy of FileMaker Pro 5–6 on the same computer as Excel 2004. (If you have FileMaker Pro 7, you can export your data as a tab-delimited text file and then use the procedure described in Chapter 9 to open or import it into Excel.)

◆ Although the *results* of FileMaker calculations can be imported, the actual *formulas* are not imported.

◆ The worksheet will probably need to be re-sorted following the import because Excel does not retain FileMaker's sort order.

◆ Because of a worksheet's maximum allowable size, only the first 65,535 records and 256 fields can be imported.

◆ If any cell contains more than 35,767 characters, the additional characters will be truncated.

To import a FileMaker Pro database:

1. *Do one of the following:*

   ▲ Drag and drop a FileMaker Pro 5.0, 5.5, or 6.0 file onto the Excel program icon.

   ▲ Choose File > Open and select the FileMaker database from the Open dialog box.

   ▲ Choose Data > Get External Data > Import from FileMaker Pro. In the Choose a Database File dialog box that appears, select the database and click Choose. (This procedure can only be used if a worksheet is open.)

   FileMaker launches, the chosen database opens, and the FileMaker Import Wizard appears (**Figure 14.13**).

2. Specify the fields to import by moving them to the Fields to import list.

   From the Layouts drop-down list, select a layout in which one or more of the fields appears. Move each field to the Fields to import list by clicking the > button. (To simultaneously move *all* fields from a layout, click the >> button.)

3. Fields are imported in the order in which they are listed. To change the position of a field in the Fields to import list, select it and click the up or down button.

4. Click Next to continue.

5. In the new screen (**Figure 14.14**), you can specify up to three criteria for record selection (if you don't want to import the entire database). Click Finish.

   If you used drag-and-drop or File > Open to start this procedure, a new worksheet is automatically created. If you used the Get External Data procedure, a dialog box appears. You can create a new worksheet or add the imported data to the current worksheet starting in a cell of your choice.

Figure 14.13 In the wizard's first screen, specify the fields to import and their order.

Figure 14.14 If you don't want to import the entire database, you can enter up to three record-selection criteria.

✔ Tip

■ When using a date as a record selection criterion in Step 5, enter a four-digit year (6/12/2004) rather than a two-digit year (6/12/04).

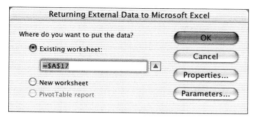

Figure 14.15 You can import query results into a new worksheet or the current one.

Figure 14.16 Enter the symbols for the stocks and mutual funds, separated by commas.

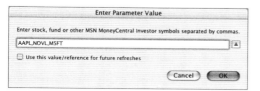

Figure 14.17 Excel connects to the Web site, downloads the data, and adds it to your worksheet.

Importing data from the Web

You can copy selected data from a table on a Web page and paste it into an Excel worksheet, but it doesn't always work as expected. A more precise method of retrieving data from the Web is to create a *Web query* using HTML forms.

Office includes several sample queries that you can edit. They're found in the Microsoft Office 2004:Office:Queries folder. The following example shows how to use one of the sample queries.

To retrieve Web data using a query:

1. Choose Data > Get External Data > Run Saved Query.

    The Choose a Query dialog box appears, open to the Queries folder.

2. Select the MSN Money Stock Quotes query and click Get Data.

    The Returning External Data to Microsoft Excel dialog box appears (**Figure 14.15**).

3. *Do one of the following:*

    ▲ To import the data into the current worksheet, click the Existing worksheet radio button. Type or click the starting cell address which will receive the import data.

    ▲ To import the data into a new, empty worksheet, click New worksheet.

4. Click OK to continue.

    The Enter Parameter Value dialog box appears (**Figure 14.16**).

5. Enter one or more stock or mutual fund symbols. (To enter multiple symbols, separate them with commas.) Click OK.

    The query report appears in the worksheet (**Figure 14.17**).

✔ Tips

■ Copying and pasting data from a Web table in Internet Explorer works as you'd expect. Doing the same using Safari from Apple Computer results in a single column of data (**Figure 14.18**).

■ To create your own database query, choose Data > Get External Data > New Database Query. In order for this to work, you must install the necessary ODBC (Open Database Connectivity) driver. For information on creating queries, review "Import or connect to data in a database" in Excel Help.

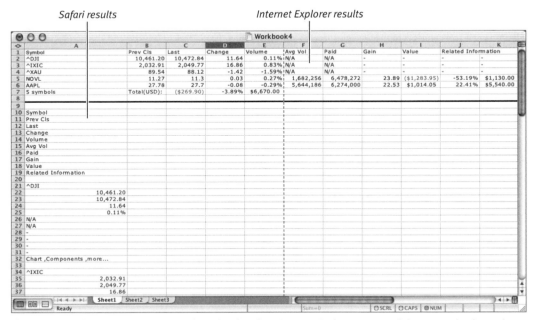

Safari results   Internet Explorer results

Figure 14.18 In this example, copying and pasting data from Internet Explorer gave much better results than using Safari. (It wasn't perfect however; some column headings shifted to the left.)

WORKING WITH EXTERNAL DATABASES

15

DATA ANALYSIS

Excel provides several excellent tools to help you analyze worksheet data. In this chapter, you'll be introduced to the following data analysis tools:

- ◆ **PivotTables.** An interactive table that you can use to view the relationships between variables.

- ◆ **Goal seeking.** Solve for a specific result in a calculation by determining how one of its components must change.

- ◆ **What-if analysis.** *Data tables* are used to calculate an equation with one or two unknown variables by substituting user-provided test values. *Scenarios* are named, saved sets of input test values for a data table.

- ◆ **Solver.** For a given formula cell, maximize, minimize, or set it to a specific value by varying the values of other cells.

Working with PivotTables

A *PivotTable* is an interactive table that helps you summarize and analyze data from existing lists and tables. PivotTables enable you to easily examine large amounts of data in different ways.

Starting with a long list or database, you can create a PivotTable summary of the data. By taking advantage of the PivotTable features, you can easily change columns into rows, drill down from the summary numbers to the data elements, and find the presentation format that best reveals the information you want to see.

PivotTables are rich with functionality. A complete discussion of how to use them is beyond the scope of this book. However, we'll cover the essentials here, and you can explore them further on your own.

To create a PivotTable:

1. Choose Data > PivotTable Report.

   The PivotTable Wizard appears (**Figure 15.1**).

2. Click a radio button to specify the data source. Click Next to continue.

3. Specify the cell range within the data source (**Figure 15.2**). Click Next to continue.

4. Indicate whether to place the PivotTable report in a new worksheet or an existing one (**Figure 15.3**).

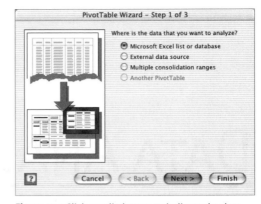

Figure 15.1 Click a radio button to indicate the data source.

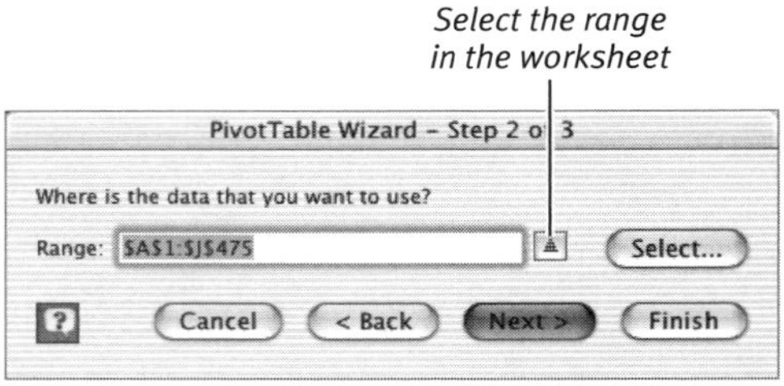

Select the range in the worksheet

Figure 15.2 Type or paste the data range in this text box. You can also specify the range by selecting it in the worksheet.

Figure 15.3 Indicate where you'd like the PivotTable to be placed.

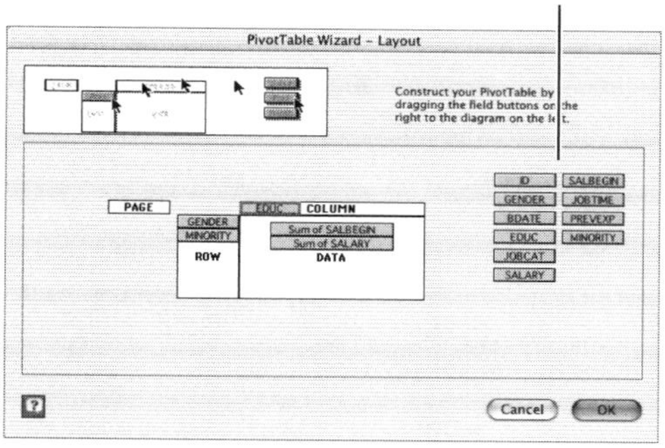

Data elements

Figure 15.4 Create the initial PivotTable layout by dragging fields into position in the diagram.

PivotTable toolbar

Figure 15.5 After the PivotTable appears, you can modify and experiment with it—as has been done here.

5. *Optional:* Rather than start with an empty layout, you can specify the initial PivotTable layout by clicking the Layout button. The PivotTable Wizard–Layout dialog box appears.

Drag data elements into the desired spots on the layout (**Figure 15.4**). (Note that numeric items normally go into the Data area.) Click OK when you're done.

6. *Optional:* To set data and formatting options, click the Options button. Click OK when you're done.

7. Click Finish in the final Wizard screen. The PivotTable report and PivotTable toolbar appear (**Figure 15.5**).

✔ Tips

- Choose a categorical field with few categories as a *page field*. In Figure 15.5, the Jobcat page field has only three categories: line staff, middle management, and upper management. By selecting a category other than Show All from the page field's drop-down list, you are electing to show only the data for that specific category.

- When a PivotTable is generated, Excel ignores any filters you've applied to the data. If you are only interested in examining a subset of your data, use the Advanced Filter command to extract the data to another area of the worksheet. Then create the PivotTable based on that new range.

To customize a PivotTable:

◆ *Do any of the following:*

▲ To add a field to the PivotTable, drag it into position from the PivotTable toolbar. (If the field list isn't visible, click the Display Fields toolbar icon.)

▲ To remove a field, drag it into an unused portion of the worksheet.

▲ To reorganize currently used fields in a PivotTable, drag each one to the desired area. You can move a column field to the rows area, for instance.

▲ To change the summary statistic used for a field, select the summary label in the PivotTable (such as Sum of Salary) and click the Field Settings toolbar icon. In the PivotTable Field dialog box (**Figure 15.6**), select a new Summarize by statistic and click OK. To set a display format for the statistic (**Figure 15.7**), click the Number button.

▲ If you've modified the original Excel list by adding fields, you can display them in the field list on the PivotTable toolbar by clicking the Refresh icon. Once displayed, you can then add them to the PivotTable.

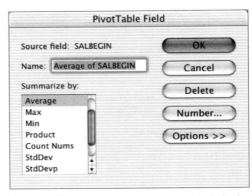

Figure 15.6 You can change the summary statistics in use in the PivotTable. In the example, an average is considerably more useful than a sum.

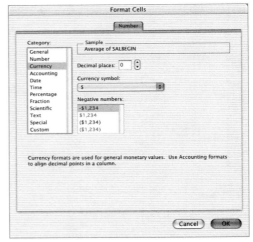

Figure 15.7 It can be a lot easier reading the data in the PivotTable if you specify an optimal format for it.

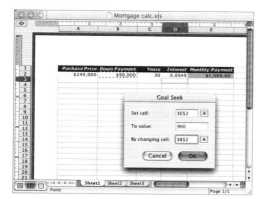

Figure 15.8 Type or point to values and cell addresses to fill in the Goal Seek text boxes.

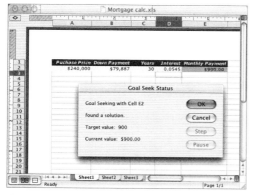

Figure 15.9 The Goal Seek Status dialog box indicates whether a solution was found. If so, the worksheet is changed as specified.

Goal Seeking

You use *goal seeking* to force a particular result in a calculation by changing one of its components. For example, if you know how much you can afford for a monthly payment on a loan, you can use goal seeking to find the down payment necessary to produce that monthly payment.

To use goal seeking:

1. Choose Tools > Goal Seek.

2. In the Goal Seek dialog box (**Figure 15.8**), enter the following:
   ▲ **Set cell.** The cell whose value you want to set (Monthly Payment or E2, in this example).
   ▲ **To value.** The value you want the Set cell to become ($900, in this example).
   ▲ **By changing cell.** The cell whose value will change in order to make the Set cell result (E2) equal the To value ($900). In this example, the By changing cell is Down Payment (B2).

3. Click OK to perform the calculation.

   The Goal Seek Status dialog box appears (**Figure 15.9**) and displays the result. The By changing cell is altered, as specified.

✔ Tips

■ Rather than typing cell addresses in the Goal Seek dialog box, you can just click the appropriate cells on the worksheet.

■ To prevent Goal Seek from modifying the worksheet with the found result, click Cancel in the Goal Seek Status dialog box.

■ The same Goal Seek dialog box can easily be modified to answer other questions. You could find out what the interest rate would have to be in the event that you had a fixed amount available as a down payment, for instance.

What-If Analyses

If you're uncertain of some elements in your calculations, Excel provides tools you can use to play "what if?"

◆ *Data tables* are used to calculate an equation with either one or two unknown variables. You provide the test values for each unknown variable. Excel then calculates the result(s) by substituting the test value(s).

◆ *Scenarios* are saved sets of input values for one or more variables that can be substituted into an equation. For example, when calculating profit, you can see what happens if sales exceed expectations or if advertising costs rise dramatically.

The first example below shows how to create a one-variable, column-oriented data table. (In a *column-oriented data table,* test values are arranged in a column; in a *row-oriented data table,* test values are arranged in a row.) The second example illustrates the creation of a two-variable, row- and column-oriented data table. Finally, this section concludes with a scenario example.

To create a one-variable data table:

1. Set up the worksheet as shown in **Figure 15.10**.

   The set of test values (in this case, interest rates) extends down a column one cell below and to the left of the cell that contains the formula.

2. Select the range of cells that covers the formula and the test values (**Figure 15.11**).

   In this example, the range is C3:D12.

3. Choose Data > Table.

   The Table dialog box appears.

Test values (C4:C12)   Formula (D3)

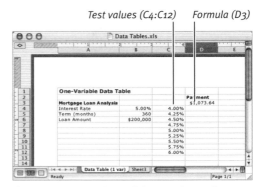

Figure 15.10 Set up the worksheet as directed.

Input cell (B4)   Formula and test values

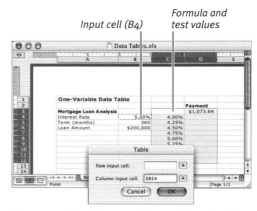

Figure 15.11 Select the test values and formula cell, choose Data > Table, and specify the single input cell in the Table dialog box.

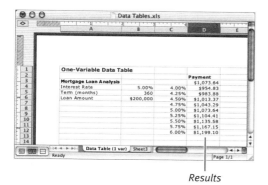

Results

Figure 15.12 The results are displayed. (Each result is to the right of the corresponding test value.)

4. *Do one of the following:*

▲ If this is a row-oriented data table, click in the Row input cell text box. Enter or point to the input cell.

▲ If this is a column-oriented data table, click in the Column input cell text box. Enter or point to the input cell.

The *input cell* is the initial value referred to in the formula for which the test values will be substituted. In our column-oriented example, the input cell is the initial interest rate (B4).

5. Click OK.

The cells beneath the formula are filled with the results of substituting the test values (**Figure 15.12**).

To create a two-variable data table:

1. Set up the worksheet (**Figure 15.13**).

   The two sets of test values (in this case, interest rates and loan term) are entered as follows:

   ▲ *Interest rates (C4:C12)* extend down a column directly below the cell that contains the formula *(C3)*.

   ▲ *Loan term values (D3:E3)* are entered in the same row as the formula, beginning one cell to the right.

2. Select the range of cells that covers the formula and the test values.

   In this example, the range is C3:E12.

3. Choose Data > Table.

   The Table dialog box appears.

4. Enter or point to the Row input cell and the Column input cell (**Figure 15.14**).

   In this example, the Row input cell is B5 and the Column input cell is B4. (These are the original cells referred to in the formula.)

5. Click OK to display the results (**Figure 15.15**).

✔ Tip

■ For assistance in creating these data table examples, refer to Excel Help. The same formula was used in both the one- and two-variable examples (found in cell D3 and C3, respectively):

   =PMT(B4/12,B5,-B6)

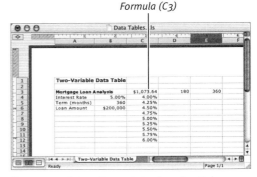

Formula (C3)

Figure 15.13 Set up the worksheet as directed.

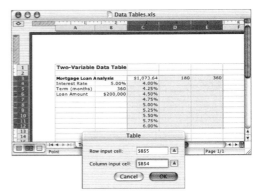

Figure 15.14 Select the test values and formula cell (C3:E12), choose Data > Table, and specify the row (B5) and column (B4) input cells in the Table dialog box.

Figure 15.15 The results are displayed (D4:E12).

WHAT-IF ANALYSES

Figure 15.16 Name the scenario, specify the cells into which new data will be substituted, and edit the comment text (if desired).

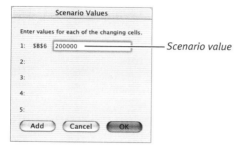

Figure 15.17 Specify value(s) to substitute in this scenario.

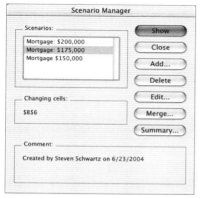

Figure 15.18 The Scenario Manager lists all defined scenarios.

To create scenarios:

1. Choose Tools > Scenarios.
   The Scenario Manager dialog box appears.

2. Click Add to create the first scenario.
   The Add Scenario dialog box appears (**Figure 15.16**).

3. Name the scenario. Click in the Changing cells text box and select the cell(s) that will change with this scenario. Edit the default comment, if you like. Click OK.
   The Scenario Values dialog box appears (**Figure 15.17**).

4. Specify the new values for the changing variables in the current scenario. Click Add to create another scenario.

5. Repeat Steps 3 and 4 until all scenarios have been defined. After defining the final scenario, click OK (rather than Add).
   The Scenario Manager dialog box appears (**Figure 15.18**). All defined scenarios are shown in the scrolling list box.

6. To dismiss the Scenario Manager, click the Close button.

WHAT-IF ANALYSES

To view scenarios:

1. If the Scenario Manager isn't open, choose Tools > Scenarios.

2. To view the results of any scenario, select its name in the Scenario Manager dialog box (see Figure 15.18) and click Show.

   Excel substitutes the scenario value(s) for the specified worksheet cell(s) and displays the results. Repeat as desired to view other scenarios.

3. To see a summary of *all* scenarios, click Summary.

   The Scenario Summary dialog box appears (**Figure 15.19**).

4. Click the Scenario summary or Scenario PivotTable radio button. Specify the *result cells* (the ones that will change as a result of the scenario data) to include in the report. Click OK.

   The chosen report appears in a new sheet in the current workbook (**Figure 15.20**).

✔ Tip

- After generating the report, you are free to edit it to make it more readable. For example, in the report in Figure 15.20, you could copy and paste the mortgage rates from column D of the original worksheet rather than show result cell addresses in column C.

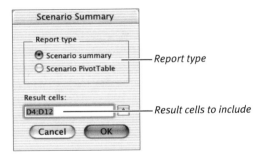

Figure 15.19 Request a summary report of all scenarios.

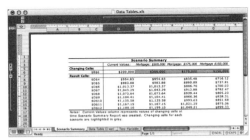

Figure 15.20 A summary report allows you to see all scenarios side by side.

WHAT-IF ANALYSES

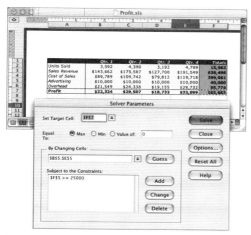

Figure 15.21 Enter the target cell and criteria in the Solver Parameters dialog box.

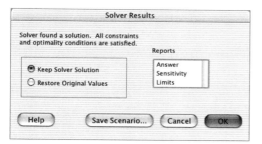

Figure 15.22 Select options for handling the Solver solution and click OK.

Using Solver

Using a tool called Solver, Excel can find the optimal value for a formula (in the *target cell*) by systematically varying the values in a group of cells (called the *changing cells*) that reference or are referenced by the target cell. Solver can maximize (find the largest value), minimize (find the smallest value), or solve for a specific value of the target cell.

In the following example, we want to maximize annual profit (F7) by varying advertising expenditures. However, total advertising costs must be at least $25,000.

To maximize, minimize, or equal a value:

1. Choose Tools > Solver.

The Solver Parameters dialog box appears (**Figure 15.21**).

2. Specify the target cell; indicate whether you want Solver to maximize, minimize, or arrive at a particular value; and enter any necessary constraints by clicking the Add button.

The target cell in our example is total Profit (F7), which we want to maximize. The cells which Solver can change in order to arrive at the desired value are the Advertising amounts (B5:E5), specified in the By Changing Cells box. The Subject to the Constraints list box shows that the total amount for Advertising (F5) must be greater than or equal to $25,000.

3. Click the Solve button.

Excel tries different values for the By changing cells until it finds a combination that meets the target criteria and constraints. It enters the new figures in the worksheet and displays the Solver Results dialog box (**Figure 15.22**).

continues on next page

4. *Do one of the following:*

▲ Select Keep Solver Solution to replace your worksheet data with the Solver solution.

▲ Select Restore Original Values to discard the Solver solution.

5. *Optional:* To view one or more of the reports generated by Solver, select them in the Reports box.

A separate sheet is used to display each selected report.

6. Click OK.

✔ Tip

■ If the Solver command isn't listed in the Tools menu (in Step 1), you'll have to install Solver from the Office 2004 CD.

SHARING
WORKBOOKS

Individuals in workgroups often need to share workbooks. Excel provides tools to distribute workbooks on the Web, intranet, or over an internal network; protect parts of workbooks that shouldn't be changed; and track and review the changes that have been made.

Publishing Excel Data on the Web

Excel makes it easy to save workbooks or worksheets for display on the Web. One advantage of publishing in this manner is that those who only need to view the contents don't need Excel to open the file. All they need is a browser. You can also *preview* any Excel file as it will look saved as a Web page.

To preview a file's Web appearance:

1. Open the workbook in Excel (**Figure 16.1**).

2. Choose File > Web Page Preview.

   The active worksheet opens in your Web browser as it would appear on the Web (**Figure 16.2**).

✔ Tips

■ To avoid surprises, it's a good idea to use Web Page Preview until you're satisfied with the file's appearance and formatting. *Then* save it as a Web page. (Note, however, that a Web page preview does *not* always produce identical results to saving the file as a Web page.)

■ Comment indicators are displayed in a Web preview as bracketed numbers. Click a comment indicator to go to the spot on the Web page where the comment is explained (see Figure 16.2).

■ Comments are handled differently when you use the Save as Web Page command (see the following page). When you pass the cursor over an embedded comment, a yellow box pops up that contains the comment text.

Figure 16.1 Create or open a workbook.

Comment

Comment explanation

Figure 16.2 When you choose Web Page Preview, a temporary HTML file is created and opens in your default browser.

Figure 16.3 Specify the filename, destination, and options.

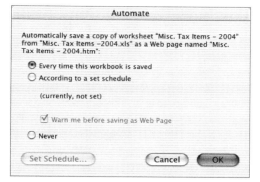

Figure 16.4 Indicate the condition under which a new HTML file will automatically be generated.

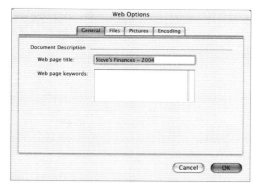

Figure 16.5 Click the Web Options button to enter a title for the generated Web page, as well as set other options.

To save a file as a Web page:

1. *Optional:* To save a specific worksheet or only a range of a worksheet as a Web page, select the worksheet and/or range.

2. Choose File > Save as Web Page.

A Save As panel appears (**Figure 16.3**). Web Page (HTML) file format is automatically selected and the Windows filename extension (.htm) is added.

3. Click a radio button to indicate whether you want to save the entire workbook, only the active worksheet, or only the currently selected cell range.

4. *Optional:* If this workbook, sheet, or range is updated regularly, you can instruct Excel to automatically create a new HTML file whenever you save the workbook or according to a particular schedule. Click the Automate button.

The Automate dialog box appears (**Figure 16.4**). Select one of the following:

▲ **Every time this workbook is saved.** Automatically generate a new HTML file when you save the workbook.

▲ **According to a set schedule.** Generate a new HTML file daily, weekly, or on some other schedule. Click the Set Schedule button to set the schedule.

▲ **Never.** Disable the automatic generation of new HTML files.

Click OK to close the Automate dialog box.

5. *Optional:* Click the Web Options button to set Web-specific settings, such as the page title and keywords that will be used by search engines (**Figure 16.5**). Review the information on the various tabs and click OK.

6. *Optional:* Click Compatibility Report to check for potential problems.

7. Click Save to create the Web (HTML) file.

Sharing Workbooks on a Network

When *sharing* has been enabled for an Excel workbook, up to 256 network users can simultaneously view and edit the workbook. (For information on storing files on your network so they can be accessed by others, contact your network administrator.)

To enable sharing for a workbook:

1. Choose Tools > Share Workbook.

   The Share Workbook dialog box appears (**Figure 16.6**).

2. On the Editing tab, click Allow changes by more than one user at the same time.

3. Click the Advanced tab to review or set options for managing changes by multiple users.

4. Click OK to dismiss the dialog box.

   A confirmation dialog box appears (**Figure 16.7**).

5. Click OK to save the workbook and enable sharing.

✔ Tip

■ To later disable sharing for a workbook, choose Tools > Share Workbook, remove the checkmark from Allow changes by more than one user at the same time, click OK to close the dialog box, and then click Yes in the confirmation dialog box that appears (**Figure 16.8**).

Enable sharing

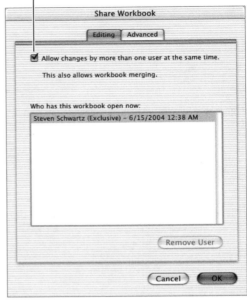

Figure 16.6 Enable sharing by clicking this check box.

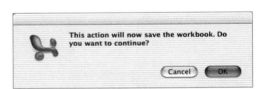

Figure 16.7 Confirm that you want to share the workbook by clicking OK.

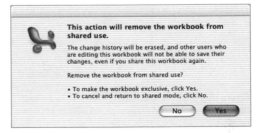

Figure 16.8 To disable sharing for the workbook, click the Yes button.

SHARING WORKBOOKS ON A NETWORK

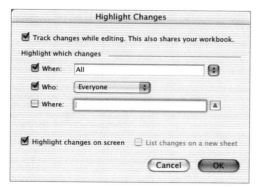

Figure 16.9 Specify criteria for tracking and displaying changes.

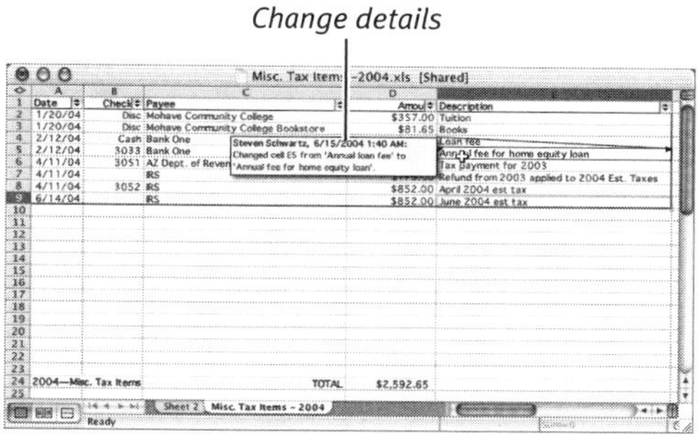

Change details

Figure 16.10 To view the details for a given change, move the cursor over the changed cell.

Tracking Changes

When sharing Excel workbooks, you can automatically track the changes made by the various users. In addition to marking each changed cell with an explanation of the change, you can review and then accept or reject each change.

To enable change tracking:

1. Choose Tools > Track Changes > Highlight Changes.

   The Highlight Changes dialog box appears (**Figure 16.9**).

2. Click the Track changes while editing check box.

   Doing so simultaneously enables change tracking and sharing of the workbook.

3. Set any of these tracking options, as appropriate:

   ▲ **When.** Specify which changes to track, based on a time period or a save.

   ▲ **Who.** Indicate whose changes to track.

   ▲ **Where.** If you're interested in only a particular cell range, click this check box and drag-select the range.

4. Modified cells will have a colored triangle in their upper-left corner. To view a change explanation, move the pointer over the cell (**Figure 16.10**).

To review changes:

1. Choose Tools > Track Changes > Accept or Reject Changes.

   The Select Changes to Accept or Reject dialog box appears (**Figure 16.11**).

2. Use the When, Who, and Where criteria to specify the changes you want to review. Click OK.

   The Accept or Reject Changes dialog box appears (**Figure 16.12**).

3. Excel displays each change, while simultaneously selecting the affected cell in the worksheet. For each proposed change, click Accept, Reject, Accept All, or Reject All.

   To end the review process immediately (even if there are still unreviewed changes), click Close.

✔ Tip

■ To indicate a cell range for the Where criterion (see Figure 16.11), you can drag-select the desired cells.

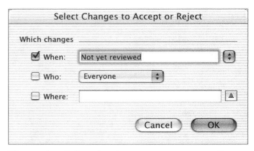

Figure 16.11 Select the changes you want to review.

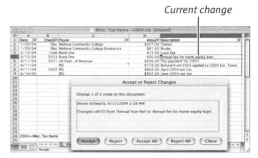

Figure 16.12 For each change, click a button to indicate how you want to handle it.

Figure 16.13 The Protect Sheet dialog box.

Figure 16.14 The Protect Workbook dialog box.

Figure 16.15 The Protect Shared Workbook dialog box.

Protecting Your Data

When working in a sharing environment or if you're afraid others might be able to view your data without permission, you can assign passwords to protect entire workbooks, individual worksheets, or specific cell ranges from changes.

To protect a workbook or worksheet:

1. If the workbook is currently open in shared mode, temporarily disable sharing by following the tip at the end of "Sharing Workbooks on a Network," earlier in this chapter.

2. *Do one of the following:*
   ▲ To protect the current sheet, choose Tools > Protection > Protect Sheet (**Figure 16.13**).
   ▲ To protect an entire workbook, choose Tools > Protection > Protect Workbook (**Figure 16.14**).
   ▲ To simultaneously protect a workbook and enable sharing, choose Tools > Protection > Protect and Share Workbook (**Figure 16.15**).

3. Click the check boxes of the elements you wish to protect.

4. *Optional:* To add password protection to the worksheet or workbook, enter a password in the text box.
   A password is an additional layer of protection. In addition to preventing the changes specified in Step 3, each user must supply the password whenever accessing the worksheet or workbook.

5. Click OK to dismiss the dialog box and enact the new protection settings.

6. If you assigned a password, you'll be prompted to re-enter it.

✔ Tips

- In general, the protected elements are those that are locked or hidden at the time that protection is enabled. For specific details, see "About protecting workbooks and worksheets from changes" in Excel Help.

- To remove protection, choose Tools > Protection, followed by Unprotect Sheet, Unprotect Workbook, or Unprotect Shared Workbook, as appropriate. If you assigned a password to the worksheet or workbook, you'll be prompted to supply it (**Figure 16.16**). Otherwise, unprotection will occur immediately.

- Unprotecting a shared workbook does *not* disable sharing. If you wish to do this, too, choose Tools > Share Workbook. In the Share Workbook dialog box (see Figure 16.6), remove the checkmark from Allow changes by more than one user at the same time, click OK to close the dialog box, and then click Yes in the confirmation dialog box that appears (see Figure 16.8).

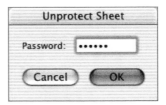

Figure 16.16 To unprotect a worksheet or workbook that has a password associated with it, you must supply the password.

Part IV: Microsoft PowerPoint

CREATING A PRESENTATION

PowerPoint provides you with all the tools necessary to create impressive onscreen, Web-based, and traditional slide presentations. You can choose from a variety of templates designed to help you create a presentation with a compelling visual message.

The first part of this chapter explains the essentials of creating a new presentation, working in different views, adding and deleting slides, and working with text and graphics. The second part shows how to use slide masters to add a background design, static images, and color to your presentation. You'll find that customizing presentations in PowerPoint is as straightforward as it has always been.

Starting a Presentation

As in Word and Excel, the Project Gallery serves as the starting point for a PowerPoint presentation. You can design a presentation completely from scratch, base it on a template, or use the AutoContent Wizard.

The AutoContent Wizard offers a variety of presentation outlines in which you can replace sample text with your own. Each outline generates a presentation with a particular look. You can change the look by choosing a different template.

To create a presentation from scratch or by using a template:

1. If the Project Gallery isn't already open, choose File > Project Gallery (Shift ⌘ P). Click the New tab.

2. *Do one of the following:*

   ▲ To create a presentation from scratch, click the PowerPoint Presentation thumbnail (**Figure 17.1**).

   ▲ To create a presentation from a template, expand the Presentations item in the Groups list. Pick the template from the Content or Designs group that best matches the type of presentation you want to create (**Figure 17.2**).

3. Click Open.

4. If you're creating a presentation based on a Content template, the presentation appears immediately.

   or

   If you're creating a blank presentation or one based on a Designs template, a new presentation opens, containing a single slide (**Figure 17.3**).

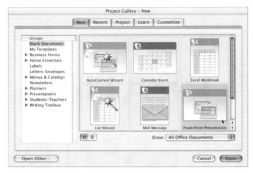

Figure 17.1 Click the PowerPoint Presentation thumbnail to create a presentation entirely from scratch.

Figure 17.2 To create a presentation from a template, select the Contents or Designs group and select a thumbnail from the ones displayed.

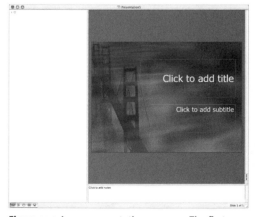

Figure 17.3 A new presentation appears. The first slide is automatically created for you.

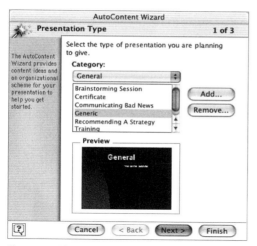

Figure 17.4 The AutoContent Wizard walks you through the process of generating the framework for a template-based presentation.

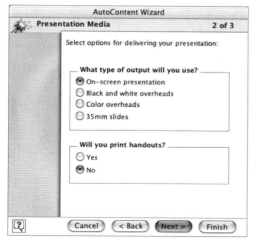

Figure 17.5 On the second screen of the AutoContent Wizard, select output options for the presentation.

✔ Tips

■ You can also start a blank presentation by choosing File > New Presentation (⌘Ⓝ).

■ The difference between Content and Designs templates is that the former group provides an entire set of suggested slides and topics.

To create a presentation using the AutoContent Wizard:

1. Open the Project Gallery window by choosing File > Project Gallery (Shift⌘Ⓟ).

2. In the Groups list, choose Blank Documents, click the AutoContent Wizard thumbnail, and then click Open.

   The AutoContent Wizard appears (**Figure 17.4**).

3. Choose a category from the drop-down menu, and then select a presentation type and format from the list presented. Click Next to continue.

4. Choose an output option for your presentation and indicate whether you will need to create handouts (**Figure 17.5**). Click Next to continue.

5. Enter the text for the title slide. You can also specify information to print in the footer of each slide. Click Finish.

   The structure of your chosen presentation appears.

✔ Tips

■ To return to a previous step, you can click the Back button in any Wizard dialog box.

■ You can click Finish at any time to skip the remaining steps and accept the default choices.

About Views

Changing views is like getting a different perspective on your presentation. You can change your view to focus on specific elements of your work. For instance, if you need to rearrange slides, you can use the Slide Sorter view. Each view shows a different aspect of the presentation. You can switch views at any time.

◆ *Normal view* (see Figure 17.3) displays the text, slide, and notes, enabling you to work on all parts of your presentation in one window.

◆ *Outline view* (**Figure 17.6**) focuses on the text of the presentation in outline form.

◆ *Slide view* (**Figure 17.7**) displays one slide at a time so you can concentrate on modifying the text and graphics of each slide.

Figure 17.6 Outline view.

Figure 17.7 Slide view.

Figure 17.8 Slide Sorter view.

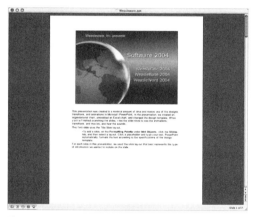

Figure 17.9 Notes Page view.

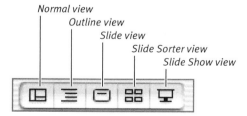

Figure 17.10 To change views, click one of these icons in the bottom-left corner of the presentation window.

◆ *Slide Sorter view* (**Figure 17.8**) displays miniatures (or thumbnails) of all slides. You can reorganize them by clicking and dragging or go directly to any slide by double-clicking it. You can also add and edit the transition effects within and between slides.

◆ *Notes Page view* (**Figure 17.9**) lets you enter and edit the speaker's notes that accompany the slides.

◆ *Slide Show view* displays the presentation as an onscreen slide show.

To change views:

◆ Click an icon in the lower-left corner of the presentation window (**Figure 17.10**) or choose a view from the View menu.

✔ Tip

■ Outline view is only accessible from the icons, while Notes Page view is only provided as a View menu command. You can access any other view in either manner.

About Views

Adding and Deleting Slides

Designing presentations is seldom a linear process. Along the way, you'll have many occasions where you will need to add or delete slides. You can do so in any view other than Slide Show. The following steps explain how to accomplish this in Outline view.

To add a slide:

1. A new slide is always inserted after the currently active slide. In the outline, click anywhere in a slide's title or text to make it the current slide.

   A thumbnail of the selected slide appears in the right side of the presentation window.

2. Click the New Slide icon on the Standard toolbar (**Figure 17.11**), choose Insert > New Slide, or press Control M.

3. Depending on the Preferences setting for New slide dialog (**Figure 17.12**), one of two things will happen:

   ▲ A new slide of the same type as the current slide will be created.

   ▲ The New Slide dialog box will appear (**Figure 17.13**). Select a layout for the new slide and click OK.

   The insertion point is automatically positioned in the outline so you can enter a title for the new slide.

✔ Tip

■ You can also add a new slide by expanding the Add Objects section of the Formatting Palette, clicking the Slides tab, and clicking the desired slide layout.

Figure 17.11 You can add a slide to the presentation by clicking this icon on the Standard toolbar.

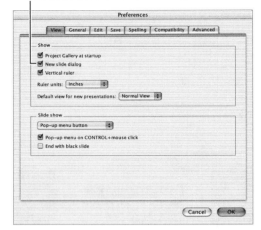

Figure 17.12 Set this preference to determine whether the New Slide dialog box will appear.

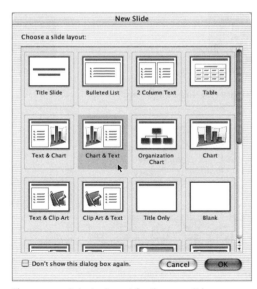

Figure 17.13 Select a layout for the new slide.

Click this icon

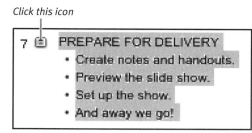

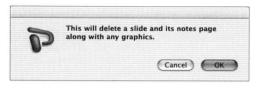

Figure 17.14 To select a slide in Outline view, click its slide icon.

![dialog]
This will delete a slide and its notes page along with any graphics.

Cancel | OK

Figure 17.15 To confirm the deletion, click OK.

To delete a slide:

1. Click the slide icon to the right of the slide number.

   This selects all outline text for the slide (**Figure 17.14**).

2. *Do one of the following:*

   ▲ Choose Edit > Delete Slide. The active slide is immediately deleted.

   ▲ Press (Delete). A warning dialog box appears (**Figure 17.15**). Click OK to confirm the deletion.

✔ Tips

■ When using the Edit > Delete Slide command, it's sufficient to place the insertion point in any part of the slide's outline text.

■ To recover a slide you mistakenly deleted, choose Edit > Undo Delete Slide, choose Edit > Undo Clear, or press ⌘Z.

ADDING AND DELETING SLIDES

Adding Text to Slides

Many slides have specific areas where you can enter a title or other text.

To create a text slide:

1. Choose Insert > New Slide or click the New Slide icon on the Standard toolbar (see Figure 17.11).

2. In the New Slide dialog box (see Figure 17.13), select a slide style that contains text and then click OK.

   The new slide appears (**Figure 17.16**).

3. Click the "Click to add title" or "Click to add text" placeholder and type the text.

4. Click the next placeholder and continue typing text (**Figure 17.17**).

✔ Tips

- If the New Slide dialog box doesn't appear, see the previous section for help.

- When you finish typing text in a placeholder, you can press (Option)(Return) to jump to the next placeholder.

- When you finish typing the text in the bottommost placeholder on a slide, you can press (Option)(Return) to automatically create another slide of the same type.

- To format text, set paragraph alignment, or create additional bullet or numbered lists, you can choose commands from the Format menu, the Formatting toolbar, or the Formatting Palette.

Bullet-point list placeholder   *Title text placeholder*

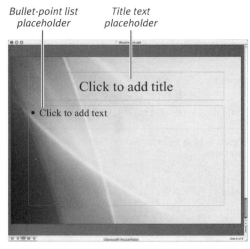

Figure 17.16 The new slide appears, ready for you to enter text into the placeholders.

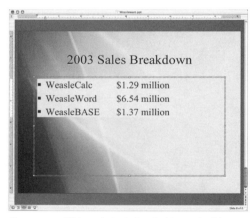

Figure 17.17 Click each text placeholder and add your text.

(side margin) ADDING TEXT TO SLIDES

Frame   *Handle*

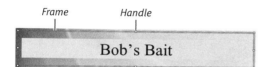

Bob's Bait

Figure 17.18 When a text block is selected, a frame and handles appear around it.

Working with Text Blocks

You can select characters, words, or paragraphs within a text block the same way you do in a Word document (see "Working with Text" in Chapter 1). However, PowerPoint differs a bit in the manner in which you move and format text blocks.

To select a text block:

◆ Click anywhere in the text block. The selected text block is surrounded by a border and handles (**Figure 17.18**), enabling you to move and resize it as necessary.

To move or resize a text block:

◆ To move a selected text block, move the cursor over the border until it changes to an open hand, and then drag the block to a new position on the slide.

◆ To resize a selected text block, click any handle and drag.

✔ Tips

■ To resize a text block proportionately, hold down (Shift) as you drag a corner handle.

■ To resize a text block from its center, hold down (Option) as you drag a corner handle. (If the block was originally centered on the slide, this procedure will keep it centered.)

■ Once a text block is selected, you can select text within it using normal editing procedures.

■ Text inside a resized text block automatically rewraps to fit the new size of the block.

Adding Images to Slides

You can embellish slides by adding images from any of the following sources:

◆ Clip Gallery (Microsoft-supplied clip art)

◆ Other image files stored on disk

◆ Image files from a digital camera or memory card reader

◆ Images scanned directly into Office 2004

◆ Images created with the Office drawing tools

Inserting image files from disk

As explained above, you can insert most types of image files into PowerPoint slides. Many will already be stored on disk.

To add clip art to a slide:

1. Create a new slide, choosing Text & Clip Art or Clip Art & Text as the format.

   The new slide appears (**Figure 17.19**).

2. Double-click the clip art placeholder.

   The Clip Gallery: PowerPoint window appears (**Figure 17.20**).

3. Select a category from the list on the left or perform a search by entering a keyword in the Search text box.

   Relevant clip art appears in the panel on the right.

4. Select an image and click Insert.

   The picture is inserted into the placeholder.

Text placeholder   *Clip art placeholder*

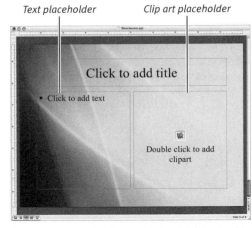

Figure 17.19 This slide layout is intended for a combination of text and clip art.

Figure 17.20 Select a clip art image from the Clip Gallery.

ADDING IMAGES TO SLIDES

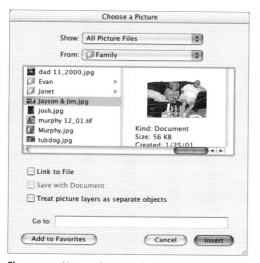

Figure 17.21 You can insert an image from disk by selecting it in the Choose a Picture dialog box.

Picture toolbar

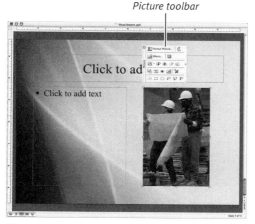

Figure 17.22 Display the Picture toolbar to assist you with image editing.

✔ Tips

■ Even if you haven't created a slide with a placeholder for clip art, you can manually insert clip art into *any* slide by choosing Insert > Picture > Clip Art.

■ To insert a *different* type of image (such as a photo), follow the same procedure but create a new slide that contains a picture placeholder. When you double-click the placeholder, the Choose a Picture dialog box appears (**Figure 17.21**), allowing you to select a picture from your hard disk.

■ If you want to edit a picture, you can use commands in the Formatting Palette, the Format menu, or the Picture toolbar. To display the toolbar (**Figure 17.22**), choose View > Toolbars > Picture.

■ Click the Format Picture icon on the Picture toolbar to open the Format Picture dialog box and access more tools that you can use to control the look and location of clip art and other images.

■ You can insert any type of graphic by clicking an icon (Insert Clip Art, Insert Image from File, Insert Picture from Scanner or Camera, or Insert Movie) in the Graphics section of the Formatting Palette.

ADDING IMAGES TO SLIDES

Inserting an image from a digital camera or scanner

There are several ways to insert images from a scanner, digital camera, or memory card reader into a PowerPoint slide. Depending on your particular device and its capabilities, one or more of the following options should be available to you.

To insert an image from a digital camera, card reader, or scanner:

◆ *Do one of the following:*

▲ Choose Insert > Picture > From Scanner or Camera. In the Insert Picture from Scanner or Camera dialog box, choose your connected scanner, camera, or memory card reader from the Device pop-up menu, and then click Acquire. Your device's software will run, enabling you to scan the image or download the photo(s).

▲ Certain devices, such as memory card readers, may mount on the Desktop, acting exactly like a removable drive. To import pictures from the device, double-click the picture placeholder on the slide. In the Choose a Picture dialog box (**Figure 17.23**), navigate to the device, select the picture to import, and click Insert.

▲ Perform a scan using your scanner software (or a compatible image-editing program) and save the scanned image to disk. Then insert the image into a slide by double-clicking a picture placeholder or by choosing Insert > Picture > From File.

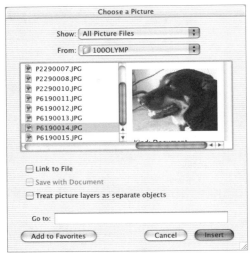

Figure 17.23 Select a photo and click Insert to insert it into the picture placeholder.

ADDING IMAGES TO SLIDES

Device name *Download location*

Figure 17.24 If Image Capture recognizes the connected device, this dialog box is displayed.

Figure 17.25 Select the photos to download and click the Download button.

Click for column view

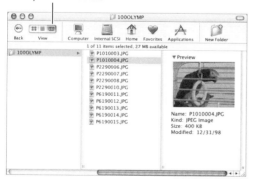

Figure 17.26 If a device appears on the Desktop, you can open it like any other disk in order to find the picture you want to import.

▲ Run Apple's Image Capture utility (found in the Applications folder). Assuming that it finds your connected device (**Figure 17.24**), select a download location from the Download To drop-down list, set Automatic Task to None, and click Download Some. The window expands to show thumbnails of all images found on the device (**Figure 17.25**). Select the desired images by clicking or ⌘-clicking their thumbnails and then click Download.

After downloading, you can insert any of these images into a slide by double-clicking a picture placeholder or by choosing Insert > Picture > From File.

✔ Tips

- You can also insert a stored picture from a Desktop-mounted device by choosing Insert > Picture > From File.

- Here's another trick for a Desktop-mounted device. Since it *does* act like a removable drive, treat it like one. Open the device by double-clicking its icon. Switch to column view and continue opening items until you see the image files (**Figure 17.26**). Then either drag them onto your hard disk (to save them) or drag one directly into a slide's picture placeholder.

- You can drag *any* compatible image that's stored on disk directly into a slide's picture placeholder.

- Don't import or drag *multiple* pictures into the same placeholder. Rather than replacing the previous image, this places the new image on top of the old one! Delete the original image first.

ADDING IMAGES TO SLIDES

Drawing objects

If you can't find images that you like or if you want to design your own artwork, you can use the drawing tools to create objects for your slides.

To draw an object:

1. If the Drawing toolbar isn't visible, display it by choosing View > Toolbars > Drawing (**Figure 17.27**).

2. Switch to a view that clearly displays the slide and select a drawing tool.

3. Click and drag to create the object (**Figure 17.28**). The outline appears as you drag.

   Depending on the tool selected, you can draw basic shapes (such as rectangles, lines, and ovals) or special shapes (such as smiley faces, banners, flowchart objects, and 3D shapes).

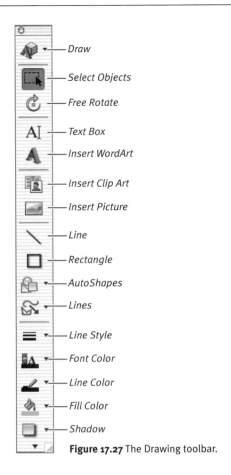

— Draw

— Select Objects

— Free Rotate

— Text Box

— Insert WordArt

— Insert Clip Art

— Insert Picture

— Line

— Rectangle

— AutoShapes

— Lines

— Line Style

— Font Color

— Line Color

— Fill Color

— Shadow

Figure 17.27 The Drawing toolbar.

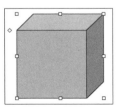

Figure 17.28 Click and drag to create the object.

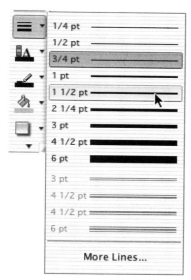

Figure 17.29 You can select a line style, line color, fill color, or shadow from pop-up palettes on the Drawing toolbar.

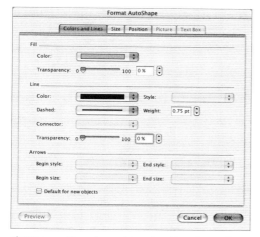

Figure 17.30 If you have elaborate object-formatting needs, you may want to use the Format AutoShape dialog box.

4. To format the drawn object, select it and do one of the following:

▲ Select formatting options from the Line Style, Line Color, Fill Color, and Shadow pop-up palettes on the Drawing toolbar (**Figure 17.29**).

▲ You can also set formatting options in the Format AutoShape dialog box (**Figure 17.30**). To open the dialog box, choose Format > AutoShape or double-click the object.

✔ Tips

■ AutoShapes, lines, and WordArt objects can also be selected from the Add Objects section of the Formatting Palette. Many common formatting commands can also be found on the Formatting Palette.

■ To add text to a drawn object, select the Text Box tool, click inside the object, and type. (Some objects, such as the Callouts in the AutoShapes menu, are automatically enclosed in a text box.)

■ To group shapes, hold down Shift as you click each object for the group, click the Draw button on the Drawing toolbar, and choose Group from the drop-down menu.

■ To change the layering for a selected object, click the Draw tool's drop-down menu. Choose Arrange > Send to Back or another layering command.

ADDING IMAGES TO SLIDES

Slide Backgrounds and Themes

By judiciously choosing graphics and colors for your slide background, you can create a presentation with a consistent theme.

Creating a common graphic background

An image placed on a slide master will appear in the background of every slide in the presentation. You can choose graphics from the art collections included with Office or use your own images.

To add graphics to the background:

1. Choose View > Master > Slide Master or press (Shift) as you click the Slide View icon at the bottom of the document window.

   The Slide Master window appears (**Figure 17.31**).

2. *Do one of the following:*

   ▲ To use your own image, choose Insert > Picture > From File. The Choose a Picture dialog box appears (see Figure 17.21). Select a picture file and click Insert. As necessary, modify, resize, or move the image.

   ▲ Choose Format > Slide Design. Select a new slide design from the ones listed (**Figure 17.32**).

   You can also select a new design in the Formatting Palette. Expand the Change Slides section, click the Slide Design tab, and click a design thumbnail (**Figure 17.33**).

3. Click a View icon (or choose a command from the View menu) to leave Slide Master view and see the effect of your changes.

Figure 17.31 Graphics and text added to the slide master appear on every slide in the presentation.

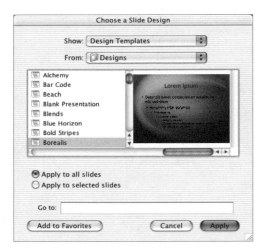

Figure 17.32 You can select a new slide design from the ones provided with PowerPoint.

SLIDE BACKGROUNDS AND THEMES

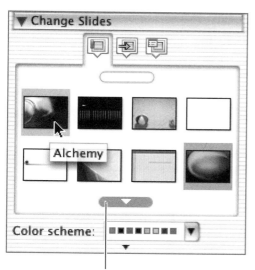

Scroll through designs

Figure 17.33 You can also select a new slide design from the Formatting Palette.

✔ Tips

- You can copy and paste a graphic image from another program onto the slide master, or copy and paste graphics from the slide master of another presentation onto the slide master of the current one.

- Any graphics that are already on the slide master as part of the template background must be ungrouped before you can modify them.

- You aren't restricted to adding only a single image or one that fills the entire slide. You might add your corporate logo to the slide master and set its transparency level high, enabling it to blend into the existing background, for example.

SLIDE BACKGROUNDS AND THEMES

Applying a background color and fill effects

You can add color to the background of your presentation to make it more appealing or compelling. Partner the color with a fill (such as a gradient) to create depth and a polished, professional look. (Background color and fill effects can vary from slide to slide or can be applied to all the slides in the presentation.)

To change the background color or fill effects:

1. If you intend to apply a background color or fill effect to only a specific slide in the presentation, display or select that slide.

    When you're applying the color or fill effect to all slides in the presentation, the specific slide displayed doesn't matter.

2. Choose Format > Slide Background. The Background dialog box appears.

3. *Do one of the following:*

    ▲ Choose a color from the ones shown in the drop-down menu (**Figure 17.34**)

    ▲ Choose More Colors to select a color using a color picker (**Figure 17.35**).

    ▲ Choose Fill Effects. Select the desired features from the Fill Effects dialog box (**Figure 17.36**). Click OK when you're done.

    If you selected a color, some fill effects will be applied to that color.

4. *Optional:* To preview the chosen color and effects in the current slide, click the Preview button.

5. *Do one of the following:*

    ▲ To apply the color and effects to only the displayed slide, click Apply.

    ▲ To apply them to all slides in the presentation, click Apply to All.

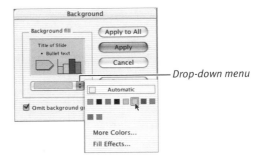

Figure 17.34 You can set a solid fill color or a fill effect using this drop-down menu.

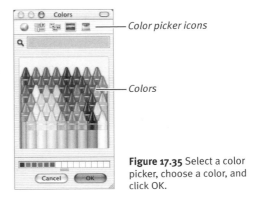

Figure 17.35 Select a color picker, choose a color, and click OK.

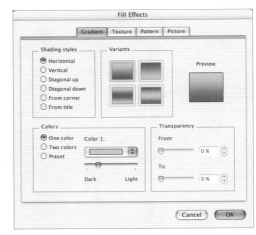

Figure 17.36 Select fill effect settings, such as a gradient, texture, or pattern fill.

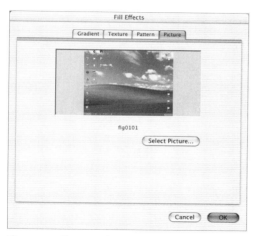

Figure 17.37 To use a photo or other image as a background, click the Picture tab, and click Select Picture.

Figure 17.38 A traditional Windows XP desktop makes an unusual presentation background.

✔ Tips

■ Another way to apply a background color and fill effects to all slides in a presentation is to add them to the slide master.

■ Using the Background dialog box, you can also insert an image as a background. Choose Fill Effects from the drop down-menu, click the Picture tab, and click the Select Picture button (**Figure 17.37**). In the Choose a Picture dialog box, select an image and click Insert. Click OK (**Figure 17.38**).

SLIDE BACKGROUNDS AND THEMES

Changing the color scheme

You can also add consistency to a presentation by selecting a color scheme for it. The eight colors of the color scheme are applied to all the elements on the current slide or all slides in the presentation—unless you change the color of a specific element. You can pick from the predefined color schemes or create your own.

To set a color scheme:

1. If you intend to apply the color scheme to only a specific slide in the presentation, display or select that slide.

   When you're applying the color scheme to all the slides in the presentation, the specific slide displayed doesn't matter.

2. Choose Format > Slide Color Scheme. The Color Scheme dialog box appears.

3. *Do one of the following:*
   - ▲ Select a predefined color scheme from the Standard tab (**Figure 17.39**).
   - ▲ To customize the current color scheme, click the Custom tab (**Figure 17.40**). Specify new colors by selecting an element's color box and then clicking the Change Color button.

4. *Optional:* To preview the chosen color scheme on the current slide, click the Preview button.

5. *Do one of the following:*
   - ▲ To apply the color scheme to only the displayed slide, click Apply.
   - ▲ To apply it to all slides in the presentation, click Apply to All.

✔ Tip

- ■ The color scheme is stored in a template, so if you switch templates, you'll switch color schemes, too.

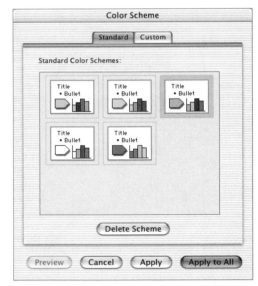

Figure 17.39 You can select a predefined color scheme from the Standard tab of the dialog box.

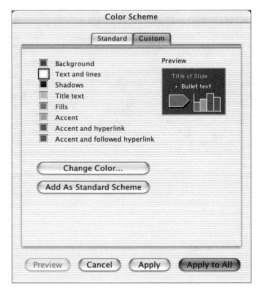

Figure 17.40 To customize the current color scheme, specify colors for the eight types of effects shown on the Custom tab of the Color Scheme dialog box.

Choose Design Template as the format

Figure 17.41 You can save the current presentation as a reusable Design Template.

Saving and Reusing a Custom Design

After spending hours modifying a PowerPoint template or creating a presentation from scratch, you can optionally save its design elements as a custom template that you can use as the basis for future presentations.

To save a presentation as a template:

1. Choose File > Save As.

   The Save As panel appears.

2. Choose Design Template from the Format drop-down menu (**Figure 17.41**).

3. Name the template and click Save.

   By default, the template is stored in the My Templates folder, making it available to you as a choice in the Project Gallery window.

Saving Presentations

Don't forget to save a presentation you're working on, especially if you need to use it again or share it with others. PowerPoint allows you to save presentations in a variety of formats that can be used in different ways. For example, you can save a presentation in HTML format for viewing on the Web in any browser, save it as a slide show, or save it as a QuickTime movie. **Table 17.1** lists some of the supported save formats.

To save a presentation:

1. Choose File > Save, press ⌘⑤, or click the Save icon on the Standard toolbar.

2. If you've previously saved the presentation, the new version overwrites the old one and you can continue working.

   or

   If this is the first time you've saved the presentation, the Save As panel appears (see Figure 17.41). Enter a name for the presentation, choose the format in which you'd like to save it, select a location on disk, and click the Save button.

✔ Tips

- If you want to save a previously saved presentation with a new name, in a different format, or in another location on disk, use the File > Save As command rather than File > Save.

- Another way to save a presentation as a Web page is to choose File > Save as Web Page.

- See Chapter 19 for an in-depth discussion of other Save options.

Table 17.1

PowerPoint File Formats	
FILENAME EXTENSION	FORMAT
.ppt	PowerPoint presentation
.pps	PowerPoint slide show
[no extension]	PowerPoint package
.pot	Design template
.mov	PowerPoint movie (QuickTime)
.htm	Web page
.rtf	Outline (Rich Text Format)

18

CHARTS AND TABLES

A chart or graph can make complex numerical information easier to interpret by expressing it visually. To create or edit a chart, PowerPoint uses Graph, the same charting program used by Excel. When creating a new chart or editing an existing one, you temporarily leave PowerPoint and work directly in Graph.

The following instructions will help you add and modify charts and graphs for use in a presentation. Note that the terms *chart* and *graph* are used interchangeably throughout the chapter. It's also important to note that all editing of the chart type and its elements are done within Graph, *not* PowerPoint.

Creating a New Chart

You can use either of the following procedures to add a chart to a slide.

To add a chart to a chart layout:

1. Click the New Slide icon on the Standard toolbar, choose Insert > New Slide, or press (Control)(M).

   The New Slide dialog box appears (**Figure 18.1**).

2. Select a layout that includes a chart placeholder: Chart, Text & Chart, or Chart & Text.

3. Click OK.

   The chart slide appears (**Figure 18.2**).

4. To add a chart to the new slide, double-click where you see the "Double click to add chart" text.

   Graph launches. A sample chart and datasheet appear (**Figure 18.3**).

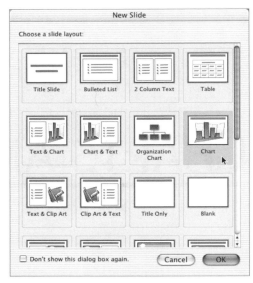

Figure 18.1 In the New Slide dialog box, choose a layout that includes a chart placeholder.

Double-click in this area

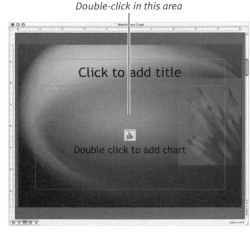

Figure 18.2 To launch Graph, double-click the chart placeholder on the slide.

CREATING A NEW CHART

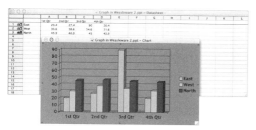

Figure 18.3 A sample chart and datasheet appear in Graph.

Figure 18.4 Click the Insert Chart icon on the Standard toolbar.

Figure 18.5 You can click the Graph or PowerPoint icon in the OS X Dock to switch to that program.

To add a chart to a non-chart layout:

1. Select the slide to which you'd like to add the chart.

   The particular layout of the current slide is unimportant; layout elements are merely guidelines you can use or ignore as you see fit.

2. Choose Insert > Chart or click the Insert Chart icon on the Standard toolbar (**Figure 18.4**).

   Graph launches. A sample chart and datasheet appear (see Figure 18.3).

✔ Tips

- You can add a chart from any *view* (see "About Views" in Chapter 17).

- While working on a chart, Graph adds its icon to the Dock (**Figure 18.5**). To switch between PowerPoint and Graph, click the appropriate Dock icon.

Entering Chart Data

Now that you have a chart started, you can replace the sample data in the Graph datasheet with your own data (**Figure 18.6**).

To enter your data:

1. Click any cell in the Excel-like datasheet, and then replace its contents. As you make new entries, the chart automatically changes to reflect the new data.

   or

   Drag from the top left to the bottom right to select the range of cells that will contain your data (**Figure 18.7**). Complete each cell entry by pressing [Return] or [Tab]. The former will move the cursor down the columns in the selected range, while the latter will move the cursor across the rows in the range. When the cursor reaches the bottom of a column or the end of a row, it will jump to the top of the next column or the beginning of the next row, respectively.

2. To send the datasheet to the background and view the graph, click the View Datasheet icon on the Standard toolbar (**Figure 18.8**) or click any visible part of the graph.

✔ Tips

■ Rather than typing your data, you may want to import existing data into the datasheet using the File > Import File command. Graph understands a variety of common data formats, such as Excel worksheets and tab-delimited text files.

■ To exclude a row or column of data from the graph (effectively hiding that row or column), double-click the row or column heading. Double-click the heading again to include the row or column data in the graph.

Selected cell

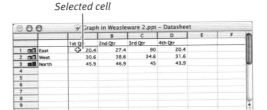

Figure 18.6 On the datasheet, you'll replace the sample data, column headers, and row headers with your own data. Click any cell and begin typing.

Active cell   *Selected cell range*

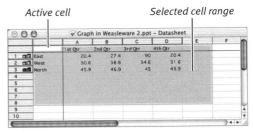

Figure 18.7 To enter data by rows or columns, begin by selecting all the cells necessary to contain the data.

View Datasheet

Figure 18.8 Click the View Datasheet toolbar icon to switch between the graph and datasheet.

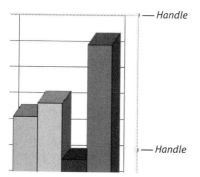

Figure 18.10 Handles appear when a chart is selected.

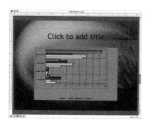

Figure 18.11 Click the Chart Type toolbar icon and select a chart type.

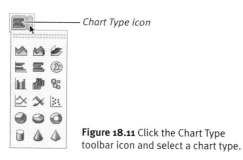

Figure 18.12 The new chart type replaces the old one on the slide.

Setting the Chart Type

After creating a chart in Graph, you're free to change its type or modify its appearance by choosing commands and options from the Standard toolbar (**Figure 18.9,** page bottom).

To change a chart's type:

1. In Graph, switch to the datasheet window or select the chart (handles appear around it, as shown in **Figure 18.10**).

2. Click the down arrow beside the Chart Type icon on the Standard toolbar and select another chart style (**Figure 18.11**). The revised chart appears in the Graph window and on the PowerPoint slide (**Figure 18.12**).

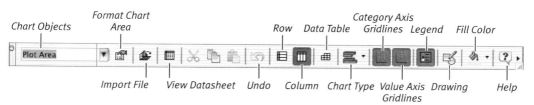

Figure 18.9 You can format a chart in Graph using the commands on the Standard toolbar.

✔ Tips

- Choose Chart > Chart Type to select from additional chart styles in the Chart Type dialog box (**Figure 18.13**).

- Be sure to check out the additional chart styles on the Custom Types tab of the Chart Type dialog box. Many of them are truly stunning.

- If you want to experiment with several chart styles, you can turn the Chart Type drop-down list in Step 2 into a floating palette. Open the Chart Type list and click the double line at its top. You can then drag the palette to any point on the screen. When you're ready to dismiss the palette, click its close button.

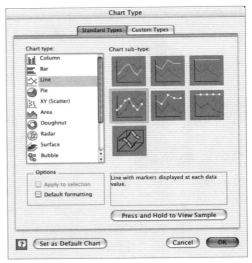

Figure 18.13 The Chart Type dialog box presents many additional chart types that are not available from the Standard toolbar's Chart Type palette.

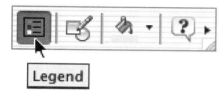

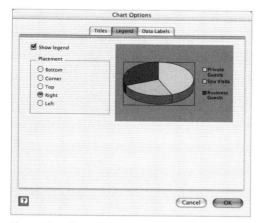

Figure 18.14 You can show or hide the legend by clicking the Legend toolbar icon.

Figure 18.15 You can also show or hide the legend, as well as specify its placement, on the Legend tab of the Chart Options dialog box.

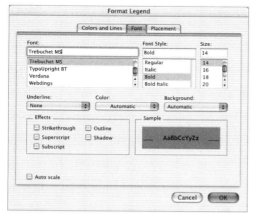

Figure 18.16 Use the Format Legend dialog box to specify formatting options for the legend.

Chart Appearance Options

Graph allows you to easily embellish charts and make them easier to interpret by adding a legend, gridlines, and data point labels.

Legends

A *legend* graphically explains the meaning of the various data series on a chart or graph.

To show or hide the legend:

◆ Switch to Graph and click the Legend icon on the Standard toolbar (**Figure 18.14**).

The Legend icon works as a toggle, hiding or displaying the chart's legend with each click. When the legend is visible, the icon is dark.

✔ Tips

■ You can also add a legend and specify its position by choosing Chart > Chart Options. In the Chart Options dialog box, switch to the Legend tab (**Figure 18.15**), select a legend position, and click OK.

■ As is the case with other objects in Office, after selecting the legend you can modify it in many ways:

   ▲ To move the legend, click in its center and then drag it to a new position.

   ▲ To change the legend size, drag any handle.

   ▲ To change the legend text, edit it in the datasheet.

   ▲ To change the font, size, or style of the legend text, you can either double-click the legend, choose Format > Selected Legend, or Control-click the legend and choose Format Legend from the pop-up menu. In the Format Legend dialog box, select options from the Font tab (**Figure 18.16**) and click OK.

Gridlines

You can elect to display or hide gridlines on any chart. Gridlines can help viewers interpret the data, since they make it easier to see the approximate size or value of each data point. You can add gridlines to any chart other than pie and doughnut charts.

To use a gridline:

◆ Switch to Graph. Click the Category Axis Gridlines (vertical) and/or the Value Axis Gridlines (horizontal) icon on the Standard toolbar (**Figure 18.17**).

The Gridlines icons work as toggles, hiding or displaying the gridlines with each click. When a gridline option is enabled, its icon is dark.

✔ Tips

■ You can also add gridlines by choosing Chart > Chart Options. On the Gridlines tab of the Chart Options dialog box (**Figure 18.18**), you can specify Major Gridlines or Minor Gridlines for each axis.

■ To format a set of gridlines (changing their style, color, or weight), select a Category Axis or Value Axis gridline on the chart. Double-click the gridline (or choose Format > Selected Gridlines) and then set options in the Format Gridlines dialog box that appears (**Figure 18.19**).

Category Axis Gridlines

Value Axis Gridlines

Figure 18.17 Click the Category Axis Gridlines or the Value Axis Gridlines toolbar icon to activate or deactivate a gridline class. When a class is active, its icon is dark.

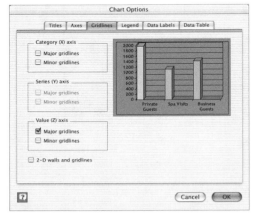

Figure 18.18 You can specify Major and Minor gridlines for each axis on the Gridlines tab of the Chart Options dialog box.

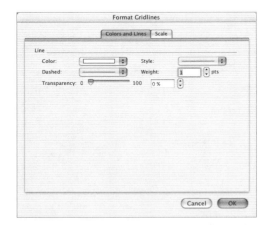

Figure 18.19 You can accept the default gridline style or specify custom formatting in the Format Gridlines dialog box.

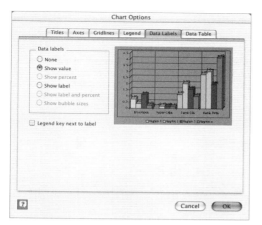

Figure 18.20 Select a data label format and click OK.

Formatting Data Labels

You can format the data labels (changing the font, number format, or alignment) for each data series. Open the Format Data Labels dialog box by double-clicking a data label, selecting a data label and choosing Format > Selected Data Labels, or (Control)-clicking a data label and choosing Format Data Labels. Make the desired formatting changes and click OK. Repeat the process for each data series.

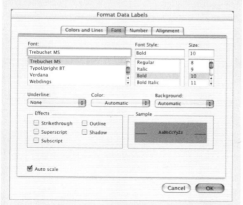

You can adjust the placement, number format, or font used for data labels.

Data point labels

You can label the data values in your chart to highlight the differences between them or to make it simpler for readers to interpret the chart.

To add a label for every data point:

1. Choose Chart > Chart Options.

2. In the Chart Options dialog box, click the Data Labels tab, select the desired labeling option (**Figure 18.20**), and click OK. The chart is redrawn with data labels.

To add labels for a single data series:

1. In Graph, select a data series on the chart. (In a bar or column chart, for example, you can click any colored bar to select all members of that data series.)

2. Choose Format > Selected Data Series. The Format Data Series dialog box appears.

3. On the Labels tab (see Figure 18.20), select a label option and click OK. The chart is redrawn as specified.

✔ Tips

■ You can also specify a label for a single data point, enabling you to label only the highest and lowest values on a chart, for example. Click to select a single data value on the chart and then choose Format > Selected Data Point.

■ To remove all data labels from a chart, choose None on the Data Labels tab of the Chart Options dialog box (see Figure 18.20). To remove data labels from only a selected series, choose None on the Data Labels tab of the Format Data Series dialog box.

CHART APPEARANCE OPTIONS

Specifying the Data Arrangement

You can arrange the data in your datasheet by rows or by columns. To indicate whether each row or each column is a data series, do one of the following:

◆ Click the Row or Column icon on the Standard toolbar (**Figure 18.21**).

◆ Choose Data > Series in Rows or Data > Series in Columns (**Figure 18.22**). The checked command represents the current choice.

Row

Column

Figure 18.21 Click the Row or Column toolbar icon to indicate the arrangement of your data series in the datasheet.

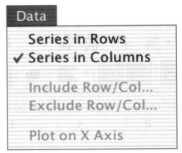

Figure 18.22 You can also specify the arrangement of your data by choosing Data > Series in Rows or Data > Series in Columns.

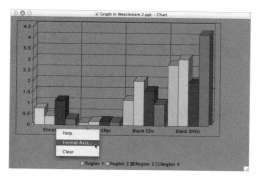

Figure 18.23 To set formatting for a particular chart element, (Control)-click it and choose the Format command from the pop-up menu that appears.

Formatting a Chart Element

You can modify the appearance of any chart element, such as a single set of bars, a line, or an axis. You can also change the style of any data series in the chart by formatting the series.

To format a chart element:

1. In Graph, click the chart to make it active, if necessary.

2. Click to select the chart element that you want to format and then double-click it.

   The appropriate dialog box for the chosen element appears, such as Format Chart Area (with the entire chart selected), Format Axis, Format Data Labels, Format Data Series, or Format Legend.

3. Choose formatting options and click OK.

✔ Tips

- To avoid opening the *wrong* dialog box, (Control)-click an element and choose the command from the pop-up menu that appears (**Figure 18.23**). Alternatively, you can simply select a chart element and then choose the relevant command from the Format menu.

- One of the quickest ways to select a chart element is to choose its name from the Chart Objects drop-down menu on the Standard toolbar (see Figure 18.9).

Special Graph Options

There are many other chart types and procedures available to Graph users. Here are a few of the most interesting, useful ones.

Exploding a pie chart

If you've created a pie chart in Graph, you can *explode* the chart (pull all the pieces out from the center to make it more visually interesting) or pull out an individual piece (to emphasize a particular data value).

To explode or cut a pie chart:

1. In Graph, click the chart to make it active, if necessary.

2. *Do one of the following:*

▲ To explode the pie chart, click once to select the entire pie (**Figure 18.24**) and then drag outward (**Figure 18.25**).

▲ To pull a selected slice away from the pie, click once to select the entire pie, and then click a second time to select only the slice you want to cut. Drag the selected slice outward (**Figure 18.26**).

✔ Tip

■ To rejoin a cut slice with the pie, drag the slice back to the center of the pie. To rejoin an exploded pie, drag *any* slice back to the center of the pie.

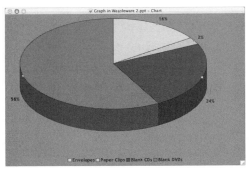

Figure 18.24 Click the pie chart to select it. Handles appear around the edges of the pie.

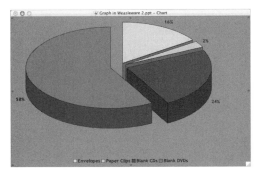

Figure 18.25 Drag outward to explode the entire pie.

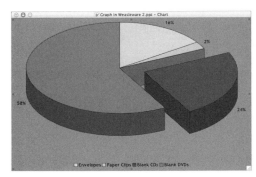

Figure 18.26 If you select a single slice and drag it, you can separate that slice from the rest of the pie.

Figure 18.27 This datasheet has daily prices for Apple Computer.

Stock chart subtypes   *Subtype description*

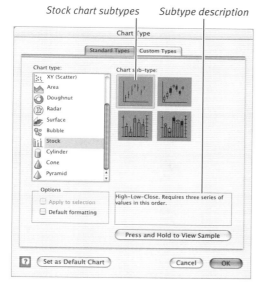

Figure 18.28 Select Stock as the chart type and select one of the four subtypes. (The data requirements for each subtype appears in the text box below.)

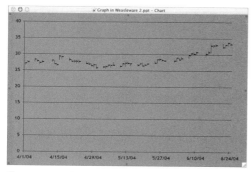

Figure 18.29 This is the high-low-close chart for the Apple stock data.

Creating stock charts

Stock charts (also known as *high-low-close charts*) can display daily prices and, optionally, the opening price and daily volume for a given stock. Stock charts can also be used to present other types of numeric data, such as daily temperatures or barometric pressure readings.

To create a stock chart:

1. In Graph, switch to the datasheet and arrange the data in columns. Depending on the type of chart you intend to create, you should arrange the columns in one of the following manners:
   - ▲ Date, High, Low, Close (**Figure 18.27**)
   - ▲ Date, Open, High, Low, Close
   - ▲ Date, Volume, High, Low, Close
   - ▲ Date, Volume, Open, High, Low, Close

2. Choose Data > Series in Columns (if it isn't already chosen).

3. Choose Chart > Chart Type.
   The Chart Type dialog box appears.

4. Click the Standard Types tab, select Stock from the Chart type list, and select the type of stock chart that matches your datasheet (**Figure 18.28**). Click OK.
   The graph appears (**Figure 18.29**).

✔ Tips

- You can download historical trading data at http://finance.yahoo.com. After the data appears, click the Download To Spreadsheet link to generate an Excel worksheet that you can rearrange to match Graph's requirements. (Be sure to sort by Date in ascending order.) Copy and paste the data into the Graph datasheet.

- You can add a variety of trendlines to a stock chart by choosing Chart > Add Trendline.

Working with 3-D charts

In modern graphing programs, the most impressive charts are three-dimensional—adding depth and perspective to an otherwise flat-looking image.

To modify a 3-D chart:

1. In Graph, click the chart to make it active, if necessary.

2. Choose Chart > 3-D View.

   The 3-D View dialog box appears (**Figure 18.30**).

3. Click the large arrows on the left to raise or lower the elevation. Click the rotation axes beneath the preview to change the angle on the horizontal plane.

   You can see the effect of the elevation and rotation changes in the preview window.

4. *Optional:* To change the perspective, remove the checkmark from the Right angle axes check box and click the perspective arrows that appear.

5. *Optional:* To alter the height of the chart and the chart elements, remove the checkmark from the Auto scaling check box and enter a percentage (such as 40 or 120) in the Height text box.

6. To view the effect of your settings on the graph, click the Apply button. When you are satisfied with the settings, click OK.

   The graph is reformatted to match the 3-D View settings (**Figure 18.31**).

✔ Tip

■ For greater precision, you can enter an exact numeric value in any text box.

Preview

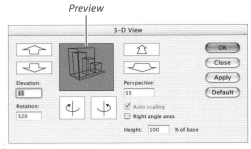

Figure 18.30 Specify elevation, rotation, and perspective settings in the 3-D View dialog box.

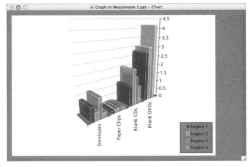

Figure 18.31 Here's a column chart with new 3-D settings applied.

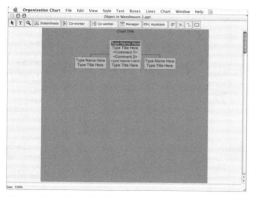

Figure 18.32 Organization Chart launches and displays the framework of a new org chart.

Figure 18.33 Create a new Microsoft Organization Chart in the Insert Object dialog box.

Organization Charts

Organization charts (or *org charts*) can be a very useful part of a business presentation. They are created within Organization Chart, a separate application. You launch the program from PowerPoint and then create or edit your org chart. To make it easy to add an organization chart to a slide, PowerPoint provides a special org chart slide layout.

To add an org chart to an Organization Chart layout slide:

1. To create a new slide, click the New Slide icon on the Standard toolbar, choose Insert > New Slide, or press (Control)(M). The New Slide dialog box appears.

2. Select the Organization Chart layout and click OK.

3. On the new slide, double-click the "Double click to add org chart" placeholder. Organization Chart launches (**Figure 18.32**).

To add an org chart to a slide with a different layout:

1. Select the slide on which you'd like to add the org chart and make that slide active.

2. Choose Insert > Object. The Insert Object dialog box appears (**Figure 18.33**).

3. Click Create new, select Microsoft Organization Chart as the Object type, and click OK. Organization Chart launches.

✔ Tip

- While you're working on an org chart, Organization Chart adds its icon to the Dock. To switch between PowerPoint and Organization Chart, click the appropriate Dock icon.

ORGANIZATION CHARTS

Entering people

Adding people's names to an organization chart is straightforward. Each person's name and title appear in his or her own box. A person's placement in the org chart depends on his or her position in the organizational hierarchy.

To add people:

1. Type the name of the organization's head in the text box that is preselected when Organization Chart launches.

2. Press Tab , Return , or Enter to highlight the next line within the same box and then type the person's title or position.

3. Click a different box. Enter that person's name and title (**Figure 18.34**).

✔ Tips

■ When you are done entering the names and titles for these initial positions, you may wish to transfer the information to your PowerPoint slide by choosing one of the File > Update commands (or by pressing Option ⌘ S). Unlike Microsoft Graph, Organization Chart doesn't update slides automatically—you must do so manually (**Figure 18.35**).

■ To edit the information in a box, click the box, pause briefly, and then click again to place the insertion mark in the text. If you double-click too quickly, the program may think you want to select the current box and all others at the same level.

Figure 18.34 Click a different box and type the person's information.

Figure 18.35 To transfer the org chart to your slide, choose one of the File > Update commands.

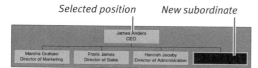
Selected position   New subordinate

Figure 18.37 A new subordinate box appears.

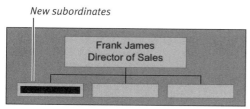
New subordinates

Figure 18.38 By clicking the Subordinate icon three times and then clicking Frank James' box, you can simultaneously create three new subordinate boxes.

Adding subordinates

The initial org chart structure contains only a manager and three *subordinates*, but you can add other subordinates as needed.

To add a subordinate:

1. Click the Subordinate icon on the Icon bar (**Figure 18.36**, page bottom).

2. Click the box of the position that requires a new subordinate.

   A subordinate box appears (**Figure 18.37**).

✔ Tips

■ To add multiple subordinates beneath a position, click the Subordinate icon once for each subordinate, and then click the box of the position to which you are adding the subordinates (**Figure 18.38**).

■ To add a coworker box beside a box, click one of the Co-worker icons on the Icon bar (depending on whether you want to display the coworker to the left or right), and then click the box of the position to which the coworker will be added.

■ To move a subordinate box beneath another member's box, drag the subordinate box on top of the other member's box, and then release the mouse button.

   Whether a moved person will be added as a subordinate, left coworker, or right coworker depends on which *edge* of the box you drag him or her onto. Drag onto the left edge of the box to add the person as a left coworker, onto the right edge to add the person as a right coworker, or onto the bottom edge to add the person as a subordinate.

Figure 18.36 To create a new subordinate, coworker, manager, or assistant, click the relevant icon on the Icon bar and then click the box associated with that person.

ORGANIZATION CHARTS

Adding assistants

Adding assistants is like adding subordinates. There is no limit to the number of assistants you can add.

To add an assistant:

1. Click the Assistant icon on the Icon bar.

2. Click the box of the member who is to receive the assistant.

   An assistant box appears (**Figure 18.39**).

✔ Tips

- You can assign several assistants to an organization member by clicking the Assistant icon once for every assistant you want to add before clicking the box of the member who will receive the assistants.

- To delete an assistant box (or any other box on the org chart), click the box and press Delete.

- Note that if you delete the box of someone who is not one of the lowest members in a group (a supervisor, for instance), the program will do its best to reorganize the remaining boxes. You may have to make some corrections.

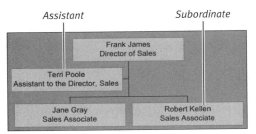

Figure 18.39 Note that an assistant is denoted by a different connecting line (from the side) than a subordinate (from the top).

Figure 18.40 If you want to format several boxes simultaneously, drag a selection rectangle around them.

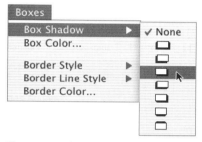

Figure 18.41 Choose commands from the Boxes menu to set a box's shadow, fill color, and border characteristics.

Formatting an org chart

You can change the look of an organization chart to suit your taste. If the chart will be an important part of your presentation, you may want to spend some extra time formatting its boxes, lines, and text.

To format selected boxes:

1. *Do one of the following:*
   - ▲ Click to select a box.
   - ▲ Shift-click to select multiple boxes.
   - ▲ Drag a selection rectangle to enclose multiple boxes (**Figure 18.40**).

   The selected boxes are blackened.

2. Choose formatting commands from the Boxes menu (**Figure 18.41**).

To format selected text:

1. Select the text that you want to format.

2. Choose formatting commands from the Text menu.

   The new formatting is applied to the selected text.

To format connecting lines:

◆ Select one or more connecting lines, and then choose options from the Lines menu.

✔ Tips

■ To apply the same formatting to all text in a box, simply select the box and then choose formatting commands. You can also apply text formatting to selected text within a box, such as only a person's name or title.

■ To select multiple line segments, draw a selection rectangle around them or Shift-click the segments.

■ To save the formatted org chart and transfer it to the slide, choose one of the File > Update commands.

ORGANIZATION CHARTS

295

More org chart tips

Organization Chart has many capabilities the preceding pages didn't touch on. Here are some more tips and areas for you to explore:

◆ You can add text anywhere on an org chart—to include comments, titles, and so forth. Select the Text tool (T) on the Icon bar, click an empty space on the chart, and begin typing. The resulting text is an object that you can format and move as you wish.

◆ The right end of the icon bar contains a set of drawing tools you can use to embellish your org chart (**Figure 18.42**). In order, they are the Horizontal/Vertical Line tool, Diagonal Line tool, Connecting Line tool, and Rectangle tool.

All but the Connecting Line tool are for drawing additional objects on the org chart. The Connecting Line tool is used to draw additional connections between member boxes (showing shared subordinates, for example). To use it, click one box and then drag to the second box.

◆ You can change a chart's background color by choosing Chart > Background Color.

◆ You might also want to experiment with different chart styles using options in the Style menu. For example, you can select the boxes of several people in a department and display them using one of the alternate "group" styles, such as Style > Stacked Group No Boxes (**Figure 18.43**).

◆ In addition to (Shift)-clicking or dragging a selection rectangle to select multiple boxes, you can select specific *classes* of boxes and objects by choosing commands from the Edit > Select submenu (**Figure 18.44**).

◆ You can launch Organization Chart at any time by double-clicking the org chart on your slide.

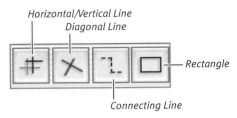

Figure 18.42 The Icon bar also has several useful drawing tools.

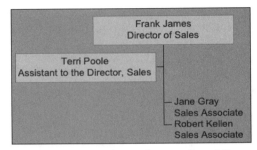

Figure 18.43 You can choose alternate ways of displaying groups in your org chart, such as Stacked Group No Boxes (shown at the bottom).

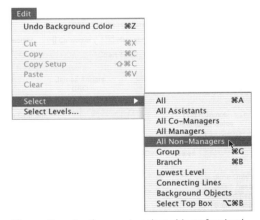

Figure 18.44 Another way to select objects for simultaneous formatting is to choose a command from the Edit >Select submenu.

ORGANIZATION CHARTS

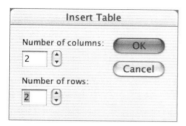

Figure 18.45 Specify the number of columns and rows for the new table.

Table   Tables and Borders toolbar

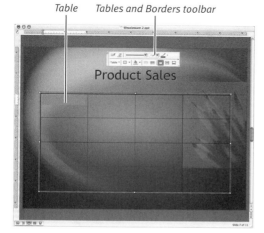

Figure 18.46 A blank table with the specified number of columns and rows appears on the slide. Use the Table and Borders toolbar to format the cells and modify the table.

Adding a Table to a Slide

Tables can help you present information efficiently. Creating and formatting a table in PowerPoint is similar to performing the same tasks in Word. See Chapter 7 for more details.

To add a table to a new slide:

1. To create a new slide, click the New Slide icon on the Standard toolbar, choose Insert > New Slide, or press (Control)(M). The New Slide dialog box appears.

2. In the New Slide dialog box, select the Table layout and click OK. The new slide appears.

3. Double-click the "Double click to add table" placeholder on the new slide. The Insert Table dialog box appears (**Figure 18.45**).

4. Specify the number of columns and rows, and then click OK. The table is added to the slide, and the Tables and Borders toolbar appears (**Figure 18.46**).

5. Enter the table's text. Format it as desired by selecting cells and choosing commands from the Tables and Borders toolbar.

To add a table to an existing slide:

1. Select the slide to which you want to add the table and make that slide active.

2. *Do one of the following:*

   ▲ Click the Insert Table icon on the Standard toolbar, and then drag to select the desired number of rows and columns (**Figure 18.47**).

   ▲ Choose Insert > Table, specify the number of columns and rows in the Insert Table dialog box (see Figure 18.45), and click OK.

✔ Tip

■ You can also format selected table cells by choosing the Format > Table command.

Insert Table icon

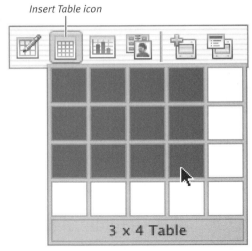

Figure 18.47 You can add a table to *any* slide by clicking the Insert Table toolbar icon, and then dragging to set the number of rows and columns.

ADDING A TABLE TO A SLIDE

19

THE PRESENTATION

When you've finished constructing your presentation, it's time to get it ready to be viewed by an audience. This is when you make final decisions about details such as slide order and design, and whether to also save the presentation as a QuickTime movie or for viewing on the Web.

The first part of the chapter discusses preparing the presentation. The second part covers the options and tools for giving and sharing the presentation.

Using the Slide Sorter

Use Slide Sorter View to get an overview of your presentation. It's similar to viewing 35mm slides on a light table. You can reorder slides, switch templates to change the look of the presentation, and delete or duplicate slides.

To switch to Slide Sorter View:

◆ Choose View > Slide Sorter or click the Slide Sorter View icon in the bottom-left corner of the PowerPoint document window (**Figure 19.1**).

✔ Tip

■ To switch to viewing a single slide, double-click the slide in the Slide Sorter, or select the slide and click the Slide View icon (see Figure 19.1).

To reorder slides:

1. Click the slide you want to move, and then drag it to a new position.

2. A vertical line appears, indicating where the slide will be inserted when you release the mouse button (**Figure 19.2**).

3. Release the mouse button to drop the slide into its new position.

✔ Tips

■ To move a contiguous group of slides, click and drag the mouse across the slides to select them (**Figure 19.3**), and then drag the group to the new position.

■ To move a noncontiguous group, ⌘-click each slide, and then drag the group to the new position. All selected slides will appear in sequence and in the same relative order.

Figure 19.1 One way to switch to Slide Sorter View is to click this icon at the bottom of the document window.

Destination   *Selected slide*

Figure 19.2 When rearranging slides, a line indicates where the slide(s) will be moved when you release the mouse button.

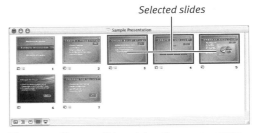

Selected slides

Figure 19.3 You can click and drag the mouse across multiple slides to move them as a group. In this example, slides 3, 4, and 5 are selected.

Figure 19.4 Click the Slide Design icon on the Standard toolbar to apply a different template to the current presentation.

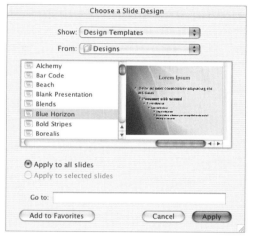

Figure 19.5 Pick the design you want from the Choose a Slide Design dialog box.

Figure 19.6 The new design is applied to the slides.

To delete or duplicate slides:

1. Select the slide(s) that you want to delete or duplicate.

2. *Do one of the following:*
   ▲ To delete the slide(s), choose Edit > Delete Slide or press [Delete].
   ▲ To duplicate the slide(s), choose Edit > Duplicate or press [⌘][D].

✔ Tip

■ You can reverse the effects of a duplication or deletion if you immediately choose the Edit > Undo command or press [⌘][Z].

To change the slide design:

1. Click the Slide Design icon on the Standard toolbar (**Figure 19.4**) or choose Format > Slide Design.

2. In the Choose a Slide Design dialog box (**Figure 19.5**), select a design from the Designs folder.

3. Click Apply.
   The slides adopt the new design (**Figure 19.6**).

✔ Tips

■ If you prefer, you can alter the slide design of only *selected* slides. Select the slides before issuing the Format > Slide Design command. In the Choose a Slide Design dialog box (see Figure 19.5), click the Apply to selected slides radio button.

■ Another way to change the appearance of part of a presentation is to select slides, choose Format > Slide Color Scheme or Format > Slide Background, and select a different color scheme or background color for the slides.

USING THE SLIDE SORTER

Adding Transition Effects

Transition effects are optional visual effects, such as dissolves, splits, and wipes, used for transitions between slides. You can apply different transitions to different slides.

1. In Slide Sorter view, select the slide for which you want to specify a transition.

2. To apply a transition to the selected slide, do one of the following:

   ▲ Choose a transition from the Slide Transition Effects menu on the Slide Sorter toolbar (**Figure 19.7**). A preview of the effect is shown on the slide.

   ▲ Click the Slide Transition icon on the Slide Sorter toolbar or choose Slide Show > Slide Transition. In the Slide Transition dialog box (**Figure 19.8**), set Effect, Sound, and Advance slide options, and then click Apply.

✔ Tips

■ PowerPoint 2001 and v.X supported QuickTime transitions. Such transitions are *not* available in PowerPoint 2004. If you open a 2001 or v.X presentation in PowerPoint 2004, similar transitions are automatically substituted. For details, see "Compatibility Report: Slide transition effects in earlier versions of PowerPoint" in PowerPoint Help.

■ To apply the same transition to multiple slides, ⌘-click the slides and choose a transition effect.

■ To preview a slide's transition, click the Transition Effect icon beneath any slide in Slide Sorter View (**Figure 19.9**).

■ If you base a presentation on a template, you may find that many slides already have transitions. To remove transitions from selected slides, choose No Transition as the slide transition effect.

Slide Transition icon
Slide Transition Effects menu

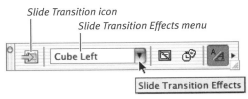

Figure 19.7 Choose a transition from the Slide Transition Effects menu on the Slide Sorter toolbar.

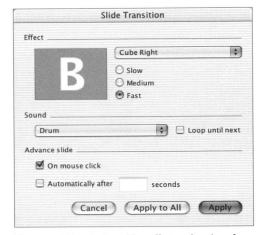

Figure 19.8 To set a transition effect and options for a slide, select them in the Slide Transition dialog box.

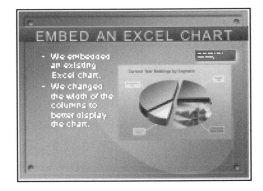

5

Figure 19.9 A clickable Transition Effect icon appears beneath any slide that has an assigned transition.

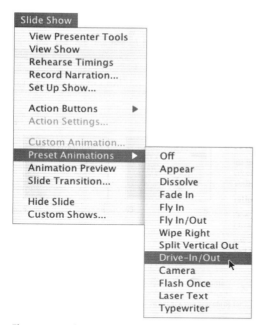

Figure 19.10 Choose an animation effect from the Preset Animations submenu. To view all animations for the current slide, choose Animation Preview.

■ For greater control when animating individual items on a slide, select the slide in Normal, Slide, or Outline View and then choose Slide Show > Custom Animation. In the Custom Animation dialog box, you can change the order of animations for a particular text string or object, set the timing and playback speed, and more.

Animation Within Slides

Motion within a slide is known as *animation*. An animation can be applied to text, objects, or charts, as well as applied selectively or to all material on a slide. You can specify multiple animations for a single object, if desired.

To add animation to a slide:

◆ *Do one of the following:*

▲ To animate all text on a slide, switch to Slide Sorter View and select the slide. Choose Slide Show > Preset Animations and pick an effect from the submenu (**Figure 19.10**).

▲ To animate selected items on a slide, display the slide in Normal, Slide, or Outline View. Select one or more items to which you want to apply the animation, choose Slide Show > Preset Animations, and pick an effect from the submenu.

✔ Tips

■ To apply a text animation to multiple slides, ⌘-click to select the slides in Slide Sorter View, and then choose the animation effect.

■ In Slide Sorter View, a slide that contains an animation has a bulleted text icon beneath it (see Figure 19.9). To preview the effect(s), click the icon or choose Slide Show > Animation Preview.

■ Like transitions, many of the templates already have animations associated with the slides. To remove all animations, select all material on the slide and choose Slide Show > Preset Animations > Off. To selectively remove some—but not all—animations, select the objects from which you want to remove animations and choose Slide Show > Preset Animations > Off.

ANIMATION WITHIN SLIDES

Adding Sound and Movies

To enliven a presentation, you can add audio, music, and movies to selected slides.

To add sound, a movie, or CD audio:

1. In Normal, Slide, or Outline View, select the slide to which you'd like to add a movie, sound, or CD audio.

2. Choose a command from the Insert > Movies and Sounds submenu:

   ▲ If you choose Movie from Gallery or Sound from Gallery, the Clip Gallery window opens.

   ▲ If you choose Movie from File or Sound from File, the Insert Movie or Insert Sound dialog box appears.

   ▲ If you choose Play CD Audio Track, the Play Options dialog box appears (**Figure 19.11**). Select a starting and ending track, and set other options.

3. Select the movie, sound clip, or audio track that you want to add to the slide.

4. Click the Insert, Choose, or OK button. (If you're inserting CD audio or a movie or sound from file, one of the dialog boxes shown in **Figure 19.12** appears. Click Yes or No to indicate whether you want the item to automatically play when the slide appears.)

   A movie frame, sound icon, or CD icon appears on the slide (**Figure 19.13**).

✔ Tips

■ You can also create your own sound clips. Choose Insert > Movies and Sounds > Record Sound. To record slide narration in the same manner, choose Slide Show > Record Narration.

■ A Sound from File item can also be a music file, such as an MP3.

Figure 19.11 To add music from a CD, load the CD into your Mac and choose Play CD Audio Track. Select tracks, indicate whether they should loop, and click OK.

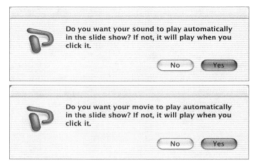

Figure 19.12 Some items can be set to automatically play when the slide appears.

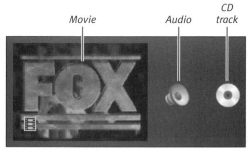

Figure 19.13 Icons for the inserted items are added to the slide.

ADDING SOUND AND MOVIES

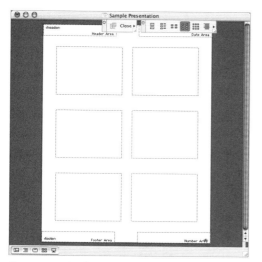

Figure 19.14 On the Handout Master, you can specify the number of slides per page and optionally edit the header and footer.

Quick Preview   *Slides per page*

Figure 19.15 To print handouts, set options in the Print dialog box.

Creating Handouts and Speaker Notes

From within PowerPoint, you can prepare *handouts* (slide printouts to give to the audience) and *speaker notes* to assist you during the presentation.

To create handouts:

1. Choose View > Master > Handout Master. The Handout Master appears (**Figure 19.14**).

2. Click an icon on the Handout Master toolbar to indicate the number of slides per page that you want to display.

3. *Optional:* Edit the header or footer text.

4. Click the Close icon on the toolbar.

5. Choose File > Print.

6. From the Print What drop-down menu in the Print dialog box (**Figure 19.15**), choose Handouts (*x* slides per page). Review the remaining settings.

   View a preview of the handout pages in the Quick Preview box. What's shown reflects the current print settings.

7. Click Print to print the handouts on the specified printer, or click Save as PDF to create an Adobe Acrobat file that you can view in Apple's Preview program or Adobe Reader.

To create speaker notes:

◆ *Do one of the following:*

  ▲ Choose View > Notes Page. Click the notes placeholder to type speaker notes for a given slide (**Figure 19.16**).

  ▲ Switch to Normal View and enter notes in the text window beneath each slide (**Figure 19.17**).

✔ Tips

■ Your notes will *not* appear on the slides during the presentation.

■ To print each slide along with its associated notes, choose Notes from the Print What drop-down menu in the Print dialog box (see Figure 19.15).

Notes area

Figure 19.16 Speaker notes are easiest to create in Notes Page View.

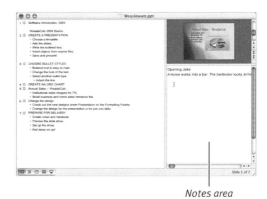

Notes area

Figure 19.17 Notes can also be entered in Normal View, although with greater difficulty because they tend to scroll off-screen.

Figure 19.18 When rehearsing a presentation, a timer is displayed in the bottom-right corner of each slide.

Figure 19.19 Choose whether to record the presentation time for use in future viewings of the slide show.

Figure 19.20 You can switch to Slide Sorter View to review the saved slide timings.

Menu icon

Figure 19.21 Click this icon to reveal a pop-up menu of helpful options.

Rehearsing a Presentation

It's always a good idea to rehearse a presentation, especially if there's a time limit. When you've finished assembling the presentation, you can rehearse it and time how long each slide must remain onscreen.

To rehearse the presentation:

1. Choose Slide Show > Rehearse Timings or click the Rehearse Timings toolbar icon.

   The first slide in the presentation appears. A timer is in the bottom-right corner (**Figure 19.18**).

2. Perform the presentation exactly as you would in front of the audience.

3. Click the mouse, press [Spacebar], or press → to advance from one action to the next within a slide, as well as to move from slide to slide.

4. At the end of the slide show, a dialog box appears, showing the presentation's total time (**Figure 19.19**). Click Yes or No to indicate whether you want to record the time for each slide (for later use in playing the slide show on automatic).

5. If you click Yes, a second dialog box appears (**Figure 19.20**). Click Yes if you'd like to switch to Slide Sorter View to review the slide timings.

✔ Tips

- You can immediately stop a rehearsal or slide show by pressing [Esc].

- You can also halt a show by moving the cursor to the lower-left corner of the screen, clicking the icon, and choosing End Show from the pop-up menu (**Figure 19.21**). There are other useful options in the menu, including a pen cursor you can use to write or draw onscreen during the presentation.

Running a Slide Show

You can view your show at any time to get an idea of how it will look to an audience. Before finalizing it, however, you should consider the available play options. For example, you can opt to control when slides change or allow the show to run automatically.

To set options for a slide show:

1. Choose Slide Show > Set Up Show.

The Set Up Show dialog box appears (**Figure 19.22**).

2. Specify the type of show, display options, the slides to be used, and the method used to advance slides.

You can advance each slide manually by clicking the mouse or display each one for a specific amount of time before advancing to the next (using the timings set in the rehearsal).

3. Click OK.

To view the slide show:

1. *Do one of the following:*

▲ To view the show from the beginning, choose Slide Show > View Show or View > Slide Show.

▲ To view the slide show but start with some slide other than the first, switch to Slide Sorter View. Select the first slide to view, and then click the Slide Show View icon in the bottom-left corner of the window.

2. Press (Esc) to end the show.

✔ Tip

■ Mac users who don't own PowerPoint can use Microsoft PowerPoint 98 Viewer to view presentations. It's available for download from Microsoft's Web site at www.microsoft.com/mac.

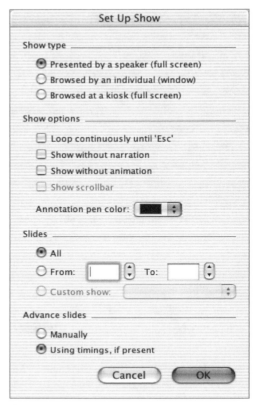

Figure 19.22 Set play options for the slide show in the Set Up Show dialog box.

Previous slide   *Next slide*

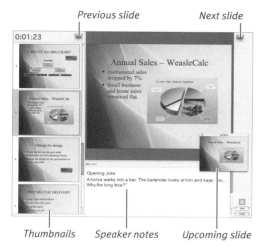

Thumbnails   *Speaker notes*   *Upcoming slide*

Figure 19.23 The presenter tools show the presenter information that is not seen by the audience, such as the notes and a preview of the next slide.

Using the Presenter Tools

If you have a dual-monitor system, you can use the new presenter tools to assist with your presentation. The presentation appears on the audience's monitor, while the tools appear on only on the presenter's monitor.

To use the presenter tools:

1. Using the Displays System Preferences, set up your Mac so it can address two monitors.

   For instructions, see "Set up your system to use the presenter tools with two monitors" in PowerPoint Help.

2. Turn on the presenter tools (**Figure 19.23**) by choosing Slide Show > View Presenter Tools.

3. Use normal slide show navigation methods to move from one slide to the next. In addition, you can do the following:
   - ▲ Click an arrow icon to move forward or backward one slide.
   - ▲ Click a slide thumbnail to move directly to that slide.

4. To change the notes magnification, select a percentage from the pop-up menu above the notes area.

5. Click the Help button to view keyboard commands for the presenter tools.

6. To end the slide show, click End, or press Esc, ⌘., or –.

✔ Tip

■ You can also use the presenter tools to rehearse a presentation. While practicing, a single monitor will suffice.

Publishing a Presentation on the Web

One way to share your presentation with a large audience is to publish it in HTML format, enabling it to be viewed with any current Web browser, such as Microsoft Internet Explorer or Safari.

To create a presentation for the Web:

1. Choose File > Save As Web Page.

   A Save As panel appears (**Figure 19.24**).

2. Select a folder in which to save the presentation. Name the output file.

3. *Optional:* If compatibility problems are noted, click the Compatibility Report button and examine the list of problems.

   In many cases, the problems will be related to opening the presentation in other versions of PowerPoint rather than its display on the Web.

4. Click the Web Options button.

   The Web Options dialog box appears (**Figure 19.25**).

5. On the General tab, type a title for the Web page. (This title will appear in the upper-left corner of the browser window.) You may also wish to enter keywords for the page, enabling Internet search engines to find and index it.

6. Click the Appearance tab and choose settings from the drop-down menus (**Figure 19.26**).

7. On the Pictures tab, pick a target monitor size.

8. When you are through changing settings, click OK to close the Web Options dialog box.

   The Save As dialog box reappears.

Figure 19.24 When saving a presentation for display on the Web, you set options in this Save As panel.

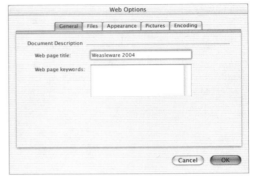

Figure 19.25 Enter a title and keywords for your Web presentation on the General tab of the Web Options dialog box.

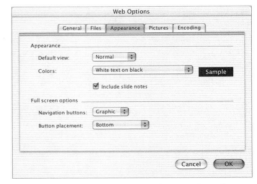

Figure 19.26 Set Appearance options, such as the text color, style of navigation buttons, and whether your notes will be displayed.

Figure 19.27 The presentation can be viewed in any current Web browser.

9. Click Save.

   The presentation is saved as an HTML file (with an .htm extension), along with a folder containing the graphics and additional pages.

10. Double-click the HTML file to view and test the presentation in your browser (**Figure 19.27**).

✔ Tips

- As you can see, you can view a Web-based presentation directly from your hard disk. This means if you want *others* to view it, all you have to do is send them the .htm file and the associated folder.

- Of course, the *real* destination of a Web presentation is typically the Internet or a corporate intranet. For instructions on publishing your presentation to the Web or to an intranet, ask your Internet Service Provider or your network administrator, respectively.

- Certain text characters, such as curved (curly) quotation marks, will not display properly in a Web browser. To scan for these and other problems before committing your presentation to the Web or intranet, choose File > Web Page Preview.

Saving a Presentation as a Movie

Another way to make a presentation easily transportable is to save it as a PowerPoint (QuickTime) movie. The resulting movie can be viewed in any QuickTime-compatible player, such as Apple's QuickTime Player.

To save a presentation as a PowerPoint movie:

1. Choose File > Make Movie.

   A Save As panel appears (**Figure 19.28**).

2. Enter a filename for the movie in the Save As text box.

3. In the Where section of the dialog box, select a location in which to save the movie.

4. To view or change the default movie settings, click the Movie Options button.

   The Movie Options dialog box appears (**Figure 19.29**).

5. Make any desired changes, such as specifying the movie size and quality, and recording details about the presentation's creators. When you've finished, click OK.

6. In the Save As panel, click Save to create the movie.

✔ Tips

- If the presentation already has a .ppt extension, Step 1 will propose the filename *filename*.ppt.mov. If the movie might be played on a Windows PC, be sure to remove the .ppt from the Save As filename.

- Not all PowerPoint presentation features are supported in movies. Refer to the Help topic: "Optimize a presentation for delivery as a PowerPoint movie."

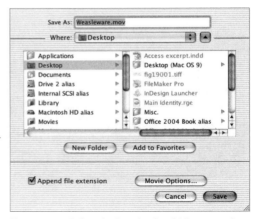

Figure 19.28 Select the location in which to save the movie.

Figure 19.29 Review and set movie options.

- In the Movie Options dialog box, uncheck Include original presentation data—unless you're sure that the recipient will require access to the actual presentation.

Part V: Microsoft Entourage

EMAIL

Since electronic mail first became available, it has been the centerpiece of most people's Internet use. Entourage is the program in Microsoft Office 2004 that handles it. Using Entourage, you can send and receive messages to and from anyone else who has an email address, attach files to outgoing messages, organize incoming and outgoing mail, and link email to other items.

In addition to email, Entourage lets you manage your contacts (Chapter 21), schedule (Chapter 22), to-do list (Chapter 23), notes (Chapter 24), and newsgroups (Chapter 25). Entourage is also command central for the new Project Center (Chapter 27).

Setting Up an Account

In order to use email, you need an account with an Internet service provider (ISP). If your account is with America Online (or a similar proprietary service), you won't be able to use Entourage for email. The literature you received with your ISP account or the ISP's tech support staff can tell you whether the service uses Post Office Protocol (POP) or Internet Message Access Protocol (IMAP) for email. There are also two other types of accounts that Entourage 2004 supports: Hotmail (Web-based email from Microsoft) and Exchange server (an email server used by many corporations).

Your first step in setting up Entourage as an email client is to import information from your current email accounts or to create a new Entourage account for each one. If your old accounts weren't imported when you first ran Entourage or you've just opened a new ISP, corporate, or Hotmail account, follow the steps below to register the account.

To set up an account:

1. Choose Tools > Accounts.

   The Accounts dialog box appears.

2. On the Mail tab, click the New toolbar icon.

   The Account Setup Assistant appears (**Figure 20.1**).

3. Enter your full email address in the form:

   `username@domain`

   (such as bob723@msn.com). If you work for an organization that uses Exchange server, click the check box, too. Click the right-arrow icon to continue.

4. Entourage should now display a screen indicating that it has determined the account type based on the information you entered. Click the right-arrow icon to continue.

Complete email address

Figure 20.1 Enter your email address. Click the check box if an Exchange server is being used.

Figure 20.2 Check your account information and enter the password for your email account.

Figure 20.3 To ensure that Entourage can both send and receive using your supplied account information, click Verify My Settings. (This test occurs online.)

Figure 20.4 Name the account and click Finish.

5. In the Verify and Complete Settings screen (**Figure 20.2** on the previous page), enter your name (or how you want your messages identified to recipients) and email password. If you want your password saved, click the Save password in Mac OS X Keychain check box. Click the right-arrow icon to continue.

   If you elect not to save your password, you'll be prompted for it every time you connect to the mail server.

6. To ensure that your account settings are correct, click the Verify My Settings button on the Optional: Verify Settings screen (**Figure 20.3**). The test results will appear in the text box. When the test has been successfully completed, click the right-arrow icon to continue.

7. On the final screen (**Figure 20.4**), enter a name for the account and click Finish. (The account name isn't critical. Its only purpose is to identify the account to you—not to others.)

   The new account is added to the list in the Accounts window.

8. Close the Accounts window.

✔ Tips

- If you have multiple accounts defined, make one of them the *default* (primary) account. Select the account name and click the Make Default button. When you create a new email message, it's assumed that you want to send it using the default account.

- You can also change settings for an account in the Accounts window. Select the account and click the Edit button.

- To delete an account (one that no longer exists or which you don't want to track with Entourage), select its name in the Accounts window and click Delete.

Creating and Sending Mail

One of the most basic functions of email is that of creating and sending messages.

To send email:

1. *Do one of the following:*
   - ▲ From the Mail section of Entourage, click the New toolbar icon or press ⌘N.
   - ▲ From any other section of Entourage, choose File > New > Mail Message, click the arrow beside the New toolbar icon and choose Mail Message from the drop-down menu (**Figure 20.5**), or press (Option)⌘N.

   A new message form appears with the address window on top (**Figure 20.6**).

2. In the To box, specify the email address to which you want to send the message by doing one of the following:
   - ▲ Type or paste a complete email address.
   - ▲ Click the Address Book icon to display the contact records you've created. Double-click or drag a contact record into the To box.
   - ▲ If you've recently received email from or the individual is in your Address Book, start typing the person's name. As you type, Entourage lists matching names and email addresses from which you can choose.

3. *Optional:* To enter more To addresses, click beneath the last address and repeat Step 2.

4. *Optional:* You can also include recipients in the Cc (carbon copy) or Bcc (blind carbon copy) boxes. Click in the appropriate box and follow Steps 2–3.

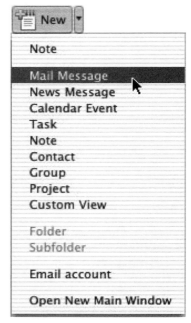

Figure 20.5 Choose Mail Message from the New icon's drop-down menu.

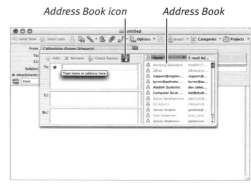

Figure 20.6 Type the recipient's address or select it from the Address Book pane.

Figure 20.7 Enter the text of your message.

Send immediately   Store in Outbox   Save as Draft

Figure 20.8 When the message is ready to send, click one of these toolbar icons.

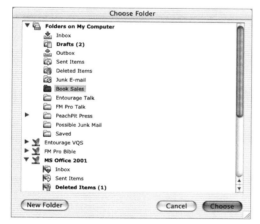

Figure 20.9 Select a folder in which to store the message and then click Choose.

5. When you finish entering addresses, click outside the address box, press ⌷Return⌷, or press ⌷Enter⌷.

The message window appears, and the insertion point is in the Subject field.

6. Enter a subject to identify the message.

7. Press ⌷Return⌷ again and the pointer appears in the message box, ready for you to begin typing (**Figure 20.7**).

8. When you've finished typing the message, click one of these icons at the top of the message window (**Figure 20.8**):

▲ **Send Now.** Click this icon if you're connected to your ISP and want to send the message immediately.

▲ **Send Later.** This option puts the message in your Outbox where it waits for the next Send/Receive.

▲ **Save as Draft.** Click this icon if you want to edit the message before sending it. The message will be stored in the Drafts folder until you open, edit, and send it.

✔ Tips

■ Entries in the Cc box represent secondary recipients—those people who you wish to receive a copy of the message. Bcc people are "invisible" recipients; that is, no other recipient will know that a Bcc recipient also received the message.

■ Sent messages are automatically stored in the Sent Items folder. To set another folder for a given message, choose Message > After Sending, Move To > Choose Folder. Select a folder (**Figure 20.9**) and click Choose.

■ Most messages are sent as plain text (single font, no formatting). To create a formatted message, choose Format > HTML or click the Use HTML toolbar icon above the message body.

Sending Attachments

In addition to sending text messages, you can optionally attach one or more files to any email message. The files can be any type, such as pictures, word processing documents, or even applications. When sent with email, these files are referred to as *attachments*.

To attach a file to an email message:

1. Click the triangle beside the word Attachments (between the Subject field and the message body) to open the Attachments pane (**Figure 20.10**).

2. *Do one of the following:*

   ▲ Click the Add button. In the Choose Attachment dialog box that appears, select a file and click Choose.

   ▲ Drag a file's icon into the Attachments pane.

3. Click the bar beneath the Attachments pane to open the Attachments options window (**Figure 20.11**). Set Encode for to Any computer (AppleDouble), unless you're sure the recipient requires another setting. If the attachments are large, you may also want to compress them.

4. Send the message.

✔ Tips

■ You can also add an attachment by clicking the Add Attachments toolbar icon.

■ To remove an attachment, select it in the Attachments pane and click Remove.

■ If you elect to compress the files (it can dramatically reduce send and receive times), make sure that the recipient has the StuffIt Expander program to decompress them. It's available free for Mac and Windows from www.aladdinsys.com.

Show/hide Attachments pane   Add an attachment

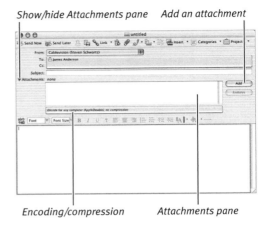

Encoding/compression   Attachments pane

Figure 20.10 When working with attachments, it can be helpful to open the Attachments pane.

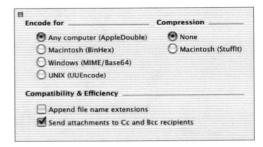

Figure 20.11 You can change the encoding and compression settings for all files attached to the current message.

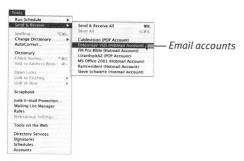

Email accounts

Figure 20.12 To retrieve email from a specific account, choose its name from the Send & Receive submenu.

Message headers   *Preview pane*

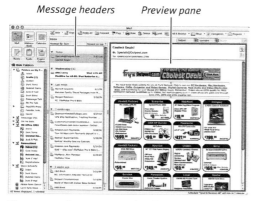

Figure 20.13 Every message header shows the subject, date/time, and the sender or recipient's name.

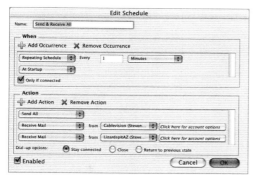

Figure 20.14 Choose Tools > Schedules to view, edit, or create mail schedules. This schedule checks my main accounts once per minute for new email.

Incoming Email

Entourage offers several options for retrieving incoming mail and attached files.

To retrieve mail from a POP account:

1. *Do any of the following:*
   - ▲ Click the Send & Receive button at the top of the main window.
   - ▲ Choose Tools > Send & Receive > Send & Receive All ([#][K]).
   - ▲ Send/receive mail from one account by choosing the account from the Send & Receive toolbar button's menu or from the Tools > Send & Receive submenu (**Figure 20.12**).

2. If you haven't set up your account to save your password, enter it when prompted.

   The waiting mail arrives in your Inbox. A message header for each incoming message appears in the message list (**Figure 20.13**).

To retrieve mail from a Hotmail, IMAP, or Exchange server account:

1. In the Folders list, click the triangle beside the Hotmail, IMAP, or Exchange server account to expand the account, displaying all of its folders.

2. Click the folder containing the messages you want to read (Inbox, for example).

3. If you haven't set up your account to save the password, enter it when prompted.

   A message header for each message in the folder appears in the message list (see Figure 20.13).

✔ Tip

- ■ Mail can be automatically retrieved at regular intervals by setting up a schedule, such as the included Send & Receive All schedule (**Figure 20.14**).

To read a message:

1. *Do one of the following:*

▲ Click a message header in the message list. The message appears in the Preview pane (see Figure 20.13).

▲ Double-click a message header in the message list. The message opens in its own window (**Figure 20.15**). Toolbar icons across the top provide message-handling options.

2. Scroll through the message using the vertical scroll bar or by pressing `Spacebar`.

✔ Tips

■ In Entourage 2004, the Preview pane can be placed below or to the right of the message list. Choose a position from the View > Preview Pane submenu.

To manage received attachments:

1. When you open or preview a message that contains an attachment (indicated by a paper clip icon), the Attachments pane opens (**Figure 20.16**).

2. Select an attachment and click one of the buttons on the right to open the file, save it to disk, or delete it (**Figure 20.17**).

✔ Tips

■ You can also open an attachment by double-clicking it in the Attachments pane. And you can save an attachment by dragging its file icon onto the Desktop.

■ If a message has multiple attachments, you can remove or save them all with a single command. From the Message menu, choose Remove All Attachments or Save All Attachments.

■ Entourage can display certain types of attachments (such as PDF and JPEG files) in the Preview pane. Thus, it's not necessary to open all files just to view them.

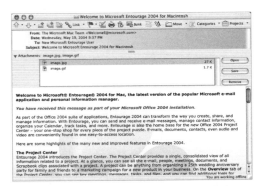

Figure 20.15 The message opens in its own window.

Attachments pane

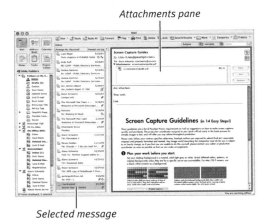

Selected message

Figure 20.16 You manage a message's attachments in the Attachments pane.

Selected attachment   Buttons

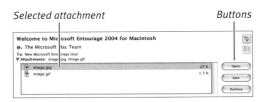

Figure 20.17 Click a button to perform an action on the selected attachment(s).

INCOMING EMAIL

Addressed to original author

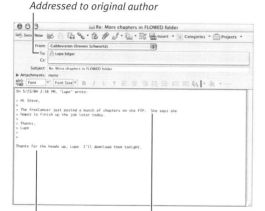

Reply text   *Original, quoted message text*

Figure 20.18 Edit the original, quoted text (if desired), add your reply, and send the message.

Replying to Email

There are several ways to reply to email you receive. This section explains the options.

To reply to a message:

1. Select the message header in the message list or open the message in its own window.

2. Click the Reply toolbar icon, choose Message > Reply, or press ⌘ R.

   A message window opens, addressed to the recipient (**Figure 20.18**). The default Subject is the original one preceded by RE.

3. Enter your reply text and send the message.

✔ Tips

- By default, the entire original message is quoted when a reply is generated. However, it's polite to quote only relevant parts. The typical approach is to delete unnecessary text from the original message.

  Another option is to select the text that you want to quote and *then* issue the Reply command. Only the selected text will be quoted in the reply.

- There are *three* Reply commands:
  - ▲ **Reply.** Use when replying only to the person who sent the message to you.
  - ▲ **Reply to All.** Reply to the message's author, as well as to all others listed in the To and Cc lines.
  - ▲ **Reply to Sender.** When replying to a message from a mailing list, this command allows you to address the reply to the message author, rather than to the list.

- Text underlined with a red squiggly line has been flagged by the spelling checker. Control-click flagged words to view the spelling checker's options, including suggested corrections.

Grouping Messages

Long a feature of newsgroup readers, the ability to *group* email messages in any way that's convenient is now a feature of Entourage. For instance, if you group messages by Subject, you can view all related messages together rather than scattered throughout the message list.

To group messages, choose a grouping method (such as From, Date, or Subject) from the View > Arrange By submenu or by clicking the Arrange By bar above the message list. Then choose View > Arrange By > Show in Groups.

Forwarding or Redirecting

If you receive mail that you want to send to others, you can forward or redirect it. When you *forward* mail, you can add your own comments, the recipients see a message that came from you, and any replies will go to you.

If you *redirect* email, on the other hand, you cannot alter or add to the message, the email appears to have come from the original sender, and any replies go to that sender. (As a result, redirection is generally used only to pass on email that was mistakenly sent to you or when there's a more suitable recipient.)

To forward email:

1. With the message selected in the message list or opened in its own window, click the Forward toolbar icon, choose Message > Forward, or press (⌘ J).

2. In the address box, enter the address or addresses to which you want to forward the message.

3. By default, the Subject is the original subject preceded by FW (as in, FW: Today's Joke). You may edit the Subject line, if you wish.

4. *Optional:* Add an introductory note to the message body, edit the forwarded text, and/or add attachments.

5. Click the Send Now toolbar icon to forward the message to its recipients.

✔ Tip

■ You can also forward a message as an attachment. Select the message header in the message list and choose Message > Forward as Attachment. A new message window appears. Instead of quoting the original message text, it's automatically included as an attached file (**Figure 20.19**).

Attached message

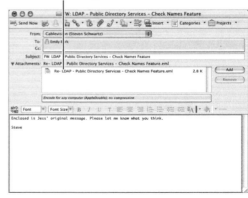

Figure 20.19 You can also forward a message as an attached file. Doing so allows you to separate your own message text from the forwarded material.

To redirect email:

1. With the message selected in the message list or opened in its own window, choose Message > Redirect (⌘ Option J).

2. In the address window that appears, enter or select the addresses to which you want to redirect the message.

   You may not edit the subject or message text, nor can you add attachments.

3. Click the Send Now toolbar icon to send the message to the specified recipient(s).

FORWARDING OR REDIRECTING

Organizing the Mail

Once you start receiving a significant amount of email, you'll want to organize it. Entourage provides several tools for this purpose.

◆ You can store selected mail in folders you've created. (To create a folder, choose File > New > Folder or press (Shift)(⌘)(N)).

◆ You can assign various attributes to messages, such as categories and projects with which they're associated. You can then sort or filter your messages based on these attributes.

◆ You can define Rules that take specific actions when messages matching your criteria are received.

To organize mail in folders:

1. In the Folders list, select the folder that contains the message you want to move.

2. *Do one of the following:*

   ▲ To move messages directly from one folder to another, drag the selected message header(s) onto the destination folder in the Folders list.

   ▲ To pick the destination folder from a dialog box, select one or more messages and choose Message > Move To > Move To Folder, press (Shift)(⌘)(M), click the Move toolbar icon and choose Move To Folder (**Figure 20.20**), or (Control)-click the message header and choose Move To > Move To Folder.

   The Move *message name* dialog box appears (**Figure 20.21**). Select a destination folder and click Move.

✔ Tip

■ The Move To submenu also lists recently used destination folders. You can move the current message to any listed folder by choosing its name from the submenu.

Figure 20.20 Click the Move toolbar icon and choose Move To Folder or one of the listed folders (if any).

Figure 20.21 Select the destination folder and click Move. (To create a new folder, click the New Folder button.)

Figure 20.22 You can choose a category by clicking the Categories toolbar icon.

Figure 20.23 Choose the categories to assign to the message and set one as Primary.

To assign categories to messages:

◆ To assign a single category to a message, select the message header in the message list, and do one of the following:

▲ Click the down arrow beside the Categories toolbar icon and choose a category (**Figure 20.22**).

▲ Choose a category from the Edit > Categories submenu.

▲ Control-click the message header. In the pop-up menu that appears, choose a category from the Categories sub-menu.

◆ To assign *multiple* categories to a single message, select the message header in the message list and do one of the following:

▲ Click the down arrow beside the Categories toolbar icon and choose Assign Categories (see Figure 20.22).

▲ Choose Edit > Categories > Assign Categories (⌘;).

In the Assign Categories dialog box that appears (**Figure 20.23**), click the check box beside each category you wish to assign. Then click OK.

✔ Tips

■ Although it is possible to assign multiple categories to a single message, there's room to display only one category. This is the message's *primary category*. If you want to change the primary category for an item, select the category in the Assign Categories dialog box (see Figure 20.23), and then click the Set Primary button.

■ To clear all categories currently set for an item, select None.

■ If you assign a category to a contact in your Address Book, future email from that contact will have that category as its primary one.

To edit the category list:

1. *Do one of the following:*
   ▲ Click the down arrow beside the Categories toolbar icon and choose Edit Categories (see Figure 20.22).
   ▲ Choose Edit > Categories > Edit Categories (Shift ⌘ ;).
   The Categories dialog box appears (**Figure 20.24**).

2. To create a new category, click the Add Category toolbar icon. An Untitled category appears. Name the category and select a color for it by clicking the Color icon to the right of its name.

3. To rename a category, double-click it. Doing so makes the name editable.

4. To change a category's color, choose a color from the Color pop-up menu to the right of its name.

5. To delete a category, select it, click the Delete Category toolbar icon, and confirm the deletion in the dialog box that appears (**Figure 20.25**).

6. Close the Categories dialog box when you are done making changes.

✔ Tip

- Try not to duplicate category colors. To assign a custom color to a category, choose Other from the Color pop-up menu.

Figure 20.24 You can edit existing categories and create new ones in the Categories dialog box.

Figure 20.25 You must confirm a category deletion by clicking the Delete button.

Current sort column

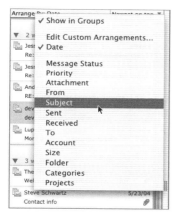

Figure 20.26 When the message list is above the Preview pane or the Preview pane is hidden, click a column heading to sort on that column.

Figure 20.27 When the message list is to the right of the Preview pane, click the Arrange By heading and choose a sort field.

Clear

Figure 20.28 Specify a filtering criterion by choosing menu options and typing. Messages that match the criterion are shown, while all others are hidden.

To sort the mail in a folder:

1. Select a folder in the Folders list.

2. *Do one of the following:*

   ▲ If the Preview pane is below the message list (**Figure 20.26**) or is hidden, click a column heading to sort by that column. (The current sort column is always displayed in blue.)

   To toggle between an ascending and descending sort, click the column heading again.

   ▲ If the Preview pane is to the right of the message list, click the Arrange By heading above the message list and choose the information on which you want to sort (**Figure 20.27**).

   To toggle between an ascending and descending sort, click the heading to the right of Arrange By.

✔ Tip

■ Every folder can have a different sort field.

To filter the mail in a folder:

1. Select the folder in the Folders list.

2. In the bar beneath the toolbar (**Figure 20.28**), choose a filtering field from the leftmost drop-down menu. Use the other drop-down menu and/or text box to specify a filter value.

   Only messages that match the filter criterion are displayed.

✔ Tip

■ To clear the filter criterion and restore the full message list, click the Clear icon.

To create rules for processing email:

1. Choose Tools > Rules.

   The Rules dialog box appears (**Figure 20.29**).

2. Click a Mail tab for the type of mail to which you want the rule to apply, and then click the New toolbar icon.

   The Edit Rule dialog box appears (**Figure 20.30**).

3. Name the rule, specify the criteria that will trigger the rule, and set actions to take.

4. Ensure that the Enabled check box is checked.

   Only enabled rules are processed.

5. Click OK.

   You're returned to the Rules dialog box and the new rule is added to the list.

6. Close the Rules dialog box.

✔ Tips

- You can also click toolbar icons in the Rules dialog box to edit or delete rules, as well as move them up or down in the processing order.

- Another way to disable a rule is by clearing its Enabled check box in the Rules dialog box.

Create a new rule

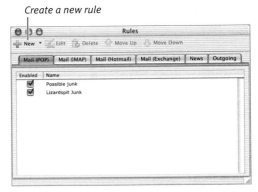

Figure 20.29 To create a new message rule, click the appropriate Mail tab and then click New.

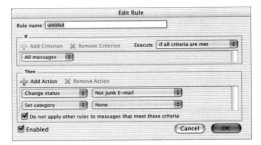

Figure 20.30 Name the message rule, specify criteria, and set actions.

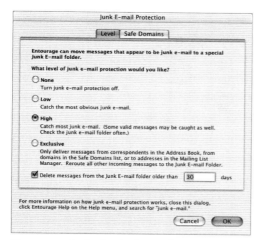

Figure 20.31 On the Level tab, specify a filtering level to use to identify incoming junk email.

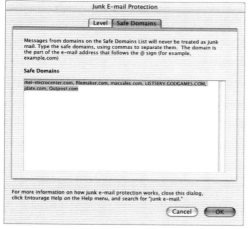

Figure 20.32 On the Safe Domains tab, enter a comma-delimited list of trusted domains. Doing so prevents their messages from being classified as junk.

Handling Junk Email

Anyone who has an email account will eventually receive junk mail (*spam*). If you use your regular email address to register on Web sites or if you send email to corporations, newsgroups, or mailing lists, your volume of received junk mail is liable to increase. Using the Junk E-mail Protection feature, you can filter out much of this time-wasting, annoying mail.

To filter out possible junk mail:

1. Choose Tools > Junk E-mail Protection. The Junk E-mail Protection dialog box appears.

2. On the Level tab (**Figure 20.31**), click a radio button to specify the level of protection desired.

   When received, suspected junk email is automatically assigned the Junk category and is moved to the Junk E-mail folder.

3. To instruct Entourage to automatically delete junk mail after a period of time, click the Delete messages from the Junk E-mail folder older than *X* days check box and enter a number in the text box.

4. *Optional:* On the Safe Domains tab of the dialog box (**Figure 20.32**), you can enter a list of *domains* (the part of an email address after the @ sign) that should never be classified as junk. Separate the domains with commas.

5. Click OK to save the new settings.

✔ Tips

■ You can specify other actions for junk mail by creating message rules (as discussed previously in this chapter).

■ To prevent Entourage from classifying mail from certain individuals as junk, create Address Book records for them.

Managing Mailing Lists

Internet mailing lists allow people with a common interest to connect. They provide subscribers with an email-based forum for conducting discussions, asking questions, and sharing experiences. When you're a member of a mailing list, you receive copies of all messages sent to the list. And when you post a message, everyone who subscribes to the list will receive a copy of your message. Entourage provides a Mailing List Manager to handle your mailing list messages.

To manage a mailing list subscription:

1. Choose Tools > Mailing List Manager.
   The Mailing List Manager dialog box appears (**Figure 20.33**).

2. Click the New toolbar icon.
   The Edit Mailing List Rule dialog box appears (**Figure 20.34**).

3. Enter a name for the mailing list, type or paste the list address, and indicate what should be done with messages from and to the list.

4. *Optional:* Review the options on the Advanced tab and make any desired changes.

5. Click OK.
   The new mailing list is recorded in the Mailing List Manager dialog box.

✔ Tips

- To change the settings for a mailing list, select it in the Mailing List Manager dialog box and click the Edit toolbar icon.

- A mailing list subscription will flood your Inbox with dozens of individual messages per day. If it's allowed by the list, subscribe in *digest mode* to request that each day's messages be combined into one message.

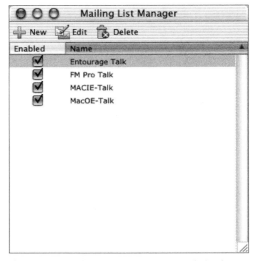

Figure 20.33 In the Mailing List Manager dialog box, you can record new mailing list subscriptions, edit existing ones, and delete others.

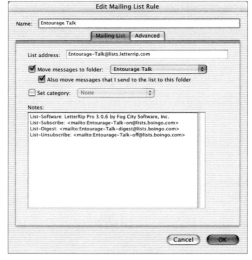

Figure 20.34 Specify the list address and actions to take on received messages from the list.

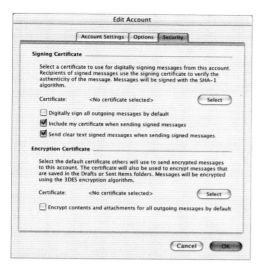

Figure 20.35 On the Security tab of the Edit Account dialog box, record your digital ID and set encryption and signature options.

Certificate list

Figure 20.36 Select a certificate from the drop-down list and click Choose.

Email Security

Entourage 2004 provides two types of security for your messages. First, you can *digitally sign* messages, assuring recipients that they actually came from you. Second, messages can be *encrypted*, allowing only recipients with the proper software key to decode and read them. While most users won't bother with either of these features, corporate and government employees are likely to find them very attractive.

Before you can employ either feature, you must obtain a *digital ID* from an authorized issuer, such as VeriSign (www.verisign.com). The digital ID can be used for both encryption and digital signing.

To enable encryption and/or a digital signature for an email account:

1. Choose Tools > Accounts.

   The Accounts dialog box appears.

2. On the Mail tab of the Accounts dialog box, double-click the account for which you want to enable encryption or a digital signature.

   The Edit Account dialog box for that account appears.

3. Click the Security tab (**Figure 20.35**).

4. To specify a certificate for digital signing, click the top Select button.

5. In the dialog box that appears (**Figure 20.36**), select an installed certificate from the drop-down list and click Choose.

6. To select a certificate to use for encryption, click the bottom Select button and repeat Step 5.

7. Set encryption and digital signing options by clicking check boxes. Then click OK to close the Edit Account dialog box.

✔ Tip

- To manually enable encryption or a digital signature for an outgoing message, do one of the following:

  ▲ From the Message > Security submenu, choose Digitally Sign Message or Encrypt Message.

  ▲ Click the Options toolbar icon (**Figure 20.37**). From the Security submenu, choose Digitally Sign Message or Encrypt Message.

Options icon

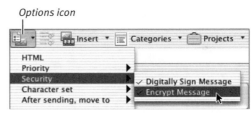

Figure 20.37 You can encrypt and/or digitally sign an outgoing message by choosing Security commands from the Options toolbar icon's drop-down menu.

Figure 20.38 A message folder in MBOX format.

Figure 20.39 If you double-click an MBOX file on a Mac that has Entourage 2004 installed, you'll be given an opportunity to import the message data.

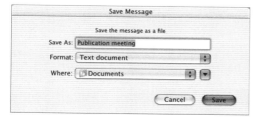

Figure 20.40 In the Save Message dialog box, choose a message format and a location in which to save the message.

Backing Up Email

Entourage 2004 provides an extraordinarily simple way to create a backup of any message folder. If necessary, the backed-up folder can later be imported into the same copy of Entourage, into a different copy (when copying messages to your laptop, for example), or into any other Mac or Windows program that supports the MBOX text format.

To back up a message folder:

1. Select a folder in the Folders list (such as the Inbox, for example) and drag it onto the Desktop.

   Entourage creates a backup of all messages in the folder using the MBOX text format (**Figure 20.38**).

2. If the dragged folder also contains subfolders that you want to back up, they must be dragged separately onto the Desktop.

To import an MBOX message folder:

◆ *Do one of the following:*

   ▲ Drag the MBOX file into Entourage's Folders list.

   ▲ Double-click the MBOX file. In the dialog box that appears (**Figure 20.39**), click Import. A new folder (named after the MBOX filename) appears in the Folders list.

✔ Tips

■ To back up only selected messages, drag their message headers onto the Desktop.

■ You can also back up a single message by selecting its message header and choosing File > Save As (**Figure 20.40**).

■ Backing up your entire Entourage database must be done via a manual file copy. See "Back up and restore the Entourage database" in Entourage Help.

BACKING UP EMAIL

Printing Messages

As is the case with other Entourage components, printing messages is accomplished using a nonstandard Print dialog box (**Figure 20.41**). The Quick Preview box reflects the selected print options and settings.

To print a message:

1. Switch to the Mail section of Entourage.

2. Select the header of the message you want to print or open the message in its own window.

3. *Optional:* To print only selected text from the message, select the text.

4. Click the Print toolbar icon, choose File > Print, or press ⌘ P.
   The Print dialog box appears (**Figure 20.41**).

5. Select a printer to use from the Printer drop-down list.

6. Indicate the number of copies to print, whether copies should be collated (when printing multiple copies), and whether to print all pages or a page range.

   If you preselected message text, Print Selection will automatically be chosen, rather than a page range.

7. Set options in the Style, Header, and Footer sections.

8. If you need to specify a different paper size or orientation, click Page Setup.

9. Click Print to generate the printout.

✔ Tip

■ To decide which pages to print, click through the pages in the Quick Preview box.

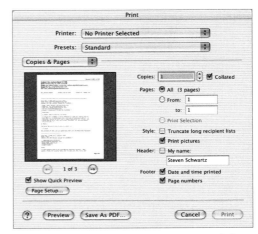

Figure 20.41 Specify print options in the Print dialog box and then click Print.

PRINTING MESSAGES

ADDRESS BOOK

The Office Address Book is the repository of your contact information for people, companies, and organizations. In addition to the standard information normally stored in an address book (such as names, home and work addresses, phone numbers, and email addresses), an Address Book record can store a birth date, picture, anniversary date, spouse's name, children's names, and notes. You can even define custom fields if you feel that an important bit of data is missing.

✔ Tips

- While you will probably create and edit most of your contact records from within Entourage, the contact information is also available to you from Word's Contact toolbar. Using the toolbar, you can create new records, insert contact data into your documents (to address letters, for example), and perform mail merges. For more information, refer to Chapter 8.

- Office 2004 supports multiple users (called *identities*). In addition to having separate email, each user who shares a copy of Office on a single Mac has a separate Address Book. To learn how to switch from one user to another, see the tip at the end of "Emailing an Office Document" in Chapter 2.

Adding Contacts

You may have been using a different program to manage your address book until now. Entourage can help you import address data from several of the most popular programs, as well as from a text file. You can also add contact records manually or create them from received email messages.

Importing an address book

There's nothing more painful than having to re-create an address book simply because you've changed programs or upgraded to a new version. Happily, Entourage can import contact data from many programs.

To import an existing address book:

1. Choose File > Import.

   The Import wizard appears, displaying the Begin Import screen (**Figure 21.1**).

2. Click the Import information from a program radio button, and then click the right-arrow icon to continue.

   The Choose a Program screen appears (**Figure 21.2**).

Click to continue

Figure 21.1 In the Import wizard's first screen, select Import information from a program and click the right arrow icon.

Figure 21.2 Select the program in which your address data is currently stored.

ADDING CONTACTS

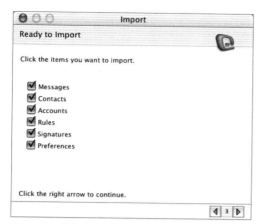

Figure 21.3 Select Contacts and any other data you wish to import. (The choices vary from program to program.)

3. If your address data is stored in one of the listed programs, select the program and click the right arrow to continue.

   The Ready to Import screen appears (**Figure 21.3**).

4. From the list of options, make sure that Contacts is checked—this is your address data. Depending on the program selected, you may also be able to import other Entourage-compatible data, such as calendar events. After making your selections, click the right arrow and follow the remaining instructions.

✔ **Tip**

■ If your current address book program *isn't* listed in Step 3, open the program and export its data as a tab- or comma-delimited text file, if possible. Then return to the Import wizard, select Import information from a text file, and select Import contacts from a tab- or comma-delimited text file.

Creating contact records from email messages

You can extract email addresses from received messages and use them as the basis for new contact records.

To create a contact record from a received email message:

1. *Do one of the following:*
   - ▲ Select the message header in the message list and choose Tools > Add to Address Book (⌘=).
   - ▲ Control-click the message header in the message list and choose Add Sender To Address Book from the pop-up menu that appears (**Figure 21.4**).
   - ▲ Select the message header in the message list and Control-click any email address in the header section of the message above the Preview pane. Choose Add to Address Book from the pop-up menu that appears (**Figure 21.5**). (You can also select other recipients—not just the sender.)

   The contact record for the new address book entry appears (**Figure 21.6**).

2. Fill in as much additional contact information for the person, company, or organization as you like. Click tabs to move from one record section to another. If you make additions or changes, click the Save toolbar icon when you are done.

Figure 21.4 You can Control-click a message header and choose Add Sender To Address Book.

Figure 21.5 You can Control-click an email address above the Preview Pane and choose Add to Address Book from the pop-up menu.

Figure 21.6 Complete the rest of the information for the contact and then save the record.

Click to view menu

Figure 21.7 You can create a new contact record by clicking the down arrow beside the New icon and choosing Contact.

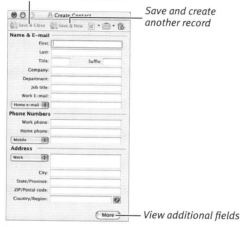

Save and close the record

Save and create another record

View additional fields

Figure 21.8 Enter the basic contact information in the Create Contact dialog box.

Manually creating new records

You can manually create new contact records as needed.

To create a contact record manually:

1. *Do one of the following:*

   ▲ If the Address Book window is currently displayed, click the New toolbar icon or press ⌘N.

   ▲ Regardless of the part of Entourage that is displayed, you can choose File > New > Contact or click the down arrow beside the New toolbar icon and choose Contact (**Figure 21.7**).

   The Create Contact dialog box appears (**Figure 21.8**).

2. Enter the basic information for the contact.

3. *Do one of the following:*

   ▲ If you are done entering information, click the Save & Close icon. (Or click Save & New if you want to create additional records.)

   ▲ If you want to enter more detailed information, click the More button. The individual's full record appears (see Figure 21.6). Enter any other information you like, clicking tabs to view other sections of the record. When you've finished, click the Save toolbar icon.

ADDING CONTACTS

Deleting Contacts

There are several ways to delete contacts from your Address Book.

To delete contacts:

1. Switch to the Address Book by clicking the Address Book icon in the upper-left corner of the Entourage window.

2. In the address list, select one or more contact records to delete. (You can [Shift]-click to select contiguous records or [⌘]-click to select noncontiguous records.)

3. Click the Delete toolbar icon (**Figure 21.9**), choose Edit > Delete Contact, press [Delete], or press [⌘][Delete].

   A confirmation dialog box appears (**Figure 21.10**).

4. To delete the selected contact(s), click Delete. Or if you've changed your mind, click Cancel .

✔ Tips

- If a contact record is open in its own window, you can delete it by clicking the Delete toolbar icon, choosing Edit > Delete Contact, or pressing [⌘][D].

- Deleting a contact record is immediate and permanent. The records are *not* moved to the Deleted Items folder.

Figure 21.9 Click the Delete toolbar icon to delete the selected record(s).

Figure 21.10 Record deletions must be confirmed.

DELETING CONTACTS

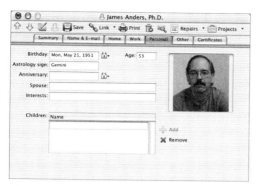

Figure 21.11 Click the various tabs to display and edit the person's contact data.

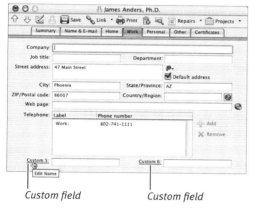

Custom field   *Custom field*

Figure 21.12 Click a Custom field's label to rename it.

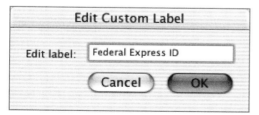

Figure 21.13 Rename the custom field and click OK.

Editing Contact Records

People occasionally move, change jobs, or get new email addresses. You're free to make additions and changes to your contact records.

To edit contact information:

1. Switch to the Address Book.

2. In the address list, double-click the contact you want to edit.

   The person's contact record opens in a separate window.

3. Click a tab at the top of the window to select the type of information you want to edit (**Figure 21.11**) and then make the desired changes.

4. Click other tabs as necessary to make additional changes. When you're done editing, click the Save toolbar icon.

✔ Tips

- If you have a Palm or Palm-compatible personal digital assistant (PDA), you can synchronize Entourage data with your PDA. To install the required *conduit,* run the Handheld Sync Installer (found in the Additional Tools folder inside the Microsoft Office 2004 folder).

- To help you better identify people, you can also store a picture as part of any contact record (see Figure 21.11). Open the record, click the Personal tab, and drag the file icon for any image file into the gray square. To remove a picture, drag it to the Trash.

- Many tabs contain Custom fields. You can rename a Custom field by clicking the underlined Custom label (**Figure 21.12**). Name the field in the Edit Custom Label dialog box (**Figure 21.13**). The new field name is added to all contact records.

Electronic Business Cards (vCards)

You may occasionally receive electronic business cards (vCards) as attachments to email. You can recognize them by the .vcf filename extension. Entourage can read and create new contact records from vCards. You can also email contact records to others as vCard attachments.

To add a received vCard to the Address Book:

1. Select the message header in the message list. If necessary, click the Attachments triangle to open the Attachments pane and display the vCard attachment (**Figure 21.14**).

2. Double-click the vCard attachment.

   A new contact record containing the vCard information opens.

3. Make any necessary changes to the contact data and click the Save toolbar icon.

   The vCard is added to your Address Book as a new contact record.

✔ Tips

- There's another way to add a received vCard to your Address Book. Open the email message in its own window, switch to the Address Book section of Entourage, and drag the vCard attachment into the address list.

- In some cases, you may receive vCards as files on disk (**Figure 21.15**) rather than as email attachments. To create a new record from such a vCard, open Entourage, switch to the Address Book section, and drag the vCard file icon into the address list.

Show/hide Attachments pane

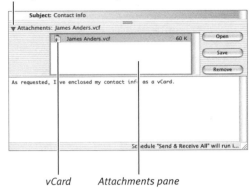

vCard   Attachments pane

Figure 21.14 A vCard (.vcf) attachment in an incoming message will be listed in the Attachments pane like any other attachment.

Figure 21.15 This is an example of a vCard file icon.

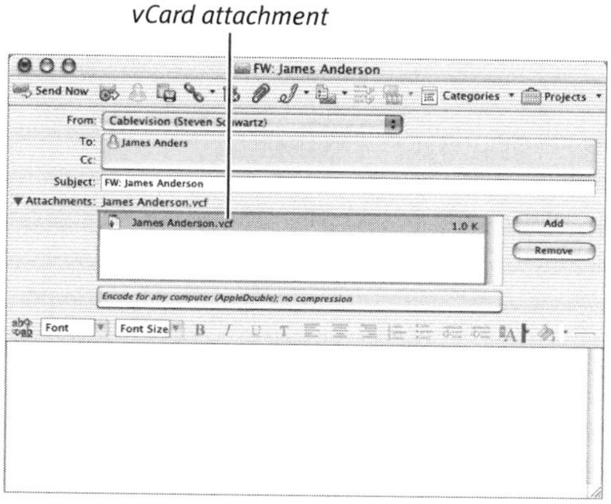

vCard attachment

Figure 21.16 The selected contact record is added as a vCard attachment to a new message.

To email a vCard to someone:

1. Switch to the Address Book section of Entourage. In the address list, select the contact record you want to send as a vCard.

   You can select your own record or any other record in your Address Book.

2. Choose Contact > Forward as vCard.

   A new email message opens, containing the vCard attachment.

3. Fill in the address information and body of the message. (The subject is already filled in for you, although you are free to change it.) You can add other attachments, if you like.

   The selected address record is included in the Attachments pane as a vCard (**Figure 21.16**).

4. To send the message and the vCard immediately, click the Send Now toolbar icon. If you'd rather just place the message in your Outbox to be sent at a more convenient time, click the Send Later icon.

✔ Tips

■ To send *multiple* contact records as vCards, simply select all the desired records from the address list before choosing Contact > Forward as vCard.

■ You can also send a contact record as a vCard by dragging the record from the address list into an open email message. (Note that *any* file dragged into an email message is automatically treated as an attachment.)

ELECTRONIC BUSINESS CARDS (vCARDS)

Addressing Email from the Address Book

In Chapter 20, you learned the most common methods of addressing email. You can also address email directly from the Address Book.

To address email from the Address Book:

1. Switch to the Address Book section of Entourage.

2. In the address list, select the person or people to whom you want to send the message.

3. *Do one of the following:*

   ▲ Choose Contact > New Message To.

   ▲ Click the New Message To toolbar icon.

   ▲ [Control]-click the contact record in the address list and choose New Message To from the pop-up menu that appears.

   A new message window opens, addressed to the selected contact.

✔ Tips

■ To rearrange contacts in the To, Cc, and Bcc areas of the address pane, drag the contacts to where you want them.

■ You can also address messages by dragging contact records from the address list into the To, Cc, or Bcc area of any outgoing message's address pane.

■ Regardless of how you're creating a message, it can be convenient to have the address list displayed when selecting recipients. Open the address pane of an outgoing message and click the Address Book icon (**Figure 21.17**). To add a new recipient, click in the To, Cc, or Bcc area, and double-click the name in the address list. You can also drag names from the address list into the address pane.

Address Book icon (show/hide address list)   *Address list*

Figure 21.17 When addressing email, you can optionally display your address list.

Unknown person   *Click to request directory services*

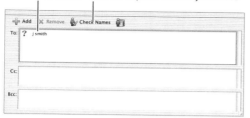

Figure 21.18 If you enter the name of a person who has no contact record and hasn't recently emailed you, Entourage marks it with a green question mark.

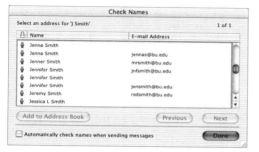

Figure 21.19 Potential matches are displayed in the Check Names dialog box.

Using Directory Services

If you don't have someone's email address, you may be able to find it in a *directory service*. Entourage supports Lightweight Directory Access Protocol (LDAP) and can consult LDAP servers to search for email addresses. Recently, many of the big name public directory services (such as Bigfoot) have been directing users to their Web sites to perform searches. They are no longer accessible through programs like Entourage. Now the most common use of this feature is to find email addresses of employees on a corporate server. Contact your network administrator for configuration instructions.

You can search for unknown email addresses from the address pane of an outgoing message or in the Directory Services dialog box.

To search from the address pane:

1. Address an outgoing email message by typing the person's name in the To, Cc, or Bcc area of the address pane.

   If Entourage does not know the person's email address, a green question mark will precede it (**Figure 21.18**).

2. Click the Check Names toolbar icon.

   Entourage contacts the default directory service and displays a list of potential matches (**Figure 21.19**).

3. If you see the correct name in the list, select it.

4. *Optional:* Click Add to Address Book to create a new contact record from the selected data record.

5. Click Done to dismiss the dialog box.

   If a record is currently selected, the new email address is substituted for the formerly unknown one. If no record is selected, the unknown address is left unchanged.

USING DIRECTORY SERVICES

347

To search from the Directory Services dialog box:

1. Choose Tools > Directory Services.

   The Directory Services dialog box appears (**Figure 21.20**).

2. In the Server List pane, select the directory service you want to search.

3. *Do one or both of the following:*

   ▲ In the Search for name field, type all or part of the person's name.

   ▲ In the E-mail field, type all or part of the person's email user name.

4. Click the Find button.

   Entourage contacts the selected directory service and displays a list of possible matches.

5. Click a record in the results list.

   The available information for the record appears in the pane below the list.

6. If you believe this is the correct person and email address, click the New Message To or Add to Address Book toolbar icon.

✔ Tips

■ You can add other directory services as needed. For example, your company may have an LDAP server you'd like to use. To create a new LDAP server account (**Figure 21.21**), click the New icon on the Directory Service tab of the Accounts dialog box.

■ When you're conducting a directory service search from an email message's address pane, Entourage automatically uses the *default* directory service. If you have another preferred directory service, you can make that one the default. Select its name on the Directory Services tab of the Accounts dialog box and click the Make Default icon.

Selected server   Results   Search string(s)

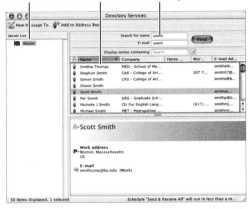

Figure 21.20 Select a directory service to consult and enter the search text. Matches are returned in a list. You can sort the list by clicking any column heading.

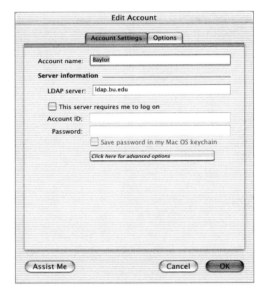

Figure 21.21 To add a directory service, enter a name for the account and the server address. In the Search base text box on the Options tab, enter the root information for the directory service.

Quick Preview area

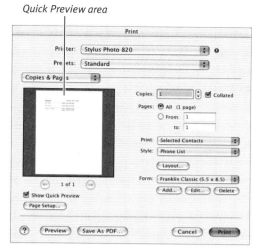

Figure 21.22 Select print settings and click Print.

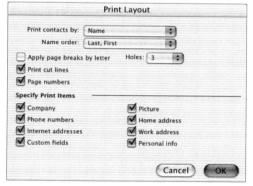

Figure 21.23 Special print options can be set in the Print Layout dialog box.

Printing the Address Book

Using the Print command, you can print one contact record, selected records, or all records (in phone list or address book format).

To print one or more contact records:

1. Switch to the Address Book section.

2. *Optional:* To print one or selected records, select the records in the Address Book list.

   You can ⌘-click or Shift-click to select multiple records.

3. Click the Print toolbar icon, choose File > Print, or press ⌘P.

   The Print dialog box appears (**Figure 21.22**).

4. Select a printer to use from the Printer drop-down list.

5. From the Print drop-down menu, choose what you want to print: Selected Contacts, All Contacts, or Flagged Contacts.

6. Choose a print format (Address Book or Phone List) from the Style drop-down menu.

7. If you intend to print on nonstandard paper, select a paper style from the Form drop-down list.

8. To review or change print options, click the Layout button. In the Print Layout dialog box (**Figure 21.23**), make any necessary changes and click OK.

9. Indicate the number of copies to print, whether copies should be collated (when printing multiple copies), and whether to print all pages or a page range.

10. If you need to specify a different paper size or orientation, click Page Setup.

11. Click Print to generate the printout.

✔ Tips

- You can use these same Print procedures when a contact record is open in its own window.

- When a record to be printed is open in its own window, the File > Print One Copy (Option ⌘ P) command is also available. You can use it to print the open record using the current print settings.

- To get an idea of what the printout will look like, click the Show Quick Preview check box. The preview changes as you select different print options. Click the arrow buttons beneath the Quick Preview to review other pages, if any.

- As with other OS X applications, you can create a PDF (Portable Document Format) file from a contacts printout. You can click Save As PDF to save the printout as a PDF file or click Preview to create a temporary PDF file that will open in the default viewer (Preview or Adobe Reader).

22

CALENDAR

Entourage provides a calendar you can use to
record upcoming appointments and events,
whether they occur only once or many times.
You can schedule reminders for events, send
and receive meeting invitations, and view
your calendar in a variety of formats.

Viewing the Calendar

You can change the calendar display in several ways: viewing a day, work week, week, or month at a time; hiding or showing the Tasks pane; or showing only a sequential list of events rather than a calendar. In addition to setting the view, you can select a particular date or range of dates you wish to see.

To change the calendar view:

1. Switch to the calendar by clicking its icon in the upper-left corner of the window, choosing View > Go To > Calendar, or pressing ⌘ 3.

   The Views pane contains a list of custom calendar views. Beneath it is a mini-calendar. To the right is the calendar view (showing events for the current day, work week, week, or month), and on the far right is the Tasks pane (**Figure 22.1**).

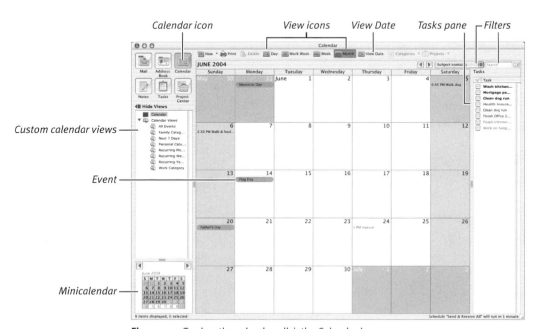

Figure 22.1 To view the calendar, click the Calendar icon.

Figure 22.2 You can change the view by choosing a command from the Calendar menu.

Figure 22.3 Choose Calendar > List if all you'd like to see is a list of events for the selected time period.

2. To change the current view, do one of the following:

▲ Click the Day, Work Week, Week, or Month toolbar icon.

▲ Choose a command from the Calendar menu (**Figure 22.2**).

The current date range is displayed using the new view. The active view is indicated by a darkened toolbar icon.

✔ Tips

■ Displaying the Tasks pane is optional. To make it appear, choose Calendar > Tasks Pane. Choose the command again to hide the pane.

■ To display only the list of events for the current view (**Figure 22.3**), choose Calendar > List. To return to a normal calendar view, click a toolbar icon or choose a Calendar command.

■ You can also display a custom view (in list form) by selecting it from the Views pane on the left side of the Entourage window (**Figure 22.4**). To restore a normal view, click the Calendar text above the Calendar Views list.

■ In some cases, you may not be able to read the full text of an event by just glancing at the calendar. However, if you hover the cursor over the event for a couple of seconds, the full text will be displayed.

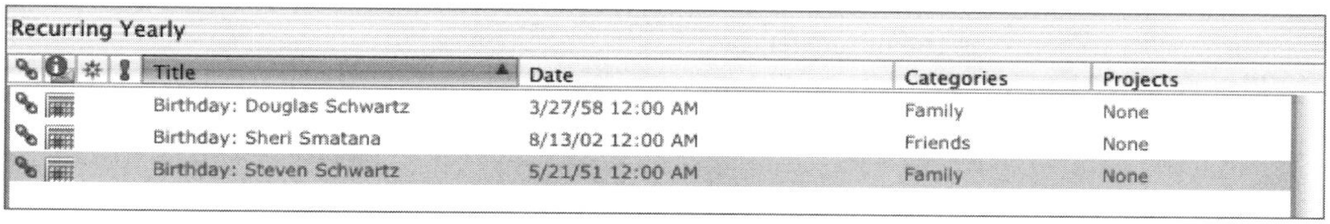

VIEWING THE CALENDAR

Figure 22.4 To see a list of upcoming events, select a custom view. Here are the results of the Recurring Yearly custom view.

To view a specific date:

1. To select a date to view, you can do any of the following:

   ▲ Click the left and right arrows above the calendar window to scroll until the desired date is visible (**Figure 22.5**).

   ▲ Click the left and right arrows above the minicalendar to scroll until the date you want is visible. (Holding down the mouse button over either arrow makes the calendar scroll quickly through the months.) Click the desired date.

   ▲ Choose Calendar > Previous (⌘[) or Calendar > Next (⌘]) to view the previous or next day, work week, week, or month (depending on the current view).

   ▲ To jump to a specific date, click the View Date icon in the toolbar or choose Calendar > View Date. In the View Date dialog box that appears, type a date or select one from the pop-up calendar (**Figure 22.6**). Click OK.

   The selected date is displayed using the view currently in effect.

2. To display the current date, choose Calendar > Go to Today, press ⌘T, or click the View Date icon and click OK in the View Date dialog box. (The default date is always today.)

✔ Tip

■ To restrict the calendar to showing a particular range of dates, you can drag-select from one to six weeks in the minicalendar (**Figure 22.7**). Unlike other date-selection methods, this one changes the view to match the number of weeks selected.

Figure 22.5 Click an arrow icon to move backward or forward. The amount moved (a day, week, or month) is determined by the calendar view that's in effect.

Figure 22.6 You can select a particular date to view by choosing it from the pop-up calendar in the View Date dialog box.

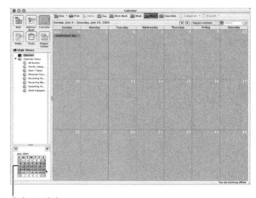

Selected date range

Figure 22.7 To view a specific range of dates (up to six weeks), drag-select the range in the minicalendar.

VIEWING THE CALENDAR

Figure 22.8 Enter the event information in this dialog box.

Figure 22.9 If this is a recurring event, you can specify a custom recurrence pattern and an end date for it.

Adding and Deleting Events

As you might expect, there are multiple ways to create calendar events. And when a scheduled event has passed, you can delete it.

To create a calendar event:

1. *Do one of the following:*
   - ▲ When viewing the calendar, click the New toolbar icon or press ⌘N. When viewing any other part of Entourage, click the down arrow beside the New toolbar icon and choose Calendar Event from the drop-down menu.
   - ▲ Choose File > New > Calendar Event.
   - ▲ On the calendar, double-click the date or time of the event.

   If you first select the event's date on the calendar, the event will default to that date.

2. In the event window that appears (**Figure 22.8**), enter the information for the event.

3. To assign a category to the event or associate it with a project:
   - ▲ Click the Categories or Projects toolbar icon.
   - ▲ Choose Edit > Categories or Edit > Projects, and then choose a category or project from the submenu.

4. To set the start or end date, type the date in the appropriate field. Or click a Calendar icon to the right of the field and select a date.

5. If this is a recurring event, choose a recurrence schedule from the Occurs drop-down menu. To set a different schedule, choose Custom, specify the schedule details in the Recurring Event dialog box (**Figure 22.9**), and click OK.

6. Save the event by clicking the Save toolbar icon, choosing File > Save, or pressing ⌘S.

To create a calendar event from an Entourage item:

1. *Do one of the following:*

   ▲ Select an item and choose Tools > Link to New > Calendar Event.

   ▲ Open an item, such as a note or email message, click the Link toolbar icon, and choose Link to New > Calendar Event from the drop-down menu.

2. Enter the event information (as described on the previous page).

To create a calendar event from a date on a contact record:

1. Switch to the Address Book by clicking its icon in the upper-left corner of the Entourage window, choosing View > Go To > Address Book, or pressing ⌘②.

2. Double-click the contact record to open it in its own window.

3. Click the Personal or Other tab (whichever contains the date field you want to add to the calendar).

4. Click the Calendar icon beside the date field and choose Add to Calendar from the pop-up menu (**Figure 22.10**).

   A new event window opens (**Figure 22.11**), containing the information required to add the date as an annual event.

5. Make any necessary changes, save the event by clicking the Save toolbar icon, and close the event window.

✔ Tip

■ To view annual events created from contact records (such as birthdays and anniversaries), as well as other annual events you've added to the calendar, click the Recurring Yearly custom view in the Views pane (see Figure 22.4).

Calendar icon

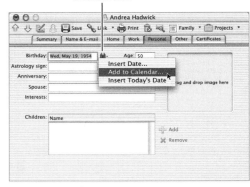

Figure 22.10 To create a calendar event from a date field of any contact record (such as this birthday), click the Calendar icon and choose Add to Calendar.

Figure 22.11 A new event is automatically created for the date. Edit it as necessary and click the Save icon.

Entourage and PDAs

If you have a Palm-compatible personal digital assistant (PDA), you can synchronize data on the device with Entourage calendar events, contacts, tasks, and notes. To do this, you must install the Entourage *conduit*. Run the Handheld Synch Installer, found in the Additional Tools folder within the Microsoft Office 2004 folder.

Note that the Entourage conduit requires Palm Desktop 4.0.

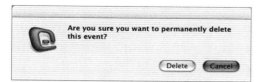

Figure 22.12 You must confirm the deletion of a normal, onetime event.

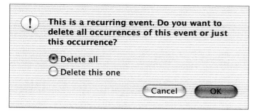

Figure 22.13 When deleting a recurring event, you can delete just the selected occurrence or the complete event series.

Automatically delete old events

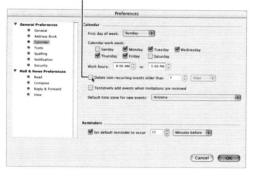

Figure 22.14 If you set this preference, Entourage will automatically delete expired events.

To delete a calendar event:

1. In the Calendar window, switch to a view that displays the event you want to delete, and select the event.

2. *Do one of the following:*
   ▲ Click the Delete toolbar icon.
   ▲ Choose Edit > Delete Event.
   ▲ Press ⌘ Delete or Delete.
   ▲ Control-click the event and choose Delete Event from the pop-up menu that appears.

   A confirmation dialog box appears. The specific dialog box displayed depends on whether this is a onetime or a recurring event.

3. *Do one of the following:*
   ▲ If this is a onetime event (**Figure 22.12**), click the Delete button.
   ▲ If this is a recurring event (**Figure 22.13**), click a radio button to indicate whether you want to delete this and all future occurrences of the event or just this occurrence. Then click OK.

✔ Tips

■ If an event is open in its own window, you can delete it by clicking the Delete toolbar icon, choosing Edit > Delete Event, or pressing ⌘ Delete.

■ You can instruct Entourage to delete old calendar events automatically. Choose Entourage > Preferences (⌘ ;), select the Calendar category, and check the option to Delete non-recurring events older than X days (**Figure 22.14**). Click OK to dismiss the dialog box.

■ Be careful when deleting events. There is no Undo command that you can choose to restore a deleted event.

ADDING AND DELETING EVENTS

Modifying Events

You can edit any aspect of a saved event.

To edit an event:

1. Switch to a calendar view that displays the event you want to change.

2. To open the event for editing, do one of the following:

   ▲ Double-click the event.

   ▲ Select the event and choose File > Open Event (or press ⌘O).

   ▲ Control-click the event and choose Open Event from the pop-up menu that appears.

3. If the event you are editing is part of a recurring series, a dialog box appears (**Figure 22.15**). Select an option and click OK.

4. In the event window, make any necessary changes.

5. Save the edited event by clicking the Save toolbar icon, choosing File > Save, or pressing ⌘S.

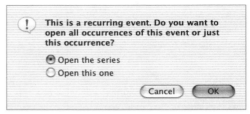

Figure 22.15 When editing a recurring event, you can edit just the selected occurrence or the entire event series.

Invite icon

Figure 22.16 To invite others to attend an event, click the Invite toolbar icon.

Display Address Book

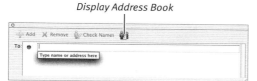

Figure 22.17 Specify invitiation recipients as you do an email recipient. To select people from your address book, click the Address Book icon.

Sending and Responding to Invitations

Entourage makes it easy to send invitations to your events via email, as well as to reply to event invitations.

To invite others to an event:

1. Switch to the Calendar window, and double-click the event to open it in a separate window (**Figure 22.16**).

   If it's a repeating event, indicate in the dialog box that appears whether you're editing just this instance or the entire event series (see Figure 22.15).

2. Click the Invite toolbar icon.

3. In the address pane (**Figure 22.17**), specify the people to whom you wish to send an invitation and close the address pane.

   The full event invitation is displayed.

4. If you have multiple email addresses, click the From drop-down list to select the address from which you want to send the invitation.

5. Edit the invitation as necessary.

   To change the event from all day to a specific time span, for example, uncheck the All-day event check box. Note that you can also attach files, if you wish.

6. Click the Send Now toolbar icon to email the invitation to the designated people.

   Recipients receive a message to which, if they are using Entourage, they can respond by simply clicking an Accept, Decline, or Tentative toolbar icon. Entourage then relays a response to the person who sent the invitations.

   Recipients who don't use Entourage can reply with a normal email message.

✔ Tips

- Recipients who use Microsoft Outlook 2004 (**Figure 22.18**) can also respond to an invitation by clicking an icon.

- Invitation recipients can change their minds at any time by opening the invitation message again and clicking a different response icon.

- To cancel an invitation you've already sent, double-click the event to open its window and click the Cancel Invitations toolbar icon. Participants will receive a cancellation email message.

- If you're the person who sent out the invitations, you can check the responses by opening the event and clicking the View attendee status text beneath the toolbar (**Figure 22.19**).

- If your organization's email is managed by an Exchange Server, you can appoint a *delegate* to manage your material on the server. Delegate access, however, must be enabled using Outlook (Windows). After a delegate has been designated, he or she can use Entourage to handle your messages, invitations, and calendar events.

Invitation response icons

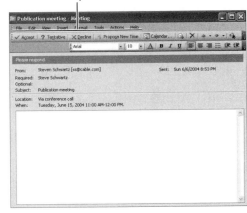

Figure 22.18 Outlook 2004 (Windows) users can also respond to an invitation by clicking an icon.

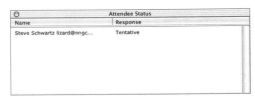

Figure 22.19 You can review invitation responses in the Attendee Status window.

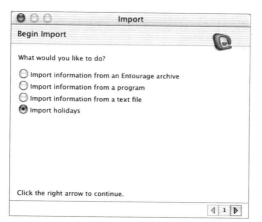

Figure 22.20 On the first screen of the Import wizard, click the Import holidays radio button.

Figure 22.21 Click the check boxes of the countries and religions whose holidays you want to import.

Adding and Removing Holidays

If you like, you can add country-specific and religious holidays to the calendar. You can also decide later to remove all or some of the holidays.

To add holidays to the calendar:

1. Choose File > Import.

   The Import wizard appears (**Figure 22.20**).

2. Click the Import holidays radio button, and then click the right-arrow icon to continue to the next screen.

3. After Entourage finishes building the list of available country-specific and religious holiday sets, make your selections by entering checkmarks (**Figure 22.21**). Click the right arrow icon to continue.

   The chosen holidays are imported into the calendar.

To remove holidays from the calendar:

1. Switch to the calendar.

2. Choose Edit > Advanced Find or press Option ⌘ F.
   The Find window appears.

3. Select only Calendar Events as Item Types and set the criterion as Category Is Holiday using the Criteria drop-down menus (**Figure 22.22**).

4. Click Find.
   A Search Results window appears, listing the found holiday events (**Figure 22.23**).

5. Select the holidays you want to delete. (Note that each holiday is listed multiple times, representing the different years for which it was added to the calendar.)

6. Click the Delete toolbar icon, choose Edit > Delete, or press Delete or ⌘ Delete.

7. Click the Delete button in the confirmation dialog box that appears.

8. Close the Search Results window.

✔ Tips

- Setting the criterion as Category Is Holiday will find *all* imported holidays. If you imported multiple holiday sets, you can find any one set (for example, Holiday–United States) by setting the search category to that specific set.

- If you want to delete *all* found holidays, click to select any one of them, choose Edit > Select All, and then perform the deletion.

- You can also remove individual holidays (marked in red on the calendar) by selecting and then deleting them as you would any other event.

Figure 22.22 In the Find dialog box, select Calendar Events and set the criterion to Category Is Holiday.

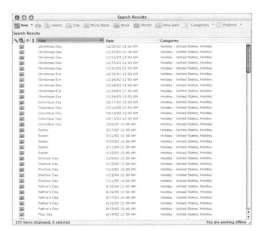

Figure 22.23 Select the holidays you want to delete from the list in the Search Results window.

ADDING AND REMOVING HOLIDAYS

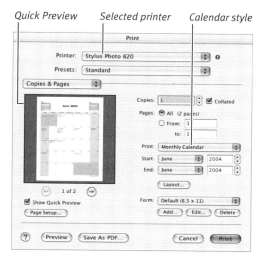

Quick Preview   *Selected printer*   *Calendar style*

Figure 22.24 All setup options for printing a calendar are specified in the Print dialog box.

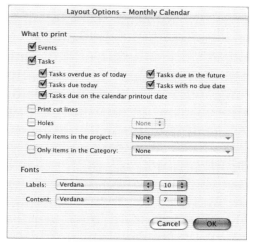

Figure 22.25 In the Layout Options dialog box, specify the types of information to include in the printout and special print options.

Printing a Calendar

As is the case with other Entourage components, printing a calendar is accomplished via a nonstandard Print dialog box (**Figure 22.24**). The Quick Preview box reflects your print selections.

To print a calendar:

1. Switch to the Calendar.

2. Click the Print toolbar icon, choose File > Print, or press ⌘P.

    The Print dialog box appears (see Figure 22.24).

3. Select a printer to use from the Printer drop-down list.

4. From the Print drop-down menu, choose the form of calendar you want to print: Daily Calendar, Calendar List, Weekly Calendar, or Monthly Calendar.

5. Specify the range of dates to include.

6. If you intend to put the printout in a personal planner, choose a paper style from the Form drop-down menu. Otherwise, select Default (8.5 x 11).

7. To review print options, click the Layout button. In the Layout Options dialog box (**Figure 22.25**), make any necessary changes and click OK.

    For example, you can specify the fonts to use, include/exclude tasks, and restrict events to those that meet certain criteria, such as belonging to a project.

8. Indicate the number of copies to print, whether copies should be collated (when printing multiple copies), and whether to print all pages or a page range.

9. If you need to specify a different paper size or orientation, click Page Setup.

10. Click Print to generate the printout.

TASKS
(TO-DO LISTS)

23

You can use Entourage to track your to-do items (referred to as *tasks*). You can mark tasks as completed, be reminded of tasks that are due, and connect tasks to other Office documents and Entourage items. You can also set tasks as *repeating*. For example, a monthly mortgage payment or weekly staff meeting can appear in your to-do list at specified intervals.

Creating and Deleting Tasks

You can create new tasks by adding them directly to the Tasks list or by linking them to other events. When you've completed a task or you're no longer interested in tracking it, you can delete it from the Tasks list.

To create a new task:

1. To create a new task from Tasks view, click the New toolbar icon at the top of the Entourage window, choose File > New > Task, or press ⌘Ⓝ.

   or

   To create a new task from any other view, choose File > New > Task or click the arrow beside the New toolbar icon and choose Task (**Figure 23.1**).

   A new task window appears (**Figure 23.2**).

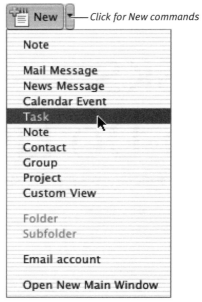

Figure 23.1 Regardless of the active Entourage component, you can create a new task by choosing this command from the New toolbar menu.

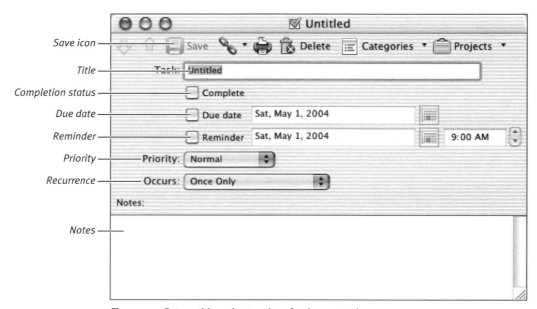

Figure 23.2 Enter a title and set options for the new task.

Main category

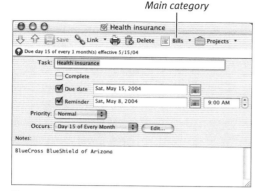

Figure 23.3 This is an example of a task with a category, due date, reminder, occurrence, and notes.

Figure 23.4 Choose common recurrence schedules from the Occurs drop-down menu.

Figure 23.5 Specify more complex recurrence schedules in the Recurring Task dialog box.

2. Enter a name for the task in the Task box.

3. *Optional:* Choose a category from the Categories pull-down menu, associate the task with a project, assign a priority, set a due date, schedule a reminder, and/or add a note (**Figure 23.3**).

4. If this is a recurring task, do one of the following:

▲ Choose a recurrence schedule from the Occurs drop-down menu (**Figure 23.4**).

▲ To set a schedule other than the ones listed, choose Custom from the Occurs drop-down menu. The Recurring Task window appears (**Figure 23.5**). Set the recurrence pattern and select an end criterion from the options in the Start and End pane. Click OK.

5. To save the task, click the Save toolbar icon, choose File > Save, or press ⌘Ⓢ. Close the task window.

The task is inserted into the Tasks list in the current sort order.

✔ Tips

■ For a task that doesn't have a specific due date and doesn't recur, it's often sufficient to enter only the task's name. Everything else (such as assigning a priority, reminder, and category) is optional.

■ Recurring tasks, due dates, and reminders are covered in depth later in this chapter.

CREATING AND DELETING TASKS

To create a new task as a link to another Entourage item:

1. *Do one of the following:*

   ▲ Select an Entourage item (an email message or note, for example) and choose Tools > Link to New > Task.

   ▲ If the Entourage item is open in its own window, choose Tools > Link to New > Task or choose the same command from the pop-up menu that appears when you click the Link toolbar icon (**Figure 23.6**).

   A new Task window opens.

2. Enter the new task information.

3. Save the task by clicking the Save toolbar icon, choosing File > Save, or pressing ⌘ S. Close the task window.

   The new task is created, and a link is established between it and the item. The link is indicated by a link icon (**Figure 23.7**). For more information about linking Entourage items, see Chapter 26.

✔ Tips

■ If an email message is already linked to at least one other item, you can also create a new link for it by clicking the link icon to the right of the message header.

■ To the left of each item in the Tasks list and Notes list is a Links column. You can create a new link item by clicking in the Links column and choosing an Entourage item (such as Task) from the Link to New submenu (**Figure 23.8**).

■ To determine what links exist between an item and other Entourage items, click the item's link icon (**Figure 23.9**).

■ You can create a task from an email messages by selecting its message header and choosing Create Task from Message from the Scripts menu (Control T).

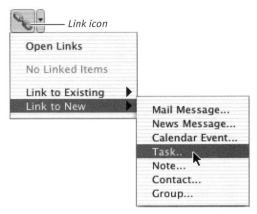

Link icon

Figure 23.6 In an open message window, click the arrow beside the Link icon, and choose Link to New > Task.

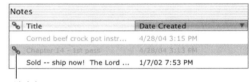

Link icon

Figure 23.7 Linked items are displayed with a link icon. Shown here is the note that was linked to the new task.

Figure 23.8 To create a new link from an item in the Notes or Tasks list, you can click in the Links column for the note or task.

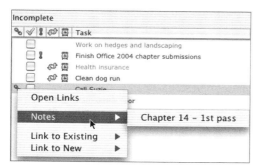

Figure 23.9 To determine what Entourage items are linked to the current item, click its link icon.

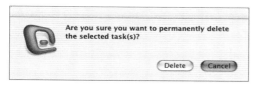

Figure 23.10 You must confirm task deletions.

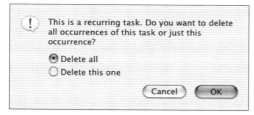

Figure 23.11 You can elect to delete this occurrence only (Delete this one) or the entire series (Delete all).

To delete a task:

1. Select one or more tasks in the Tasks list. To select multiple tasks, ⌘-click (for noncontiguous tasks) or Shift-click (for contiguous tasks).

2. *Do one of the following:*
   ▲ Click the Delete toolbar icon, choose Edit > Delete Task, press Delete, or press ⌘ Delete.
   ▲ With the task open in its own window, click the Delete toolbar icon, choose Edit > Delete Task, or press ⌘ Delete.

   A confirmation dialog box appears (**Figure 23.10**).

3. Click Delete to delete the task.

4. If a selected task is a recurring one, a second dialog box appears, offering the option to delete only this instance or the entire series of tasks (**Figure 23.11**). Click a radio button to indicate your choice and then click OK. (To cancel the deletion, click Cancel.)

Viewing the Tasks List

You can view your tasks in several ways, sort them by any important characteristic, and filter the list of visible tasks to make it more manageable.

To view the Tasks list:

1. Click the Tasks icon in the upper-left corner of the Entourage window, choose View > Go To > Tasks, or press ⌘ 5 .
   The Tasks list appears (**Figure 23.12**).

2. You can sort the list on any column (except the first) by clicking that column heading. To reverse the sort order, click the same column heading again.
   The current sort column's heading is shown in blue.

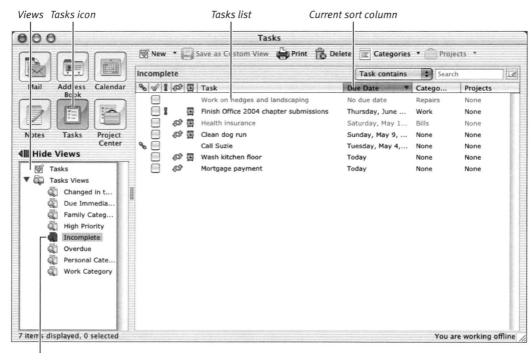

Views Tasks icon   *Tasks list*   *Current sort column*

Current view

Figure 23.12 Click the Tasks icon to display the Tasks list.

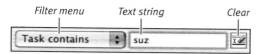

Figure 23.13 You can filter the Tasks list by entering a text string.

Figure 23.14 You can specify which tasks to view by choosing a command from the View menu.

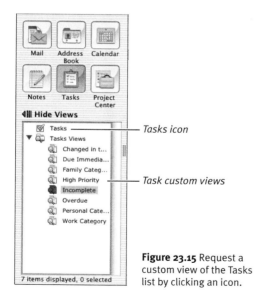

Figure 23.15 Request a custom view of the Tasks list by clicking an icon.

3. You can filter the Tasks list to show only tasks that match a criterion: matching text, an assigned category, or an associated project. You can also filter the list by selecting a predefined view, such as overdue or incomplete tasks.

Do any of the following:

▲ Choose Task contains from the drop-down menu above the Tasks list, and type a string in the text box (**Figure 23.13**). As you type, Entourage filters the list to show only the tasks which contain the typed characters. To restore the Tasks list, click the Clear icon or delete the typed text.

▲ Choose Category is from the drop-down menu and choose a category from the second drop-down menu. To restore the Tasks list, click the Clear icon or set the category to All.

▲ Choose Project is from the drop-down menu and choose a project from the second drop-down menu. To restore the Tasks list, click the Clear icon or set the project to All.

▲ Choose a completion command (All Tasks, Incomplete Tasks, or Complete Tasks) or a due date command (Due Today or Due This Week) from the View menu (**Figure 23.14**). To restore the Tasks list after choosing a completion command, choose All Tasks. To restore the Tasks list after choosing a due date command, choose the same command again.

▲ In the Views pane, select a custom view by clicking an item in the Tasks Views folder (**Figure 23.15**). To restore the Tasks list, click the Tasks icon.

VIEWING THE TASKS LIST

Editing Tasks

You can easily change any aspect of a task.

To edit a task:

1. In the Tasks list, double-click the task you want to edit. Alternately, you can select the task and choose File > Open, press ⌘O, or press Return.

   The task opens in its own window.

2. Make whatever changes you like.

3. Click the Save toolbar icon, choose File > Save, or press ⌘S.

To edit a task's attributes:

- To change a task's completion status, click the check box that precedes the task. Completed items are displayed in strike-through text (**Figure 23.16**).

- To change a task's title, select the task in the Tasks list. Click the title to select it for editing (**Figure 23.17**), make any necessary changes, and press Return or click elsewhere in the Entourage window to save the new title.

- To assign a category to a task, click the Categories section of any task in the Tasks list and choose a category from the pop-up menu (**Figure 23.18**).

   Note that because any Entourage item can be assigned multiple categories, choosing a category in this manner assigns it as an *additional* category; previously assigned categories are *not* removed. If that's your intent, choose Assign Categories from the Categories pop-up menu.

✔ Tip

- When creating a task that's similar to an existing one, it may be quicker to create a duplicate task and edit the copy. Select the task, and choose Edit > Duplicate Task.

Completed item   Incomplete

Figure 23.16 Completed items in the Tasks list are displayed in strike-through text and have a checkmark in their Status check box.

Title selected for editing

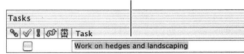

Figure 23.17 You can edit the title of any task by clicking its title in the Tasks list.

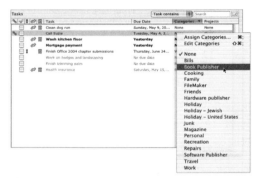

Figure 23.18 To assign a category to a task, click its Categories entry in the Tasks list and choose a category from the pop-up menu.

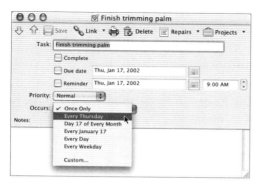

Figure 23.19 Select a recurrence schedule from the Occurs drop-down menu.

Edit recurrence schedule

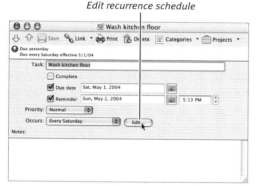

Figure 23.20 To change an existing recurrence schedule to a different custom schedule, click Edit.

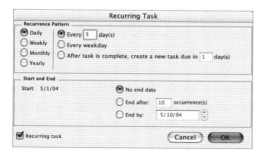

Figure 23.21 Complex recurrence schedules are set in the Recurring Task dialog box. This example schedules a floor mopping every five days.

Recurring Tasks

You can set a task to recur at any regular interval, repeating as many times as you like. You can also change a normal task to a recurring one or vice versa, as well as alter the recurrence pattern for any task.

To set a task as recurring:

1. Create a new task (as described previously), or edit an existing task by double-clicking it in the Tasks list.

2. To accept one of the preset schedules, choose one from the Occurs drop-down menu (**Figure 23.19**). Go to Step 7.

3. To specify a different schedule, do one of the following:
   ▲ If this is a new task or an existing non-recurring task, choose Custom from the Occurs drop-down menu.
   ▲ If this is an existing recurring task, click the Edit button (**Figure 23.20**).
   The Recurring Task dialog box opens (**Figure 23.21**).

4. At the top of the dialog box, specify the recurrence pattern. The options presented depend on whether you select Daily, Weekly, Monthly, or Yearly.

5. In the Start and End pane, specify whether the task will recur indefinitely, end after a certain number of occurrences, or end by a specific date.

6. Click OK to close the Recurring Task dialog box.
   The task window reappears.

7. Save the task and close its window.

✔ Tip

■ To stop a task from recurring, open the task window and choose Once Only from the Occurs drop-down menu.

Due Dates and Reminders

Many tasks don't have a due date—you just need to wash the car *sometime*, for example. Nevertheless, you can optionally assign a due date and/or schedule a reminder for any task. (Due dates and reminders are independent of one another. A task can have a due date, a reminder, both, or neither.)

Setting task due dates

A *due date* specifies when a task must be completed. Unlike an appointment, a due date is associated only with a date, not a time.

To set or modify a task due date:

1. Create a new task or open an existing one.

2. In the task's window, click the Due date check box (**Figure 23.22**), if it isn't already checked.

3. Choose a date from the pop-up calendar (**Figure 23.23**) or edit the current or suggested date.

4. Save the task and close its window.

Setting task reminders

Setting a reminder for a task is different from setting a reminder for a calendar event. Rather than specifying how far in advance you wish to be reminded, you select a specific time at which the task reminder will appear onscreen.

Office 2004 handles reminders for both tasks and calendar events using a separate program called Office Notifications. This enables reminders to appear any time your Mac is on, regardless of whether an Office application is running.

Set due date

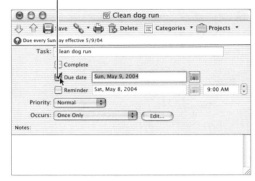

Figure 23.22 To set a due date for a task, click the Due date check box.

Next month
Previous month

Today's date

Figure 23.23 You can edit a due date by typing in the Due date text box or by selecting a date from the pop-up calendar.

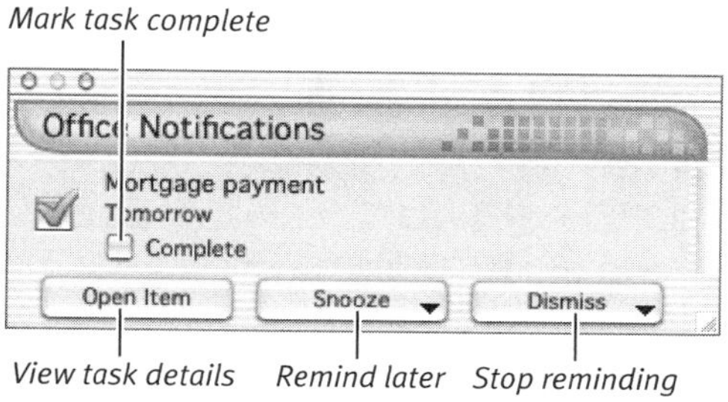

Mark task complete

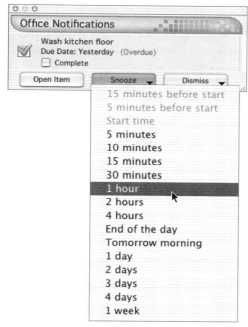

View task details   Remind later   Stop reminding

Figure 23.24 When a task or calendar reminder is due, Office Notifications presents this dialog box.

Figure 23.25 Click the Snooze button to be reminded again in 5 minutes (the default) or choose another Snooze period from the drop-down menu.

To set or modify a task reminder:

1. Create a new task or open an existing one.

2. In the task window, click the Reminder check box (see Figure 23.22), if it isn't already checked.

3. Choose a reminder date from the pop-up calendar (see Figure 23.23) or edit the current or suggested date.

4. Specify a time for the reminder.

   Select the hour, minute, or AM/PM segment of the time. To change the selected segment, click the up- and down-arrow buttons or type new numbers.

5. Save the task and close its window.

To respond to a reminder:

1. At the appointed time, the Office Notifications dialog box appears (**Figure 23.24**).

   If more than one task or event is listed, scroll to select the one to which you want to respond.

2. *Do one of the following:*

   ▲ If you've already performed the task, click the Complete check box. Doing so dismisses the reminder and marks the task as complete in the Tasks list.

   ▲ To dismiss the reminder so it doesn't reappear, click the Dismiss button.

   ▲ If this is a recurring task, you can dismiss this and all future occurrences of the task by holding down the Dismiss button and choosing Dismiss all.

   ▲ To delay the reminder for 5 minutes (when it will reappear onscreen), click the Snooze button.

   ▲ If you want to be reminded later (from 5 minutes to 1 week from now), hold down the Snooze button and choose a delay interval (**Figure 23.25**).

DUE DATES AND REMINDERS

375

✔ Tips

- If there are multiple reminders to be processed—indicated by the presence of a scroll bar and a number in the icon on the Dock (**Figure 23.26**)—the Office Notifications dialog box remains open until you've responded to each reminder. You can view the other reminders by clicking the scroll arrows.

- If you want to open the task's window and view or edit its details, click the Open Item button (see Figure 23.24).

- You can also view the Tasks list in the Calendar window (**Figure 23.27**) by choosing Calendar > Tasks Pane. To mark a task as complete, click its check box. To view the details for a task, double-click it.

- Although the Tasks list is displayed in the Calendar window and some of your tasks may have due dates or reminders, tasks are *not* listed as events on the calendar. This is why it is especially important to decide carefully which items should be created as tasks and which items should be recorded as calendar events.

Office Notification icon

Figure 23.26 Office Notifications adds its icon to the Dock. The number shows the number of current reminders that haven't been handled.

Tasks pane

Figure 23.27 The Calendar can also display the Tasks list, but shows only incomplete tasks.

Status column

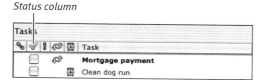

Figure 23.28 You can mark a task as complete by clicking its Status check box in the Tasks list.

Status

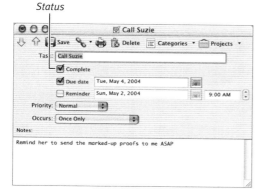

Figure 23.29 You can also mark a task as complete by opening the task in its own window and clicking the Complete check box.

Marking Tasks as Complete

If you mark a task as complete rather than deleting it, the task will still be visible in the Tasks list. This is the appropriate approach when you want to retain a history of a task, as when you're checking off completed project milestones, for example.

To mark a task as complete:

1. Display the Tasks list by clicking the Tasks icon in the upper-left corner of the Entourage window, choosing View > Go To > Tasks, or pressing ⌘ 5.

2. *Do one of the following:*

   ▲ In the Tasks list, click the task's Status check box (**Figure 23.28**) to add a checkmark to it.

   ▲ Open the task in its own window. Click the Complete check box (**Figure 23.29**), save the task, and close its window.

✔ Tips

- The Status and Complete check boxes work as toggles. To reverse the state of a task from incomplete to complete or vice versa, click the check box again.

- You can also mark tasks as completed in the Calendar window.

- You can filter the Tasks list to hide the completed tasks by choosing View > Incomplete Tasks. Conversely, to view *only* tasks you have completed, choose View > Complete Tasks. Other custom filtering options can be selected from the Views pane (see Figure 23.12).

Printing Tasks

As is the case with other Entourage components, printing tasks is accomplished via a nonstandard Print dialog box (**Figure 23.30**). The Quick Preview box reflects your selections.

To print tasks:

1. Switch to Tasks view.

   The Tasks list appears in the main pane.

2. In the Tasks list, select the title of the task you want to print. To print multiple tasks in one printout, ⌘-click each task title.

3. Click the Print toolbar icon, choose File > Print, or press ⌘P.

   The Print dialog box appears.

4. Select a printer to use from the Printer drop-down list.

5. From the Print drop-down list, indicate what you want to print, such as All Tasks, Selected Tasks, or Tasks Due This Week.

6. If you intend to put the printout in a personal planner, select a paper style from the Form drop-down list.

7. To review print options, click the Layout button. In the Print Layout dialog box (**Figure 23.31**), make any necessary changes and click OK.

8. Indicate the number of copies to print, whether copies should be collated (when printing multiple copies), and whether to print all pages or a page range.

9. If you need to specify a different paper size or orientation, click Page Setup.

10. Click Print to generate the printout.

✔ Tip

■ You can also use these Print procedures when a task is open in its own window.

Quick Preview

Figure 23.30 Select print settings and click Print.

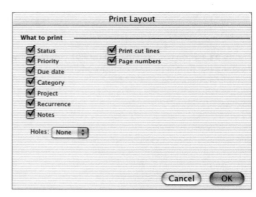

Figure 23.31 Special print options can be set in the Print Layout dialog box.

NOTES

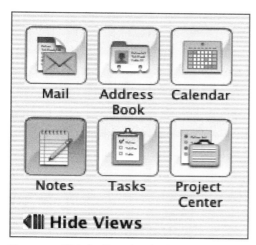

Figure 24.1 Click the Notes icon in the upper-left corner of the Entourage window to see your Notes list.

Entourage's Notes section is designed as a freeform note-taking utility. You can combine text, images, and sounds in notes, and assign categories to them. Unlike most simple note-taking applications, Entourage creates formatted text notes. Any note can contain multiple fonts, sizes, styles, colors, and paragraph formatting.

To view or work with your notes, switch to Notes view by clicking the Notes icon (**Figure 24.1**), choosing View > Go To > Notes, or pressing ⌘4.

Creating and Deleting Notes

Click for New commands

Figure 24.2 Regardless of the active Entourage component, you can create a new note by choosing this command from the New toolbar menu.

You can create as many notes as you wish. And when notes cease to be useful, you can delete them.

To create a new note:

1. To create a new note from Notes view, click the New toolbar icon at the top of the Entourage window, choose File > New > Note, or press ⌘N.

   or

   To create a new note from any other view, click the down arrow beside the New toolbar icon and choose Note (**Figure 24.2**), or choose File > New > Note.

   A new note window appears (**Figure 24.3**).

2. Enter a title for the note and fill in the body by typing, pasting, or dragging and dropping the text. You can optionally assign categories to the note to classify it and/or associate it with a project.

Figure 24.3 A new note window appears, ready to receive a title and the note text.

CREATING AND DELETING NOTES

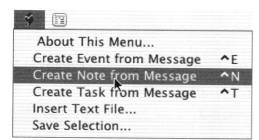

Figure 24.5 You can save the current email message as a note by choosing the Create Note from Message AppleScript.

Figure 24.6 You can add pictures, sounds, movies, or a background picture to a note by choosing commands from the Insert toolbar icon.

3. You can use the Formatting toolbar (**Figure 24.4,** bottom) to format the note's text, or you can choose commands from the Format menu.

4. To save the note, click the Save toolbar icon, choose File > Save, or press ⌘ S.

✔ Tips

■ To save an email message for future reference, you can create a note from it. Select the email message's header in the message list, open the Scripts menu, and choose Create Note from Message (**Figure 24.5**) or press Control N. You can edit the message text if necessary.

■ You can add a background color to a note by clicking the Background Color icon on the Formatting toolbar or by choosing a color from the Format > Background Color submenu.

■ Notes can optionally contain images, sounds, movies, or a background picture. Position the text insertion mark and click the Insert icon on the note window's toolbar (**Figure 24.6**) to add one of these items to the current note.

■ You can keep track of important Web site addresses by dragging them from Internet Explorer or Safari into a note. You can drag any link you find in the body of a Web page or the current Web page's address from the Address box.

CREATING AND DELETING NOTES

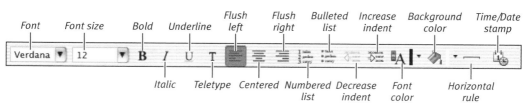

Figure 24.4 You can format note text by choosing commands and options from the Formatting toolbar.

To delete a note:

1. Switch to Notes view and select the note's heading in the Notes list.

2. Click the Delete toolbar icon, choose Edit > Delete Note, or press `Delete` or `⌘ Delete`.

3. In the dialog box that appears (**Figure 24.7**), confirm the deletion by clicking the Delete button.

✔ Tips

- You can also delete a note that is open in its own window. Click the Delete toolbar icon, choose Edit > Delete Note, or press `⌘ Delete`.

- Note deletions cannot be reversed. There is no Undo Delete command.

- You can simultaneously delete multiple notes. Hold down `⌘` to select additional notes from the Notes list and perform the deletion as you would for an individual note. (You can also press `Shift` to select multiple contiguous notes.)

Figure 24.7 You must confirm any note deletion.

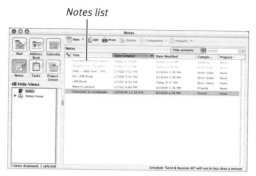

Figure 24.8 The Notes list is displayed in the main window. Double-click a note title to view the note.

Reading Notes

You can view notes, sort the Notes list, and filter the list to see notes that match a particular title or category.

To view notes:

1. Switch to Notes view.

   The Notes list appears in the main pane (**Figure 24.8**).

2. To view a note (**Figure 24.9**), double-click its title. Or you can select the note title and then choose File > Open Note, press ⌘O, or click the Edit toolbar icon.

continues on next page

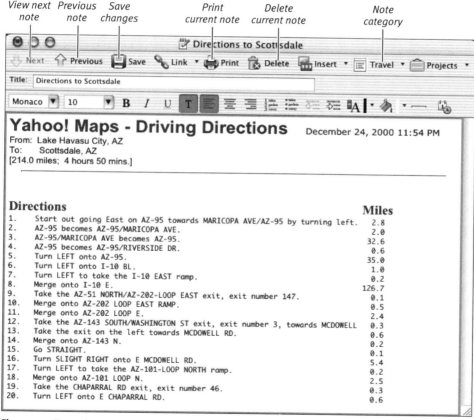

Figure 24.9 To read a note, you must first open it.

READING NOTES

3. You can sort the Notes list by the contents of any column by clicking the column name. To reverse the sort order, click the column name again.

The sort column is indicated by a blue column heading. The sort direction is indicated by the triangle following the column name (**Figure 24.10**).

4. *Optional:* You can filter the Notes list to show only titles that contain a particular text string or those to which a specific category or project has been assigned (**Figure 24.11**).

- ▲ To filter by title, choose Title contains from the drop-down menu above the Notes list, and type a string in the text box.

- ▲ To filter by category, choose Category is from the drop-down menu, and choose a category from the menu to its right.

- ▲ To filter by project, choose Project is from the drop-down menu, and choose a project from the menu to its right.

✔ Tips

- ■ To reverse the effects of filtering (to see the entire Notes list), click the Clear icon beside the filter, delete the text in the text box, set the Category to All, or set the Project to All.

- ■ You can also search for a particular note by choosing Edit > Find (⌘F) and entering search criteria in the Find dialog box (**Figure 24.12**). The matching notes are displayed in a separate Search Results window.

- ■ Once a note is displayed in its own window, you can view other notes by clicking the Next or Previous toolbar icon (see Figure 24.9).

Sort column   *Sort direction indicator*

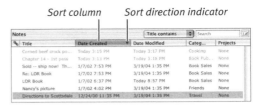

Figure 24.10 Click any column name to sort the Notes list by the information in that column.

Filter menu   *Text string*   *Clear*

Figure 24.11 To restrict the Notes list, you can filter it by title, category, or project.

Search string

Restrict search to Notes

Figure 24.12 For more advanced filtering and selection needs, you can perform a Find.

Custom Views

Another way to filter the Notes list is to create a *custom view* (a set of saved Find criteria that you can replay over and over). Entourage provides several ready-to-use custom views, such as Created in the Past 7 Days. Custom views are listed in the lower-left pane of the Entourage window.

For more information, see "Create a custom view" in Entourage Help.

READING NOTES

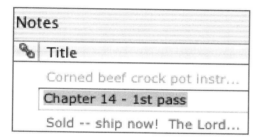

Figure 24.13 You can edit any note's title by clicking its title in the Notes list.

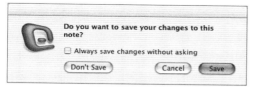

Figure 24.14 If you close a changed note without first saving it, this dialog box appears.

Editing Notes

You can easily change any aspect of a note—its text, formatting, assigned categories, or even its title.

To edit a note:

1. Switch to Notes view.

2. In the Notes list, open the note you want to edit.

   Double-click the note title. Or select the note title and choose File > Open Note, press ⌘O, or click the Edit toolbar icon.

3. Make any desired changes.

4. Click the Save toolbar icon, choose File > Save, or press ⌘S.

To change a note's title:

1. Select the note in the Notes list.

2. Click the note's title.

   The title is selected and ready for editing (**Figure 24.13**).

3. Edit the title.

4. To save the revised title, press [Return] or [Enter], or click elsewhere on the page.

✔ Tip

■ If you modify a note and try to close its window without saving it, a dialog box automatically appears (**Figure 24.14**).

   Do one of the following:

   ▲ Click Save to save the note's changes.

   ▲ Click Cancel if you want to continue editing the note.

   ▲ Click Don't Save to close the note and discard all changes.

   To instruct Entourage to save all changed notes *automatically* (without forcing you to use the Save command), click the Always save changes without asking check box.

Printing Notes

As is the case with the other Entourage components, printing options abound. You can print individual notes or combine several into a single print job. You can even generate printouts that are designed to fit a personal planner, such as a Day Runner.

To print notes:

1. Switch to Notes view.

   The Notes list appears in the main pane (see Figure 24.8).

2. In the Note list, select the title of the note you want to print. To print multiple notes in one printout, ⌘-click each note title.

3. Click the Print toolbar icon, choose File > Print, or press ⌘P.

   The Print dialog box appears (**Figure 24.15**).

4. Select a printer to use from the Printer drop-down list.

5. From the Print drop-down list, indicate what you want to print by selecting Selected Notes or All Notes.

6. If you intend to print on nonstandard paper, select its style from the Form drop-down list.

7. To review print options, click the Layout button. In the Print Layout dialog box (**Figure 24.16**), make any necessary changes and click OK.

8. Indicate the number of copies to print, whether copies should be collated (when printing multiple copies), and whether to print all pages or a page range.

9. If you need to specify a different paper size or orientation, click Page Setup.

10. Click Print to generate the printout.

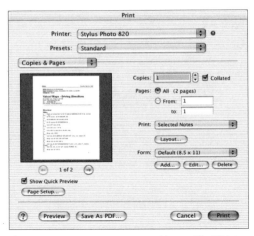

Figure 24.15 Entourage presents this modified Print dialog box for printing notes.

Shows where to cut pages for a planner

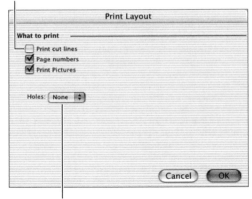

Hole-punched paper

Figure 24.16 Several special print options can be set in the Print Layout dialog box.

PRINTING NOTES

✔ Tips

- You can use these same Print procedures when a note is open in its own window.

- When the note to be printed is open in its own window, the File > Print One Copy ((Option)(⌘)(P)) command is also available. You can use it to print the open note with the current print settings.

- To get an idea of what the printout will look like, click the Show Quick Preview check box. The preview changes as you select different print options. Click the arrow buttons beneath the Quick Preview to review other pages, if any.

- As with other OS X applications, you can create a PDF (Portable Document Format) file from a notes printout. You can click Save As PDF to save the printout as a PDF file or click Preview to create a temporary PDF file that will open in the default viewer (Preview or Adobe Reader).

PRINTING NOTES

INTERNET NEWSGROUPS

Internet newsgroups (sometimes called Usenet newsgroups) are like computerized public bulletin boards. There are tens of thousands of newsgroups on the Internet, each focused on a particular topic. Messages—resembling email messages—are posted to newsgroups. Anyone with access to the newsgroup can read them. If you respond to a message you've read, your reply is posted along with it. Some newsgroups include *binaries* (files associated with messages, similar to email attachments) that you can download.

Creating a News Server Account

To use Entourage for working with newsgroups, you need access to a news server that uses Network News Transfer Protocol (NNTP). Your Internet service provider (ISP) may have one. Check its sign-up instructions for the name of its news server.

If your ISP doesn't offer newsgroups, you can use a search engine to locate one of the many free public news servers. Visit www.google.com, for example, and search for "public news servers." There are also Web-based news servers, such as groups.google.com, but you view these in a Web browser, not Entourage.

To set up a news server account in Entourage, you'll need the name or IP (Internet Protocol) address of a news server that you can access. In some cases, you may also need a user name and password. Once you have the necessary information, you're ready to set Entourage as your newsreader.

To create a news server account:

1. Choose Tools > Accounts.

   The Accounts window appears.

2. Click the News tab (**Figure 25.1**).

3. Click the New toolbar icon to create a new account.

   The Account Setup Assistant appears (**Figure 25.2**).

4. People who reply to your newsgroup posts can respond to your email address and/or post a public reply on the newsgroup. If you have multiple email accounts in Entourage, open the Mail account drop-down list and select the address you want to use for sending newsgroup posts and receiving replies.

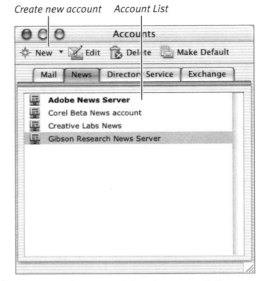

Create new account   *Account List*

Figure 25.1 The News tab lists the names of all news servers that you've set up, plus those imported from previous versions of Office.

Continue

Figure 25.2 Select a reply-to email address from the Mail account list and enter an organization name (optional).

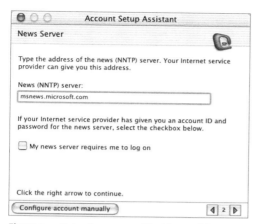

Figure 25.3 Enter the name or IP address of the news server.

Figure 25.4 If this news server requires you to have an account, enter your account ID (user name) and password.

5. The header information included with your posts can include an organization with which you're affiliated. Enter its name in the Organization text box, if you like.

6. Click the right-arrow button to continue.

7. Enter the name or IP address of the news server to which you want to connect (**Figure 25.3**). If the server requires you to enter a user name and password, check My news server requires me to log on. Click the right-arrow button.

8. If you indicated that a user name and password are required, enter them here (**Figure 25.4**). To have the password automatically entered each time you access the news server, check Save password in my Mac OS keychain. Click the right-arrow button to continue.

9. On the final screen, enter a name for the news server account and click Finish. The news server account is added to the Accounts list and the Folders list.

✔ Tips

- To get you started, you can configure Entourage to access the Microsoft News Server for Microsoft's product-related newsgroups: msnews.microsoft.com.

- To add other news servers, repeat these steps for each account. Your default news account is displayed in bold in the Accounts list. To set a different default, select the account and click Make Default (see Figure 25.1). Note that you can also *delete* news server accounts here.

- People who send junk email (*spam*) often collect the email addresses of people who post messages to newsgroups. To avoid receiving unwanted email in your primary account, consider using Hotmail or another free email account as your email address.

The Newsgroup List

Once you have set up at least one news server account, you can download the list of newsgroups available on that server. You can also specify the newsgroups you'd like to read on a regular basis.

Figure 25.5 Click Receive to download the newsgroup list from the server.

To view the newsgroups on a server:

1. Click a news server name in the Folders list.

2. If this is the first time you've selected this news server, Entourage will ask if you want to receive the list of the newsgroups carried on the server (**Figure 25.5**).

3. Click the Receive button.

   The list of available newsgroups will appear in Entourage's right pane (**Figure 25.6**). It may take a while to receive the entire list, depending on the speed of your Internet connection and the number of newsgroups the server offers.

Figure 25.6 The list of newsgroups appears.

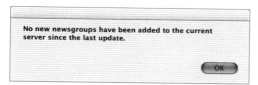

Figure 25.7 If there are no new newsgroups, this message appears.

Filter text   *Clear*

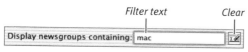

Figure 25.8 Type a text string to filter the newsgroup list to show only the ones that contain the string.

Updating the newsgroup list

The newsgroups available on any given news server can—and often do—change over time. If it's been awhile since you last downloaded the list of newsgroups on a server, you can refresh the list.

To update the list of newsgroups on a server:

1. Click the news server account in the Folders list.

2. Click the Update List icon on the toolbar or choose View > Get New Newsgroups.

   If no new newsgroups have been added, you will be informed (**Figure 25.7**). Otherwise, any new newsgroups will be added to the list.

Filtering the newsgroup list

Many news servers carry thousands of newsgroups. It can be a daunting task to find a particular one that you may want to read. Entourage lets you *filter* the list of newsgroup names to show only the ones of interest.

To filter the list of newsgroup names:

1. Click the name of the news server account in the Folders list.

2. Type a search string (**Figure 25.8**) in the box labeled Display newsgroups containing (located above the newsgroup list).

3. Only newsgroups that contain the search string in their titles are displayed; all others are temporarily hidden.

   To restore the complete list, click the Clear icon or delete the filter text.

THE NEWSGROUP LIST

Subscribing to Newsgroups

If you find some newsgroups you'd like to read regularly, you can *subscribe* to them. This isn't the same as subscribing to a magazine; you don't receive anything automatically. And subscribing to a newsgroup doesn't add you to a list anywhere, as subscribing to an email mailing list does. Subscribing simply makes it easier to follow a newsgroup by adding its name to the Folders list (beneath the news server), as well as displaying its name in bold in the newsgroup list.

To subscribe to newsgroups:

1. Click the news server account in the Folders list.

2. *Optional:* Filter the newsgroup list (as described on the previous page) to make it simpler to find the newsgroup to which you want to subscribe.

3. Select a newsgroup in the right pane to which you want to subscribe.

4. Click the Subscribe icon on the toolbar (**Figure 25.9**) or choose Edit > Subscribe. Or you can Control-click the newsgroup name and choose Subscribe from the pop-up menu that appears.

   The newsgroup name is added to the Folders list beneath the news server and is displayed in bold in the newsgroup list.

To view only subscribed-to newsgroups:

1. With a news server's newsgroup list displayed, choose View > Subscribed Only.

   Newsgroups to which you haven't subscribed are hidden (**Figure 25.10**).

2. To see the entire newsgroup list, choose View > Subscribed Only again.

   The command works as a toggle.

Figure 25.9 Click the Subscribe icon to subscribe to the selected newsgroup.

Microsoft News Server
microsoft.public.mac.office.entourage
microsoft.public.office.mac.entourage

Figure 25.10 Only subscribed-to newsgroups remain visible. Their names are shown in bold type.

Figure 25.11 You can [Control]-click a newsgroup and choose Unsubscribe from the pop-up menu that appears.

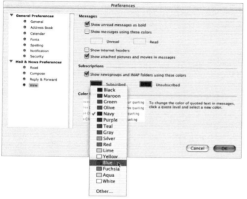

Figure 25.12 Click the Subscribed icon to display this pop-up color list, and then select a new color.

To unsubscribe from a newsgroup:

1. Click the news server account in the Folders list.

2. *Optional:* To make it simpler to find the newsgroup, choose View > Subscribed Only or filter the list.

3. Select the newsgroup from the list in the right pane.

   The names of subscribed-to newsgroups are shown in bold text.

4. Click the Unsubscribe toolbar icon (see Figure 25.9) or choose Edit > Unsubscribe. Or you can [Control]-click the newsgroup name and choose Unsubscribe from the pop-up menu (**Figure 25.11**).

✔ Tip

■ Names of newsgroups to which you have subscribed appear in bold and color in the newsgroup list. The color used is determined by a Preferences setting. To change the color, choose Entourage > Preferences, click the View topic in the left pane, click the Subscribed color box, select a new color from the pop-up list, and click OK (**Figure 25.12**).

Managing Newsgroup Messages

Once you've set up a news server account, retrieved the list of newsgroups, and found a newsgroup you'd like to read, the next step is to retrieve the current list of messages (also known as *posts*) and read the ones that interest you.

Older messages are periodically deleted from the news server to make room for new ones. Messages are usually updated several times a day.

To manage the current list of messages in a newsgroup:

1. *Do one of the following:*
   - ▲ If you subscribe to the newsgroup, click its name in the Folders list. The initial list of message headers for the newsgroup appears (**Figure 25.13**).
   - ▲ If you don't subscribe to the newsgroup, select the news server in the Folders list and then double-click the name of the desired newsgroup in the right pane. The list of message headers appears in a new window.

2. If additional messages for this newsgroup are available on the server, you can retrieve the next batch by clicking the More toolbar icon or by choosing View > Get More News Messages.

3. You can sort the messages in the message list by clicking any but the first column head (Online Status). Clicking the same column head again reverses the sort order.

Download additional message headers

Message list   *Preview pane*

Figure 25.13 Current message headers for the selected newsgroup appear in the message list.

MANAGING NEWSGROUP MESSAGES

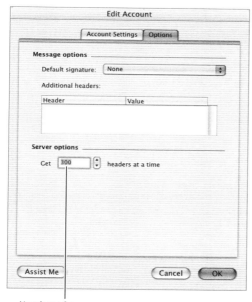

Number of messages
to download

Figure 25.14 You can change the number of messages downloaded each time from a given news server.

Figure 25.15 When Show in Groups is enabled, you can group messages by Subject, Sent (date posted), or almost anything else that you want.

✔ Tips

■ The number of message headers downloaded in each pass is a news server-specific setting. The default is 300. To increase or decrease the number, choose Tools < Accounts, click the News tab in the Accounts dialog box, and double-click the name of the news server. Click the Options tab, specify a new number for Server options (**Figure 25.14**), click OK, and then close the Accounts dialog box.

■ To make it easier to follow a particular message conversation (called a *thread* or *group*), choose View > Arrange By > Subject and ensure that the View > Arrange By > Show in Groups command is checked. This groups every original message with all responses to it (**Figure 25.15**).

■ Messages can be grouped by many other useful criteria, such as Sent (date posted) or From (message author).

■ To simultaneously reveal or hide all grouped messages in the message list, choose View > Expand All or View > Collapse All.

Reading Messages

When Entourage displays the message list for a newsgroup or updates the list, it downloads only the message headers—not the message body or attachments. After you've selected one or more message headers, Entourage downloads their text.

To read a message:

1. *Do one of the following:*

   ▲ Click the message header to view the message text in the Preview pane (**Figure 25.16**).

   ▲ Double-click the message header to open the message in its own window (**Figure 25.17**).

2. To read additional messages, do any of the following:

   ▲ Click another message header in the message list.

   ▲ Choose View > Next (⌘⟧) or View > Previous (⌘⟦).

   ▲ Click the Next or Previous toolbar icon (only available when you're reading messages in a separate window).

Selected message header   Message text

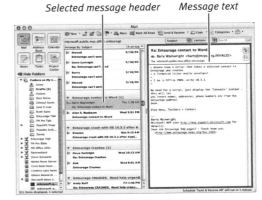

Figure 25.16 Click a message header in the list to read the message in the Preview pane.

Previous
Next

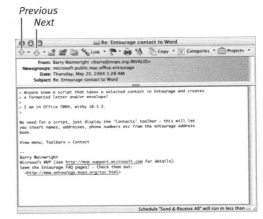

Figure 25.17 Double-click a message to open it in its own window.

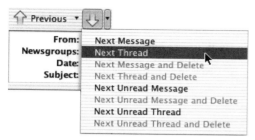

Figure 25.18 Click the down arrow beside the Previous or Next toolbar icon for more options.

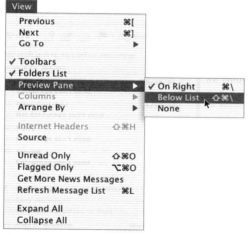

Figure 25.19 You can choose a location for the Preview pane or elect to hide it.

✔ Tips

- You can also use the cursor keys to select messages to read. Press ⟶ and ⟵ to expand or collapse a group, and press ⟱ and ⟰ to read the next or previous message. Note, however, that any message the cursor touches—even momentarily—will be downloaded.

- When reading messages in a separate window, you can click the down arrow beside the Next or Previous toolbar icon to reveal a menu of other message navigation options (**Figure 25.18**).

- You can scroll through a lengthy message by holding down (Spacebar) or scroll up by pressing (Shift)(Spacebar). When you reach the end of the message, press (Spacebar) to jump to the next unread message in the message list.

- You cannot *delete* newsgroup messages as you can email. However, you can set the message list to display only messages you haven't read by choosing View > Unread Only. To revert to seeing the entire list, choose the command again.

- You can select the headers of messages you want to ignore and mark them as read by choosing Message > Mark as Read ((⌘)(T)). Then set the view to Unread Only to hide these messages in the message list.

- In Entourage 2004, the location of the Preview pane is up to you. Choose a location from the View > Preview Pane submenu (**Figure 25.19**).

Posting to Newsgroups

You can post messages to newsgroups by either replying to an existing message or creating a new one.

It is common courtesy (and in your own best interest) to read the messages in the newsgroup for a while before posting. Also be sure to read the FAQ for the newsgroup. The FAQ—if one exists—usually explains what constitutes an appropriate posting. Messages the group's regular participants deem inappropriate are likely to be on the receiving end of *flames* (attacking or insulting messages).

To reply to a message:

1. Select a message in the message list to view it in the Preview pane, or double-click the message to open it in its own window.

2. *Do one of the following:*

   ▲ To post a reply to the newsgroup, click the Reply to Newsgroup toolbar icon (**Figure 25.20**), choose Message > Reply, or press ⌘R.

   ▲ To send an email message to the author of the newsgroup post, click the Reply to Sender toolbar icon, choose Message > Reply to Sender, or press Option ⌘R.

   ▲ To post a reply to the newsgroup *and* send an email message to the author, choose Message > Reply to All or press Shift ⌘R.

   A new message window opens, containing a copy of the message to which you are replying. The message is pre-addressed to the newsgroup, the author, or both, as appropriate.

Figure 25.20 Click Reply to Newsgroup to post a reply to the newsgroup. (Whether the icon labels are displayed depends on the current width of the window.)

POSTING TO NEWSGROUPS

Original message   Newsgroup   Reply

Figure 25.21 A pre-addressed reply message opens. Remove any unnecessary text and add your reply.

3. Delete any of the original message text that's irrelevant to your response, but quote the part of the message to which you're replying.

4. Add your comments in the body of the message (**Figure 25.21**).

5. *Do one of the following:*

▲ Click the Post Now or Post Later toolbar icon at the top of the message window. (If one of these icons is missing, you can expand the message window to display it.)

▲ Choose Message > Post Message Now (⌘ Return) or Message > Post Message Later (Shift ⌘ Return).

To post a new message to a newsgroup:

1. Open the newsgroup list to which you want to post a message by selecting it in the Folders list or by double-clicking it in the news server's newsgroup list.

2. Click the New toolbar icon, choose File > New > News Message, or press ⌘N.

   A blank message window opens, pre-addressed to the newsgroup (**Figure 25.22**).

3. Add other desired recipients to the address field (additional newsgroups go in the To line and email recipients go in the Cc line), enter a subject, and type the body of the message as you would an email message.

4. *Optional:* You can add attachments just as you would with an email message. It is polite to compress large attachments to save retrieval time for the recipients.

5. *Optional:* Click the Use HTML icon on the Formatting toolbar (see Figure 25.22) to toggle between unformatted and formatted text. (You can also choose Format > HTML).

   Be aware, however, that many people use text-only newsreaders and may find formatted text unreadable.

6. *Do one of the following:*
   ▲ When you're through composing your message, click the Post Now or Post Later toolbar icon.
   ▲ Choose Message > Post Message Now (⌘Return) or Message > Post Message Later (Shift ⌘ Return).

Server   Newsgroup

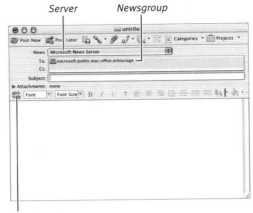

Use HTML

Figure 25.22 Compose your message in the new window that appears.

POSTING TO NEWSGROUPS

Attachments icon   *Attachments pane*

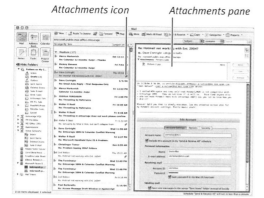

Figure 25.23 The Attachments icon and pane appear after the message is downloaded from the server.

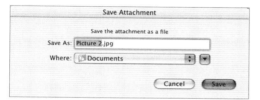

Figure 25.24 Select a destination disk and folder, and then click Save.

✔ Tips

- Picture attachments that are in a format Entourage supports (such as JPEG, GIF, and PDF) appear as pictures in the body of the message (see Figure 25.23).

- Newsgroups that actively promote attachments (such as pictures, movies, or song files) often have the word *binaries* in their name.

Downloading Files from Newsgroups

Attached files show up in newsgroup message headers as attachments, just as they do in email messages. However, the paper-clip icon does not appear in the message header in the Attachments column until you've clicked the message header and downloaded the message.

You can usually tell if a message contains an attachment by its size—anything over a few kilobytes is almost certain to include an attachment. After you've previewed or opened the message, you can handle its attachments in the same way as you would in email (see Chapter 20).

To download a file from a newsgroup:

1. Click the news server account in the Folders list.

2. Select the newsgroup in the Folders list or double-click the newsgroup's name in the newsgroup list.

3. Select or double-click the header of a message that contains an attachment.

   After your Mac downloads the message and attachment(s) from the news server (this can take a while), the Attachments pane appears (**Figure 25.23**).

4. Select the attachment and click the Save button beside the Attachments pane.

   The Save Attachment dialog box appears (**Figure 25.24**).

5. Navigate to the disk and folder in which you want to save the file, and then click Save.

Part VI: Combining the Applications

USING

PROGRAMS TOGETHER

Separately, each Office application is impressive. But when combined, they form a powerful system for sharing information.

One simple way of combining information from different Office applications is by copying, embedding, and linking. You can copy a table of numeric data from Excel into a Word document—to add some relevant numbers to a memo, for instance. Or to ensure that later changes to the Excel data automatically flow to the table in the Word document, you can link the data between the documents.

In addition to explaining copying, linking, and embedding, this chapter provides some specific examples of ways to share data among Office applications. It also explains how to link Entourage items to Office documents.

Copying, Linking, and Embedding

Office lets you easily share information among its applications. The three main methods are to copy, embed, or link information from one application to another.

The simplest method is to *copy and paste* or *drag and drop* information from one program to another. For example, you can copy Excel data and paste it into a Word document. The data becomes part of the Word document as an editable table. Similarly, after switching to Slide Sorter View in PowerPoint, you can drag a copy of a slide into a Word document. Data added via the copy-and-paste or drag-and-drop method becomes a part of—and is saved with—the destination document.

If you want to maintain a link between the original data or object and the new document, you can use *embedding* or *linking*. The difference between the two procedures lies in where the data is stored. Embedded data becomes part of the destination document, making it transportable. Linked data, on the other hand, is stored only in the original document and is *referenced* by the destination document. Thus, linking is an excellent choice for working with files on a network.

Table 26.1

Common Objects to Drag and Drop	
SOURCE APPLICATION	OBJECT
Word	Selected text or a table
Excel	A cell, cell range, graphic, or table
PowerPoint	A slide from Slide Sorter view

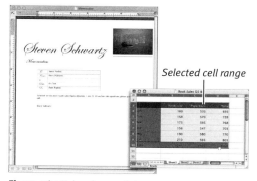

Selected cell range

Figure 26.1 Using drag and drop, you can copy a selected cell range from an Excel worksheet into a Word document.

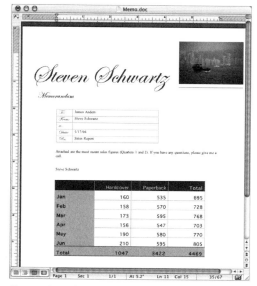

Figure 26.2 Release the mouse button when the Excel object is properly positioned in the Word document.

Using Drag and Drop

The easiest way to move something from one application to another is by using drag and drop. Dragging and dropping *between* applications works just like doing so *within* an application. Arrange the document windows of the two applications so you can see them both. Then drag selected text or an object from one application window to its destination in the other application's document window. **Table 26.1** lists the types of items you can drag and drop between applications.

To drag and drop an object:

1. Arrange the document windows of the two applications so you can see both the source object and its destination.

2. Select the object or text—in this example, a worksheet range (**Figure 26.1**).

3. Drag the border of the object or text to the destination in the other window.

4. Release the mouse button.

   The object or text appears in the destination document (**Figure 26.2**).

✔ Tips

- When you drag and drop an item, it becomes embedded in the destination application. The copy will not reflect any changes made to the original material unless you establish a link. See "Linking Objects," later in this chapter.

- You are free to modify the object or text in the destination document.

- If you hold down (Option)(⌘) as you drag an object between applications, a pop-up menu allows you to either copy or move the object. (Moving deletes the original object.)

Embedding objects

An *embedded object* is one that is copied or moved from its source application to a target application. All data for the object is copied to the target application. As a result, if you move the target file to another computer, the object will be moved, too. Objects that are copied and pasted or dragged and dropped also become embedded.

This section explains how to embed an existing object in a target application, as well as how to create an embedded object from scratch. The examples embed an Excel object in a Word document, but the procedures are the same for the other applications.

To embed an existing object:

1. Select the object or text in its source application (**Figure 26.3**).

2. Choose Edit > Copy or press ⌘C.

3. Switch to the target application (Word, in this example) and click to set the destination for the object.

   The embedded object will appear at the insertion point.

4. Choose Edit > Paste Special.

   The Paste Special dialog box appears (**Figure 26.4**).

5. Select the item labeled as an Object (in this case, the Microsoft Excel Worksheet Object). Ensure that Paste is selected and then click OK.

   The embedded object appears in the document (**Figure 26.5**).

To create an embedded object:

1. Click to set the destination for the object.

   The embedded object will appear at the insertion point.

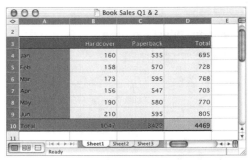

Figure 26.3 Select the material you want to embed (in this case, a portion of an Excel worksheet).

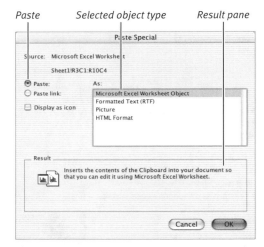

Figure 26.4 In the Paste Special dialog box, select the appropriate object type from the As list. The Result pane indicates the type of object that will be inserted.

	Hardcover	Paperback	Total
Jan	160	535	695
Feb	158	570	728
Mar	173	595	768
Apr	156	547	703
May	190	580	770
Jun	210	595	805
Total	1047	3422	4469

Figure 26.5 The embedded object appears in the Word document.

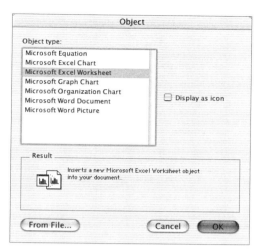

Figure 26.6 Select Microsoft Excel Worksheet as the type of object you want to create.

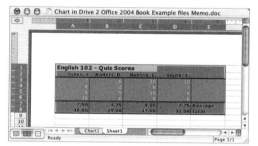

Figure 26.7 Create the new object—in this instance, a formatted Excel worksheet.

2. Choose Insert > Object.

   The Object dialog box appears (**Figure 26.6**).

3. Select the type of object and click OK.

   The appropriate Office application opens and a new document appears.

4. Delete the sample data and create the object (**Figure 26.7**).

5. *Optional:* Save the object document by choosing File > Save Copy As.

6. Close the object document.

   The object appears in the document at the insertion point. (You may need to alter the text wrap setting in order for the object to display correctly.)

To edit an embedded object:

1. *Do one of the following:*

   ▲ Double-click the object (in this case, the worksheet embedded in the Word document).

   ▲ Select the object and choose Edit > *object type* > Edit.

   The source application launches and the object appears in a new document window.

2. As you modify the object, the changes automatically appear in the embedded object, too. When you are finished editing, close the document window and return to the original document.

   It is *not* necessary to save changes when editing an object. Any changes you make to the object are automatically conveyed to the document in which the object is embedded.

✔ Tip

■ You can show the embedded object as an icon by checking Display as icon in the Object dialog box.

Linking objects

When you link rather than embed an object, the object remains in the original application's document. A *copy* of the object—linked to the original—is displayed in the second application. Think of the copy as representing the linked object; it is merely a reference to the original. Any changes made to the original object also appear in the linked copy.

You create linked objects using the Copy and Paste Special commands. The object is updated whenever you reopen the destination file. In addition to (or instead of) automatically updating a link, you can manually update a link.

The example below shows how to link an Excel chart into a Word document.

To link an object:

1. In the original document, select the object to link (**Figure 26.8**).

2. Choose Edit > Copy or press ⌘C.

3. Open the destination document and click where you want the linked object to appear.

4. Choose Edit > Paste Special.
   The Paste Special dialog box appears (**Figure 26.9**).

5. Click the Paste link radio button, select the object to link, and click OK.
   The linked object appears in the destination document (**Figure 26.10**).

✔ Tips

■ You can double-click a linked object (in the destination document) to edit the original object.

■ When you open a document containing links that automatically update, the links are checked for any necessary updates.

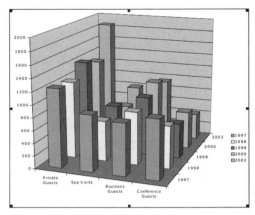

Figure 26.8 Select the object you want to link, such as this Excel chart.

Figure 26.9 Click the Paste link radio button, select the specific object type, and click OK.

COPYING, LINKING, AND EMBEDDING

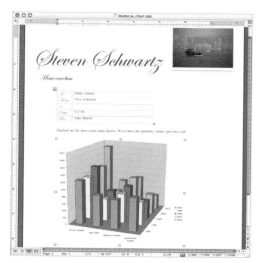

Figure 26.10 The linked Excel object appears in the Word document.

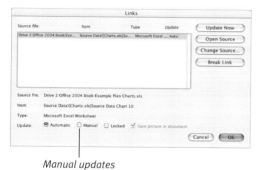

Manual updates

Figure 26.11 In the Links dialog box, click Update Now to update the selected link.

To manually update a link:

1. Choose Edit > Links.

   The Links dialog box appears (**Figure 26.11**).

2. Select the link from the list and click Update Now.

   The linked object is updated.

3. Click OK to close the Links dialog box.

✔ Tips

- The linked object will appear in the target document at its original size. You can resize it as necessary.

- To set the link so that it updates *only* when you click Update Now, select Manual as the Update option.

- To change a linked object into an embedded object, select the link and click the Break Link button.

COPYING, LINKING, AND EMBEDDING

Combining Word and Excel

Word and Excel work well together, especially when you're creating Word documents that display structured numerical data. The previous sections explained how to copy and link Excel data into Word documents. In this section, you'll learn how to do the reverse—copy a Word table into an Excel worksheet. Later in this chapter, we'll cover copying text from Word into Excel and PowerPoint.

To copy a Word table into Excel:

1. In Word, click any cell within the table you intend to copy.

2. Choose Table > Select > Table.
   The table is selected (**Figure 26.12**).

3. Choose Edit > Copy or press ⌘C.

4. Switch to Excel and select the cell in which the Word table will start.

5. Choose Edit > Paste or press ⌘V.
   The Word table is pasted into the Excel document. Adjust the column widths as necessary to fully display the contents of each column (**Figure 26.13**).

✔ Tip

- A table copied in this manner is fully editable within Excel. You can also change the formatting, if necessary. The data maintains no link to the Word document.

Figure 26.12 To select a table in Word, click any cell of the table and choose Table > Select > Table.

Figure 26.13 The Word table appears in the Excel worksheet.

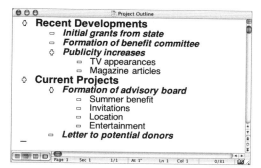

Figure 26.14 A presentation outline created in Word.

Figure 26.15 The Word outline opens as a new presentation in PowerPoint.

Combining Word and PowerPoint

You can use Word and PowerPoint together, too. This section covers importing outlines from one application to the other.

To use a Word outline file in a PowerPoint presentation:

1. Open or create a presentation outline in Word (**Figure 26.14**).

   Each Heading 1 paragraph will become the title of a new slide. Heading 2 paragraphs will become first-level text.

2. Choose File > Send To > Microsoft PowerPoint.

   PowerPoint launches and the Word outline appears as a new presentation (**Figure 26.15**). No link is maintained to the original Word outline.

3. Apply a slide design and other formatting to the new presentation.

✔ Tips

- Generating the outline in Word allows you to use Word tools, such as the thesaurus. Most people find writing and editing easier to do in Word than in PowerPoint.

- If heading styles haven't been applied to the Word paragraph, PowerPoint uses the paragraph indentations to determine the presentation's structure.

To copy a PowerPoint presentation outline into a Word document:

1. In PowerPoint, switch to Outline View (**Figure 26.16**).

2. Choose File > Send To > Microsoft Word. The PowerPoint outline opens as a new Word document (**Figure 26.17**).

3. In Word, switch to Outline view by choosing View > Outline or by clicking the Outline View icon in the bottom-left corner of the document window.

Outline View

Figure 26.16 Create or open a PowerPoint presentation in Outline View.

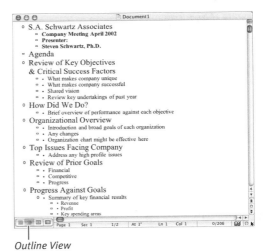

Outline View

Figure 26.17 A new Word document opens to display the PowerPoint outline.

Destination cell

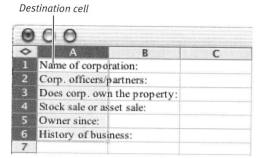

Figure 26.18 Drag or paste the selected text into an Excel cell range.

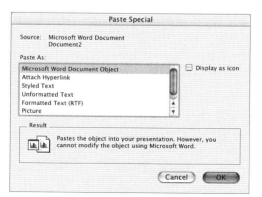

Figure 26.19 You can also drag or paste it into a text placeholder on a PowerPoint slide.

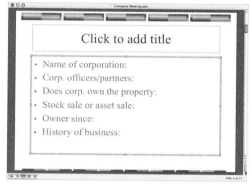

Figure 26.20 Using the Edit > Paste Special command, you can transfer copied Word text as an object.

Copying Text from Word

You can copy text from Word into Excel or PowerPoint via copy/paste or drag and drop.

To copy text from Word or PowerPoint:

1. Arrange the Word document window so you can also see the Excel or PowerPoint document window.

2. In Word, select the text to be copied.

3. *Do one of the following:*
   - ▲ Choose Edit > Copy (⌘C). Paste the text into an Excel cell or a PowerPoint slide by choosing Edit > Paste (⌘V).
   - ▲ Drag the text to a destination cell in Excel or onto a slide in PowerPoint (**Figures 26.18** and **26.19**).

   The text is copied to the destination.

✔ Tips

- ■ Formatting, such as font, size, and style, is also copied and will appear in the Excel worksheet. In PowerPoint, however, the formatting of the destination placeholder text determines the font size.

- ■ In Excel, pasted Word text frequently overflows the cells. Expand the width or enable text wrapping for the affected cells, if necessary.

- ■ Excel attempts to mimic the paragraph formatting of copied Word text. A tab within a paragraph is treated as an instruction to place the text in the next cell; a return is treated as an instruction to move down to the next row.

- ■ You can also paste Word text as a floating object. In Excel or PowerPoint, choose Edit > Paste Special and select Microsoft Word Document Object as the format (**Figure 26.20**). The result is an embedded text object that is editable in Word.

Combining Excel and PowerPoint

Excel and PowerPoint can share information, too. You can copy and paste material from either application into the other. You can also import Excel files into a PowerPoint presentation.

To create a PowerPoint chart from imported Excel data:

1. Create a chart slide in PowerPoint and double-click the "Double click to add chart" placeholder (**Figure 26.21**). Graph launches (**Figure 26.22**).

2. If you want the imported data to begin in any cell other than the upper-left corner of the datasheet, click to select the starting cell.

3. Choose File > Import File.
   The Choose a File dialog box appears.

4. Select the Excel file to import and click Choose.
   The Import Data Options dialog box appears (**Figure 26.23**).

5. Select the sheet to import, specify the range (if you want to import only part of the worksheet), and click OK.

6. Edit and rearrange the data as necessary.

7. Select a chart type from the Chart Type drop-down palette on the toolbar or choose Chart > Chart Type.

8. Format the chart elements as desired. When the chart is satisfactory, choose Graph > Quit & Return to *presentation name*.
   The finished chart appears on the slide (**Figure 26.24**).

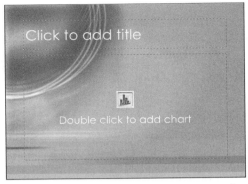

Figure 26.21 Create a chart slide in PowerPoint and double-click the chart placeholder to launch Graph.

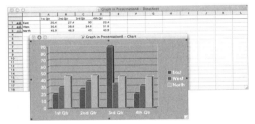

Figure 26.22 Graph opens, displaying sample data and a temporary chart.

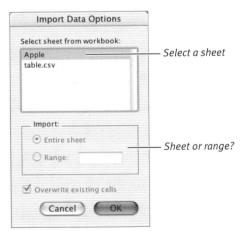

Figure 26.23 Select a sheet to import. By clicking a radio button, you can import the entire sheet or only a specific range.

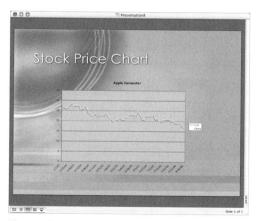

Figure 26.24 Quit Graph. The finished chart appears on the PowerPoint slide. If you later need to alter the chart, double-click it on the slide.

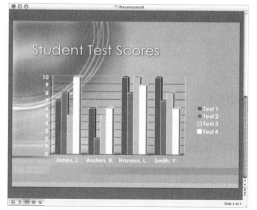

Figure 26.25 After you complete the chart and quit Graph, the linked chart appears on the slide.

✔ Tip

■ As long as Graph is running, the chart will reflect any changes made to the data in Excel. Otherwise, to update the link, double-click the chart on the slide. Graph launches and updates the figures based on the current version of the Excel data.

✔ Tip

■ You can consolidate data from several worksheets by repeating the import procedure with different destination cells. Be sure to remove the checkmark from Overwrite existing cells in the Import Data Options dialog box.

To link Excel data to a PowerPoint chart:

1. Create a chart slide in PowerPoint and double-click the "Double click to add chart" placeholder (see Figure 26.21). Graph launches (see Figure 26.22).

2. Switch to Excel and select the cell range you want to use to generate the chart.

3. Choose Edit > Copy or press ⌘C.

4. Switch to Graph and select the datasheet cell in the upper-left corner.

    This is where the Excel data will appear.

5. Choose Edit > Paste Link.

    A dialog box appears, informing you that the sample data will be replaced.

6. Click OK.

    The data appears in the datasheet.

7. Edit and rearrange the data as necessary.

8. Select a chart type from the Chart Type drop-down palette on the toolbar or by choosing Chart > Chart Type.

9. Format the chart elements as desired. When the chart is satisfactory, choose Graph > Quit & Return to *presentation name*.

    The finished chart appears on the slide (**Figure 26.25**).

COMBINING EXCEL AND POWERPOINT

419

Entourage Linking

In Entourage, you can link files, calendar events, or notes to any other Entourage item. Links in Entourage are especially useful when planning meetings, for example. You can link a document pertaining to the meeting to a contact record in your Address Book. This enables you to open the document directly from the Address Book, as shown in the following example.

To link an Entourage contact to an Office document:

1. In Entourage, switch to the Address Book by clicking its icon in the upper-left corner of the window, choosing View > Go To > Address Book, or pressing ⌘②.

2. Select the record in the contact list.

3. *Do one of the following:*
   ▲ Choose Tools > Link to Existing > File.
   ▲ Click in the Links column for the contact record and choose Link to Existing > File from the pop-up menu.

   The Link to file dialog box appears (**Figure 26.26**).

4. Select the file to which you want to link the contact information and click Link.

   A link indicator appears beside the contact name in the Address Book, showing that the contact is linked to a file or an Entourage item. To later view the linked file, click the link indicator in the person's record and choose the linked file from the pop-up menu that appears (**Figure 26.27**).

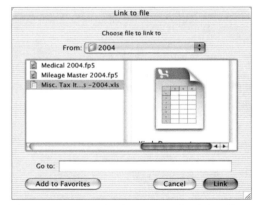

Figure 26.26 Select the document in the Link to file dialog box.

Link indicator

Figure 26.27 The link indicator appears beside the contact name in the Address Book. To open the linked document, click the indicator and choose the file from the pop-up menu.

Break the selected link

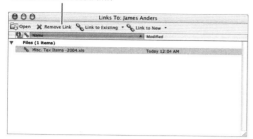

Figure 26.28 You can break a link by selecting it in the Links To dialog box and clicking the Remove Link toolbar icon.

✔ Tips

■ You can link Entourage items to files created in *any* application—not just Office.

■ You can also link notes, calendar events, and tasks to any document, as well as to each other.

■ When a link ceases to be useful, you can break it. Click the link icon and choose Open Links from the pop-up menu that appears (see Figure 26.27). The Links To dialog box appears, listing all links to the selected item. Select the link to break (**Figure 26.28**), click the Remove Link toolbar icon, and close the dialog box.

THE PROJECT CENTER

The Project Center is a new feature, exclusive to Office 2004 users. Its purpose is to help you manage projects and to provide a convenient place in which to gather all project-related Office and non-Office documents, email messages, tasks, appointments, and notes. A project can be something that you're working on alone (such as a school paper or trip planning) or shared with others (such as a business report or product launch).

The Project Center is accessible from any Office application, although it's an Entourage component.

Creating a Project

Of course, the first step is to create a new project. All projects are created and managed from within Entourage's Project Center.

To create a new project:

1. Launch Entourage.

2. *Do one of the following:*

   ▲ Click the Project Center icon in the upper-left corner (**Figure 27.1**). Click the New Project toolbar icon, choose File > New > New Project, or press ⌘N.

   ▲ From any other part of Entourage, click the down arrow beside the New toolbar icon and choose Project, or choose File > New > Project.

   The New Project Wizard appears (**Figure 27.2**).

3. To identify the project, enter a name for it in the Name text box.

4. *Optional:* If there is a due date for project completion, select a date by clicking the calendar icon. Ensure that the Due Date check box is checked.

5. *Optional:* To associate a color with all project-related items, click the Color icon and select a color from the pop-up list. You can also add an identifying picture by dragging its file icon into the designated area. If you have general notes about the project which you'd like to record, enter them in the Notes to Self text box.

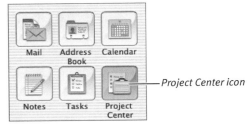

Figure 27.1 Click the Project Center icon to view and manage your projects.

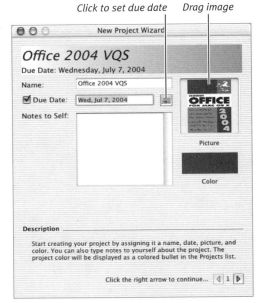

Figure 27.2 The New Project Wizard will step you through the process of setting up a new project.

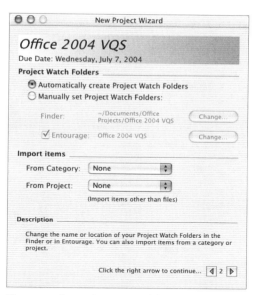

Figure 27.3 Create the two Watch folders and optionally import existing items into the new project.

6. Click the right-arrow icon to continue.

   The next Wizard screen appears (**Figure 27.3**).

7. Every project has two *Watch folders*. The purpose of these folders is to enable Entourage to make note of documents and items that are part of the project.

   ▲ **Entourage Project Watch Folder.** When an email message is moved or copied to this folder, it is associated with the project.

   ▲ **Finder Project Watch Folder.** This folder contains the actual documents (or aliases to them) that have been associated with the project.

   Click a radio button in the Project Watch Folders area to indicate whether the folders will be created for you (Automatically create Project Watch Folders) or whether you wish to create them (Manually set Project Watch Folders). In the latter case, click each of the Change buttons to select an existing folder or to create a new one.

8. To import items that are already assigned to an existing category or project, select a category and/or project from the dropdown lists. Click the right-arrow icon to continue.

   The next Wizard screen appears.

   continues on next page

Project Setup: The Aftermath

After a project has been created, you can revisit your New Project Wizard settings whenever you like. You can do so to review the choices you made or to modify them. In the Project Center, click the Overview tab and then click the Properties button at the bottom of the window.

9. Set rules for associating email messages with the project (**Figure 27.4**):

▲ **Associate e-mail from Project contacts.** If you later designate project contacts, any email from them will automatically be associated with the project.

▲ **Associate e-mail with the following subjects.** Enter up to three keywords that—if found in an incoming message's Subject—will be used to classify the message as project-related.

▲ **Don't apply other rules to these messages.** When checked, this prevents other message rules that you've created from performing their processing on project-related messages.

▲ **Apply Rules to existing messages.** Check this box if you want to use the specified rules to attempt to reclassify current Entourage messages as being project-related.

10. In the Finder Tools section, click the check box to place an alias to the Project Watch folder on the Desktop.

Creating the folder alias will give you easy access to project documents. It will also enable you to add new documents to the project by simply dragging them into the folder.

11. Click the right-arrow icon to continue. The final Wizard screen appears (**Figure 27.5**).

12. Read the information presented and click the right-arrow icon to create the project.

The project is generated, and you are taken to the Project Center.

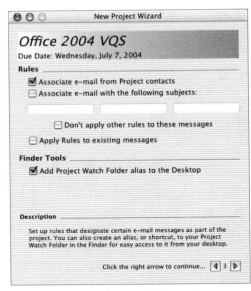

Figure 27.4 Set rules for associating email messages with the project.

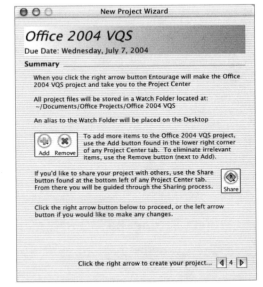

Figure 27.5 Review this material and then click the right-arrow icon to create the project.

CREATING A PROJECT

The Project Center

In Entourage's Project Center area (**Figure 27.6**), you can view the status and all components of your active projects. Above each project is a series of tabs that you can click to view, add, or remove project-related items.

To view a project:

1. In Entourage, click the Project Center icon to open the Project Center.

2. Click the project name in the Folders list.

   The project appears, open to the most recently used tab.

Folders list   *Project Center icon*   *Tabs*   *Display options*   *Display options*   *Watch folders*

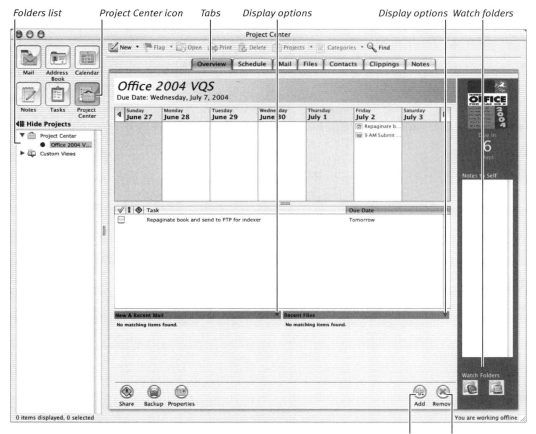

Add a new item   *Remove an item*

Figure 27.6 The Project Center, open to a project overview.

Adding and Removing Contacts

People are often—but not always—associated with a project. You can add any person from your Address Book to a project.

To add contacts to a project:

◆ In the Project Center, you can add new contacts to the currently selected project by doing either of the following:

▲ On the Overview or Schedule tab of the Project Center, click the Add button (at the bottom right) and choose Contact from the pop-up menu (**Figure 27.7**).

▲ On the Contacts tab of the Project Center, click the Add button.

In the Add Contact dialog box (**Figure 27.8**), select contacts from your Address Book and click Add. (To select multiple contacts, ⌘-click each one.)

◆ In the Address Book area of Entourage, select a contact from the list. Then choose Edit > Projects > *project name*, or click the Projects toolbar icon and select the project name from the drop-down list.

◆ If an Address Book record is open in its own window, click the Projects toolbar icon and select the project name from the drop-down list (**Figure 27.9**).

✔ Tip

■ Not every project participant will already be in your Address Book. To associate new people with a project, you'll first have to create a contact record for each person.

Add Button

Figure 27.7 You can add a contact to the project by clicking the Add button on the Overview or Schedule tab.

Figure 27.8 In the Add Contact dialog box, select contact records and click the Add button.

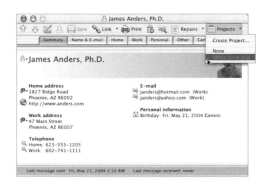

Figure 27.9 You can add a selected or open contact to a project by clicking the Projects toolbar icon.

ADDING AND REMOVING CONTACTS

To remove a contact from a project:

◆ *Do one of the following:*

▲ In the Project Center, select the project in the Folders list and click the Contacts tab. Select the contact you want to remove and then click the Remove button, click the Projects toolbar icon and choose *current project*, or choose Edit > Projects > *current project*. (The project name is a toggle; select it again to reverse its state.)

▲ In the Address Book, select the contact record or open it in its own window. Click the Projects toolbar icon and choose *current project* from the drop-down list (see Figure 27.9), or choose Edit > Projects > *current project*.

✔ Tips

■ You use these same techniques to remove *any* project item, not just contacts.

■ To simultaneously remove a contact from *all* projects, choose None. (If this is the only project with which the person is associated, choosing None has the same effect as choosing *current project*.)

■ Do *not* delete a contact to remove the person from a project. Any of the various Delete commands deletes the person's contact record from the Address Book.

■ As you probably noticed (see Figure 27.9), you can also create a new project by clicking the Projects toolbar icon and choosing Create Project.

ADDING AND REMOVING CONTACTS

Adding Email Messages to a Project

Being able to see all project-related email messages in one place can vastly simplify your project management and tracking duties. When you created the project, Entourage made a new email folder for storing project messages.

To add an email message to a project:

◆ *Do any of the following:*

▲ From the Mail tab of the Project Center, click the Add button at the bottom of the window. In the Add Mail dialog box (**Figure 27.10**), select an email folder from the list, select one or more messages from those displayed, and click Add. A copy of each message is added to the project's email folder.

▲ In the Mail area of Entourage, switch to the folder that contains the messages you want to associate with the project. To move or copy a message, drag or (Option)-drag its header into the project folder in the Folders list.

▲ In the Mail area of Entourage, you can copy any message from the message list into a project folder. Select its header, click the Projects toolbar icon, and select the project name from the drop-down list. You can also (Control)-click a message header and choose Projects > *project name* from the pop-up menu. Finally, with a message header selected, you can choose Edit > Projects > *project name*.

✔ Tip

■ You can also move a selected message by clicking the Move toolbar icon (**Figure 27.11**). If the project folder is listed, choose it. If not, choose Move to Folder and then select the project folder.

Email folders   *Email messages*

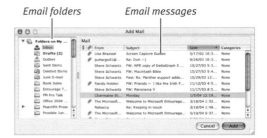

Figure 27.10 Select a folder, select one or more message headers, and click Add.

Figure 27.11 You can also move messages into the project folder by clicking the Move toolbar icon or choosing Message > Move To.

More Help for Project Email

Manually copying/moving messages into a project can be very time-consuming. Here are two tips for speeding things up:

◆ Create some clever Entourage *message rules* (Tools > Rules) to screen incoming and/or outgoing email. For example, you can automatically move all email received from or sent to a particular person into the project message folder.

◆ To make it easier to find existing messages to move to the project folder, filter the message list to show a project-related subject or sender.

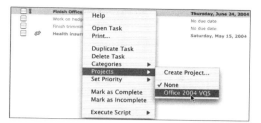

Figure 27.12 You can also (Control)-click any note, task, or calendar event to associate it with a project.

Adding Notes, Tasks, and Events to a Project

A given project is also likely to have associated notes, tasks, and calendar events (such as appointments and meetings). It's simple to add any of these items to a project.

To add an Entourage note, task, or event to a project:

◆ *Do any of the following:*

▲ From the Notes, Tasks, or Calendar section of Entourage, select a note, task, or event. Click the Projects toolbar icon and select the project with which you want to associate the item.

▲ From the Notes, Tasks, or Calendar section of Entourage, select a note, task, or event. Choose Edit > Projects > *project name*.

▲ From the Notes, Tasks, or Calendar section of Entourage, (Control)-click a note, task, or event. Choose Projects > *project name* from the pop-up menu that appears (**Figure 27.12**).

▲ On the various Project Center tabs, you can click Add to add an existing note, task, or event to the project. On the Schedule and Notes tabs, you can click the New button to simultaneously create a new note, task, or event and add it to the current project.

✔ Tip

■ The Add and New icons on the Project Center tabs are of two different types. Some (such as those on the Notes tab) are section-specific. That is, you simply click them to add or create an item. Others (such as those on the Overview and Schedule tabs) contain a drop-down menu with which you can set the item type.

Adding Documents to a Project

Projects frequently rely on Office documents (presentations, worksheets, and word processing files), as well as documents from other programs, such as images, statistics, Acrobat PDFs, or desktop publishing publications. The Project Center allows *any* file to be associated with a project. By including key files in a project, you can quickly open them for editing or viewing.

To add a document to a project:

◆ *Do any of the following:*

▲ On the Files tab of the Project Center, click the Add button. In the Add File dialog box that appears, select the file that you want to add to the current project and click Open.

▲ On the Overview or Schedule tab of the Project Center, click the Add button and choose File from the drop-down menu.

▲ On the Schedule tab of the Project Center, click the New button and choose File from the drop-down menu. The Project Gallery appears. Select the type of new Office document you wish to create, simultaneously adding it to the current project.

▲ In Word, Excel, or PowerPoint, open the Office Toolbox by choosing Tools > Project Palette. To add the current document to a project (**Figure 27.13**), select the project from the drop-down menu at the top of the Toolbox and then click the Add current file icon (the plus). Click OK in the confirmation dialog box that appears (**Figure 27.14**).

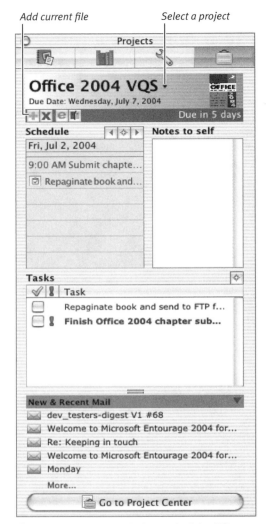

Add current file   Select a project

Figure 27.13 You can use Projects tab of the Office Toolbox to add the current Office file to a project.

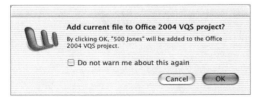

Figure 27.14 Confirm the file addition by clicking OK.

Figure 27.15 To open a project-related document, double-click its name in the Files tab list.

▲ Drag the original document icon (or an alias) into the Project Watch folder on the Desktop.

▲ Drag the original document icon (or an alias) into the files list on the Files tab of the Project Center.

✔ Tips

■ To open any project-related file, go to the Files tab of the Project Center and double-click the filename (**Figure 27.15**). Note that this technique will open *any* Project Center item, such as events, notes, email messages, and so on.

■ If you believe that the file list has gotten out of synch with the contents of the Project Watch folder, click the Refresh button on the Files tab.

ADDING DOCUMENTS TO A PROJECT

Sharing a Project

A project and its materials can be shared with others, if you wish. In order to share a project, you and your colleagues must have access to a file server. All shared materials are moved from their original location to a shared location on the designated file server.

To share a project:

1. *Do one of the following:*

▲ At the bottom of any Project Center tab, click the Share icon and choose Start Sharing Project.

▲ Choose File > Share a Project.

The Project Sharing Assistant appears (**Figure 27.16**).

2. Provide the information requested by the Project Sharing Assistant, such as the project you wish to share and a destination location on the file server. Click the right-arrow icon to move from one screen to the next.

✔ Tips

■ To invite colleagues via email to join the current project, click the Share icon and choose Invite people to join project.

■ To join someone else's project, choose File > Subscribe to a Project, select a project (.rge) file from the file list, and click Choose.

■ Materials that you elect to share will be made available to other project participants. To set the sharing status of any project item, switch to the Project Center, select the item, click the Share icon, and choose Share *item type* or Do Not Share *item type*.

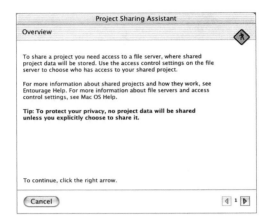

Figure 27.16 You use the Project Sharing Assistant to set up sharing for a given project.

Selected project

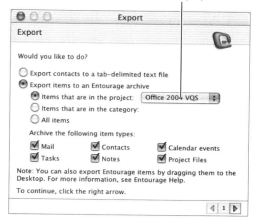

Figure 27.17 Select a project and specify the types of items that you wish to archive.

Figure 27.18 Following the archive procedure, you can delete or retain the data within Entourage.

Figure 27.19 Select a location for the archive file and click Save.

Archiving a Project

To ensure that your project data is secure or to clear it from your hard disk at the project's conclusion, the Project Center provides its own backup/archive procedure.

To back up or archive a project:

1. In the Project Center, select the project and click the Overview tab. Click the Backup button at the bottom of the page. The Export wizard appears (**Figure 27.17**).

2. Ensure that the correct project is selected. If you wish, you can elect *not* to archive some project item classes by clearing their check boxes. Click the right-arrow icon.

    The Delete Archived Items? screen appears (**Figure 27.18**).

3. Click a radio button to indicate whether the project items should remain intact within Entourage (when performing a backup) or deleted (when making an archive at a project's conclusion). Click the right-arrow icon.

    If you choose to delete the items, you can click the check box to prevent the wizard from deleting any items that are associated with other projects or categories.

4. In the Save dialog box (**Figure 27.19**), select a location for the archive file, edit its name (if desired), and click Save.

    The project archive is created.

5. Click Done to dismiss the Export wizard.

✔ Tips

- You can also archive a project using the File > Export command. However, the Export wizard automatically leaves all project items intact; i.e., no deletions.

- To restore an archived project, choose File > Import and elect to Import information from an Entourage archive.

ARCHIVING A PROJECT

INDEX

Graph program

changing chart type in, 281–282
data formats understood by, 280
formatting chart elements in, 287
launching, 278
purpose of, 277
showing/hiding legends with, 283, 284
special options, 288–290
switching between PowerPoint and, 279

graphics-related features (PowerPoint), 264–271

adding clip art to slides, 264–265
adding graphics to background, 270–271
drawing lines/shapes, 268–269
inserting images from camera, 266–267
inserting scanned images, 266–267

graphics-related features (Word), 101–113

creating text boxes, 111
drawing lines/shapes, 105–106
editing images/shapes, 107–110
inserting clip art, 102–103
inserting/modifying WordArt, 112–113
setting text wrap, 104

graphs. *See also* charts

Excel, 211
PowerPoint, 277

gridlines

in Excel charts, 217
in PowerPoint charts, 284

Groups list, 6
Gutter margins (Word), 73

H

Handheld Sync Installer, 343
handouts (PowerPoint), 305
hanging indents (in Word documents), 86, 87, 88
Header and Footer toolbar (Word), 74
headers (in Word documents), 74, 75
headings

in Excel worksheets, 178
in Word documents, 52

Help menu, 34, 44
high-low-close charts, 289
Highlight Changes dialog box (Excel), 249
holidays (in Entourage calendars), 361–362
Hotmail accounts, 316, 321, 391
.htm file extension, 311
HTML format, 311

hyperlinks, 38–42. *See also* linking objects

and AutoCorrect feature, 42
creating, 38–41
editing, 41
purpose of, 37, 38
removing, 41, 42

I

I-beam cursor, 16
icons, 4
identities, switching, 43, 337
Image Capture utility, 267
images. *See also* graphics-related features; photos

adding to documents, 102–103
adding to slides, 264–269
copyright considerations, 101
editing, 109–110
resizing, 103
scanning, 101
wrapping text around, 104

IMAP accounts, 316, 321
Import wizard (Entourage), 338–339, 361
importing

contacts (into Address Book), 338–339
data (into Excel), 158, 202, 229–232
data (into PowerPoint), 280
from Web (into Excel), 231–232

in-line objects, 104
Increase Indent icon (Word), 88
indenting paragraphs (in Word documents), 86–88
Insert Cells dialog box (Word), 125
Insert dialog box (Excel), 176
Insert Table dialog box (Word), 117
insertion point, blinking, 16, 53
interest-rate calculations, 240
International icon, 29
Internet. *See also* Web

links. *See* hyperlinks
mailing lists, 332
newsgroups, 389. *See also* newsgroups

Internet Explorer, 232
Internet Message Access Protocol. *See* IMAP accounts
Internet Protocol addresses, 390, 391
Internet Service Providers. *See* ISPs
invitations, sending/responding to, 359–360
IP addresses, 390, 391
ISPs, 316, 390

INDEX

creating, 424–426
creating Watch folders for, 425
defined, 423
entering due dates for, 424
examples of, 423
file extension for, 434
naming, 424
sharing, 434
viewing, 427
Protect Sheet dialog box (Excel), 251
Protect Workbook dialog box (Excel), 251
publishing, Web. *See* Web publishing

Q

Queries folder, 231
QuickTime movies, 312
QuickTime transitions, 302

R

ranges (in Excel worksheets)
formatting, 22, 180
naming, 156–157
Read-Only option, Open dialog, 14
Recent Items submenu, 14
Recent tab, Project Gallery, 6, 7, 10, 14
records
Address Book. *See* contacts
Excel, 223, 225
Recurring Task dialog box (Entourage), 367
red eye, 110
Redirect command (Entourage), 324, 325
Redo command, 28
Redo icon, 28
Reference Tools section, Office Toolbox, 65
references
cell, 190, 191
linked data, 408
Rehearse Timings command (PowerPoint), 307
relational databases, 223
reminders, 30, 374–375
Remove Split command (Excel), 179
Repeat command, 28
Replace command. *See* Find and Replace feature
Reply commands (Entourage), 323
reply envelopes, 134
Reviewing toolbar
Excel, 155
Word, 67
.rge file extension, 434
Right alignment icon (Word), 85, 121

rows. *See also* cells; tables
in Excel worksheets, 174–175, 193–194
in Word tables, 120, 122, 123, 125
royalty-free clip art. *See* clip art
ruler (Word), 50, 87
rules, email-message, 330, 430
Rules dialog box (Entourage), 330

S

Safari, 232
Safe Domains tab, Junk E-mail Protection, 331
sales reports, 115
sample files, 35
Save As dialog box, 15
Save As PDF button, 70, 350
Save as Web Page command, 44, 247
Save icon, 15
scanners, 266–267
Scenario Manager dialog box (Excel), 241
Scenario Values dialog box (Excel), 241
scenarios (Excel), 238, 241–242
schedules. *See* Calendar
Scrapbook, 24–26
ScreenTips, 34
Scribble tool (Word), 141, 142
section breaks (Word), 77–78
security features (Entourage), 333–334
selecting text, 17–18
Send To commands, 43
Set Up Show dialog box (PowerPoint), 308
shading
in Excel worksheets, 185–186
in Word documents, 92–93
in Word tables, 127
Shading Color icon, 127
shadows, 108
shapes (in Word documents), 105–108
applying color to, 107
applying shadow/3-D effects to, 108
drawing, 105, 106
resizing, 107
setting wrapping style for, 104
Share Workbook dialog box (Excel), 248, 252
Sharing Assistant, Project, 434
sheets (Excel), 148. *See also* worksheets
Show Heading commands (Word), 52
Show/Hide ¶ icon (Word), 55
Slide Background command (PowerPoint), 272
Slide Color Scheme command (PowerPoint), 274
Slide Design icon (PowerPoint), 301